ANTHROPOLOGY 94/95

Seventeenth Edition

Editor

Elvio Angeloni
Pasadena City College

Elvio Angeloni received his B.A. from UCLA in 1963, his
M.A. in anthropology from UCLA in 1965, and his M.A. in
communication arts from Loyola Marymount University in
1976. He has produced several films, including "Little
Warrior," winner of the Cinemedia VI Best Bicentennial
Theme, and "Broken Bottles," shown on PBS. He most
recently served as an academic advisor on the instructional
television series "Faces of Culture."

A Library of Information from the Public Press

Cover illustration by Mike Eagle

The Dushkin Publishing Group, Inc.
Sluice Dock, Guilford, Connecticut 06437

The Annual Editions Series

Annual Editions is a series of over 60 volumes designed to provide the reader with convenient, low-cost access to a wide range of current, carefully selected articles from some of the most important magazines, newspapers, and journals published today. Annual Editions are updated on an annual basis through a continuous monitoring of over 300 periodical sources. All Annual Editions have a number of features designed to make them particularly useful, including topic guides, annotated tables of contents, unit overviews, and indexes. For the teacher using Annual Editions in the classroom, an Instructor's Resource Guide with test questions is available for each volume.

VOLUMES AVAILABLE

Africa
Aging
American Foreign Policy
American Government
American History, Pre-Civil War
American History, Post-Civil War
Anthropology
Biology
Business Ethics
Canadian Politics
Child Growth and Development
China
Comparative Politics
Computers in Education
Computers in Business
Computers in Society
Criminal Justice
Drugs, Society, and Behavior
Dying, Death, and Bereavement
Early Childhood Education
Economics
Educating Exceptional Children
Education
Educational Psychology
Environment
Geography
Global Issues
Health
Human Development
Human Resources
Human Sexuality
India and South Asia
International Business
Japan and the Pacific Rim

Latin America
Life Management
Macroeconomics
Management
Marketing
Marriage and Family
Mass Media
Microeconomics
Middle East and the Islamic World
Money and Banking
Multicultural Education
Nutrition
Personal Growth and Behavior
Physical Anthropology
Psychology
Public Administration
Race and Ethnic Relations
Russia, Eurasia, and Central/Eastern Europe
Social Problems
Sociology
State and Local Government
Third World
Urban Society
Violence and Terrorism
Western Civilization, Pre-Reformation
Western Civilization, Post-Reformation
Western Europe
World History, Pre-Modern
World History, Modern
World Politics

Library of Congress Cataloging in Publication Data
Main entry under title: Annual editions: Anthropology. 1994/95.
1. Anthropology—Periodicals. I. Angeloni, Elvio, *comp.* II. Title: Anthropology.
301.2   74–84595   ISBN 1–56134–265–3
GN 325.A53

Seventeenth Edition

Printed in the United States of America

Printed on Recycled Paper

Editors/ Advisory Board

To the Reader

In publishing ANNUAL EDITIONS we recognize the enormous role played by the magazines, newspapers, and journals of the *public press* in providing current, first-rate educational information in a broad spectrum of interest areas. Within the articles, the best scientists, practitioners, researchers, and commentators draw issues into new perspective as accepted theories and viewpoints are called into account by new events, recent discoveries change old facts, and fresh debate breaks out over important controversies.

Many of the articles resulting from this enormous editorial effort are appropriate for students, researchers, and professionals seeking accurate, current material to help bridge the gap between principles and theories and the real world. These articles, however, become more useful for study when those of lasting value are carefully *collected, organized, indexed,* and *reproduced* in a *low-cost format,* which provides easy and permanent access when the material is needed. That is the role played by *Annual Editions.* Under the direction of each volume's *Editor,* who is an expert in the subject area, and with the guidance of an *Advisory Board,* we seek each year to provide in each *ANNUAL EDITION* a current, well-balanced, carefully selected collection of the best of the public press for your study and enjoyment. We think you'll find this volume useful, and we hope you'll take a moment to let us know what you think.

The seventeenth edition of *Annual Editions: Anthropology* contains a variety of articles on contemporary issues in social and cultural anthropology. In contrast to the broad range of topics and minimum depth typical of standard textbooks, this anthology provides an opportunity to read firsthand accounts by anthropologists of their own research. By allowing scholars to speak for themselves about the issues on which they are expert, we are better able to understand the kinds of questions anthropologists ask, the ways in which they ask them, and how they go about searching for answers. Where there is disagreement among anthropologists, this format allows readers to draw their own conclusions.

Given the very broad scope of anthropology—in time, space, and subject matter—the present collection of highly readable articles has been selected according to certain criteria. The articles have been chosen from both professional and nonprofessional publications for the purpose of supplementing the standard textbook that is used in introductory courses in cultural anthropology. Some of the articles are considered classics in the field, while others have been selected for their timely relevance.

Included in this volume are a number of features designed to be useful for students, researchers, and professionals in the field of anthropology. While the articles are arranged along the lines of broadly unifying themes, the *topic guide* can be used to establish specific reading assignments tailored to the needs of a particular course of study. Other useful features include the *table of contents abstracts,* which summarize each article and present key concepts in bold italics, and a comprehensive *index.* In addition, each unit is preceded by an *overview* that provides a background for informed reading of the articles, emphasizes critical issues, and presents *challenge questions.*

Annual Editions: Anthropology 94/95 will continue to be updated annually. Those involved in producing this volume wish to make the next one as useful and effective as possible. Your criticism and advice are welcomed. Please fill out the article rating form on the last page of the book, and let us know your opinions. Any anthology can be improved. This continues to be—annually.

Elvio Angeloni

Elvio Angeloni
Editor

Contents

Unit 1

Anthropological Perspectives

Five selections examine the role of anthropologists in studying different cultures. The innate problems in developing productive relationships between anthropologists and exotic cultures are considered by reviewing a number of fieldwork experiences.

The concepts in bold italics are developed in the article. For further expansion please refer to the Topic Guide and the Index.

Unit 2

Culture and Communication

Five selections discuss communication as an element of culture. Ingrained social and cultural values have a tremendous effect on an individual's perception or interpretation of both verbal and nonverbal communication.

Unit 3

The Organization of Society and Culture

Six selections discuss the influence of the environment and culture on the organization of the social structure of groups.

The concepts in bold italics are developed in the article. For further expansion please refer to the Topic Guide and the Index.

Unit 4

Other Families, Other Ways

Six selections examine some of the influences on the
family structure of different cultures. The strength of
the family unit is affected by both economic and
social pressures.

20. Family Planning, Amazon Style, Warren M. Hern, *Natural History,* December 1992.
Among the Shipibo of the Peruvian Amazon, the coming of the **market economy** has meant changes in **family structure** and methods of **population control,** and caused **resource depletion.** The result has been higher rates of fertility, disease, and poverty.

107

21. Death Without Weeping, Nancy Scheper-Hughes, *Natural History,* October 1989.
In the shantytowns of Brazil, the seeming indifference of mothers who allow some of their **children** to die is a **survival strategy** geared to circumstances in which only some may live.

112

22. Arranging a Marriage in India, Serena Nanda, from *The Naked Anthropologist,* Wadsworth, 1992.
Arranging a marriage in India is far too serious a business for the young and inexperienced. Instead the parents make decisions on the basis of the families' social position, reputation, and ability to get along.

117

Overview

122

23. Society and Sex Roles, Ernestine Friedl, *Human Nature,* April 1978.
The author relates the extent of **male domination** over **women** to the degree to which men control the exchange of valued goods with people outside the family. As women gain increasing access to positions of power in industrial society, they may regain the **equality** that seems to have been prevalent among our foraging ancestors.

124

24. Why Don't We Act Like the Opposite Sex? Anthony Layng, *USA Today Magazine (Society for the Advancement of Education),* January 1993.
While the field of **sociobiology** has prompted arguments as to whether the behavioral differences between **men and women** are inherited or learned, Anthony Layng claims the truth to be somewhere in between.

130

25. The Global War Against Women, Lori Heise, *The Washington Post,* April 9, 1989.
Violence against women is perhaps the most pervasive, yet least recognized, **human-rights** issue in the world. Although rooted in such traditions as **female infanticide** and **female circumcision** and, in some ways, made even more prevalent by **social change**, its seeming inevitability, says the author, can and must be challenged.

134

Unit 5

Sex Roles and Statuses

Six selections discuss some of the sex roles prescribed by the social, economic, and political forces of a culture.

The concepts in bold italics are developed in the article. For further expansion please refer to the Topic Guide and the Index.

Unit 6

Religion, Belief, and Ritual

Eight selections examine the role of ritual, religion, and
belief in a culture. The need to develop a religion is
universal among societies.

The concepts in bold italics are developed in the article. For further expansion please refer to the Topic Guide and the Index.

Unit 7

Sociocultural Change: The Impact of the West

Eight articles examine the influence that the developed world has had on primitive cultures. Exposure to the industrial West often has disastrous effects on the delicate balance of a primitive society.

The concepts in bold italics are developed in the article. For further expansion please refer to the Topic Guide and the Index.

Topic Guide

This topic guide suggests how the selections in this book relate to topics of traditional concern to students and professionals involved with the study of anthropology. It can be very useful in locating articles that relate to each other for reading and research. The guide is arranged alphabetically according to topic. Articles may, of course, treat topics that do not appear in the topic guide. In turn, entries in the topic guide do not necessarily constitute a comprehensive listing of all the contents of each selection.

TOPIC AREA	TREATED IN:	TOPIC AREA	TREATED IN:
Aculturation	9. Cross-Cultural Experience 16. Unsettled People 38. Growing Up as a Fore 42. Lost Tribes, Lost Knowledge 43. Bicultural Conflict	Cultural Relativity and Ethnocentrism	1. Doing Fieldwork Among the Yąnomamö 3. "White Man Will Eat You!" 4. Eating Christmas in the Kalahari 5. Naked Truth 9. Cross-Cultural Experience 22. Arranging a Marriage in India 35. Body Ritual Among the Nacirema 39. Civilization and Its Discontents 43. Bicultural Conflict
Aggression and Violence	25. Global War Against Women 34. Rituals of Death 40. Dark Dreams About the White Man 41. People at Risk 43. Bicultural Conflict		
		Culture Shock	1. Doing Fieldwork Among the Yąnomamö 5. Naked Truth 39. Civilization and Its Discontents 43. Bicultural Conflict
Children and Child Care	17. Memories of a !Kung Girlhood 19. Young Traders of Northern Nigeria 20. Family Planning, Amazon Style 21. Death Without Weeping 24. Why Don't We Act Like the Opposite Sex? 26. Little Emperors 27. Parental Favoritism Toward Daughters 31. Mbuti Pygmies 43. Bicultural Conflict	Ecology and Society	11. Understanding Eskimo Science 12. Blood in Their Veins 13. Mystique of the Masai 15. Life Without Chiefs 18. When Brothers Share a Wife 20. Family Planning, Amazon Style 23. Society and Sex Roles 27. Parental Favoritism Toward Daughters 37. Why Can't People Feed Themselves? 39. Civilization and Its Discontents 41. People at Risk 42. Lost Tribes, Lost Knowledge 44. Easter Island
Cooperation, Sharing, and Altruism	4. Eating Christmas in the Kalahari 12. Blood in Their Veins 14. Too Many Bananas		
Cross-Cultural Experience	1. Doing Fieldwork Among the Yąnomamö 2. Doctor, Lawyer, Indian Chief 3. "White Man Will Eat You!" 4. Eating Christmas in the Kalahari 8. Shakespeare in the Bush 9. Cross-Cultural Experience 11. Understanding Eskimo Science 14. Too Many Bananas 21. Death Without Weeping 22. Arranging a Marriage in India 39. Civilization and Its Discontents 40. Dark Dreams About the White Man 43. Bicultural Conflict	Economic and Political Systems	2. Doctor, Lawyer, Indian Chief 13. Mystique of the Masai 14. Too Many Bananas 15. Life Without Chiefs 16. Unsettled People 18. When Brothers Share a Wife 19. Young Traders of Northern Nigeria 21. Death Without Weeping 23. Society and Sex Roles 26. Little Emperors 27. Parental Favoritism Toward Daughters 37. Why Can't People Feed Themselves? 39. Civilization and Its Discontents 41. People at Risk 44. Easter Island
Cultural Diversity	5. Naked Truth 9. Cross-Cultural Experience 16. Unsettled People 22. Arranging a Marriage in India 27. Parental Favoritism Toward Daughters 30. Body's War and Peace 42. Lost Tribes, Lost Knowledge 43. Bicultural Conflict	Ethnographic Fieldwork	1. Doing Fieldwork Among the Yąnomamö 2. Doctor, Lawyer, Indian Chief 3. "White Man Will Eat You!" 4. Eating Christmas in the Kalahari 14. Too Many Bananas 41. People at Risk
Cultural Identity	5. Naked Truth 9. Cross-Cultural Experience 13. Mystique of the Masai 16. Unsettled People 39. Civilization and Its Discontents 42. Lost Tribes, Lost Knowledge 43. Bicultural Conflict	Health and Welfare	20. Family Planning, Amazon Style 21. Death Without Weeping 25. Global War Against Women 26. Little Emperors 27. Parental Favoritism Toward Daughters 29. Psychotherapy in Africa

TOPIC AREA	TREATED IN:	TOPIC AREA	TREATED IN:
Health and Welfare (cont'd)	30. Body's War and Peace 35. Body Ritual Among the Nacirema 37. Why Can't People Feed Themselves? 39. Civilization and Its Discontents 41. People at Risk 42. Lost Tribes, Lost Knowledge	**Rituals (cont'd)**	31. Mbuti Pygmies 32. Initiation of a Maasai Warrior 33. Secrets of Haiti's Living Dead 34. Rituals of Death 35. Body Ritual Among the Nacirema 36. Superstition and Ritual in American Baseball
Hunter-Collectors	11. Understanding Eskimo Science 12. Blood in Their Veins 15. Life Without Chiefs 17. Memories of a !Kung Girlhood 31. Mbuti Pygmies	**Sex Roles/Sexuality**	17. Memories of a !Kung Girlhood 18. When Brothers Share a Wife 23. Society and Sex Roles 24. Why Don't We Act Like the Opposite Sex? 25. Global War Against Women 26. Little Emperors 28. Blaming the Victim 43. Bicultural Conflict
Language	6. World's Language 7. Language, Appearance, and Reality 8. Shakespeare in the Bush 9. Cross-Cultural Experience 30. Body's War and Peace 43. Bicultural Conflict	**Social, Cultural, and Industrial Change**	16. Unsettled People 26. Little Emperors 27. Parental Favoritism Toward Daughters 29. Psychotherapy in Africa 37. Why Can't People Feed Themselves? 38. Growing Up as a Fore 39. Civilization and Its Discontents 40. Dark Dreams About the White Man 41. People at Risk 42. Lost Tribes, Lost Knowledge 43. Bicultural Conflict 44. Easter Island
Magic	33. Secrets of Haiti's Living Dead 34. Rituals of Death 35. Body Ritual Among the Nacirema 36. Superstition and Ritual in American Baseball		
Marriage, Kinship, and Family Systems	9. Cross-Cultural Experience 16. Unsettled People 17. Memories of a !Kung Girlhood 18. When Brothers Share a Wife 19. Young Traders of Northern Nigeria 21. Death Without Weeping 22. Arranging a Marriage in India 23. Society and Sex Roles 24. Why Don't We Act Like the Opposite Sex? 25. Global War Against Women 26. Little Emperors 27. Parental Favoritism Toward Daughters 43. Bicultural Conflict	**Social Equality**	15. Life Without Chiefs 16. Unsettled People 25. Global War Against Women 28. Blaming the Victim 31. Mbuti Pygmies
		Social Relationships	1. Doing Fieldwork Among the Yąnomamö 2. Doctor, Lawyer, Indian Chief 3. "White Man Will Eat You!" 4. Eating Christmas in the Kalahari 5. Naked Truth 9. Cross-Cultural Experience 14. Too Many Bananas 16. Unsettled People 22. Arranging a Marriage in India 24. Why Don't We Act Like the Opposite Sex? 25. Global War Against Women 26. Little Emperors 28. Blaming the Victim 31. Mbuti Pygmies 33. Secrets of Haiti's Living Dead
Medicine and Healing	29. Psychotherapy in Africa 30. Body's War and Peace 35. Body Ritual Among the Nacirema 42. Lost Tribes, Lost Knowledge		
Participant Observation	1. Doing Fieldwork Among the Yąnomamö 2. Doctor, Lawyer, Indian Chief 3. "White Man Will Eat You!" 4. Eating Christmas in the Kalahari 8. Shakespeare in the Bush 14. Too Many Bananas 39. Civilization and Its Discontents		
		Values	4. Eating Christmas in the Kalahari 5. Naked Truth 9. Cross-Cultural Experience 16. Unsettled People 17. Memories of a !Kung Girlhood 21. Death Without Weeping 22. Arranging a Marriage in India 26. Little Emperors 31. Mbuti Pygmies 35. Body Ritual Among the Nacirema 38. Growing Up as a Fore 41. People at Risk 42. Lost Tribes, Lost Knowledge 43. Bicultural Conflict
Patriarchy	23. Society and Sex Roles 28. Blaming the Victim		
Poverty	16. Unsettled People 20. Family Planning, Amazon Style 21. Death Without Weeping 27. Parental Favoritism Toward Daughters 37. Why Can't People Feed Themselves?		
Rituals	16. Unsettled People 29. Psychotherapy in Africa		

Anthropological Perspectives

For at least a century the goals of anthropology have been to describe societies and cultures throughout the world and to compare the differences and similarities among them. Anthropologists study in a variety of settings and situations, ranging from small hamlets and villages to neighborhoods and corporate offices of major urban centers throughout the world. They study hunters and gatherers, peasants, farmers, labor leaders, politicians, and bureaucrats. They examine religious life in Latin America as well as revolutionary movements.

Wherever practicable, anthropologists take on the role of the "participant observer," for it is through active involvement in the lifeways of the people that they hope to gain an insider's perspective without sacrificing the objectivity of the trained scientist. Sometimes the conditions for achieving such a goal may seem to form an almost insurmountable barrier, but anthropologists' persistence, adaptability, and imagination may be employed to overcome the odds against them.

The diversity of focus in anthropology means that it is earmarked less by its particular subject matter than by its perspective. Although the discipline relates to both the biological and social sciences, anthropologists also know that the boundaries drawn between such disciplines are highly artificial. For example, although it may be possible to examine only the social organization of a family unit or the organization of political power in a nation-state, in reality, it is impossible to separate the biological from the social from the economic from the political. The explanatory perspective of anthropology, as the articles in this section exemplify, is to seek out interrelationships among all these factors.

The articles in this section illustrate varying degrees of difficulty an anthropologist may encounter in taking on the role of the participant observer. Napoleon Chagnon's "Doing Fieldwork Among the Yąnomamö" shows, for instance, the hardships imposed by certain physical conditions, the unwillingness of the people to provide needed information, and the vast differences in values and attitudes to be bridged by the anthropologist just in order to get along.

Richard Kurin ("Doctor, Lawyer, Indian Chief"), Richard Lee ("Eating Christmas in the Kalahari"), and William Wormsley ("The White Man Will Eat You!") apparently had few problems with the physical conditions and the personalities of the people they were studying. However, they were not completely accepted by the communities until they modified their behavior to conform to the expectations of their hosts and found ways to participate as equals in the socioeconomic exchange systems.

Finally, as Roger Welsch shows, whenever anyone enters a new situation without understanding and abiding by the generally accepted rules, embarrassment and moral indignation are the inevitable results.

Much is at stake in these discussions, since the purpose of anthropology is not only to describe and explain, but to develop a special vision of the world in which cultural alternatives (past, present, and future) can be measured against one another and used as a guide for human action.

Looking Ahead: Challenge Questions

What is culture shock?

How can anthropologists who become personally involved with a community through participant observation maintain their objectivity as scientists?

In what ways do the results of fieldwork depend on the kinds of questions asked?

How does cross-cultural experience help us to understand ourselves?

In what sense is sharing intrinsic to egalitarianism?

How can we avoid the pitfalls of cultural relativity and ethnocentrism in dealing with what we think of as harmful practices in other cultures?

Who decides that human nakedness is an obscenity, and why?

Doing Fieldwork among the Yąnomamö[1]

Napoleon A. Chagnon

VIGNETTE

The Yąnomamö are thinly scattered over a vast and verdant tropical forest, living in small villages that are separated by many miles of unoccupied land. They have no writing, but they have a rich and complex language. Their clothing is more decorative than protective. Well-dressed men sport nothing more than a few cotton strings around their wrists, ankles, and waists. They tie the foreskins of their penises to the waiststring. Women dress about the same. Much of their daily life revolves around gardening, hunting, collecting wild foods, collecting firewood, fetching water, visiting with each other, gossiping, and making the few material possessions they own: baskets, hammocks, bows, arrows, and colorful pigments with which they paint their bodies. Life is relatively easy in the sense that they can 'earn a living' with about three hours' work per day. Most of what they eat they cultivate in their gardens, and most of that is plantains—a kind of cooking banana that is usually eaten green, either roasted on the coals or boiled in pots. Their meat comes from a large variety of game animals, hunted daily by the men. It is usually roasted on

coals or smoked, and is always well done. Their villages are round and open—and very public. One can hear, see, and smell almost everything that goes on anywhere in the village. Privacy is rare, but sexual discreetness is possible in the garden or at night while others sleep. The villages can be as small as 40 to 50 people or as large as 300 people, but in all cases there are many more children and babies than there are adults. This is true of most primitive populations and of our own demographic past. Life expectancy is short.

The Yąnomamö fall into the category of Tropical Forest Indians called 'foot people'. They avoid large rivers and live in interfluvial plains of the major rivers. They have neighbors to the north, Carib-speaking Ye'kwana, who are true 'river people': They make elegant, large dugout canoes and travel extensively along the major waterways. For the Yąnomamö, a large stream is an obstacle and can be crossed only in the dry season. Thus, they have traditionally avoided larger rivers and, because of this, contact with outsiders who usually come by river.

They enjoy taking trips when the jungle abounds with seasonally ripe wild fruits and vegetables. Then, the large village—the *shabono*—is abandoned for a few weeks and everyone camps out for from one to several days

away from the village and garden. On these trips, they make temporary huts from poles, vines, and leaves, each family making a separate hut.

Two major seasons dominate their annual cycle: the wet season, which inundates the low-lying jungle, making travel difficult, and the dry season—the time of visiting other villages to feast, trade, and politic with allies. The dry season is also the time when raiders can travel and strike silently at their unsuspecting enemies. The Yąnomamö are still conducting intervillage warfare, a phenomenon that affects all aspects of their social organization, settlement pattern, and daily routines. It is not simply 'ritualistic' war: At least one-fourth of all adult males die violently in the area I lived in.

Social life is organized around those same principles utilized by all tribesmen: kinship relationships, descent from ancestors, marriage exchanges between kinship/descent groups, and the transient charisma of distinguished headmen who attempt to keep order in the village and whose responsibility it is to determine the village's relationships with those in other villages. Their positions are largely the result of kinship and marriage patterns; they come from the largest kinship groups within the village. They can, by their personal wit, wisdom, and charisma, become autocrats, but most of them are largely 'greaters' among equals. They, too, must clear gardens, plant crops, collect wild foods, and hunt. They are simultaneously peacemakers and valiant warriors. peacemaking often requires the threat or actual use of force, and most headmen have an acquired reputation for being *waiteri*: fierce.

The social dynamics within villages are involved with giving and receiving marriageable girls. Marriages are arranged by older kin, usually men, who are brothers, uncles, and the father. It is a political process, for girls are promised in marriage while they are young, and the men who do this attempt to create alliances with other men via marriage exchanges. There is a shortage of women due in part to a sex-ratio imbalance in the younger age categories, but also complicated by the fact that some men have multiple wives. Most fighting within the village stems from sexual affairs or failure to deliver a promised woman—or out-and-out seizure of a married woman by some other man. This can lead to internal fighting and conflict of such an intensity that villages split up and fission, each group then becoming a new village and, often, enemies to each other.

But their conflicts are not blind, uncontrolled violence. They have a series of graded forms of violence that ranges from chest-pounding and club-fighting duels to out-and-out shooting to kill. This gives them a good deal of flexibility in settling disputes without immediate resort to lethal violence. In addition, they have developed patterns of alliance and friendship that serve to limit violence—trading and feasting with others in order to become friends. These alliances can, and often do, result in intervillage exchanges of marriageable women, which leads to additional amity between villages. No good thing lasts forever, and most alliances crumble. Old friends become hostile and, occasionally, treacherous. Each village must therefore be keenly aware that its neighbors are fickle and must behave accordingly. The thin line between friendship and animosity must be traversed by the village leaders, whose political acumen and strategies are both admirable and complex.

Each village, then, is a replica of all others in a broad sense. But each village is part of a larger political, demographic, and ecological process, and it is difficult to attempt to understand the village without knowing something of the larger forces that affect it and it's particular history with all its neighbors.

COLLECTING THE DATA IN THE FIELD

I have now spent over 60 months with Yąnomamö, during which time I gradually learned their language and, up to a point, submerged myself in their culture and way of life.[2] As my research progressed, the thing that impressed me most was the importance that aggression played in shaping their culture. I had the opportunity to witness a good many incidents that expressed individual vindictiveness on the one hand and collective bellicosity on the other hand. These ranged in seriousness from the ordinary incidents of wife beating and chest pounding to dueling and organized raids by parties that set out with the intention of ambushing and killing men from enemy villages. One of the villages . . . was raided approximately twenty-five times during my first 15 months of fieldwork—six times by the group among whom I was living. And, the history of every village I investigated, from 1964 to 1991, was intimately bound up in patterns of warfare with neighbors that shaped its politics and determined where it was found at any point in time and how it dealt with it's current neighbors.

The fact that the Yąnomamö have lived in a chronic state of warfare is reflected in their mythology, ceremonies, settlement pattern, political behavior, and marriage practices. Accordingly, I have organized this case study in such a way that students can appreciate the effects of warfare on Yąnomamö culture in general and on their social organization and political relationships in particular.

I collected the data under somewhat trying circumstances, some of which I will describe to give a rough idea of what is generally meant when anthropologists speak of 'culture shock' and 'fieldwork.' It should be borne in mind, however, that each field situation is in many respects unique, so that the problems I encountered do not necessarily exhaust the range of possible problems other anthropologists have confronted in other areas. There are a few problems, however, that seem to be nearly universal among anthropological fieldworkers, particularly those having to do with eating, bathing, sleeping, lack of privacy, loneliness, or discovering that the people you are living with have a lower opinion of you than you have of them—or you yourself are not as culturally or emotionally 'flexible' as you assumed.

The Yąnomamö can be difficult people to live with at times, but I have spoken to colleagues who have had difficulties living in the communities they studied. These things vary from society to society, and probably from one anthropologist to the next. I have also done limited fieldwork among the Yąnomamö's northern neighbors, the Carib-speaking Ye'kwana Indians. By contrast to many experiences I had among the Yanomamö, the Ye'kwana were very pleasant and charming, all of them anxious to help me and honor bound to show any visitor the numerous courtesies of their system of etiquette. In short, they approached the image of 'primitive man' that I had conjured up in my mind before doing fieldwork, a kind of 'Rousseauian' view, and it was sheer pleasure to work with them. Other anthropologists have also noted sharp contrasts in the people they study from one field situation to another. One of the most startling examples of this is in the work of Colin Turnbull, who first studied the Ituri Pygmies (1965, 1983) and found them delightful to live with, but then studied the Ik (1972) of the desolate outcroppings of the Kenya/Uganda/Sudan border region, a people he had difficulty coping with intellectually, emotionally, and physically. While it is possible that the anthropologist's reactions to a particular people are personal and idiosyncratic, it nevertheless remains true that there are enormous differences between whole peoples, differences that affect the anthropologist in often dramatic ways.

Hence, what I say about some of my experiences is probably equally true of the experiences of many other field-workers. I describe some of them here for the benefit of future anthropologists—because I think I could have profited by reading about the pitfalls and field problems of my own teachers. At the very least I might have been able to avoid some of my more stupid errors. In this regard there is a growing body of excellent descriptive work on field research. Students who plan to make a career in anthropology should consult these works, which cover a wide range of field situations in the ethnographic present.[3]

The Longest Day: The First One
My first day in the field illustrated to me what my teachers meant when they spoke of 'culture shock.' I had traveled in a small, aluminum rowboat propelled by a large outboard motor for two and a half days. This took me from the territorial capital, a small town on the Orinoco River, deep into Yąnomamö country. On the morning of the third day we reached a small mission settlement, the field 'headquarters' of a group of Americans who were working in two Yąnomamö villages. The missionaries had come out of these villages to hold their annual conference on the progress of their mission work and were conducting their meetings when I arrived. We picked up a passenger at the mission station, James P. Barker, the first non-Yąnomamö to make a sustained, permanent contact with the tribe (in 1950). He had just returned from a year's furlough in the United States, where I had earlier visited him before leaving for Venezuela. He agreed to accompany me to the village I had selected for my base of operations to introduce me to the Indians. This village was also his own home base, but he had not been there for over a year and did not plan to join me for another three months. Mr. Barker had been living with this particular group about five years.

We arrived at the village, Bisaasi-teri, about 2:00 P.M. and docked the boat along the muddy bank at the terminus of the path used by Yąnomamö to fetch their drinking water. It was hot and muggy, and my clothing was soaked with perspiration. It clung uncomfortably to my body, as it did thereafter for the remainder of the work. The small biting gnats, *bareto,* were out in astronomical numbers, for it was the beginning of the dry season. My face and hands were swollen from the venom of their numerous stings. In just a few moments I was to meet my first Yąnomamö, my first primitive man. What would he be like? I had visions of entering the village and seeing 125 social facts running about altruistically calling each other kinship terms and sharing food, each waiting and anxious to have me collect his genealogy. I would wear them out in turn. Would they like me? This was important to me; I wanted them to be so fond of me that they would adopt me into their kinship system and way of life. I had heard that successful anthropologists always get adopted by their people. I had learned during my seven years of anthropological training at the University of Michigan that kinship was equivalent to society in primitive tribes and that it was a moral way of life, 'moral' being something 'good' and 'desirable.' I was determined to work my way into their moral system of kinship and become a member of their society—to be 'accepted' by them.

How Did They Accept You?
My heart began to pound as we approached the village and heard the buzz of activity within the circular compound. Mr. Barker commented that he was anxious to see if any changes had taken place while he was away and wondered how many of them had died during his absence. I nervously felt my back pocket to make sure that my notebook was still there and felt personally more secure when I touched it.

The entrance to the village was covered over with brush and dry palm leaves. We pushed them aside to expose the low opening to the village. The excitement of meeting my first Yąnomamö was almost unbearable as I duck-waddled through the low passage into the village clearing.

I looked up and gasped when I saw a dozen burly, naked, sweaty, hideous men staring at us down the shafts of their drawn arrows! Immense wads of green tobacco were stuck between their lower teeth and lips making them look even more hideous, and strands of dark-green slime dripped or hung from their nostrils—strands so long that they clung to their pectoral muscles or drizzled down their chins. We arrived at the village while the men were blowing a hallucinogenic drug up their noses. One of the side effects of the drug is a runny nose. The mucus is always saturated with the green powder and they usually let it run freely from their nostrils. My next discovery was that there were a dozen or so vicious, underfed dogs snapping at my legs, circling me as if I were to be their next meal. I just stood there holding my notebook, helpless and pathetic. Then the stench of the decaying vegetation and filth hit me and I almost got sick. I was horrified. What kind of welcome was this for the person who came here to live with you and learn your way of life, to become friends with you? They put their weapons down when they recognized Barker and returned to their chanting, keeping a nervous eye on the village entrances.

We had arrived just after a serious fight. Seven women had been abducted the day before by a neighboring group, and the local men and their guests had just that morning recovered five of them in a brutal club fight that nearly ended in a shooting war. The abductors, angry because they had lost five of their seven new captives, vowed to raid the Bisaasi-teri. When we arrived and entered the village unexpectedly, the Indians feared that we were the raiders. On several occasions during the next two hours the men in the village jumped to their feet, armed themselves, nocked their arrows and waited nervously for the noise outside the village to be identified. My enthusiasm for collecting ethnographic facts diminished in proportion to the number of times such an alarm was raised. In fact, I was relieved when Barker suggested that we sleep across the river for the evening. It would be safer over there.

As we walked down the path to the boat, I pondered the wisdom of having decided to spend a year and a half with these people before I had even seen what they were like. I am not ashamed to admit that had there been a diplomatic way out, I would have ended my fieldwork then and there. I did not look forward to the next day—and months— when I would be left alone with the Yąnomanö; I did not speak a word of their language, and they were decidedly different from what I had imagined them to be. The whole situation was depressing, and I wondered why I ever decided to switch from physics and engineering in the first place. I had not eaten all day, I was soaking wet from perspiration, the *bareto* were biting me, and I was covered with red pigment, the result of a dozen or so complete examinations I had been given by as many very pushy Yąnomamö men. These examinations capped an otherwise grim day. The men would blow their noses into their hands, flick as much of the mucus off that would separate in a snap of the wrist, wipe the residue into their hair, and then carefully examine my face, arms, legs, hair, and the contents of my pockets. I asked Barker how to say, 'Your hands are dirty'; my comments were met by the Yąnomamö in the following way: They would 'clean' their hands by spitting a quantity of slimy tobacco juice into them, rub them together, grin, and then proceed with the examination.

Mr. Barker and I crossed the river and slung our hammocks. When he pulled his hammock out of a rubber bag, a heavy, disagreeable odor of mildewed cotton and stale wood smoke came with it. 'Even the missionaries are filthy,' I thought to myself. Within two weeks, everything I owned smelled the same way, and I lived with that odor for the remainder of the fieldwork. My own habits of personal

cleanliness declined to such levels that I didn't even mind being examined by the Yąnomamö, as I was not much cleaner than they were after I had adjusted to the circumstances. it is difficult to blow your nose gracefully when you are stark naked and the invention of hankerchiefs is millenia away.

Life in the Jungle: Oatmeal, Peanut Butter, and Bugs

It isn't easy to plop down in the Amazon Basin for a year and get immediately into the anthropological swing of things. You have been told about horrible diseases, snakes, jaguars, electric eels, little spiny fish that will swim up your urine into your penis, quicksand, and getting lost. Some of the dangers are real, but your imagination makes them more real and threatening than many of them really are. What my teachers never bothered to advise me about, however, was the mundane, nonexciting, and trivial stuff—like eating, defecating, sleeping, or keeping clean. These turned out to be the bane of my existence during the first several months of field research. I set up my household in Barker's abandoned mud hut, a few yards from the village of Bisaasi-teri, and immediately set to work building my own mud/thatch hut with the help of the Yąnomamö. Meanwhile, I had to eat and try to do my 'field research.' I soon discovered that it was an enormously time-consuming task to maintain my own body in the manner to which it had grown accustomed in the relatively antiseptic environment of the northern United States. Either I could be relatively well fed and relatively comfortable in a fresh change of clothes and do very little fieldwork, or I could do considerably more fieldwork and be less well fed and less comfortable.

It is appalling how complicated it can be to make oatmeal in the jungle. First, I had to make two trips to the river to haul the water. Next, I had to prime my kerosene stove with alcohol to get it burning, a tricky procedure when you are trying to mix powdered milk and fill a coffee pot at the same

time. The alcohol prime always burned out before I could turn the kerosene on, and I would have to start all over. Or, I would turn the kerosene on, optimistically hoping that the Coleman element was still hot enough to vaporize the fuel, and start a small fire in my palm-thatched hut as the liquid kerosene squirted all over the table and walls and then ignited. Many amused Yąnomanö onlookers quickly learned the English phrase 'Oh, Shit!', and, once they discovered that the phrase offended and irritated the missionaries, they used it as often as they could in their presence. I usually had to start over with the alcohol. Then I had to boil the oatmeal and pick the bugs out of it. All my supplies, of course, were carefully stored in rat-proof, moisture-proof, and insect-proof containers, not one of which ever served its purpose adequately. Just taking things out of the multiplicity of containers and repacking them afterward was a minor project in itself. By the time I had hauled the water to cook with, unpacked my food, prepared the oatmeal, milk, and coffee, heated water for dishes, washed and dried the dishes, repacked the food in the containers, stored the containers in locked trunks, and cleaned up my mess, the ceremony of preparing breakfast had brought me almost up to lunch time!

Eating three meals a day was simply out of the question. I solved the problem by eating a single meal that could be prepared in a single container, or, at most, in two containers, washed my dishes only when there were no clean ones left, using cold river water, and wore each change of clothing at least a week to cut down on my laundry problem—a courageous undertaking in the tropics. I reeked like a jockstrap that had been left to mildew in the bottom of some dark gym locker. I also became less concerned about sharing my provisions with the rats, insects, Yąnomamö, and the elements, thereby eliminating the need for my complicated storage process. I was able to last most of the day on *café con leche,* heavily sugared espresso coffee diluted about five to one with hot milk. I would prepare this in the evening and store it in a large thermos. Frequently, my single meal was no more complicated than a can of sardines and a package of soggy crackers. But at least two or three times a week I would do something 'special' and sophisticated, like make a batch of oatmeal or boil rice and add a can of tuna fish or tomato paste to it. I even saved time by devising a water system that obviated the trips to the river. I had a few sheets of tin roofing brought in and made a rain water trap; I caught the water on the tin surface, funneled it into an empty gasoline drum, and then ran a plastic hose from the drum to my hut. When the drum was exhausted in the dry season, I would get a few Yąnomamö boys to fill it with buckets of water from the river, 'paying' them with crackers, of which they grew all too fond all too soon.

I ate much less when I traveled with the Yąnomamö to visit other villages. Most of the time my travel diet consisted of roasted or boiled green plantains (cooking bananas) that I obtained from the Yąnomamö, but I always carried a few cans of sardines with me in case I got lost or stayed away longer than I had planned. I found peanut butter and crackers a very nourishing 'trail' meal, and a simple one to prepare. It was nutritious and portable, and only one tool was required to make the meal: a hunting knife that could be cleaned by wiping the blade on a convenient leaf. More importantly, it was one of the few foods the Yąnomamö would let me eat in relative peace. It looked suspiciously like animal feces to them, an impression I encouraged. I referred to the peanut butter as the feces of babies or 'cattle'. They found this disgusting and repugnant. They did not know what 'cattle' were, but were increasingly aware that I ate several canned products of such an animal. Tin cans were thought of as containers made of 'machete skins', but how the cows got inside was always a mystery to them. I went out of my way to describe my foods in such a way as to make them sound unpalatable to them, for it gave me some peace of mind while I ate: They wouldn't beg for a share of something that was too horrible to contem-

plate. Fieldworkers develop strange defense mechanisms and strategies, and this was one of my own forms of adaptation to the fieldwork. On another occasion I was eating a can of frankfurters and growing very weary of the demands from one of the onlookers for a share in my meal. When he finally asked what I was eating, I replied: 'Beef.' He then asked: 'Shąki![4] What part of the animal are you eating?' To which I replied, 'Guess.' He muttered a contemptuous epithet, but stopped asking for a share. He got back at me later, as we shall see.

Meals were a problem in a way that had nothing to do with the inconvenience of preparing them. Food sharing is important to the Yąnomamö in the context of displaying friendship. 'I am hungry!' is almost a form of greeting with them. I could not possibly have brought enough food with me to feed the entire village, yet they seemed to overlook this logistic fact as they begged for my food. What became fixed in their minds was the fact that I did not share my food with whomsoever was present—usually a small crowd—at each and every meal. Nor could I easily enter their system of reciprocity with respect to food. Every time one of them 'gave' me something 'freely', he would dog me for months to 'pay him back', not necessarily with food but with knives, fishhooks, axes, and so on. Thus, if I accepted a plantain from someone in a different village while I was on a visit, he would most likely visit me in the future and demand a machete as payment for the time that he 'fed' me. I usually reacted to these kinds of demands by giving a banana, the customary reciprocity in their culture—food for food—but this would be a disappointment for the individual who had nursed visions of that single plantain growing into a machete over time. Many years after beginning my fieldwork I was approached by one of the prominent men who demanded a machete for a piece of meat he claimed he had given me five or six years earlier.

Despite the fact that most of them knew I would not share my food with them at their request, some of them

always showed up at my hut during mealtime. I gradually resigned myself to this and learned to ignore their persistent demands while I ate. Some of them would get angry because I failed to give in, but most of them accepted it as just a peculiarity of the subhuman foreigner who had come to live among them. If or when I did accede to a request for a share of my food, my hut quickly filled with Yąnomamö, each demanding their share of the food that I had just given to one of them. Their begging for food was not provoked by hunger, but by a desire to try something new and to attempt to establish a coercive relationship in which I would accede to a demand. If one received something, all others would immediately have to test the system to see if they, too, could coerce me.

A few of them went out of their way to make my meals downright unpleasant—to spite me for not sharing, especially if it was a food that they had tried before and liked, or a food that was part of their own cuisine. For example, I was eating a cracker with peanut butter and honey one day. The Yąnomamö will do almost anything for honey, one of the most prized delicacies in their own diet. One of my cynical onlookers—the fellow who had earlier watched me eating frankfurters—immediately recognized the honey and knew that I would not share the tiny precious bottle. It would be futile to even ask. Instead, he glared at me and queried icily, 'Shąki! What kind of animal semen are you pouring onto your food and eating?' His question had the desired effect and my meal ended.

Finally, there was the problem of being lonely and separated from your own kind, especially your family. I tried to overcome this by seeking personal friendships among the Yąnomamö. This usually complicated the matter because all my 'friends' simply used my confidence to gain privileged access to my hut and my cache of steel tools and trade goods—and looted me when I wasn't looking. I would be bitterly disappointed that my erstwhile friend thought no more of me than to finesse our personal relationship exclusively with the intention of getting at my locked up possessions, and my depression would hit new lows every time I discovered this. The loss of the possessions bothered me much less than the shock that I was, as far as most of them were concerned, nothing more than a source of desirable items. No holds were barred in relieving me of these, since I was considered something subhuman, a non-Yąnomamö.

The hardest thing to learn to live with was the incessant, passioned, and often aggressive demands they would make. It would become so unbearable at times that I would have to lock myself in my hut periodically just to escape from it. Privacy is one of our culture's most satisfying achievements, one you never think about until you suddenly have none. It is like not appreciating how good your left thumb feels until someone hits it with a hammer. But I did not want privacy for its own sake; rather, I simply had to get away from the begging. Day and night for almost the entire time I lived with the Yąnomamö I was plagued by such demands as: 'Give me a knife, I am poor!'; 'If you don't take me with you on your next trip to Widokaiyateri, I'll chop a hole in your canoe!'; 'Take us hunting up the Mavaca River with your shotgun or we won't help you!'; 'Give me some matches so I can trade with the Reyaboböwei-teri, and be quick about it or I'll hit you!'; 'Share your food with me, or I'll burn your hut!'; 'Give me a flashlight so I can hunt at night!'; 'Give me all your medicine, I itch all over!'; 'Give me an ax or I'll break into your hut when you are away and steal all of them!' And so I was bombarded by such demands day after day, month after month, until I could not bear to see a Yąnomamö at times.

It was not as difficult to become calloused to the incessant begging as it was to ignore the sense of urgency, the impassioned tone of voice and whining, or the intimidation and aggression with which many of the demands were made. It was likewise difficult to adjust to the fact that the Yąnomamö refused to accept 'No' for an answer until or unless it seethed with passion and intimidation—which it did after a few

months. So persistent and characteristic is the begging that the early 'semi-official' maps made by the Venezuelan Malaria Control Service (*Malarialogía*) designated the site of their first permanent field station, next to the village of Bisaasi-teri, as *Yababuhii:* 'Gimme.'I had to become like the Yąnomamö to be able to get along with them on their terms: somewhat sly, aggressive, intimidating, and pushy.

It became indelibly clear to me shortly after I arrived there that had I failed to adjust in this fashion I would have lost six months of supplies to them in a single day or would have spent most of my time ferrying them around in my canoe or taking them on long hunting trips. As it was, I did spend a considerable amount of time doing these things and did succumb often to their outrageous demands for axes and machetes, at least at first, for things changed as I became more fluent in their language and learned how to defend myself socially as well as verbally. More importantly, had I failed to demonstrate that I could not be pushed around beyond a certain point, I would have been the subject of far more ridicule, theft, and practical jokes than was the actual case. In short, I had to acquire a certain proficiency in their style of interpersonal politics and to learn how to imply subtly that certain potentially undesirable, but unspecified, consequences might follow if they did such and such to me. They do this to each other incessantly in order to establish precisely the point at which they cannot goad or intimidate an individual any further without precipitating some kind of retaliation. As soon as I realized this and gradually acquired the self-confidence to adopt this strategy, it became clear that much of the intimidation was calculated to determine my flash point or my 'last ditch' position—and I got along much better with them. Indeed, I even regained some lost ground. It was sort of like a political, interpersonal game that everyone had to play, but one in which each individual sooner or later had to give evidence that his bluffs and implied threats could be backed up with a sanction. I suspect

that the frequency of wife beating is a component in this syndrome, since men can display their *waiteri* (ferocity) and 'show' others that they are capable of great violence. Beating a wife with a club is one way of displaying ferocity, one that does not expose the man to much danger—unless the wife has concerned, aggressive brothers in the village who will come to her aid. Apparently an important thing in wife beating is that the man has displayed his presumed potential for violence and the intended message is that other men ought to treat him with circumspection, caution, and even deference.

After six months, the level of Yąnomamö demand was tolerable in Bisaasi-teri, the village I used for my base of operations. We had adjusted somewhat to each other and knew what to expect with regard to demands for food, trade goods, and favors. Had I elected to remain in just one Yąnomamö village for the entire duration of my first 15 months of fieldwork, the experience would have been far more enjoyable than it actually was. However, as I began to understand the social and political dynamics of this village, it became patently obvious that I would have to travel to many other villages to determine the demographic bases and political histories that lay behind what I could understand in the village of Bisaasi-teri. I began making regular trips to some dozen neighboring Yąnomamö villages as my language fluency improved. I collected local genealogies there, or rechecked and cross-checked those I had collected elsewhere. Hence, the intensity of begging was relatively constant and relatively high for the duration of my fieldwork, for I had to establish my personal position in each village I visited and revisited.

For the most part, my own 'fierceness' took the form of shouting back at the Yąnomamö as loudly and as passionately as they shouted at me, especially at first, when I did not know much of the language. As I became more fluent and learned more about their political tactics, I became more sophisticated in the art of bluffing and brinksmanship. For example, I paid one young man a machete (then worth about $2.50) to cut a palm tree and help me make boards from the wood. I used these to fashion a flooring in the bottom of my dugout canoe to keep my possession out of the water that always seeped into the canoe and sloshed around. That afternoon I was working with one of my informants in the village. The long-awaited mission supply boat arrived and most of the Yąnomamö ran out of the village to see the supplies and try to beg items from the crew. I continued to work in the village for another hour or so and then went down to the river to visit with the men on the supply boat. When I reached the river I noticed, with anger and frustration, that the Yąnomamö had chopped up all my new floor boards to use as crude paddles to get their own canoes across the river to the supply boat.[5] I knew that if I ignored this abuse I would have invited the Yąnomamö to take even greater liberties with my possessions in the future. I got into my canoe, crossed the river, and docked amidst their flimsy, leaky craft. I shouted loudly to them, attracting their attention. They were somewhat sheepish, but all had mischievous grins on their impish faces. A few of them came down to the canoe, where I proceeded with a spirited lecture that revealed my anger at their audacity and license. I explained that I had just that morning paid one of them a machete for bringing me the palmwood, how hard I had worked to shape each board and place it in the canoe, how carefully and painstakingly I had tied each one in with vines, how much I had perspired, how many *bareto* bites I had suffered, and so on. Then, with exaggerated drama and finality, I withdrew my hunting knife as their grins disappeared and cut each one of their canoes loose and set it into the strong current of the Orinoco River where it was immediately swept up and carried downstream. I left without looking back and huffed over to the other side of the river to resume my work.

They managed to borrow another canoe and, after some effort, recovered their dugouts. Later, the headman of the village told me, with an approving chuckle, that I had done the correct thing. Everyone in the village, except, of course, the culprits, supported and defended my actions—and my status increased as a consequence.

Whenever I defended myself in such ways I got along much better with the Yąnomamö and gradually acquired the respect of many of them. A good deal of their demeanor toward me was directed with the forethought of establishing the point at which I would draw the line and react defensively. Many of them, years later, reminisced about the early days of my fieldwork when I was timid and *mohode* ("stupid") and a little afraid of them, those golden days when it was easy to bully me into giving my goods away for almost nothing.

Theft was the most persistent situation that required some sort of defensive action. I simply could not keep everything I owned locked in trunks, and the Yąnomamö came into my hut and left at will. I eventually developed a very effective strategy for recovering almost all the stolen items: I would simply ask a child who took the item and then I would confiscate that person's hammock when he was not around, giving a spirited lecture to all who could hear on the antisociality of thievery as I stalked off in a faked rage with the thief's hammock slung over my shoulder. Nobody ever attempted to stop me from doing this, and almost all of them told me that my technique for recovering my possessions was ingenious. By nightfall the thief would appear at my hut with the stolen item or send it over with someone else to make an exchange to recover his hammock. He would be heckled by his covillagers for having got caught and for being embarrassed into returning my item for his hammock. The explanation was usually, 'I just borrowed your ax! I wouldn't think of stealing it!'

Collecting Yąnomamö Genealogies and Reproductive Histories
My purpose for living among Yąnomamö was to systematically collect certain kinds of information on genealogy, reproduction, marriage practices, kinship, settlement patterns, migrations, and politics. Much of the fundamental data was genealogical—who was the parent of whom, tracing these connections as far back in time as Yąnomamö knowledge and memory permitted. Since 'primitive' society is organized largely by kinship relationships, figuring out the social organization of the Yąnomamö essentially meant collecting extensive data on genealogies, marriage, and reproduction. This turned out to be a staggering and very frustrating problem. I could not have deliberately picked a more difficult people to work with in this regard. They have very stringent name taboos and eschew mentioning the names of prominent living people was well as all deceased friends and relatives. They attempt to name people in such a way that when the person dies and they can no longer use his or her name, the loss of the word in their language is not inconvenient. Hence, they name people for specific and minute parts of things, such as 'toenail of sloth,' 'whisker of howler monkey,' and so on, thereby being able to retain the words 'toenail' or 'whisker' but somewhat handicapped in referring to these anatomical parts of sloths and monkeys respectively. The taboo is maintained even for the living, for one mark of prestige is the courtesy others show you by not using your name publicly. This is particularly true for men, who are much more competitive for status than women in this culture, and it is fascinating to watch boys grow into young men, demanding to be called either by a kinship term in public, or by a teknonymous reference such as 'brother of Himotoma'. The more effective they are at getting others to avoid using their names, the more public acknowledgment there is that they are of high esteem and social standing. Helena Valero, a Brazilian woman who was captured as a child by a Yąnomamö raiding party, was married for many years to a Yąnomamö headman before she discovered what his name was (Biocca, 1970; Valero, 1984). The sanctions behind the taboo are more complex than just this, for they involve

a combination of fear, respect, admiration, political deference, and honor.

At first I tried to use kinship terms alone to collect genealogies, but Yąnomamö kinship terms, like the kinship terms in all systems, are ambiguous at some point because they include so many possible relatives (as the term 'uncle' does in our own kinship system). Again, their system of kin classification merges many relatives that we 'separate' by using different terms: They call both their actual father and their father's brother by a single term, whereas we call one 'father' and the other 'uncle.' I was forced, therefore, to resort to personal names to collect unambiguous genealogies or 'pedigrees'. They quickly grasped what I was up to and that I was determined to learn everyone's 'true name', which amounted to an invasion of their system of prestige and etiquette, if not a flagrant violation of it. They reacted to this in a brilliant but devastating manner: They invented false names for everybody in the village and systematically learned them, freely revealing to me the 'true' identities of everyone. I smugly thought I had cracked the system and enthusiastically constructed elaborate genealogies over a period of some five months. They enjoyed watching me learn their names and kinship relationships. I naively assumed that I would get the 'truth' to each question and the best information by working in public. This set the stage for converting my serious project into an amusing hoax of the grandest proportions. Each 'informant' would try to outdo his peers by inventing a name even more preposterous or ridiculous than what I had been given by someone earlier, the explanations for discrepancies being 'Well, he has two names and this is the other one.' They even fabricated devilishly improbable genealogical relationships, such as someone being married to his grandmother, or worse yet, to his mother-in-law, a grotesque and horrifying prospect to the Yanomamö. I would collect the desired names and relationships by having my informant whisper the name of the person softly into my ear, noting that he or she was the parent of such and

such or the child of such and such, and so on. Everyone who was observing my work would then insist that I repeat the name aloud, roaring in hysterical laughter as I clumsily pronounced the name, sometimes laughing until tears streamed down their faces. The 'named' person would usually react with annoyance and hiss some untranslatable epithet at me, which served to reassure me that I had the 'true' name. I conscientiously checked and rechecked the names and relationships with multiple informants, pleased to see the inconsistencies disappear as my genealogy sheets filled with those desirable little triangles and circles, thousands of them.

My anthropological bubble was burst when I visited a village about 10 hours' walk to the southwest of Bisaasi-teri some five months after I had begun collecting genealogies on the Bisaasi-teri. I was chatting with the local headman of this village and happened to casually drop the name of the wife of the Bisaasi-teri headman. A stunned silence followed, and then a villagewide roar of uncontrollable laughter, choking, gasping, and howling followed. It seems that I thought the Bisaasi-teri headman was married to a woman named "hairy cunt." It also seems that the Bisaasi-teri headman was called 'long dong' and his brother 'eagle shit.' The Bisaasi-teri headman had a son called "asshole" and a daughter called 'fart breath.' And so on. Blood welled up my temples as I realized that I had nothing but nonsense to show for my five months' of dedicated genealogical effort, and I had to throw away almost all the information I had collected on this the most basic set of data I had come there to get. I understood at that point why the Bisaasi-teri laughed so hard when they made me repeat the names of their covillagers, and why the 'named' person would react with anger and annoyance as I pronounced his 'name' aloud.

I was forced to change research strategy—to make an understatement to describe this serious situation. The first thing I did was to begin working in private with my informants to eliminate the horseplay and distraction that

attended public sessions. Once I did this, my informants, who did not know what others were telling me, began to agree with each other and I managed to begin learning the 'real' names, starting first with children and gradually moving to adult women and then, cautiously, adult men, a sequence that reflected the relative degree of intransigence at revealing names of people. As I built up a core of accurate genealogies and relationships—a core that all independent informants had verified repetitiously—I could 'test' any new informant by soliciting his or her opinion and knowledge about these 'core' people whose names and relationships I was confident were accurate. I was, in this fashion, able to immediately weed out the mischievous informants who persisted in trying to deceive me. Still, I had great difficulty getting the names of dead kinsmen, the only accurate way to extend genealogies back in time. Even my best informants continued to falsify names of the deceased, especially closely related deceased. The falsifications at this point were not serious and turned out to be readily corrected as my interviewing methods improved (see below). Most of the deceptions were of the sort where the informant would give me the name of a living man as the father of some child whose actual father was dead, a response that enabled the informant to avoid using the name of a deceased kinsman or friend.

The quality of a genealogy depends in part on the number of generations it embraces, and the name taboo prevented me from making any substantial progress in learning about the deceased ancestors of the present population. Without this information, I could not, for example, document marriage patterns and interfamilial alliances through time. I had to rely on older informants for this information, but these were the most reluctant informants of all for this data. As I became more proficient in the language and more skilled at detecting fabrications, my informants became better at deception. One old man was particularly cunning and persuasive, following a sort of Mark Twain policy that the most effective lie is a sincere lie. He specialized in making a ceremony out of false names for dead ancestors. He would look around nervously to make sure nobody was listening outside my hut, enjoin me never to mention the name again, become very anxious and spooky, and grab me by the head to whisper a secret name into my ear. I was always elated after a session with him, because I managed to add several generations of ancestors for particular members of the village. Others steadfastly refused to give me such information. To show my gratitude, I paid him quadruple the rate that I had been paying the others. When word got around that I had increased the pay for genealogical and demographic information, volunteers began pouring into my hut to 'work' for me, assuring me of their changed ways and keen desire to divest themselves of the 'truth'.

Enter Rerebawä: Inmarried Tough Guy

I discovered that the old man was lying quite by accident. A club fight broke out in the village one day, the result of a dispute over the possession of a woman. She had been promised to a young man in the village, a man named Rerebawä, who was particularly aggressive. He had married into Bisaasi-teri and was doing his 'bride service'— a period of several years during which he had to provide game for his wife's father and mother, provide them with wild foods he might collect, and help them in certain gardening and other tasks. Rerebawä had already been given one of the daughters in marriage and was promised her younger sister as his second wife. He was enraged when the younger sister, then about 16 years old, began having an affair with another young man in the village, Bäkotawä, making no attempt to conceal it. Rerebawä challenged Bäkotawä to a club fight. He swaggered boisterously out to the duel with his 10-foot-long club, a roof-pole he had cut from the house on the spur of the moment, as is the usual procedure. He hurled insult after insult at both Bäkotawä and his father, trying to goad them into a fight.

His insults were bitter and nasty. They tolerated them for a few moments, but Rerebawä's biting insults provoked them to rage. Finally, they stormed angrily out of their hammocks and ripped out roof-poles, now returning the insults verbally, and rushed to the village clearing. Rerebawä continued to insult them, goading them into striking him on the head with their equally long clubs. Had either of them struck his head—which he held out conspicuously for them to swing at—he would then have the right to take his turn on their heads with his club. His opponents were intimidated by his fury, and simply backed down, refusing to strike him, and the argument ended. He had intimidated them into submission. All three retired pompously to their respective hammocks, exchanging nasty insults as they departed. But Rerebawä had won the showdown and thereafter swaggered around the village, insulting the two men behind their backs at every opportunity. He was genuinely angry with them, to the point of calling the older man by the name of his long-deceased father. I quickly seized on this incident as an opportunity to collect an accurate genealogy and confidentially asked Rerebawä about his adversary's ancestors. Rerebawä had been particularly 'pushy' with me up to this point, but we soon became warm friends and staunch allies: We were both 'outsiders' in Bisaasi-teri and, although he was a Yąnomamö, he nevertheless had to put up with some considerable amount of pointed teasing and scorn from the locals, as all inmarried 'sons-in-law' must. He gave me the information I requested of his adversary's deceased ancestors, almost with devilish glee. I asked about dead ancestors of other people in the village and got prompt, unequivocal answers: He was angry with everyone in the village. When I compared his answers to those of the old man, it was obvious that one of them was lying. I then challenged his answers. He explained, in a sort of 'you damned fool, don't you know better?' tone of voice that everyone in the village knew the old man was lying to me and gloating over it when I was out of earshot. The

names the old man had given to me were names of dead ancestors of the members of a village so far away that he thought I would never have occasion to check them out authoritatively. As it turned out, Rerebawä knew most of the people in that distant village and recognized the names given by the old man.

I then went over all my Bisaasi-teri genealogies with Rerebawä, genealogies I had presumed to be close to their final form. I had to revise them all because of the numerous lies and falsifications they contained, much of it provided by the sly old man. Once again, after months of work, I had to recheck everything with Rerebawä's aid. Only the living members of the nuclear families turned out to be accurate; the deceased ancestors were mostly fabrications.

Discouraging as it was to have to recheck everything all over again, it was a major turning point in my fieldwork. Thereafter, I began taking advantage of local arguments and animosities in selecting my informants, and used more extensively informants who had married into the village in the recent past. I also began traveling more regularly to other villages at this time to check on genealogies, seeking out villages whose members were on strained terms with the people about whom I wanted information. I would then return to my base in the village of Bisaasi-teri and check with local informants the accuracy of the new information. I had to be careful in this work and scrupulously select my local informants in such a way that I would not be inquiring about *their* closely related kin. Thus, for each of my local informants, I had to make lists of names of certain deceased people that I dared not mention in their presence. But despite this precaution, I would occasionally hit a new name that would put some informants into a rage, or into a surly mood, such as that of a dead 'brother' or 'sister'[6] whose existence had not been indicted to me by other informants. This usually terminated my day's work with that informant, for he or she would be too touchy or upset to continue any further, and I would be reluctant to take a chance on accidentally discovering another dead close kinsman soon after discovering the first.

These were unpleasant experiences, and occasionally dangerous as well, depending on the temperament of my informant. On one occasion I was planning to visit a village that had been raided recently by one of their enemies. A woman, whose name I had on my census list for that village, had been killed by the raiders. Killing women is considered to be bad form in Yąnomamö warfare, but this woman was deliberately killed for revenge. The raiders were unable to bushwhack some man who stepped out of the village at dawn to urinate, so they shot a volley of arrows over the roof into the village and beat a hasty retreat. Unfortunately, one of the arrows struck and killed a woman, an accident. For that reason, her village's raiders *deliberately* sought out and killed a woman in retaliation—whose name was on my list. My reason for going to the village was to update my census data on a name-by-name basis and estimate the ages of all the residents. I knew I had the name of the dead woman in my list, but nobody would dare to utter her name so I could remove it. I knew that I would be in very serious trouble if I got to the village and said her name aloud, and I desperately wanted to remove it from my list. I called on one of my regular and usually cooperative informants and asked him to tell me the woman's name. He refused adamantly, explaining that she was a close relative—and was angry that I even raised the topic with him. I then asked him if he would let me whisper the names of *all* the women of that village in his ear, and he would simply have to nod when I hit the right name. We had been 'friends' for some time, and I thought I was able to predict his reaction, and thought that our friendship was good enough to use this procedure. He agreed to the procedure, and I began whispering the names of the women, one by one. We were alone in my hut so that nobody would know what we were doing and nobody could hear us. I read the names softly, continuing to

the next when his response was a negative. When I ultimately hit the dead woman's name, he flew out of his chair, enraged and trembling violently, his arm raised to strike me: 'You son-of-a-bitch!' he screamed. 'If you say her name in my presence again, I'll kill you in an instant!' I sat there, bewildered, shocked, and confused. And frightened, as much because of his reaction, but also because I could imagine what might happen to me should I unknowingly visit a village to check genealogy accuracy without knowing that someone had just died there or had been shot by raiders since my last visit. I reflected on the several articles I had read as a graduate student that explained the 'genealogical method,' but could not recall anything about its being a potentially lethal undertaking. My furious informant left my hut, never again to be invited back to be an informant. I had other similar experiences in different villages, but I was always fortunate in that the dead person had been dead for some time, or was not very closely related to the individual into whose ear I whispered the forbidden name. I was usually cautioned by one of the men to desist from saying any more names lest I get people 'angry'.[7]

Kąobawä: The Bisaasi-teri Headman Volunteers to Help Me

I had been working on the genealogies for nearly a year when another individual came to my aid. It was Kąobawä, the headman of Upper Bisaasi-teri. The village of Bisaasi-teri was split into two components, each with its own garden and own circular house. Both were in sight of each other. However, the intensity and frequency of internal bickering and argumentation was so high that they decided to split into two separate groups but remain close to each other for protection in case they were raided. One group was downstream from the other; I refer to that group as the 'Lower' Bisaasi-teri and call Kąobawä's group 'Upper' (upstream) Bisaasi-teri, a convenience they themselves adopted after separating from each other. I spent most

of my time with the members of Kąobawä's group, some 200 people when I first arrived there. I did not have much contact with Kąobawä during the early months of my work. He was a somewhat retiring, quiet man, and among the Yąomamö, the outsider has little time to notice the rare quiet ones when most everyone else is in the front row, pushing and demanding attention. He showed up at my hut one day after all the others had left. He had come to volunteer to help me with the genealogies. He was 'poor,' he explained, and needed a machete. He would work only on the condition that I did not ask him about his own parents and other very close kinsmen who had died. He also added that he would not lie to me as the others had done in the past.

This was perhaps the single most important event in my first 15 months of field research, for out of this fortuitous circumstance evolved a very warm friendship, and among the many things following from it was a wealth of accurate information on the political history of Kąobawä's village and related villages, highly detailed genealogical information, sincere and useful advice to me, and hundreds of valuable insights into the Yąnomamö way of life. Kąobawä's familiarity with his group's history and his candidness were remarkable. His knowledge of details was almost encyclopedic, his memory almost photographic. More than that, he was enthusiastic about making sure I learned the truth, and he encouraged me, indeed, *demanded* that I learn all details I might otherwise have ignored. If there were subtle details he could not recite on the spot, he would advise me to wait until he could check things out with someone else in the village. He would often do this clandestinely, giving me a report the next day, telling me who revealed the new information and whether or not he thought they were in a position to know it. With the information provided by Kąobawä and Rerebawä, I made enormous gains in understanding village interrelationships based on common ancestors and political histories and became lifelong friends with both. And both men knew that I had to learn about his recently deceased kin from the other one. It was one of those quiet understandings we all had but none of us could mention.

Once again I went over the genealogies with Kąobawä to recheck them, a considerable task by this time. They included about two thousand names, representing several generations of individuals from four different villages. Rerebawä's information was very accurate, and Kąobawä's contribution enabled me to trace the genealogies further back in time. Thus, after nearly a year of intensive effort on genealogies, Yąnomamö demographic patterns and social organization began to make a good deal of sense to me. Only at this point did the patterns through time begin to emerge in the data, and I could begin to understand how kinship groups took form, exchanged women in marriage over several generations, and only then did the fissioning of larger villages into smaller ones emerge as a chronic and important feature of Yąomamö social, political, demographic, economic, and ecological adaptation. At this point I was able to begin formulating more sophisticated questions, for there was now a pattern to work from and one to flesh out. Without the help of Rerebawä and Kąobawä it would have taken much longer to make sense of the plethora of details I had collected from not only them, but dozens of other informants as well.

I spent a good deal of time with these two men and their families, and got to know them much better than I knew most Yąnomamö. They frequently gave their information in a way which related themselves to the topic under discussion. We became warm friends as time passed, and the formal 'informant/anthropologist' relationship faded into the background. Eventually, we simply stopped 'keeping track' of work and pay. They would both spend hours talking with me, leaving without asking for anything. When they wanted something, they would ask for it no matter what the relative balance of reciprocity between us might have been at that point. . . .

For many of the customary things that anthropologists try to communicate about another culture, these two men and their families might be considered to be 'exemplary' or 'typical'. For other things, they are exceptional in many regards, but the reader will, even knowing some of the exceptions, understand Yąnomamö culture more intimately by being familiar with a few examples.

Kąobawä was about 40 years old when I first came to his village in 1964. I say "about 40" because the Yąnomamö numeration system has only three numbers: one, two, and more-than-two. It is hard to give accurate ages or dates for events when the informants have no means in their language to reveal such detail. Kąobawä is the headman of his village, meaning that he has somewhat more responsibility in political dealings with other Yąnomamö groups, and very little control over those who live in his group except when the village is being raided by enemies. We will learn more about political leadership and warfare in a later chapter, but most of the time men like Kąobawä are like the North American Indian 'chief' whose authority was characterized in the following fashion: "One word from the chief, and each man does as he pleases." There are different 'styles' of political leadership among the Yąnomamö. Some leaders are mild, quiet, inconspicuous most of the time, but intensely competent. They act parsimoniously, but when they do, people listen and conform. Other men are more tyrannical, despotic, pushy, flamboyant, and unpleasant to all around them. They shout orders frequently, are prone to beat their wives, or pick on weaker men. Some are very violent. I have met headmen who run the entire spectrum between these polar types, for I have visited some 60 Yąnomamö villages. Kąobawä stands at the mild, quietly competent end of the spectrum. He has had six wives thus far—and temporary affairs with as many more, at least one of which resulted in a child that is publicly acknowledged as his child. When I first met him he had just two wives: Bahimi

and Koamashima. Bahimi had two living children when I first met her; many others had died. She was the older and enduring wife, as much a friend to him as a mate. Their relationship was as close to what we think of as 'love' in our culture as I have seen among the Yąnomamö. His second wife was a girl of about 20 years, Koamashima. She had a new baby boy when I first met her, her first child. There was speculation that Kąobawä was planning to give Koamashima to one of his younger brothers who had no wife; he occasionally allows his younger brother to have sex with Koamashima, but only if he asks in advance. Kąobawä gave another wife to one of his other brothers because she was *beshi* ("horny"). In fact, this earlier wife had been married to two other men, both of whom discarded her because of her infidelity. Kąobawä had one daughter by her. However, the girl is being raised by Kąobawä's brother, though acknowledged to be Kąobawä's child.

Bahimi, his oldest wife, is about five years younger than he. She is his cross-cousin—his mother's brother's daughter. Ideally, all Yąnomamö men should marry a cross-cousin. . . . Bahimi was pregnant when I began my fieldwork, but she destroyed the infant when it was born—a boy in this case—explaining tearfully that she had no choice. The new baby would have competed for milk with Ariwari, her youngest child, who was still nursing. Rather than expose Ariwari to the dangers and uncertainty of an early weaning, she chose to terminate the newborn instead. By Yąnomamö standards, this has been a very warm, enduring marriage. Kąobawä claims he beats Bahimi only 'once in a while, and only lightly' and she, for her part, never has affairs with other men.

Kąobawä is a quiet, intense, wise, and unobtrusive man. It came as something of a surprise to me when I learned that he was the headman of his village, for he stayed at the sidelines while others would surround me and press their demands on me. He leads more by example than by coercion. He can afford to be this way at his age, for he established his reputation for being forthright and as fierce as the situation required when he was younger, and the other men respect him. He also has five mature brothers or half-brothers in his village, men he can count on for support. He also has several other mature 'brothers' (parallel cousins, whom he must refer to as 'brothers' in his kinship system) in the village who frequently come to his aid, but not as often as his 'real' brothers do. Kąobawä has also given a number of his sisters to other men in the village and has promised his young (8-year-old) daughter in marriage to a young man who, for that reason, is obliged to help him. In short, his 'natural' or 'kinship' following is large, and partially because of this support, he does not have to display his aggressiveness to remind his peers of his position.

Rerebawä is a very different kind of person. He is much younger—perhaps in his early twenties. He has just one wife, but they have already had three children. He is from a village called Karohi-teri, located about five hours' walk up the Orinoco, slightly inland off to the east of the river itself. Kąobawä's village enjoys amicable relationships with Rerebawä's, and it is for this reason that marriage alliances of the kind represented by Rerebawä's marriage into Kąobawä's village occur between the two groups. Rerebawä told me that he came to Bisaasi-teri because there were no eligible women from him to marry in his own village, a fact that I later was able to document when I did a census of his village and a preliminary analysis of its social organization. Rerebawä is perhaps more typical than Kąobawä in the sense that he is chronically concerned about his personal reputation for aggressiveness and goes out of his way to be noticed, even if he has to act tough. He gave me a hard time during my early months of fieldwork, intimidating, teasing, and insulting me frequently. He is, however, much braver than the other men his age and is quite prepared to back up his threats with immediate action—as in the club fight incident just described above. Moreover, he is fascinated with political relationships and knows the details of intervillage relationships over a large area of the tribe. In this respect he shows all the attributes of being a headman, although he has too many competent brothers in his own village to expect to move easily into the leadership position there.

He does not intend to stay in Kąobawä's group and refuses to make his own garden—a commitment that would reveal something of an intended long-term residence. He feels that he has adequately discharged his obligations to his wife's parents by providing them with fresh game, which he has done for several years. They should let him take his wife and return to his own village with her, but they refuse and try to entice him to remain permanently in Bisaasi-teri to continue to provide them with game when they are old. It is for this reason that they promised to give him their second daughter, their only other child, in marriage. Unfortunately, the girl was opposed to the marriage and ultimately married another man, a rare instance where the woman in the marriage had this much influence on the choice of her husband.

Although Rerebawä has displayed his ferocity in many ways, one incident in particular illustrates what his character can be like. Before he left his own village to take his new wife in Bisaasi-teri, he had an affair with the wife of an older brother. When it was discovered, his brother attacked him with a club. Rerebawä responded furiously: He grabbed an ax and drove his brother out of the village after soundly beating him with the blunt side of the single-bit ax. His brother was so intimidated by the thrashing and promise of more to come that he did not return to the village for several days. I visited this village with Koabawä shortly after this event had taken place; Rerebawä was with me as my guide. He made it a point to introduce me to this man. He approached his hammock, grabbed him by the wrist, and dragged him out on the ground: 'This is the brother whose wife I screwed when he wasn't around!' A deadly insult, one that would usually provoke a bloody club fight among more valiant Yąnomamö. The man did nothing. He slunk sheepishly back into his hammock, shamed, but relieved to have Rerebawä release his grip.

Even though Rerebawä is fierce and capable of considerable nastiness, he has a charming, witty side as well. He has a biting sense of humor and can entertain the group for hours with jokes and clever manipulations of language. And, he is one of few Yąnomamö that I feel I can trust. I recall indelibly my return to Bisaasi-teri after being away a year—the occasion of my second field trip to the Yąnomamö. When I reached Bisaasi-teri, Rerebawä was in his own village visiting his kinsmen. Word reached him that I had returned, and he paddled downstream immediately to see me. He greeted me with an immense bear hug and exclaimed, with tears welling up in his eyes, 'Shaki! Why did you stay away so long? Did you not know that my will was so cold while you were gone that I could not at times eat for want of seeing you again?' I, too, felt the same way about him—then, and now.

Of all the Yąnomamö I know, he is the most genuine and the most devoted to his culture's ways and values. I admire him for that, although I cannot say that I subscribe to or endorse some of these values. By contrast, Kąobawä is older and wiser, a polished diplomat. He sees his own culture in a slightly different light and seems even to question aspects of it. Thus, while many of his peers enthusiastically accept the 'explanations' of things given in myths, he occasionally reflects on them—even laughing at some of the most preposterous of them. . . . Probably more of the Yąnomamö are like Rerebawä than like Kąobawä, or at least try to be. . . .

NOTES

1. The word Yąnomamö is nasalized through its entire length, indicated by the diacritical mark ' ̨'. When this mark appears on any Yąnomamö word, the whole word is nasalized. The vowel 'ö' represents a sound that does not occur in the English language. It is similar to the umlaut 'ö' in the German language or the 'oe' equivalent, as in the poet Goethe's name. Unfortunately, many presses and typesetters simply eliminate diacritical marks, and this has led to multiple spellings of the word Yąnomamö—and

multiple mispronunciations. Some anthropologists have chosen to introduce a slightly different spelling of the word Yᶏnomamö since I began writing about them, such as Yᶏnomami, leading to additional misspellings as their diacriticals are characteristically eliminated by presses, and to the *incorrect* pronunciation 'Yanomameee.' Vowels indicated as 'ä' are pronounced as the 'uh' sound in the word 'duck'. Thus, the name Kᶏobawä would be pronounced 'cow-ba-wuh,' but entirely nasalized.

2. I spent a total of 60 months among the Yᶏnomamö between 1964 and 1991. The first edition of this case study was based on the first 15 months I spent among them in Venezuela. I have, at the time of this writing, made 20 field trips to the Yᶏnomamö and this edition reflects the new information and understandings I have acquired over the years. I plan to return regularly to continue what has now turned into a life-long study.

3. See Spindler (1970) for a general discussion of field research by anthropologists who have worked in other cultures. Nancy Howell has recently written a very useful book (1990) on some of the medical, personal, and environmental hazards of doing field research, which includes a selected bibliography on other field-work problems.

4. They could not pronounce "Chagnon." It sounded to them like their name for a pesky bee, shaki, and that is what they called me: pesky, noisome bee.

5. The Yᶏnomamö in this region acquired canoes very recently. The missionaries would purchase them from the Ye'kwana Indians to the north for money, and then trade them to the Yᶏnomamö in exchange for labor, produce, or 'informant' work in translating. It should be emphasized that those Yᶏnomamö who lived on navigable portions of the Upper Orinoco River moved there recently from the deep forest in order to have contact with the missionaries and acquire the trade goods the missionaries (and their supply system) brought.

6. Rarely were there actual brothers or sisters. In Yᶏnomamö kinship classifications, certain kinds of cousins are classified as siblings. See Chapter 4.

7. Over time, as I became more and more 'accepted' by the Yᶏnomamö, they became less and less concerned about my genealogical inquiries and, now, provide me with this information quite willingly because I have been very discrete with it. Now, when I revisit familiar villages I am called aside by someone who whispers to me things like, "Don't ask about so-and-so's father."

Doctor, Lawyer, Indian Chief

*As Punjabi villagers say, "You never really know who a man is
until you know who his grandfather and his ancestors were"*

Richard Kurin

*Richard Kurin is the Deputy Director
of Folklife Programs at the Smithsonian Institution.*

I was full of confidence when—
equipped with a scholarly proposal,
blessings from my advisers, and
generous research grants—I set out
to study village social structure in the
Punjab province of Pakistan. But
after looking for an appropriate
fieldwork site for several weeks without success, I began to think that my
research project would never get off
the ground. Daily I would seek out
villages aboard my puttering motor
scooter, traversing the dusty dirt
roads, footpaths, and irrigation
ditches that crisscross the Punjab.
But I couldn't seem to find a village
amenable to study. The major problem was that the villagers I did approach were baffled by my presence.
They could not understand why anyone would travel ten thousand miles
from home to a foreign country in
order to live in a poor village, interview illiterate peasants, and then
write a book about it. Life, they were
sure, was to be lived, not written
about. Besides, they thought, what of
any importance could they possibly

tell me? Committed as I was to ethnographic research, I readily understood their viewpoint. I was a *babu
log*—literally, a noble; figuratively, a
clerk; and simply, a person of the city.
I rode a motor scooter, wore tight-
fitting clothing, and spoke Urdu, a
language associated with the urban
literary elite. Obviously, I did not
belong, and the villagers simply did
not see me fitting into their society.

The Punjab, a region about the size
of Colorado, straddles the northern
border of India and Pakistan. Parti-
tioned between the two countries in
1947, the Punjab now consists of a
western province, inhabited by Muslims, and an eastern one, populated in
the main by Sikhs and Hindus. As its
name implies—*punj* meaning "five"
and *ab* meaning "rivers"—the region
is endowed with plentiful resources to
support widespread agriculture and a
large rural population. The Punjab
has traditionally supplied grains,
produce, and dairy products to the
peoples of neighboring and considerably more arid states, earning it a
reputation as the breadbasket of
southern Asia.

Given this predilection for agriculture, Punjabis like to emphasize that
they are earthy people, having values
they see as consonant with rural life.
These values include an appreciation
of, and trust in, nature; simplicity and

directness of expression; an awareness of the basic drives and desires
that motivate men (namely, *zan, zar,
zamin*—"women, wealth, land"); a
concern with honor and shame as
abiding principles of social organization; and for Muslims, a deep faith in
Allah and the teachings of his prophet
Mohammad.

Besides being known for its fertile
soils, life-giving rivers, and superla-
tive agriculturists, the Punjab is also
perceived as a zone of transitional
culture, a region that has experienced
repeated invasions of peoples from
western and central Asia into the
Indian subcontinent. Over the last
four thousand years, numerous
groups, among them Scythians, Par-
thians, Huns, Greeks, Moguls, Per-
sians, Afghans, and Turks, have
entered the subcontinent through the
Punjab in search of bountiful land,
riches, or power. Although Punjabis—notably Rajputs, Sikhs, and
Jats—have a reputation for courage
and fortitude on the battlefield, their
primary, self-professed strength has
been their ability to incorporate new,
exogenous elements into their society
with a minimum of conflict. Punjabis
are proud that theirs is a multiethnic
society in which diverse groups have
been largely unified by a common
language and by common customs
and traditions.

1. ANTHROPOLOGICAL PERSPECTIVES

Given this background, I had not expected much difficulty in locating a village in which to settle and conduct my research. As an anthropologist, I viewed myself as an "earthy" social scientist who, being concerned with basics, would have a good deal in common with rural Punjabis. True, I might be looked on as an invader of a sort; but I was benevolent, and sensing this, villagers were sure to incorporate me into their society with even greater ease than was the case for the would-be conquering armies that had preceded me. Indeed, they would welcome me with open arms.

I was wrong. The villagers whom I approached attributed my desire to live with them either to neurotic delusions or nefarious ulterior motives. Perhaps, so the arguments went, I was really after women, land, or wealth.

On the day I had decided would be my last in search of a village, I was driving along a road when I saw a farmer running through a rice field and waving me down. I stopped and he climbed on the scooter. Figuring I had nothing to lose, I began to explain why I wanted to live in a village. To my surprise and delight, he was very receptive, and after sharing a pomegranate milkshake at a roadside shop, he invited me to his home. His name was Allah Ditta, which means "God given," and I took this as a sign that I had indeed found my village.

"My" village turned out to be a settlement of about fifteen hundred people, mostly of the Nunari *qaum*, or "tribe." The Nunaris engage primarily in agriculture (wheat, rice, sugar cane, and cotton), and most families own small plots of land. Members of the Bhatti tribe constitute the largest minority in the village. Although traditionally a warrior tribe, the Bhattis serve in the main as the village artisans and craftsmen.

On my first day in the village I tried explaining in great detail the purposes of my study to the village elders and clan leaders. Despite my efforts, most of the elders were perplexed about why I wanted to live in their village. As a guest, I was entitled to the hospitality traditionally bestowed by Muslim peoples of Asia, and during the first evening I was assigned a place to stay. But I was an enigma, for guests leave, and I wanted to remain. I was also perceived as being strange, for I was both a non-Muslim and a non-Punjabi, a type of person not heretofore encountered by most of the villagers. Although I tried to temper my behavior, there was little I could say or do to dissuade my hosts from the view that I embodied the antithesis of Punjabi values. While I was able to converse in their language, Jatki, a dialect of western Punjabi, I was only able to do so with the ability of a four-year-old. This achievement fell far short of speaking the *t'et',* or "genuine form," of the villagers. Their idiom is rich with the terminology of agricultural operations and rural life. It is unpretentious, uninflected, and direct, and villagers hold high opinions of those who are good with words, who can speak to a point and be convincing. Needless to say, my infantile babble realized none of these characteristics and evoked no such respect.

Similarly, even though I wore indigenous dress, I was inept at tying my *lungi,* or pant cloth. The fact that my *lungi* occasionally fell off and revealed what was underneath gave my neighbors reason to believe that I indeed had no shame and could not control the passions of my *nafs,* or "libidinous nature."

This image of a doltish, shameless infidel barely capable of caring for himself lasted for the first week of my residence in the village. My inability to distinguish among the five varieties of rice and four varieties of lentil grown in the village illustrated that I knew or cared little about nature and agricultural enterprise. This display of ignorance only served to confirm the general consensus that the mysterious morsels I ate from tin cans labeled "Chef Boy-ar-Dee" were not really food at all. Additionally, I did not oil and henna my hair, shave my armpits, or perform ablutions, thereby convincing some commentators that I was a member of a species of subhuman beings, possessing little in the form of either common or moral sense. That the villagers did not quite grant me the status of a person was reflected by their not according me a proper name. In the Punjab, a person's name is equated with honor and respect and is symbolized by his turban. A man who does not have a name, or whose name is not recognized by his neighbors, is unworthy of respect. For such a man, his turban is said to be either nonexistent or to lie in the dust at the feet of others. To be given a name is to have one's head crowned by a turban, an acknowledgment that one leads a responsible and respectable life. Although I repeatedly introduced myself as "Rashid Karim," a fairly decent Pakistani rendering of Richard Kurin, just about all the villagers insisted on calling me *Angrez* ("Englishman"), thus denying me full personhood and implicitly refusing to grant me the right to wear a turban.

As I began to pick up the vernacular, to question villagers about their clan and kinship structure and trace out relationships between different families, my image began to change. My drawings of kinship diagrams and preliminary census mappings were looked upon not only with wonder but also suspicion. My neighbors now began to think there might be a method to my madness. And so there was. Now I had become a spy. Of course it took a week for people to figure out whom I was supposedly spying for. Located as they were at a cross-roads of Asia, at a nexus of conflicting geopolitical interests, they had many possibilities to consider. There was a good deal of disagreement on the issue, with the vast majority maintaining that I was either an American, Russian, or Indian spy. A small, but nonetheless vocal, minority held steadfastly to the belief that I was a Chinese spy. I thought it all rather humorous until one day a group confronted me in the main square in front of the nine-by-nine-foot mud hut that I had rented. The leader spoke up and accused me of spying. The remainder of the group grumbled *jahsus! jahsus!* ("spy! spy!"), and I realized that this ad hoc committee of inquiry had the potential of becoming a mob.

To be sure, the villagers had good reason to be suspicious. For one, the times were tense in Pakistan—a national political crisis gripped the country and the populace had been anxious for months over the uncertainty of elections and effective governmental functions. Second, keenly aware of their history, some of the villagers did not have to go too far to imagine that I was at the vanguard of some invading group that had designs upon their land. Such intrigues, with far greater sophistication, had been played out before by nations seeking to expand their power into the Punjab. That I possessed a gold seal letter (which no one save myself could read) from the University of Chicago to the effect that I was pursuing legitimate studies was not enough to convince the crowd that I was indeed an innocent scholar.

I repeatedly denied the charge, but to no avail. The shouts of *jahsus! jahsus!* prevailed. Confronted with this I had no choice.

"Okay," I said. "I admit it. I am a spy!"

The crowd quieted for my long-awaited confession.

"I am a spy and am here to study this village, so that when my country attacks you we will be prepared. You see, we will not bomb Lahore or Karachi or Islamabad. Why should we waste our bombs on millions of people, on factories, dams, airports, and harbors? No, it is far more advantageous to bomb this strategic small village replete with its mud huts, livestock, Persian wheels, and one light bulb. And when we bomb this village, it is imperative that we know how Allah Ditta is related to Abdullah, and who owns the land near the well, and what your marriage customs are."

Silence hung over the crowd, and then one by one the assemblage began to disperse. My sarcasm had worked. The spy charges were defused. But I was no hero in light of my performance, and so I was once again relegated to the status of a nonperson without an identity in the village.

I remained in limbo for the next week, and although I continued my attempts to collect information about village life, I had my doubts as to whether I would ever be accepted by the villagers. And then, through no effort of my own, there was a breakthrough, this time due to another Allah Ditta, a relative of the village headman and one of my leading accusers during my spying days.

I was sitting on my woven string bed on my porch when Allah Ditta approached, leading his son by the neck. "Oh, *Angrez!*" he yelled, "this worthless son of mine is doing poorly in school. He is supposed to be learning English, but he is failing. He has a good mind, but he's lazy. And his teacher is no help, being more intent upon drinking tea and singing film songs than upon teaching English. Oh son of an Englishman, do you know English?"

"Yes, I know English," I replied, "after all, I am an *Angrez.*"

"Teach him," Allah Ditta blurted out, without any sense of making a tactful request.

And so, I spent the next hour with the boy, reviewing his lessons and correcting his pronunciation and grammar. As I did so, villagers stopped to watch and listen, and by the end of the hour, nearly one hundred people had gathered around, engrossed by this tutoring session. They were stupefied. I was an effective teacher, and I actually seemed to know English. The boy responded well, and the crowd reached a new consensus. I had a brain. And in recognition of this achievement I was given a name—"Ustad Rashid," or Richard the Teacher.

Achieving the status of a teacher was only the beginning of my success. The next morning I awoke to find the village sugar vendor at my door. He had a headache and wanted to know if I could cure him.

"Why do you think I can help you?" I asked.

Bhai Khan answered, "Because you are a *ustad,* you have a great deal of knowledge."

The logic was certainly compelling. If I could teach English, I should be able to cure a headache. I gave him two aspirins.

An hour later, my fame had spread. Bhai Khan had been cured, and he did not hesitate to let others know that it was the *ustad* who had been responsible. By the next day, and in fact for the remainder of my stay, I was to see an average of twenty-five to thirty patients a day. I was asked to cure everything from coughs and colds to typhoid, elephantiasis, and impotency. Upon establishing a flourishing and free medical practice, I received another title, *hakim,* or "physician." I was not yet an anthropologist, but I was on my way.

A few days later I took on yet another role. One of my research interests involved tracing out patterns of land ownership and inheritance. While working on the problem of figuring out who owned what, I was approached by the village watchman. He claimed he had been swindled in a land deal and requested my help. As the accused was not another villager, I agreed to present the watchman's case to the local authorities.

Somehow, my efforts managed to achieve results. The plaintiff's grievance was redressed, and I was given yet another title in the village—*wakil,* or "lawyer." And in the weeks that followed, I was steadily called upon to read, translate, and advise upon various court orders that affected the lives of the villagers.

My roles as teacher, doctor, and lawyer not only provided me with an identity but also facilitated my integration into the economic structure of the community. As my imputed skills offered my neighbors services not readily available in the village, I was drawn into exchange relationships known as *seipi. Seipi* refers to the barter system of goods and services among village farmers, craftsmen, artisans, and other specialists. Every morning Roshan the milkman would deliver fresh milk to my hut. Every other day Hajam Ali the barber would stop by and give me a shave. My next-door neighbor, Nura the cobbler, would repair my sandals when required. Ghulam the horse-cart driver would transport me to town when my motor scooter was in disrepair. The parents of my students would send me sweets and sometimes delicious meals. In return, none of my neighbors asked for direct payment for the specific actions performed. Rather, as they told me, they would call upon me when they had need of my services. And they did. Nura needed cough syrup for his children, the milkman's brother needed a job contact in the city, students wanted to continue their lessons, and so on. Through *seipi* relations, various neighbors gave goods and services to me, and I to them.

Even so, I knew that by Punjabi standards I could never be truly accepted into village life because I was not a member of either the Nunari or Bhatti tribe. As the villagers would say, "You never really know who a man is until you know who his grandfather and his ancestors were." And to know a person's grandfather or ancestors properly, you had to be a member of the same or a closely allied tribe.

The Nunari tribe is composed of a number of groups. The nucleus consists of four clans—Naul, Vadel, Sadan, and More—each named for one of four brothers thought to have originally founded the tribe. Clan members are said to be related to blood ties, also called *pag da sak,* or "ties of the turban." In sharing the turban, members of each clan share the same name. Other clans, unrelated by ties of blood to these four, have become attached to this nucleus through a history of marital relations or of continuous political and economic interdependence. Marital relations, called *gag da sak,* or "ties of the skirt," are conceived of as relations in which alienable turbans (skirts) in the form of women are exchanged with other, non-turban-sharing groups. Similarly, ties of political and economic domination and subordination are thought of as relations in which the turban of the client is given to that of the patron. A major part of my research work was concerned with reconstructing how the four brothers formed the Nunari tribe, how additional clans became associated with

it, and how clan and tribal identity were defined by nomenclature, codes of honor, and the symbols of sharing and exchanging turbans.

To approach these issues I set out to reconstruct the genealogical relationships within the tribe and between the various clans. I elicited genealogies from many of the villagers and questioned older informants about the history of the Nunari tribe. Most knew only bits and pieces of this history, and after several months of interviews and research, I was directed to the tribal genealogists. These people, usually not Nunaris themselves, perform the service of memorizing and then orally relating the history of the tribe and the relationships among its members. The genealogist in the village was an aged and arthritic man named Hedayat, who in his later years was engaged in teaching the Nunari genealogy to his son, who would then carry out the traditional and hereditary duties of his position.

The villagers claimed that Hedayat knew every generation of the Nunari from the present to the founding brothers and even beyond. So I invited Hedayat to my hut and explained my purpose.

"Do you know Allah Ditta son of Rohm?" I asked.

"Yes, of course," he replied.

"Who was Rohm's father?" I continued.

"Shahadat Mohammad," he answered.

"And his father?"

"Hamid."

"And his?"

"Chigatah," he snapped without hesitation.

I was now quite excited, for no one else in the village had been able to recall an ancestor of this generation. My estimate was that Chigatah had been born sometime between 1850 and 1870. But Hedayat went on.

"Chigatah's father was Kamal. And Kamal's father was Nanak. And Nanak's father was Sikhu. And before him was Dargai, and before him Maiy. And before him was Siddiq. And Siddiq's father was Nur. And Nur's Asmat. And Asmat was of Channa.

And Channa of Nau. And Nau of Bhatta. And Bhatta was the son of Koduk."

Hedayat had now recounted sixteen generations of lineal ascendants related through the turban. Koduk was probably born in the sixteenth century. But still Hedayat continued.

"Sigun was the father of Koduk. And Man the father of Sigun. And before Man was his father Maneswar. And Maneswar's father was the founder of the clan, Naul."

This then was a line of the Naul clan of the Nunari tribe, ascending twenty-one generations from the present descendants (Allah Ditta's sons) to the founder, one of four brothers who lived perhaps in the fifteenth century. I asked Hedayat to recite genealogies of the other Nunari clans, and he did, with some blanks here and there, ending with Vadel, More, and Saddan, the other three brothers who formed the tribal nucleus. I then asked the obvious question, "Hedayat, who was the father of these four brothers? Who is the founding ancestor of the Nunari tribe?"

"The father of these brothers was not a Muslim. He was an Indian rajput [chief]. The tribe actually begins with the conversion of the four brothers," Hedayat explained.

"Well then," I replied, "who was this Indian chief?"

He was a famous and noble chief who fought against the Moguls. His name was Raja Kurin, who lived in a massive fort in Kurinnagar, about twenty-seven miles from Delhi."

"What!" I asked, both startled and unsure of what I had heard.

"Raja Kurin is the father of the brothers who make up—"

"But his name! It's the same as mine," I stammered. "Hedayat, my name is Richard Kurin. What a coincidence! Here I am living with your tribe thousands of miles from my home and it turns out that I have the same name as the founder of the tribe! Do you think I might be related to Raja Kurin and the Nunaris?"

Hedayat looked at me, but only for an instant. Redoing his turban, he tilted his head skyward, smiled, and asked, "What is the name of your father?"

I had come a long way. I now had a name that could be recognized and respected, and as I answered Hedayat, I knew that I had finally and irrevocably fit into "my" village. Whether by fortuitous circumstances or by careful manipulation, my neighbors had found a way to take an invading city person intent on studying their life and transform him into one of their own, a full person entitled to wear a turban for participating in, and being identified with, that life. As has gone on for centuries in the region, once again the new and exogenous had been recast into something Punjabi.

Epilogue: There is no positive evidence linking the Nunaris to a historical Raja Kurin, although there are several famous personages identified by that name (also transcribed as Karan and Kurran). Estimated from the genealogy recited by Hedayat, the founding of the tribe by the four brothers appears to have occurred sometime between 440 and 640 years ago, depending on the interval assumed for each generation. On that basis, the most likely candidate for Nunari progenitor (actual or imputed) is Raja Karan, ruler of Anhilvara (Gujerat), who was defeated by the Khilji Ala-ud-Din in 1297 and again in 1307. Although this is slightly earlier than suggested by the genealogical data, such genealogies are often telescoped or otherwise unreliable.

Nevertheless, several aspects of Hedayat's account make this association doubtful. Hedayat clearly identifies Raja Kurin's conquerors as Moguls, whereas the Gujerati Raja Karan was defeated by the Khiljis. Second, Hedayat places the Nunari ancestor's kingdom only twenty-seven miles from Delhi. The Gujerati Raja Karan ruled several kingdoms, none closer than several hundred miles to Delhi.

Other circumstances, however, offer support for this identification of the Nunari ancestor. According to Hedayat, Raja Kurin's father was named Kam Deo. Although the historical figure was the son of Serung Deo, the use of "Deo," a popular title for the rajas of the Vaghela and Solonki dynasties, does seem to place the Nunari founder in the context of medieval Gujerat. Furthermore, Hedayat clearly identifies the saint (*pir*) said to have initiated the conversion of the Nunaris to Islam. This saint, Mukhdum-i-Jehaniyan, was a contemporary of the historical Raja Karan.

Also of interest, but as yet unexplained, is that several other groups living in Nunari settlement areas specifically claim to be descended from Raja Karan of Gujerat, who is said to have migrated northward into the Punjab after his defeat. Controverting this theory, the available evidence indicates that Raja Karan fled, not toward the Punjab, but rather southward to the Deccan, and that his patriline ended with him. It is his daughter Deval Devi who is remembered: she is the celebrated heroine of "Ashiqa," a famous Urdu poem written by Amir Khusrau in 1316. She was married to Khizr Khan, the son of Karan's conqueror; nothing is known of her progeny.

"The White Man Will Eat You!"

William E. Wormsley

Children are everywhere in Imbonggu. Over half the population was twelve years of age or younger when I first arrived in Tona. Almost all were extremely curious about me. I was the first white person many had ever seen. I was the only white person who had ever lived in a house in the village. On very rare occasions government and mission personnel entered the village, carried out a specific task, and returned to their enclave at the end of the project, or when the afternoon rains started, whichever occurred first. I was not only a novelty to be observed, but a mystery to be explained.

I was also a fact of daily life in the village, intent on prying into everyone's business. But I also shared my hearth, house, food, radio, torch, and other possessions with the Imbi. I had acquired a kinship niche by virtue of Yombi having given me access to some land and providing me with sugar cane plants. Nabene had given me sweet potato vines to establish my garden. And Yombi and Turi had built my house. Extended kinship ties were somewhat defined by these generally accepted nuclear ties, but not entirely. Some Imbi were uncertain whether I was best defined as a distant relative against whom some more limited claims could be made for food, money, and so forth. Others felt that I was best regarded as an outsider until I had proven my sincerity. For many of those, relationships emerged over time. For others, I was an outsider until the day I left, in much the same way that some of my upstate New York schoolmates were still "City kids" even after living for years in the town where I grew up.

Definitions of my social position were varied and fascinating. One of my dearest friends was an aging man whose house was located only a few meters from mine, but socially outside the village's inner circle. While I found him warm and sensitive, most Imbi held him in relatively low esteem. His kin relationship ties to me, had he chosen to accept common form, would have been weak and unrewarding. He confided in me early that he was concerned for me. After all, my wife was in Australia. While women are dangerous and troublesome in a variety of ways, it nonetheless remains a fact that no man should be without one. Therefore, I could marry his daughter. We could agree to a minimal brideprice payment, he would become my father-in-law, and he would protect me against some people who he feared were intent on exploiting me. My reluctance to take advantage of his proposition was the source of considerable concern to him throughout my years of residence with the Imbi.

But there is more to Imbi life than simply being related in some way to all one's fellow Imbi. Imbi are a society, and one in which everyone pulls his or her weight. That means contributing to the social health of the community. So Torol knew how to make sorcery. Kelo knew the art of muscle manipulation. Yama knew the stories of the sacred stones. Wakea knew the art of love magic. Everyone had a role. What could mine be? It is not an easy thing to place a physically mature adult in a responsible adult role when he or she exhibits the social and cultural knowledge of a two-year-old who constantly says no when he means yes and vice versa.

As time passed, however, many roles emerged for me. One the Imbi valued highly was that of tourist attraction. Visitors literally walked miles to observe the white man who chose to live in an Imbi village house. Such visitors brought with them gifts of food and welcome news of relatives living in other villages. They shared their stories and opinions and inquired into mine. I found that I was a better anthropologist than informant. This demanded attention, as the Imbi were not about to spend their evenings telling me their stories without some form of reciprocation. But my repertoire of myths and legends proved to be nearly nonexistent. Paul Bunyan and his ox held possibilities, but my incomplete familiarity with it left the Imbi unsatisfied. That a giant ox could leave depressions and lakes in his wake made considerable sense to the Imbi, whose every stride accomplished the same feat. But there was no moral to be learned, or at least none to be learned from me.

I needed something more. George Washington came to mind. He held at least the prospect of moral instruction. But I came to accept the Imbi view that throwing a coin across a river is a somewhat strange thing to do. As a feat of prowess, it left the Imbi unimpressed. Not surprising, really. After all, the widest river in the experience of most is about twelve feet. Truly adventurous men who had gone to the Nebilyer to return with wives could visualize a river as wide as fifty feet. Pawa pointed out that even his sixteen-year-old daughter could throw a stone across the Nebilyer. Being able to recall only the bare bones of the story, I was unable to explain what facts had possessed a grown man to throw a coin across a river. But the mere fact he would throw money away like that was a clear symptom of dementia in the Imbi interpretation.

But I was not yet willing to consign America's first president to the unimportant and insignificant. There remained the famous cherry tree. At last, proclaimed Pawa, we were getting somewhere. All men should carry an axe and know how to cut trees. There was hope after all for this enigmatic white hero. That he had learned to use an axe in his youth was what every Imbi father would expect. It was unsurprising that he would cut a tree whose value was greater than he thought. All Imbi boys sooner or later make the same mistake. The story was progressing well, approving heads nodding from every corner of my house. Finally we reached the moral conclusion. To the disbelief of the Imbi, George had admitted to cutting the tree that was not his to cut. The nodding stopped, and the eyes that had earlier focused on me were now turned to one another and back to me. The silence suggested that I had no more to say. It also hinted that no Imbi knew what to say or how to say it.

My mind raced through all the Imbi stories I had heard, in a frantic effort to relate my tale of the value of truth to one the Imbi could appreciate. Awareness hit me like a blow to the stomach. I had not yet heard any Imbi story suggesting that telling the truth was a worthwhile endeavor. During the remainder of my time with the Imbi no such story was destined to echo around my hearth. The Imbi refuse to accept that lying is intrinsically wrong. They are in good company. Plato questioned the notion also. One of the endearing qualities of enemies, of which the Imbi like all New Guinea Highlanders have an endless supply, is that they are indeed supposed to lie. Even when they are telling the truth, one must assume

one's enemies are lying. No matter what the Ango say, one must always be skeptical of their veracity. But this skepticism, bordering on cynicism, also places the Imbi in good company. After all, one of the primary responsibilities of the U.S. Department of State is to interpret for the American people what the world's Communists truly mean when they issue a communiqué. Exactly as the Imbi, most Americans grow up learning that our enemies are compulsive liars. If a point was to be taken away from the story of George Washington and the cherry tree, I concluded, surely it must be that American children are retarded in their social development by accepting the wisdom of such stories for even a short time before the true facts of social interaction are learned. Clearly, my inability to tell stories worth listening to caused me much concern, although my house continued to be a destination for distant friends and relatives of the Imbi. The situation took a turn for the better when I happened across a copy of Kipling's *Just So Stories*. They were very well received.

A second role of mine was that of status symbol. Many white persons lived in the Ialibu area, most commonly as government contract workers, missionaries, teachers, or foreign volunteers. But I was the only one who lived in an Imbonggu village. There was always much interest in my comings and goings. My Imbi clan mates took delight in introducing me as their *kondodl* (red man). The Imbonggu are not color blind. Far from it. They describe what they see. I am often amazed at a system of ethnic classification that demands that I and several million of my coloring tick off "white" simply because it is what we have been told we are. The Imbi and their Papua New Guinean comrades find no difficulty achieving more accurate descriptions. Wendy Patrick, a friend from Milne Bay Province, always referred to white people by the Neo-Melanesian term *dimdim*. It was never totally clear to me whether she was describing their skin or their wits. But whether white, red, or dim, one thing remained clear: I stuck out in Imbonggu crowds.

In an effort to confirm their privileged claim to me and my resources, Imbi always linked my kinship position to their proprietary interest in me. The message was clear: I was not fair game. I, and my wealth, belonged to the Imbi. My presence was also taken to mean that the Imbi enjoyed closer access to the government's resources through me. While there was no truth to this rumor, it refused to go away.

To my distress, I was also defined as something of a medical practitioner. I had spoken with numerous anthropologists and read in many books about the common phenomenon of anthropologist-as-doctor. This role concerned me a great deal. When I was discharged from the U.S. Army at Fort Lewis, Washington, in 1968, I humiliated myself by passing out as I watched an enormous quantity of my blood being sucked into a hypodermic needle the size of a baseball bat. There would be no point in taking such needles to the field with me. Beyond the personal wimp factor was the realization that I had no idea what was contained in most medicines. I had always consumed the potions prescribed by my own doctors, but I had granted them my confidence in their knowledge and training. Possessing neither, I refused to yield to the temptation to enter the field with enormous quantities of drugs and syringes. My response to all injuries was basic. I cleansed the wound with Dettol, an over-the-counter disinfectant, applied enough gauze to cover the wound, and referred the victim of the calamity to the health center about five miles away. This satisfied my concerns about a weak stomach, medical ignorance, and the moral issue of usurping the medical profession's widely accepted role of playing God. Still, I cleaned enough axe wounds, machete wounds, knife wounds, and burns to qualify as a medical doctor through a fully accredited, credit-for-life program. But one appeal of my medicine chest to the Imbi was exactly what defined its limitations to me: its mystery. All Imbi cures are in the hands of specialists in their application. That is not to say that one person knows and applies them all. Quite the contrary, few practitioners understand more than one or two cures, of which there are dozens. Under these circumstances nothing is unique about possessing or dispensing medicine. The Imbi never quite understood my reluctance to dispense my potions. Uncertainty of success was inadequate justification. After all, the Imbi had the same problem. Nothing works all the time. My ignorance of how cures worked was equally unacceptable as a justification for my apparent selfishness. No Imbi practitioner possessed such knowledge. All cures were learned from *tumbuna*. Ancestors passed on the application of medical technology rather than medical knowledge itself. "We have always done it that way" is surely the most frustrating response an anthropologist can receive. We want knowledge, not just habit. Yala, on my refusal to give him aspirin, pointed out that he didn't care how it worked. He merely wanted his headache to go away. Once again the table had been turned on me. After all, Americans gulp aspirin for the primary purpose of alleviating pain. Despite the frivolity of television commercials depicting little colored spheres bouncing around inside our bodies on some mysteriously predetermined timed-release schedule, most Americans have absolutely no knowledge of how aspirin works in the body and what it accomplishes aside from the desired alleviation of pain!

My most intriguing role, if the least personally rewarding, was that of legendary, semimythological creature. It turned out that my mere glance, or even a distant reference to me, was sufficient to frighten children into doing what all their developing urges convinced them they did not want to do. When I announced my intention to live in a village in the highlands of New Guinea, friends and relatives were normally dumbstruck. "Wasn't that where Michael Rockefeller was eaten by cannibals?" was a common response. Or, "Don't they still eat people there?" No amount of reassurance on my part could serve to allay those fears. Looking back, I am certain that the news of my trip to New Guinea

was as troublesome to my parents as my military orders sending me to Vietnam a few years earlier. The Social Security Administration need not fear making payments to Bill Wormsley if he persisted in his reckless lifestyle.

But as my stay with the Imbi lengthened, they assured me that my concerned family and friends had been correct. There were cannibals and sorcerers, the Imbi assured me. But fortunately for me, I was not living among them. Had I opted for any other village in the basin, however, that would not be the case. But there was a problem. Every Ialibu clan and village where I discussed the matter told me exactly the same thing. It seemed that only the names were changed to identify the innocent, the cannibals, and the sorcerers. Old women in the village cried when I made a trip to Mount Hagen. The Hagen people were almost certain to kill me. A trip to Wabag all but triggered my mourning rites. The Enga were an absolute certainty to kill me, even if they chose not to eat me. And, of course, a trip to the coastal town of Lae was the most inexplicable form of flirting with disaster. I would have to travel through the lands of the Chimbu. These unfathomable people were known to laugh at the death of a person and cry at the purchase of a new truck. Such demented behavior defied rational explanation. Such people could only be dangerous in the extreme. On my only return trip from Lae, one of the old women of the village froze at the sight of me. As recognition set in, she screamed, dropped her woven net bag of sweet potatoes and baby piglet, and ran toward her house yelling to all who could hear that a ghost was in the village. I could only speculate at the wild tales about my trip that must have been told in my absence.

Anthropologist William Arens (1979) has written a fascinating history and analysis of the study of cannibalism and its attribution to groups of people throughout recorded history. The book proved to be quite controversial, for no apparent reason. Reading his book in light of my experiences among the Imbonggu, I thought his argument so

basic and so obvious as to militate against the sort of debate that ensued. There are no cannibals, or at least not in the numbers reported or for the purposes reported. To say that someone else is a cannibal is to define him as less than human. Accepting the unavoidability of occasionally having to kill others in order to defend or promote one's own interests requires that some strategy be employed to redefine the basic fact of humanness on both sides of a dispute or war. So Americans were told by their government that Japanese committed every conceivable atrocity during the Second World War. The Japanese told their citizens and soldiers the same things about Americans. As historian John Dower (1986) illustrates, no one should be surprised at the realization that most atrocities committed by the combatants against one another during the Second World War occurred in the Pacific theater, between American and Japanese soldiers. German and Italian soldiers were never dehumanized to the same extent by the Allies. Likewise, the European Axis powers treated the Allies comparably. The major atrocities of the European war were committed against Jewish noncombatants. Japanese and American reciprocal charges of atrocities and cannibalism thus provided just one more form of legitimization for the need to kill one another. The cannibals of the Ialibu Basin perform that same essential role in sociopolitical conflict.

But other cannibals are afoot among the Imbi. They are horrible creatures. Some possess no mouths. The tops of their heads are hinged at the back and can be lifted up. In this manner food is consumed through the top of the heads of these mouthless monsters. In all other physical respects they closely resemble human beings. Because of their anatomy, they are limited in their consumption to smaller humans, especially children. The threat of being set outside at night to be collected and dropped into the open skull of this monster is a powerful force in Imbi behavior modification techniques. Children seldom persist in the behavior that leads an angry mother to threaten to offer her child as a spirit-meal. Such monsters are not a stock cast of supernatural characters. Imbonggu storytellers are wonderfully talented in the arts of invention and embellishment. New monsters are created as needed or desired. But the utility of all these monsters, mouthless or otherwise, is mitigated somewhat by one unfortunate fact. No one has ever seen one. And, of course, maturing children come to question their existence. Indipendo, a young girl of six or seven years of age, was displaying an unusual tendency to question authority. And just as American and European children come to forfeit belief in the bogeymen that keep them out of the cellar, Indipendo was on the verge of concluding that no mouthless, hinged-headed monsters existed in the real world.

One evening as several people sat around my hearth, Indipendo pressed her mother, Alu, beyond the limit of her patience. Indipendo was unmoved by reference to the mouthless monster. In a fit of inspiration, Alu recalled Indipendo's discomfort at the noise of airplanes, which the young girl had never seen up close but feared considerably. Indipendo often asked about the *balus* spirit when she heard planes pass overhead. In one final attempt at maintaining control of her headstrong daughter, Alu explained that *balus* was something white men knew about. It opened a giant hole in its side through which people entered the monster. People went in the monster's gut, but only spirits came out. Indipendo, skeptical of the description but still leery of the machines themselves, expressed her cautious disbelief. Alu proceeded to note that *balus* took people to the land of white men, where they were eaten. Only white men returned. The few Imbonggu who returned had become like white men, but most never returned. In the mind of a child, never is a somewhat imprecise concept. But young men often left the village to work on plantations or to seek their fortunes in the big city of Port Moresby. Such young men were often absent for years at a stretch. Village children knew of such youths but almost never saw them return. When the youths did make the trek back to Tona, they wore the white man's clothing and carried his tape cassette players and wristwatches, the latter always a mystery to the Imbi.

Alu's desperate attempt was beginning to take shape in a most unlikely way. Intent on pressing her emerging advantage, she continued. She noted that I had come to Ialibu inside *balus*. Several onlookers assented. Indipendo appraised me and shifted perceptibly closer to her mother. All the village children had heard stories of how white men "thumped" New Guineans, put them into jail, and killed them by hanging them from trees. Younger Imbi children had always given me a wide berth, but we were now on the verge of being consigned to different universes. Seeking balance, Alu assured Indipendo that I had promised not to eat anyone while I lived in Tona. But like Alu, I might be pushed beyond my tolerance, and this could not be good. Then Alu drove the final nail into my coffin when she threatened, "If you misbehave, I will give you to Kondoli, and he will eat you!"

For the remainder of my stay, young children of Tona often would run screaming in search of their mothers at my approach. As they matured, even the threat of Kondoli eating them lost its potency. But while the threat evaporated for individual children, it continued to be offered to the younger ones as they tended toward disobedience. It became a common occurrence for a song or story to be interrupted with a stern, "Be quiet. Or the White Man will eat you!"

Eating Christmas in the Kalahari

Richard Borshay Lee

Richard Borshay Lee is a full professor of anthropology at the University of Toronto. He has done extensive field-work in southern Africa, is coeditor of Man the Hunter *(1968) and* Kalahari Hunter-Gatherers *(1976), and author of* The !Kung San: Men, Women, and Work in a Foraging Society.

The !Kung Bushmen's knowledge of Christmas is thirdhand. The London Missionary Society brought the holiday to the southern Tswana tribes in the early nineteenth century. Later, native catechists spread the idea far and wide among the Bantu-speaking pastoralists, even in the remotest corners of the Kalahari Desert. The Bushmen's idea of the Christmas story, stripped to its essentials, is "praise the birth of white man's god-chief"; what keeps their interest in the holiday high is the Tswana-Herero custom of slaughtering an ox for his Bushmen neighbors as an annual goodwill gesture. Since the 1930's, part of the Bushmen's annual round of activities has included a December congregation at the cattle posts for trading, marriage brokering, and several days of trance-dance feasting at which the local Tswana headman is host.

As a social anthropologist working with !Kung Bushmen, I found that the Christmas ox custom suited my purposes. I had come to the Kalahari to study the hunting and gathering subsistence economy of the !Kung, and to accomplish this it was essential not to provide them with food, share my own food, or interfere in any way with their food-gathering activities. While liberal handouts of tobacco and medical supplies were appreciated, they were scarcely adequate to erase the glaring disparity in wealth between the anthropologist, who maintained a two-month inventory of canned goods, and the Bushmen, who rarely had a day's supply of food on hand. My approach, while paying off in terms of data, left me open to frequent accusations of stinginess and hard-heartedness. By their lights, I was a miser.

The Christmas ox was to be my way of saying thank you for the cooperation of the past year; and since it was to be our last Christmas in the field, I determined to slaughter the largest, meatiest ox that money could buy, insuring that the feast and trance-dance would be a success.

Through December I kept my eyes open at the wells as the cattle were brought down for watering. Several animals were offered, but none had quite the grossness that I had in mind. Then, ten days before the holiday, a Herero friend led an ox of astonishing size and mass up to our camp. It was solid black, stood five feet high at the shoulder, had a five-foot span of horns, and must have weighed 1,200 pounds on the hoof. Food consumption calculations are my specialty, and I quickly figured that bones and viscera aside, there was enough meat—at least four pounds—for every man, woman, and child of the 150 Bushmen in the vicinity of /ai/ai who were expected at the feast.

Having found the right animal at last, I paid the Herero £20 ($56) and asked him to keep the beast with his herd until Christmas day. The next morning word spread among the people that the big solid black one was the ox chosen by /ontah (my Bushman name; it means, roughly, "whitey") for the Christmas feast. That afternoon I received the first delegation. Ben!a, an outspoken sixty-year-old mother of five, came to the point slowly.

"Where were you planning to eat Christmas?"

"Right here at /ai/ai," I replied.

"Alone or with others?"

"I expect to invite all the people to eat Christmas with me."

"Eat what?"

"I have purchased Yehave's black ox, and I am going to slaughter and cook it."

"That's what we were told at the well but refused to believe it until we heard it from yourself."

"Well, it's the black one," I replied expansively, although wondering what she was driving at.

"Oh, no!" Ben!a groaned, turning to her group. "They were right." Turning back to me she asked, "Do you expect us to eat that bag of bones?"

"Bag of bones! It's the biggest ox at /ai/ai."

"Big, yes, but old. And thin. Everybody knows there's no meat on that old ox. What did you expect us to eat off it, the horns?"

Everybody chuckled at Ben!a's one-liner as they walked away, but all I could manage was a weak grin.

That evening it was the turn of the young men. They came to sit at our evening fire. /gaugo, about my age, spoke to me man-to-man.

"/ontah, you have always been square with us," he lied. "What has happened to change your heart? That sack of guts and bones of Yehave's will hardly feed one camp, let alone all the Bushmen around /ai/ai." And he proceeded to enumerate the seven camps in the /ai/ai vicinity, family by family. "Perhaps you have forgotten that we are not few, but many. Or are you too blind to tell the difference between a proper cow and an old wreck? That ox is thin to the point of death."

"Look, you guys," I retorted, "that is a beautiful animal, and I'm sure you will eat it with pleasure at Christmas."

"Of course we will eat it; it's food. But it won't fill us up to the point where we will have enough strength to dance. We will eat and go home to bed with stomachs rumbling."

That night as we turned in, I asked my wife, Nancy: "What did you think of the black ox?"

"It looked enormous to me. Why?"

"Well, about eight different people have told me I got gypped; that the ox is nothing but bones."

"What's the angle?" Nancy asked. "Did they have a better one to sell?"

"No, they just said that it was going to be a grim Christmas because there won't be enough meat to go around. Maybe I'll get an independent judge to look at the beast in the morning."

Bright and early, Halingisi, a Tswana cattle owner, appeared at our camp. But before I could ask him to give me his opinion on Yehave's black ox, he gave me the eye signal that indicated a confidential chat. We left the camp and sat down.

"/ontah, I'm surprised at you: you've lived here for three years and still haven't learned anything about cattle."

"But what else can a person do but choose the biggest, strongest animal one can find?" I retorted.

"Look, just because an animal is big doesn't mean that it has plenty of meat on it. The black one was a beauty when it was younger, but now it is thin to the point of death."

"Well I've already bought it. What can I do at this stage?"

"Bought it already? I thought you were just considering it. Well, you'll have to kill it and serve it, I suppose. But don't expect much of a dance to follow."

My spirits dropped rapidly. I could believe that Ben!a and /gaugo just might be putting me on about the black ox, but Halingisi seemed to be an impartial critic. I went around that day feeling as though I had bought a lemon of a used car.

In the afternoon it was Tomazo's turn. Tomazo is a fine hunter, a top trance performer . . . and one of my most reliable informants. He approached the subject of the Christmas cow as part of my continuing Bushman education.

"My friend, the way it is with us Bushmen," he began, "is that we love meat. And even more than that, we love fat. When we hunt we always search for the fat ones, the ones dripping with layers of white fat: fat that turns into a clear, thick oil in the cooking pot, fat that slides down your gullet, fills your stomach and gives you a roaring diarrhea," he rhapsodized.

"So, feeling as we do," he continued, "it gives us pain to be served such a scrawny thing as Yehave's black ox. It is big, yes, and no doubt its giant bones are good for soup, but fat is what we really crave and so we will eat Christmas this year with a heavy heart."

The prospect of a gloomy Christmas now had me worried, so I asked Tomazo what I could do about it.

"Look for a fat one, a young one . . . smaller, but fat. Fat enough to make us //gom ('evacuate the bowels'), then we will be happy."

My suspicions were aroused when Tomazo said that he happened to know of a young, fat, barren cow that the owner was willing to part with. Was Tomazo working on commission, I wondered? But I dispelled this unworthy thought when we approached the Herero owner of the cow in question and found that he had decided not to sell.

The scrawny wreck of a Christmas ox now became the talk of the /ai/ai water hole and was the first news told to the outlying groups as they began to come in from the bush for the feast. What finally convinced me that real trouble might be brewing was the visit from u!au, an old conservative with a reputation for fierceness. His nickname meant spear and referred to an incident thirty years ago in which he had speared a man to death. He had an intense manner; fixing me with his eyes, he said in clipped tones:

"I have only just heard about the black ox today, or else I would have come here earlier. /ontah, do you honestly think you can serve meat like that to people and avoid a fight?" He paused, letting the implications sink in. "I don't mean fight you, /ontah; you are a white man. I mean a fight between Bushmen. There are many fierce ones here, and with such a small quantity of meat to distribute, how can you give everybody a fair share? Someone is sure to accuse another of taking too much or hogging all the choice pieces. Then you will see what happens when some go hungry while others eat."

The possibility of at least a serious argument struck me as all too real. I had witnessed the tension that surrounds the distribution of meat from a kudu or gemsbok kill, and had documented many arguments that sprang up from a real or imagined slight in meat distribution. The owners of a kill may spend up to two hours arranging and rearranging the piles of meat under the gaze of a circle of recipients before handing them out. And I also knew that the Christmas feast at /ai/ai would be bringing together groups that had feuded in the past.

Convinced now of the gravity of the situation, I went in earnest to search for a second cow; but all my inquiries failed to turn one up.

The Christmas feast was evidently going to be a disaster, and the incessant complaints about the meagerness of the ox had already taken the fun out of it for me. Moreover, I was getting bored with the wisecracks, and after losing my temper a few times, I resolved to serve the beast anyway. If the meat fell short, the hell with it. In the Bushmen idiom, I announced to all who would listen:

"I am a poor man and blind. If I have chosen one that is too old and too thin, we will eat it anyway and see if there is enough meat there to quiet the rumbling of our stomachs."

On hearing this speech, Ben!a offered me a rare word of comfort. "It's thin," she said philosophically, "but the bones will make a good soup."

At dawn Christmas morning, instinct told me to turn over the butchering and cooking to a friend and take off with Nancy to spend Christmas alone in the bush. But curiosity kept me from retreating. I wanted to see what such a scrawny ox looked like on butchering, and if there *was* going to be a fight, I wanted to catch every word of it. Anthropologists are incurable that way.

The great beast was driven up to our dancing ground, and a shot in the forehead dropped it in its tracks. Then, freshly cut branches were heaped around the fallen carcass to receive the meat. Ten men volunteered to help with the cutting. I asked /gaugo to make the breast bone cut. This cut, which begins the butchering process for most large game, offers easy access for removal of the viscera. But it also allows the hunter to spot-check the amount of fat on the animal. A fat game animal carries a white layer up to an inch thick on the chest, while in a thin one, the knife will quickly cut to bone. All eyes fixed on his hand as /gaugo, dwarfed by the great carcass, knelt to the breast. The first cut opened a pool of solid white in the black skin. The second and third cut widened and deepened the creamy white. Still no bone. It was pure fat; it must have been two inches thick.

"Hey /gau," I burst out, "that ox is loaded with fat. What's this about the ox being too thin to bother eating? Are you out of your mind?"

"Fat?" /gau shot back, "You call that fat? This wreck is thin, sick,

dead!" And he broke out laughing. So did everyone else. They rolled on the ground, paralyzed with laughter. Everybody laughed except me; I was thinking.

I ran back to the tent and burst in just as Nancy was getting up. "Hey, the black ox. It's fat as hell! They were kidding about it being too thin to eat. It was a joke or something. A put-on. Everyone is really delighted with it!"

"Some joke," my wife replied. "It was so funny that you were ready to pack up and leave /ai/ai."

If it had indeed been a joke, it had been an extraordinarily convincing one, and tinged, I thought, with more than a touch of malice as many jokes are. Nevertheless, that it was a joke lifted my spirits considerably, and I returned to the butchering site where the shape of the ox was rapidly disappearing under the axes and knives of the butchers. The atmosphere had become festive. Grinning broadly, their arms covered with blood well past the elbow, men packed chunks of meat into the big cast-iron cooking pots, fifty pounds to the load, and muttered and chuckled all the while about the thinness and worthlessness of the animal and /ontah's poor judgment.

We danced and ate that ox two days and two nights; we cooked and distributed fourteen potfuls of meat and no one went home hungry and no fights broke out.

But the "joke" stayed in my mind. I had a growing feeling that something important had happened in my relationship with the Bushmen and that the clue lay in the meaning of the joke. Several days later, when most of the people had dispersed back to the bush camps, I raised the question with Hakekgose, a Tswana man who had grown up among the !Kung, married a !Kung girl, and who probably knew their culture better than any other non-Bushman.

"With us whites," I began, "Christmas is supposed to be the day of friendship and brotherly love. What I can't figure out is why the Bushmen went to such lengths to criticize and belittle the ox I had bought for the feast. The animal was

perfectly good and their jokes and wisecracks practically ruined the holiday for me."

"So it really did bother you," said Hakekgose. "Well, that's the way they always talk. When I take my rifle and go hunting with them, if I miss, they laugh at me for the rest of the day. But even if I hit and bring one down, it's no better. To them, the kill is always too small or too old or too thin; and as we sit down on the kill site to cook and eat the liver, they keep grumbling, even with their mouths full of meat. They say things like, 'Oh this is awful! What a worthless animal! Whatever made me think that this Tswana rascal could hunt!' "

"Is this the way outsiders are treated?" I asked.

"No, it is their custom; they talk that way to each other too. Go and ask them."

/gaugo had been one of the most enthusiastic in making me feel bad about the merit of the Christmas ox. I sought him out first.

"Why did you tell me the black ox was worthless, when you could see that it was loaded with fat and meat?"

"It is our way," he said smiling. "We always like to fool people about that. Say there is a Bushman who has been hunting. He must not come home and announce like a braggard, 'I have killed a big one in the bush!' He must first sit down in silence until I or someone else comes up to his fire and asks, 'What did you see today?' He replies quietly, 'Ah, I'm no good for hunting. I saw nothing at all [pause] just a little tiny one.' Then I smile to myself," /gaugo continued, "because I know he has killed something big.

"In the morning we make up a party of four or five people to cut up and carry the meat back to the camp. When we arrive at the kill we examine it and cry out, 'You mean to say you have dragged us all the way out here in order to make us cart home your pile of bones? Oh, if I had known it was this thin I wouldn't have come.' Another one pipes up, 'People, to think I gave up a nice day in the shade for this. At home we may be hungry but at least we have nice cool water to drink.' If the horns are big, someone says, 'Did you think that somehow you were going to boil down the horns for soup?'

"To all this you must respond in kind. 'I agree,' you say, 'this one is not worth the effort; let's just cook the liver for strength and leave the rest for the hyenas. It is not too late to hunt today and even a duiker or a steenbok would be better than this mess.'

"Then you set to work nevertheless; butcher the animal, carry the meat back to the camp and everyone eats," /gaugo concluded.

Things were beginning to make sense. Next, I went to Tomazo. He corroborated /gaugo's story of the obligatory insults over a kill and added a few details of his own.

"But," I asked, "why insult a man after he has gone to all that trouble to track and kill an animal and when he is going to share the meat with you so that your children will have something to eat?"

"Arrogance," was his cryptic answer.

"Arrogance?"

"Yes, when a young man kills much meat he comes to think of himself as a chief or a big man, and he thinks of the rest of us as his servants or inferiors. We can't accept this. We refuse one

who boasts, for someday his pride will make him kill somebody. So we always speak of his meat as worthless. This way we cool his heart and make him gentle."

"But why didn't you tell me this before?" I asked Tomazo with some heat.

"Because you never asked me," said Tomazo, echoing the refrain that has come to haunt every field ethnographer.

The pieces now fell into place. I had known for a long time that in situations of social conflict with Bushmen I held all the cards. I was the only source of tobacco in a thousand square miles, and I was not incapable of cutting an individual off for non-cooperation. Though my boycott never lasted longer than a few days, it was an indication of my strength. People resented my presence at the water hole, yet simultaneously dreaded my leaving. In short I was a perfect target for the charge of arrogance and for the Bushmen tactic of enforcing humility.

I had been taught an object lesson by the Bushmen; it had come from an unexpected corner and had hurt me in a vulnerable area. For the big black ox was to be the one totally generous, unstinting act of my year at /ai/ai,

and I was quite unprepared for the reaction I received.

As I read it, their message was this: There are no totally generous acts. All "acts" have an element of calculation. One black ox slaughtered at Christmas does not wipe out a year of careful manipulation of gifts given to serve your own ends. After all, to kill an animal and share the meat with people is really no more than Bushmen do for each other every day and with far less fanfare.

In the end, I had to admire how the Bushmen had played out the farce—collectively straight-faced to the end. Curiously, the episode reminded me of the *Good Soldier Schweik* and his marvelous encounters with authority. Like Schweik, the Bushmen had retained a thorough-going skepticism of good intentions. Was it this independence of spirit, I wondered, that had kept them culturally viable in the face of generations of contact with more powerful societies, both black and white? The thought that the Bushmen were alive and well in the Kalahari was strangely comforting. Perhaps, armed with that independence and with their superb knowledge of their environment, they might yet survive the future.

The Naked Truth

Some friends are unsuited for one another

Roger L. Welsch

Folklorist Roger L. Welsch lives on a tree farm in Dannebrog, Nebraska.

Once, when I was involved in a lawsuit with a neighbor, I attended a meeting between my lawyer and his, who were trying to forge an out-of-court resolution. I watched and listened as they maneuvered, dispassionately sorting through things that I regarded as matters of right and wrong. Finally I couldn't stand it any more. "Your client should be ashamed of himself," I blurted, "acting as if he can take advantage of me anytime he wants." My neighbor's lawyer instantly lost his dignified, professional demeanor: "Don't you talk to me about morality," he snarled. "We know what you do down there on that farm of yours!" He wadded papers into his briefcase and stomped from the office in a fury, slamming the door behind him.

My lawyer and I sat there astonished. The angry man's footsteps were still ringing down the marble hall when my lawyer turned to me and said, "I don't know what you're doing, but cut it out right now before we have trouble we can't deal with." In fact, my lawyer was showing more than just a professional concern: his son was my best friend and was at my farm almost as much as I was. He must have been wondering what wayward paths I had opened to the family scion.

I could not for the life of me figure out what I had done that had driven my neighbor's elderly, sedate lawyer into such a rage. For the next half hour I racked my mind trying to imagine what debauchery I might have missed.

"Okay," my lawyer finally said. "Walk the straight and narrow for a while. I've known Cy for a long time. I'll give him a couple days to cool down and then I'll try to find out what's upset him."

A week later, he called. "Well, I found out what agitated Cy," he chuckled. "The word is out that you guys skinny-dip!"

My tree farm includes a half mile of wooded bank on a lovely, clean river. My farm home at that time was an ancient log house without conveniences—no water, no electricity. Work on a tree farm is hard and dirty; Nebraska summers are uncomfortably hot and humid. For years it had been a part of the usual regimen at the end of the day for everyone—family and friends, whoever happened to be there, tired and dirty—to lug cold beer and towels down to the river for a long, luxurious dip in the cool, clean waters of the gentle river. Men and women. For us it was perfectly normal behavior.

What of propriety? Well, as I have always told my wife, Linda, men are all built exactly alike, and I have no knowledge whatsoever on which to base a physical comparison of women. But that wasn't the point. Neither was the fact that most of us were nearly blind without our glasses, so we wouldn't have been able to see much even if we had looked. The thing is, we skinny-dippers had arrived at a set of tacit agreements about modesty, and that, after all, is what modesty is—a matter of social understanding.

In some cultures, the sight of a woman's nose and mouth are considered irresistibly seductive. In others, the soles of a person's feet are perceived as disgusting beyond comprehension. In mainstream American culture, sex is obscene but violence is television fare for preschoolers. What is acceptable in swimwear is unacceptable in a restaurant. In an elevator we condone contact that would otherwise be actionable in criminal court. Rules of behavior are not absolute; we negotiate them constantly.

At my farm we had reached an unspoken consensus that at the river, on prescribed occasions, nakedness was to be ignored. We would have died of embarrassment if someone's pants had fallen down at the supper table and, before averting our eyes, we had caught sight of boxer shorts with hearts or pink panties with lace—on the very same bodies we could have seen completely naked a few hours earlier at the river.

I suppose the chief rule in the canon of Primrose Farm skinny-dipping was sangfroid: No staring, pointing, or laughing allowed. You were to proceed as if you didn't notice that everyone was naked. (Perhaps the only difference was that in normal conversation, one might occasionally glance, for one reason or another or for no reason at all, below a man's waist or a woman's neck, but during skinny-dipping, there was a lot more eye contact and gazing off toward the horizon.)

That was never better demonstrated than the time a bunch of us were walking along a sand bar, naked as jaybirds, whatever that means. Our custom was to walk a half mile upstream, get into the gentle current, and drift slowly downstream ("butt-bouncing," we called it). On this occasion we had stopped at the upstream end of the sand bar and were talking vigorously about something or another when around the bend of the bank came two canoes. We screamed and dived for the bushes, covering ourselves as much as possible.

After the startled canoeists passed downstream, we gathered what was left of our dignity and sought the safety of the water. It was wacky, we all agreed: Here we were, a flock of academics (almost all of us were anthropologists and folklorists!) who two days later would be dressed for success and calling each other Mr. Carter and Miss Shonsey across office desks. We were perfectly comfortable with our own nakedness but panicked when we were observed for an instant by four people we had never laid eyes on before and would in all likelihood never see again. What was that all about?!

The canoeists weren't in on the rules, that's what. They hadn't agreed not to stare, point, or laugh. And they had clothes on, another factor in the ethnology of skinny-dipping. The embarrassment of nakedness is partic-

ularly obvious when other people are wearing clothes.

One summer a bunch of friends came to help me water trees. At the end of the long day we were hot and dirty, so we headed toward the river. Six of us were familiar with the routine; two others were helping at the farm for the first time. The veterans got to the river, undressed, and plunged in. The male half of the new couple assessed the situation and did the same. His wife considered the process, hesitated a moment, and put on her swimsuit.

No problem. We were old friends. The naked folks were all comfortable. After all, in the river one is submerged most of the time anyway, so there is little cause for embarrassment. But the woman in the swimsuit was soon visibly troubled. We had trusted her not to stare, point, and laugh at our fat, skinny, lumpy, warty, flabby, pale bodies . . . but she had not offered the same trust.

I felt sorry for her in her discomfort but didn't want to make things worse by calling attention to her dilemma. My friend—the lawyer's son—swam over to me and quietly said that he could see she was uncomfortable and he was considering helping her out. "Have at it," I said. "I have a feeling she'd be grateful."

"Hey, Dot," John called. "How can you stand that swimsuit? Mine always

gets full of gravel and turns to lead." And that's true. The river's water is very sandy. Shoes, socks, swimsuits worn into the river soon become sodden sandbags.

"Gosh, that sure is the truth," Dot exploded, happy to have an excuse other than immodesty to join our Compact of Vulnerability. She was naked in moments and clearly relieved to be a part of our shared trust.

That, of course, was the foundation of Lawyer Cy's fury. Those of us who were naked were neither embarrassed nor prurient; but Cy, clothed and at long distance, was troubled by a freedom and trust in which he couldn't share. He wasn't embarrassed nearly as much by our presumed nudity as he was by his three-piece suit.

And that's what modesty and embarrassment are all about. Immodesty, indecency, obscenity are cultural factors, mutually agreed upon and negotiable. Contrary to the cliché, we don't "know obscenity when we see it"; we decide what obscenity is, sometimes even without seeing it. We are enjoined to "cover our nakedness," but there's considerable disagreement about what our nakedness is. Our noses and mouths? The bottoms of our feet? A lack of trust or mutual respect?

We can talk about it later. Right now, it's August, it's hot, I won't look if you won't, and last one in the river is a blue-nosed lawyer.

Culture and Communication

Anthropologists are interested in all aspects of human behavior and how they interrelate with each other. Language is a form of such behavior (albeit primarily verbal behavior) and therefore worthy of study. It is patterned and passed down from one generation to the next through learning, not instinct. In keeping with the idea that language is integral to human social interaction, it has long been recognized that human communication through language is by its nature different from the kind of communication found among other animals. Central to this difference is the fact that humans communicate abstractly with symbols that have meaning independent of the immediate sensory experiences of either the sender or the receiver of messages. Thus, for instance, humans are able to refer to the future and the past instead of just the here and now.

Recent experiments have shown that anthropoid apes can be taught a small portion of Ameslan, the sign language used to overcome hearing and speech disabilities. It must be remembered, however, that their very rudimentary ability has to be tapped by painstaking human effort, and that the degree of difference between apes and humans serves only to emphasize the peculiarly human need for and development of language.

Just as the abstract quality of symbols lifts our thoughts beyond immediate sense perception, it also inhibits our ability to think about and convey the full meaning of our personal experience. No categorical term can do justice to its referents—the variety of forms to which the term refers. The degree to which this is an obstacle to clarity of thought and communication relates to the degree of abstraction in the symbols involved. The word "chair," for instance, would not present much difficulty since it has rather objective referents. Consider the trouble we have, however, in thinking and communicating with words whose referents are not quite so tied to immediate sense perception—words such as "freedom," "democracy," and "justice." At best, the likely result is symbolic confusion: an inability to think or communicate in objectively definable symbols. At its worst, language may be used to purposefully obfuscate, as is shown in the article "Language, Appearance, and Reality: Doublespeak in 1984."

A related issue, in "The World's Language" by Bill Bryson, has to do with the fact that languages differ as to what is relatively easy to express within the restrictions of their particular vocabularies. Thus, although a given language may not have enough words to allow one to cope with a new situation or a new field of activity, the typical solution is to invent or borrow words. In this way, it may be said that any language can be used to teach anything. This point is illustrated by Laura Bohannan's attempt to convey the "true" meaning of Shakespeare's *Hamlet* to the West African Tiv. Much of her task is devoted to finding the most appropriate words in the Tiv language to convey her Western thoughts. At least part of her failure is due to the fact that some of the words are just not there, and her inventions are, to the Tiv at least, unacceptable.

Symbolic communication involves more than the precise and appropriate use of words, especially since it takes place on a nonverbal as well as a verbal level. Thus, Huang Shu-min ("A Cross-Cultural Experience: A Chinese Anthropologist in the United States") shows the importance of personal hygiene in the expression of American middle-class values, and Valerie Steele ("The F Word"), demonstrates how we subtly convey messages to others just by the clothes we wear.

Taken collectively, therefore, the articles in this section show how symbolic confusion may occur between individuals or groups on a verbal and a nonverbal level. They also demonstrate the tremendous potential of recent research to enhance effective communication among all of us.

Looking Ahead: Challenge Questions

Why is English becoming the most global of languages?

Does language restrict our thought processes?

In what ways is communication difficult in a cross-cultural situation?

How does an increased awareness of other cultures lead to a better understanding of your own culture?

What kinds of values and thoughts do you communicate by the clothes you wear?

What kinds of messages are transmitted through nonverbal communication?

How has this section enhanced your ability to communicate more effectively?

The World's Language

Bill Bryson

More than 300 million people in the world speak English and the rest, it sometimes seems, try to. It would be charitable to say that the results are sometimes mixed.

Consider this hearty announcement in a Yugoslavian hotel: "The flattening of underwear with pleasure is the job of the chambermaid. Turn to her straightaway." Or this warning to motorists in Tokyo: "When a passenger of the foot heave in sight, tootle the horn. Trumpet at him melodiously at first, but if he still obstacles your passage, then tootle him with vigor." Or these instructions gracing a packet of convenience food from Italy: "Besmear a backing pan, previously buttered with a good tomato sauce, and, after, dispose the cannelloni, lightly distanced between them in a only couch."

Clearly the writer of *that* message was not about to let a little ignorance of English stand in the way of a good meal. In fact, it would appear that one of the beauties of the English language is that with even the most tenuous grasp you can speak volumes if you show enough enthusiasm—a willingness to tootle with vigor, as it were.

To be fair, English is full of booby traps for the unwary foreigner. Any language where the unassuming word *fly* signifies an annoying insect, a means of travel, and a critical part of a gentleman's apparel is clearly asking to be mangled. Imagine being a foreigner and having to learn that in English one tells *a* lie but *the* truth, that a person

---

The English language is fast becoming a world language

---

who says "I could care less" means the same thing as someone who says "I couldn't care less," that a sign in a store saying ALL ITEMS NOT ON SALE doesn't mean literally what it says (that every item is *not* on sale) but rather that only some of the items are on sale, that when a person says to you, "How do you do?" he will be taken aback if you reply, with impeccable logic, "How do I do what?"

The complexities of the English language are such that even native speakers cannot always communicate effectively, as almost every American learns on his first day in Britain. Indeed, Robert Burchfield, editor of the *Oxford English Dictionary,* created a stir in linguistic circles on both sides of the Atlantic when he announced his belief that American English and English English are drifting apart so rapidly that within 200 years the two nations won't be able to understand each other at all.

That may be. But if the Briton and American of the twenty-second century baffle each other, it seems altogether likely that they won't confuse many others—not, at least, if the rest of the world continues expropriating words and phrases at its present rate. Already Germans talk about *ein Image Problem* and *das Cash-Flow,* Italians program their computers with *il software,* French motorists going away for a *weekend break* pause for *les refueling stops,* Poles watch *telewizja,* Spaniards have a *flirt,* Austrians eat *Big Mäcs,* and the Japanese go on a *pikunikku.* For better or worse, English has become the most global of languages, the lingua franca of business, science, education, politics, and pop music. For the airlines of 157 nations (out of 168 in the world), it is the agreed international language of discourse. In India, there are more than 3,000 newspapers in English. The six member nations of the European Free Trade Association conduct all their business in English, even though not one of them is an English-speaking country. When companies from four European countries—France, Italy, Germany, and Switzerland—formed a joint truck-making venture called Iveco in 1977, they chose English as their working language because, as one of the founders wryly observed, "It puts us all at an equal disadvantage." For the same reasons, when the Swiss company Brown Boveri and the Swedish company ASEA merged in 1988, they decided to make the official company language English, and when Volkswagen set up a factory in Shanghai it found that there were too few Germans who spoke Chinese and too few Chinese who spoke German, so now Volkswagen's German engineers and Chinese managers communicate in a language that is alien to both of them, English. Belgium has two languages, French and Flemish, yet on a recent visit to the country's main airport in Brussels, I counted more than fifty posters and billboards and not one of them was in French or Flemish. They were all in English.

For non-English speakers everywhere, English has become the common tongue. Even in France, the most determinedly non-English-speaking nation in the world, the war against English encroachment has largely been lost. In early 1989, the Pasteur Institute announced that henceforth it would publish its famed international medical review only in English because too few people were reading it in French.

English is, in short, one of the world's great growth industries. "English is just as much big business as the export of manufactured goods," Professor Randolph Quirk of Oxford University has written. "There are problems with what you might call 'after-sales service'; and

'delivery' can be awkward; but at any rate the production lines are trouble free." [*The Observer,* October 26, 1980] Indeed, such is the demand to learn the language that there are now more students of English in China than there are people in the United States.

It is often said that what most immediately sets English apart from other languages is the richness of its vocabulary. *Webster's Third New International Dictionary* lists 450,000 words, and the revised *Oxford English Dictionary* has 615, 000, but that is only part of the total. Technical and scientific terms would add millions more. Altogether, about 200,000 English words are in common use, more than in German (184,000) and far more than in French (a mere 100,000). The richness of the English vocabulary, and the wealth of available synonyms, means that English speakers can often draw shades of distinction unavailable to non-English speakers. The French, for instance, cannot distinguish between house and home, between mind and brain, between man and gentleman, between "I wrote" and "I have written." The Spanish cannot differentiate a chairman from a president, and the Italians have no equivalent of wishful thinking. In Russia there are no native words for efficiency, challenge, engagement ring, have fun, or take care [all cited in *The New York Times,* June 18, 1989]. English, as Charlton Laird has noted, is the only language that has, or needs, books of synonyms like *Roget's Thesaurus.* "Most speakers of other languages are not aware that such books exist." [*The Miracle of Language,* page 54]

On the other hand, other languages have facilities we lack. Both French and German can distinguish between knowledge that results from recognition (respectively *connaître* and *kennen*) and knowledge that results from understanding (*savoir* and *wissen*). Portuguese has words that differentiate between an interior angle and an exterior one. All the Romance languages can distinguish between something that leaks into and something that leaks out of. The Italians even have a word for the mark left on a table by a moist glass

(*culacino*) while the Gaelic speakers of Scotland, not to be outdone, have a word for the itchiness that overcomes the upper lip just before taking a sip of whiskey. (Wouldn't they just?) It's *sgriob.* And we have nothing in English to match the Danish *hygge* (meaning "instantly satisfying and cozy"), the French *sang-froid,* the Russian *glasnost,* or the Spanish *macho,* so we must borrow the term from them or do without the sentiment.

At the same time, some languages have words that we may be pleased to do without. The existence in German of a word like *schadenfreude* (taking delight in the misfortune of others) perhaps tells us as much about Teutonic sensitivity as it does about their neologistic versatility. Much the same could be said about the curious and monumentally unpronounceable Highland Scottish word *sgiomlaireachd,* which means "the habit of dropping in at mealtimes." That surely conveys a world of information about the hazards of Highland life—not to mention the hazards of Highland orthography.

Of course, every language has areas in which it needs, for practical purposes, to be more expressive than others. The Eskimos, as is well known, have fifty words for types of snow—though curiously no word for just plain snow. To them there is crunchy snow, soft snow, fresh snow, and old snow, but no word that just means snow. The Italians, as we might expect, have over 500 names for different types of macaroni. Some of these, when translated, begin to sound distinctly unappetizing, like strozzapreti, which means "strangled priests." Vermicelli means "little worms" and even spaghetti means "little strings." When you learn that muscatel in Italian means "wine with flies in it," you may conclude that the Italians are gastronomically out to lunch, so to speak, but really their names for foodstuffs are no more disgusting than our hot dogs or those old English favorites, toad-in-the hole, spotted dick, and faggots in gravy.

The residents of the Trobriand Islands of Papua New Guinea have a hundred words for yams, while the Maoris of New Zealand have thirty-five words for dung (don't ask me why). Meanwhile, the Arabs are said (a little unbelievably, perhaps) to have 6,000 words for camels and camel equipment. The aborigines of Tasmania have a word for every type of tree, but no word that just means "tree," while the Araucanian Indians of Chile rather more poignantly have a variety of words to distinguish between different degrees of hunger. Even among speakers of the same language, regional and national differences abound. A Londoner has a less comprehensive view of extremes of weather than someone from the Middle West of America. What a Briton calls a blizzard would, in Illinois or Nebraska, be a flurry, and a British heat wave is often a thing of merriment to much of the rest of the world. (I still treasure a London newspaper with the

---

English has a flexibility that sets it apart from other languages

---

banner headline: BRITAIN SIZZLES IN THE SEVENTIES!)

A second commonly cited factor in setting English apart from other languages is its flexibility. This is particularly true of word ordering, where English speakers can roam with considerable freedom between passive and active sense. Not only can we say "I kicked the dog," but also "The dog was kicked by me"—a construction that would be impossible in many other languages. Similarly, where the Germans can say just "ich singe" and the French must manage with "je chante," we can say "I sing," "I do sing," or "I am singing." English also has a distinctive capacity to extract maximum work from a word by making it do double duty as both noun and verb. The list of such versatile words is practically endless; *drink, fight, fire, sleep, run, fund, look, act, view, ape, silence, worship, copy, blame, comfort, bend, cut, reach, like, dislike,* and so on. Other languages sometimes show inspired flashes of versatility, as with the Ger-

man *auf,* which can mean "on," "in," "upon," "at," "toward," "for," "to," and "upward," but these are relative rarities.

At the same time, the endless versatility of English is what makes our rules of grammar so perplexing. Few English-speaking natives, however well educated, can confidently elucidate the difference between, say, a complement and a predicate or distinguish a full infinitive from a bare one. The reason for this is that the rules of English grammar were originally modeled on those of Latin, which in the seventeenth century was considered the purest and most admirable of tongues. That it may be. But it is also quite clearly another language altogether. Imposing Latin rules on English structure is a little like trying to play baseball in ice skates. The two simply don't match. In the sentence "I am swimming," swimming is a present participle. But in the sentence "Swimming is good for you," it is a gerund—even though it means exactly the same thing.

A third—and more contentious—supposed advantage of English is the relative simplicity of its spelling and pronunciation. For all its idiosyncrasies, English is said to have fewer of the awkward consonant clusters and singsong tonal variations that makes other languages so difficult to master. In Cantonese, *hae* means "yes." But, with a fractional change of pitch, it also describes the female pudenda. The resulting scope for confusion can be safely left to the imagination. In other languages it is the orthography, or spelling, that leads to bewilderment. In Welsh, the word for beer is *cwrw*—an impossible combination of letters for any English speaker. But Welsh spellings are as nothing compared with Irish Gaelic, a language in which spelling and pronunciation give the impression of having been devised by separate committees, meeting in separate rooms, while implacably divided over some deep semantic issue. Try pronouncing *geimhreadh,* Gaelic for "winter," and you will probably come up with something like "gem-reed-uh." It is in fact "gyeeryee." *Beaudhchais* ("thank

you") is "bekkas" and *O Séaghda* ("Oh-seeg-da?") is simply "O'Shea." Against this, the Welsh pronunciation of *cwrw*—"koo-roo"—begins to look positively self-evident.

In all languages pronunciation is of course largely a matter of familiarity mingled with prejudice. The average English speaker confronted with agglomerations of letters like *tchst, sthm,* and *tchph* would naturally conclude that they were pretty well unpronounceable. Yet we use them every day in the words matchstick, asthma, and *catchphrase.* Here, as in almost every other area of language, natural bias plays an inescapable part in any attempt at evaluation. No one has ever said, "Yes, my language is backward and unexpressive, and could really do with some sharpening up." We tend to regard other people's languages as we regard their cultures—with ill-hidden disdain. In Japanese, the word for foreigner means "stinking of foreign hair." To the Czechs a Hungarian is "a pimple." Germans call cockroaches "Frenchmen," while the French call lice "Spaniards." We in the English-speaking world take French leave, but Italians and Norwegians talk about departing like an Englishman, and Germans talk of running like a Dutchman. Italians call syphilis "the French disease," while both French and Italians call con games "American swindle." Belgian taxi drivers call a poor tipper "un Anglais." To be bored to death in French is "être de Birmingham," literally "to be from Birmingham" (which is actually about right). And in English we have "Dutch courage," "French letters," "Spanish fly," "Mexican carwash" (i.e., leaving your car out in the rain), and many others. Late in the last century these epithets focused on the Irish, and often, it must be said, they were as witty as they were wounding. An Irish buggy was a wheelbarrow. An Irish beauty was a woman with two black eyes. Irish confetti was bricks. An Irish promotion was a demotion. Now almost the only slur against these fine people is to get one's Irish up, and that isn't really taken as an insult.

So objective evidence, even among the authorities, is not always easy to come by. Most books on English imply in one way or another that our language is superior to all others. In *The English Language,* Robert Burchfield writes: "As a source of intellectual power and entertainment the whole range of prose writing in English is probably unequalled anywhere else in the world." I would like to think he's right, but I can't help wondering if Mr. Burchfield would have made the same generous assertion had he been born Russian or German or Chinese. There is no reliable way of measuring the quality or efficiency of any language. Yet there are one or two small ways in which English has a demonstrable edge over other languages. For one thing its pronouns are largely, and mercifully, uninflected. In German, if you wish to say *you,* you must choose between seven words: *du, dich, dir, Sie, Ihnen, ihr,* and *euch.* This can cause immense social anxiety. The composer Richard Strauss and his librettist, Hugo von Hofmannsthal, were partners for twenty-five years and apparently adored each other and yet never quite found the nerve to address each other as anything but the stiff "Sie." In English we avoid these problems by relying on just one form: *you.*

In other languages, questions of familiarity can become even more agonizing. A Korean has to choose between one of six verb suffixes to accord with the status of the person addressed. A speaker of Japanese must equally wend his way through a series of linguistic levels appropriate to the social position of the participants. When he says thank you he must choose between a range of meanings running from the perfunctory *arigato* ("thanks") to the decidedly more humble *makotoni go shinsetsu de gozaimasu,* which means "what you have done or proposed to do is a truly and genuinely kind and generous deed." Above all, English is mercifully free of gender. Anyone who spent much of his or her adolescence miserably trying to remember whether it is "la plume" or "le plume" will appreciate just what a pointless burden masculine and feminine nouns are to any language. In this regard English is a godsend to students

everywhere. Not only have we discarded problems of gender with definite and indefinite articles, we have often discarded the articles themselves. We say in English, "It's time to go to bed," where in most other European languages they say, "It's *the* time to go to *the* bed." We possess countless examples of pithy phrases—"life is short," "between heaven and earth," "to go to work"—which in other languages require articles.

English also has a commendable tendency toward conciseness, in contrast to many languages. German is full of jaw-crunching words like *Wirtschaftstreuhandgesellschaft* (business trust company), *Bundesbahnangestelltenwitwe* (a widow of a federal railway employee), and *Kriegsgefangenanentschädigungsgesetz* (a law pertaining to war reparations), while in Holland

---

English is a very concise language

---

companies commonly have names of forty letters or more, such as Douwe Egberts Koninlijke Tabaksfabriek-Koffiebranderijen-Theehandal Naamloze Vennootschap (literally Douwe Egberts Royal Tobacco Factory-Coffee Roasters-Tea Traders Incorporated; they must use fold-out business cards). English, in happy contrast, favors crisp truncations: IBM, laser, NATO. Against this, however, there is an occasional tendency in English, particularly in academic and political circles, to resort to waffle and jargon. At a conference of sociologists in America in 1977, love was defined as "the cognitive-affective state characterized by intrusive and obsessive fantasizing concerning reciprocity of amorant feelings by the object of the amorance." That is jargon—the practice of never calling a spade a spade when you might instead call it a manual earth-restructuring implement—and it is one of the great curses of modern English.

But perhaps the single most notable

characteristic of English—for better *and* worse—is its deceptive complexity. . . .

. . . English is unique in possessing a synonym for each level of our culture: popular, literary, and scholarly—so that we can, according to our background and cerebral attainments, rise, mount, or ascend a stairway, shrink in fear, terror, or trepidation, and think, ponder, or cogitate upon a problem. This abundance of terms is often cited as a virtue. And yet a critic could equally argue that English is an untidy and acquisitive language, cluttered with a plethora of needless words. After all, do we really need *fictile* as a synonym for *moldable, glabrous* for *hairless, sternutation* for *sneezing?* Jules Feiffer once drew a strip cartoon in which the down-at-heel character observed that first he was called poor, then needy, then deprived, then underprivileged, and then disadvantaged, and concluded that although he still didn't have a dime he sure had acquired a fine vocabulary. There is something in that. A rich vocabulary carries with it a concomitant danger of verbosity, as evidenced by our peculiar affection for redundant phrases, expressions that say the same thing twice: *beck and call, law and order, assault and battery, null and void, safe and sound, first and foremost, trials and tribulations, hem and haw, spick-and-span, kith and kin, dig and delve, hale and hearty, peace and quiet, vim and vigor, pots and pans, cease and desist, rack and ruin, without let or hindrance, to all intents and purposes, various different.*

Despite this bounty of terms, we have a strange—and to foreigners it must seem maddening—tendency to load a single word with a whole galaxy of meanings. *Fine,* for instance, has fourteen definitions as an adjective, six as a noun, and two as an adverb. In the *Oxford English Dictionary* it fills two full pages and takes 5,000 words of description. We can talk about fine art, fine gold, a fine edge, feeling fine, fine hair, and a court fine and mean quite separate things. The condition of having many meanings is known as *polysemy,* and it is very common. *Sound* is another polysemic word. Its vast repertory of meanings can suggest an audible noise, a state of healthiness (sound mind), an outburst (sound off), an inquiry (sound out), a body of water (Puget Sound), or financial stability (sound economy), among many others. And then there's *round*. In the *OED*, *round* alone (that is without variants like *rounded* and *roundup*) takes 7½ pages to define or about 15,000 words of text—about as much as is contained in the first hundred pages of this book. Even when you strip out its obsolete sense, *round* still has twelve uses as an adjective, nineteen as a noun, seven as a transitive verb, five as an intransitive verb, one as an adverb, and two as a proposition. But the polysemic champion must be *set*. Superficially it looks a wholly unseeming monosyllable, the verbal equivalent of the single-celled organism. Yet it has 58 uses as a noun, 126 as a verb, and 10 as a participial adjective. Its meanings are so various and scattered that it takes the *OED* 60,000 words—the length of a short novel—to discuss them all. A foreigner could be excused for thinking that to know *set* is to know English. . . .

Language, Appearance, and Reality: Doublespeak in 1984

William D. Lutz

William D. Lutz, chair of the Department of English at Rutgers University, is also chair of the National Council of Teachers of English (NCTE) Committee on Public Doublespeak and editor of the Quarterly Review of Doublespeak.

There are at least four kinds of doublespeak. The first kind is the euphemism, a word or phrase that is designed to avoid a harsh or distasteful reality. When a euphemism is used out of sensitivity for the feelings of someone or out of concern for a social or cultural taboo, it is not doublespeak. For example, we express grief that someone has *passed away* because we do not want to say to a grieving person, "I'm sorry your father is dead." The euphemism *passed away* functions here not just to protect the feelings of another person but also to communicate our concern over that person's feelings during a period of mourning.

However, when a euphemism is used to mislead or deceive, it becomes doublespeak. For example, the U.S. State Department decided in 1984 that in its annual reports on the status of human rights in countries around the world it would no longer use the word *killing*. Instead, it uses the phrase *unlawful or arbitrary deprivation of life*. Thus the State Department avoids discussing the embarrassing situation of the government-sanctioned killings in countries that are supported by the United States. This use of language constitutes doublespeak because it is designed to mislead, to cover up the

unpleasant. Its real intent is at variance with its apparent intent. It is language designed to alter our perception of reality.

A second kind of doublespeak is jargon, the specialized language of a trade, profession, or similar group. It is the specialized language of doctors, lawyers, engineers, educators, or car mechanics. Jargon can serve an important and useful function. Within a group, jargon allows members of the group to communicate with each other clearly, efficiently, and quickly. Indeed, it is a mark of membership in the group to be able to use and understand the group's jargon. For example, lawyers speak of an *involuntary conversion* of property when discussing the loss or destruction of property through theft, accident, or condemnation. When used by lawyers in a legal situation, such jargon is a legitimate use of language, since all members of the group can be expected to understand the term.

However, when a member of the group uses jargon to communicate with a person outside the group, and uses it knowing that the nonmember does not understand such language, then there is doublespeak. For example, a number of years ago a commercial airliner crashed on takeoff, killing three passengers, injuring twenty-one others, and destroying the airplane, a 727. The insured value of the airplane was greater than its book value, so the airline made a profit of three million dollars on the destroyed airplane. But the airline had two problems: it did not want to talk about one of its airplanes crashing and it had to account for the three million dollars when it issued its annual report to its stockholders. The

airline solved these problems by inserting a footnote in its annual report explaining that this three million dollars was due to "the involuntary conversion of a 727." Note that airline officials could thus claim to have explained the crash of the airplane and the subsequent three million dollars in profit. However, since most stockholders in the company, and indeed most of the general public, are not familiar with legal jargon, the use of such jargon constitutes doublespeak.

A third kind of doublespeak is gobbledygook or bureaucratese. Basically, such doublespeak is simply a matter of piling on words, of overwhelming the audience with words, the bigger the better. For example, when Alan Greenspan was chairman of the President's Council of Economic Advisors, he made this statement when testifying before a Senate committee:

It is a tricky problem to find the particular calibration in timing that would be appropriate to stem the acceleration in risk premiums created by falling incomes without prematurely aborting the decline in the inflation-generated risk premiums.

Did Alan Greenspan's audience really understand what he was saying? Did he believe his statement really explained anything? Perhaps there is some meaning beneath all those words, but it would take some time to search it out. This seems to be language that pretends to communicate but does not.

The fourth kind of doublespeak is inflated language. Inflated language designed to make the ordinary seem extraordinary, the common, uncommon; to make everyday things seem impressive; to give an air of importance to people, situations, or things

From *ETC* (Et Cetera), Winter 1987, pp. 383-391. Excerpt from *The Legacy of Language—A Tribute to Charlton Laird,* edited by Philip C. Boardman.

that would not normally be considered important; to make the simple seem complex. With this kind of language, car mechanics become *automotive internists,* elevator operators become members of the *vertical transportation corps,* used cars become not just *preowned* but *experienced cars.* When the Pentagon uses the phrase *pre-emptive counterattack* to mean that American forces attacked first, or when it uses the phrase *engage the enemy on all sides* to describe an ambush of American troops, or when it uses the phrase *tactical redeployment* to describe a retreat by American troops, it is using doublespeak. The electronics company that sells the television set with *non-multicolor capability* is also using the doublespeak of inflated language.

Doublespeak is not a new use of language peculiar to the politics or economics of the twentieth century. Thucydides in *The Peloponnesian War* wrote that

revolution thus ran its course from city to city. . . . Words had to change their ordinary meanings and to take those which were now given them. Reckless audacity came to be considered the courage of a loyal ally; prudent hesitation, specious cowardice; moderation was held to be a cloak for unmanliness; ability to see all sides of a question, inaptness to act on any. Frantic violence become the attribute of manliness; cautious plotting, a justifiable means of self-defense. The advocate of extreme measures was always trustworthy; his opponent, a man to be suspected.[1]

Caesar in his account of the Gallic Wars described his brutal conquest as "pacifying" Gaul. Doublespeak has a long history.

Military doublespeak seems always to have been with us. In 1947 the name of the War Department was changed to the more pleasing if misleading *Defense Department.* During the Vietnam War the American public learned that it was an *incursion,* not an invasion; a *protective reaction strike* or a *limited duration protective reaction strike* or *air support,* not bombing; and *incontinent ordinance,* not bombs and artillery shells, fell on civilians. This use of language continued with the invasion of Grenada, which was conducted not by the United States Army, Navy, or Air Force, but by the Caribbean Peace Keeping Forces. Indeed, according to the Pentagon, it was not an invasion of Grenada, but a *predawn, vertical insertion.* And it wasn't that the armed forces lacked intelligence data on Grenada before the invasion, it was just that "we were not micromanaging Grenada intelligencewise until about that time frame." In today's army forces, it's not a shovel but a *combat emplacement evacuator,* not a toothpick but a *wood interdental stimulator,* not a pencil but a portable, handheld communications inscriber, not a bullet hole but a *ballistically induced aperture in the subcutaneous environment.*

Members of the military and politicians are not the only ones who use doublespeak. People in all parts of society use it. Take educators, for example. On some college campuses what was once the Department of Physical Education is now the *Department of Human Kinetics* or the *College of Applied Life Studies.* Home Economics is now the *School of Human Resources and Family Studies.* College campuses no longer have libraries but *learning resource centers.* Those are not desks in the classroom, they are *pupil stations.* Teachers—*classroom managers* who apply an *action plan* to a *knowledge base*—are concerned with the *basic fundamentals,* which are *inexorably linked* to the *education user's* (not student's) *time-on-task.* Students don't take tests; now it is *criterion referencing testing* which measures whether a student has achieved the *operational curricular objectives.* A school system in Pennsylvania uses the following grading system on report cards: "no effort, less than minimal effort, minimal effort, more than minimal effort, less than full effort, full effort, better than full effort, effort increasing, effort decreasing." Some college students in New York come from *economically nonaffluent* families, while the coach at a Southern university wasn't fired, "he just won't be asked to continue in that job." An article in a scholarly journal suggests teaching students three approaches to writing to help them become better writers: "concretization of goals, procedural facilitation, and modeling planning." An article on family relationships entitled "Familial Love and Intertemporal Optimality" observes that "an altruistic utility function promotes intertemporal efficiency. However, altruism creates an externality that implies that satisfying the condition for efficiency, does not insure intertemporal optimality." A research report issued by the U.S. Office of Education contains this sentence: "In other words, feediness is the shared information between toputness, where toputness is at a time just prior to the inputness." Educations contributes more than its share to current doublespeak.

The world of business has produced large amounts of doublespeak. If an airplane crash is one of the worst things that can happen to an airline company, a recall of automobiles because of a safety defect is one of the worst things that can happen to an automobile company. So a few years ago, when one of the three largest car companies in America had to recall two of its models to correct mechanical defects, the company sent a letter to all those who had bought those models. In its letter, the company said that the rear axle bearings of the cars "can deteriorate" and that "continued driving with a failed bearing could result in disengagement of the axle shaft and adversely affect vehicle control." This is the language of nonresponsibility. What are "mechanical deficiencies"—poor design, bad workmanship? If they do, what causes the deterioration? Note that "continued driving" is the subject of the sentence and suggests that it is not the company's poor manufacturing which is at fault but the driver who persists in driving. Note, too, "failed bearing," which implies that the bearing failed, not the company. Finally, "adversely affect vehicle control" means nothing more than that the driver could lose control of the car and get killed.

If we apply Hugh Rank's criteria for examining such language, we quickly discover the doublespeak here. What the car company should be saying to its customers is that the car the company sold them has a serious defect which should be corrected immediately—otherwise the customer runs the risk of being killed. But the reader of the letter must find this message beneath the doublespeak the company has used to disguise the harshness of its message. We will probably never know how many of the customers never brought their cars in for the necessary repairs because they did not think the problem serious enough to warrant the inconvenience involved.

When it come time to fire employees, business has produced more than enough doublespeak to deal with the unpleasant situation. Employees are, of course, never fired. They are *selected out, placed out, non-retained, released, dehired, non-renewed.* A corporation will *eliminate the redundancies in the human resources area,* assign *candidates for derecruitment* to a *mobility pool,* revitalize the department by placing executives on *special assignment, enhance the efficiency of operations, streamline the field sales organization,* or *further rationalize marketing efforts.* The reality behind all this doublespeak is that companies are firing employees, but no one wants the stockholders, public, or competition to know that times are tough and people have to go.

Recently the oil industry has been hard hit by declining sales and a surplus of oil. Because of *reduced demand for product,* which results in *spare refining capacity* and problems in *down-stream operations,* oil companies have been forced to *re-evaluate and consolidate their operations* and take *appropriate cost reduction actions,* in order to *enhance the efficiency of operations,* which has meant the *elimination of marginal outlets, accelerating the divestment program,* and the *disposition of low throughput marketing units.* What this doublespeak really means is that oil companies have fired employees, cut back on expenses, and closed gas stations and oil refineries because there's surplus of oil and people are not buying as much gas and oil as in the past.

One corporation faced with declining business sent a memorandum to its employees advising them that the company's "business plans are under revi-

sion and now reflect a more moderate approach toward our operating and capital programs." The result of this "more moderate approach" is a "surplus of professional/technical employees." To "assist in alleviating the surplus, selected professional and technical employees" have been "selected to participate" in a "Voluntary Program." Note that individuals were selected to "resign voluntarily." What this memorandum means, of course, is that expenses must be cut because of declining business, so employees will have to be fired.

It is rare to read that the stock market *fell.* Members of the financial community prefer to say that the stock market *retreated, eased, made a technical adjustment* or a *technical correction,* or perhaps that *prices were off due to profit taking,* or *off in light trading,* or *lost ground.* But the stock market never falls, not if stockbrokers have their say. As a side note, it is interesting to observe that the stock market never rises because of a *technical adjustment* or *correction,* nor does it ever *ease* upwards.

The business sections of newspapers, business magazines, corporate reports, and executive speeches are filled with words and phrases such as *marginal rates of substitution, equilibrium price, getting off margin, distribution coalition, non-performing assets,* and *encompassing organizations.* Much of this is jargon or inflated language designed to make the simple seem complex, but there are other examples of business doublespeak that mislead, that are designed to avoid a harsh reality. What should we make of such expressions as *negative deficit* or *revenue excesses* for profit, *invest in* for buy, *price enhancement* or *price adjustment* for price increase, *shortfall* for a mistake in planning or *period of accelerated negative growth* or *negative economic growth* for recession?

Business doublespeak often attempts to give substance to wind, to make ordinary actions seem complex. Executives *operate* in *timeframes* within the *context* of which a *task force* will serve as the proper *conduit* for all the necessary *input* to *program a scenario* that,

within acceptable *parameters,* and with the proper *throughput,* will *generate* the *maximum output* for a *print out* of *zero defect terminal objectives* that will *enhance the bottom line.*

There are instances, however, where doublespeak becomes more than amusing, more than a cause for a weary shake of the head. When the anesthetist turned the wrong knob during a Caesarean delivery and killed the mother and unborn child, the hospital called it a *therapeutic misadventure.* The Pentagon calls the neutron bomb "an efficient nuclear weapon that eliminates an enemy with a minimum degree of damage to friendly territory." The Pentagon also calls expected civilian casualties in a nuclear war *collateral damage.* And it was the Central Intelligence Agency which during the Vietnam War created the phrase *eliminate with extreme prejudice* to replace the more direct verb *kill.*

Identifying doublespeak can at times be difficult. For example, on July 27, 1981, President Ronald Reagan said in a speech televised to the American public: "I will not stand by and see those of you who are dependent on Social Security deprived of the benefits you've worked so hard to earn. You will continue to receive your checks in the full amount due you." This speech had been billed as President Reagan's position on Social Security, a subject of much debate at the time. After the speech, public opinion polls revealed that the great majority of the public believed that President Reagan had affirmed his support for Social Security and that he would not support cuts in benefits. However, five days after the speech, on July 31, 1981, an article in the *Philadelphia Inquirer* quoted White House spokesman David Gergen as saying that President Reagan's words had been "carefully chosen." What President Reagan did mean, according to Gergen, was that he was reserving the right to decide who was "dependent" on those benefits, who had "earned" them, and who, therefore, was "due" them.[2]

The subsequent remarks of David Gergen reveal the real intent of President Reagan as opposed to his apparent intent. Thus Hugh Rank's criteria for analyzing language to determine whether it is doublespeak, when applied in light of David Gergen's remarks, reveal the doublespeak of President Reagan. Here indeed is the insincerity of which Orwell wrote. Here, too, is the gap between the speaker's real and declared aim.

In 1982 the Republican National Committee sponsored a television advertisement which pictured an elderly, folksy postman delivering Social Security checks "with the 7.4% cost-of-living raise that President Reagan promised." The postman then added that "he promised that raise and he kept his promise, in spite of those sticks-in-the-mud who tried to keep him from doing what we elected him to do." The commercial was, in fact, deliberately misleading. The cost-of-living increases had been provided automatically by law since 1975, and President Reagan tried three times to roll them back or delay them but was overruled by congressional opposition. When these discrepancies were pointed out to an official of the Republican National Committee, he called the commercial "inoffensive" and added, "Since when is a commercial supposed to be accurate? Do women really smile when they clean their ovens?"

Again, applying Hugh Rank's criteria to this advertisement reveals the doublespeak in it once we know the facts of past actions by President Reagan. Moreover, the official for the Republican National Committee assumes that all advertisements, whether for political candidates or commercial products, are lies, or in his doublespeak term, *inaccurate.* Thus, the real intent of the advertisement was to mislead while the apparent purpose was to inform the public of President Reagan's position on possible cuts in Social Security benefits. Again there is insincerity, and again there is a gap between the speaker's real and declared aims.

In 1981 Secretary of State Alexander Haig testified before congressional committees about the murder of three American nuns and a Catholic lay worker in El Salvador. The four

women had been raped and shot at close range, and there was clear evidence that the crime had been committed by soldiers of the Salvadoran government. Before the House Foreign Affairs Committee, Secretary Haig said,

I'd like to suggest to you that some of the investigations would lead one to believe that perhaps the vehicle the nuns were riding in may have tried to run a roadblock, or may accidentally have been perceived to have been doing so, and there'd been an exchange of fire and then perhaps those who inflicted the casualties sought to cover it up. And this could have been at a very low level of both competence and motivation in the context of the issue itself. But the facts on this are not clear enough for anyone to draw a definitive conclusion.

The next day, before the Senate Foreign Relations Committee, Secretary Haig claimed that press reports on his previous testimony were inaccurate. When Senator Claiborne Pell asked whether Secretary Haig was suggesting the possibility that "the nuns may have run through a roadblock." Secretary Haig replied, "You mean that they tried to violate . . .? Not at all, no, not at all. My heavens! The dear nuns who raised me in my parochial schooling would forever isolate me from their affections and respect." When Senator Pell asked Secretary Haig, "Did you mean that the nuns were firing at the people, or what did 'exchange of fire' mean?" Secretary Haig replied, "I haven't met any pistol-packing nuns in my day, Senator. What I meant was that if one fellow starts shooting, then the next thing you know they all panic." Thus did the secretary of state of the United States explain official government policy on the murder of four American citizens in a foreign land.

Secretary Haig's testimony implies that the women were in some way responsible for their own fate. By using such vague wording as "would lead one to believe" and "may accidentally have been perceived to have been," he avoids any direct assertion. The use of "inflicted the casualties" not only avoids using the word *kill* but also implies that at the worst the kill-

ings were accidental or justifiable. The result of this testimony is that the secretary of state has become an apologist for murder. This is indeed language in defense of the indefensible; language designed to make lies sound truthful and murder respectable; language designed to give an appearance of solidity to pure wind.

These last three examples of doublespeak should make it clear that doublespeak is not the product of careless language or sloppy thinking. Indeed, most doublespeak is the product of clear thinking and is language carefully designed and constructed to appear to communicate when in fact it does not. It is language designed not to lead but to mislead. It is language designed to distort reality and corrupt the mind. It is not a tax increase but *revenue enhancement* or *tax base broadening,* so how can you complain about higher taxes? It is not acid rain, but *poorly buffered precipitation,* so don't worry about all those dead trees. That is not the Mafia in Atlantic City, New Jersey, those are *members of a career offender cartel,* so don't worry about the influence of organized crime in the city. The judge was not addicted to the pain-killing drug he was taking, it was just that the drug had "established an interrelationship with the body, such that if the drug is removed precipitously, there is a reaction," so don't worry that his decisions might have been influenced by his drug addiction. It's not a Titan II nuclear-armed, intercontinental ballistic missile with a warhead 630 times more powerful than the atomic bomb dropped on Hiroshima, it is just a *very large, potentially disruptive re-entry system,* so don't worry about the threat of nuclear destruction. It is not a neutron bomb but a *radiation enhancement device,* so don't worry about escalating the arms race. It is not an invasion but a *rescue mission,* or a *predawn vertical insertion,* so don't worry about any violations of United States or international law.

Doublespeak has become so common in our everyday lives that we fail to notice it. We do not protest when we are asked to check our packages at the desk "for our convenience" when it is not for our convenience at all but for someone else's convenience. We see advertisements for *genuine imitation leather, virgin vinyl,* or *real counterfeit diamonds* and do not question the language or the supposed quality of the product. We do not speak of slums or ghettos but of the *inner city* or *substandard housing where the disadvantaged* live and thus avoid talking about the poor who have to live in filthy, poorly heated, ramshackle apartments or houses. Patients do not die in the hospital; it is just *negative patient care outcome.*

Doublespeak which calls cab drivers *urban transportation specialists,* elevator operators *members of the vertical transportation corps,* and automobile mechanics *automotive internists* can be considered humorous and relatively harmless. However, doublespeak which calls a fire in a nuclear reactor building *rapid oxidation,* an explosion in a nuclear power plant an *energetic disassembly,* the illegal overthrow of a legitimate administration *destablizing a government,* and lies *inoperative statements* is language which attempts to avoid responsibility, which attempts to make the bad seem good, the negative appear positive, something unpleasant appear attractive, and which seems to communicate but does not. It is language designed to alter our perception of reality and corrupt our minds. Such language does not provide us with the tools needed to develop and preserve civilization. Such language breeds suspicion, cynicism, distrust, and, ultimately, hostility.

Doublespeak is insidious because it can infect and ultimately destroy the function of language, which is communication between people and social groups. If this corrupting process does occur, it can have serious consequences in a country that depends upon an informed electorate to make decisions in selecting candidates for office and deciding issues of public policy. After a while we may really believe that politicians don't lie but only *misspeak,* that illegal acts are merely *inappropriate actions,* that fraud and criminal conspiracy are just *miscertification.* And if we really believe that we understand such language, then the world of *Nineteen Eighty-four* with its control of reality through language is not far away.

The consistent use of doublespeak can have serious and far-reaching consequences beyond the obvious ones. The pervasive use of doublespeak can spread so that doublespeak becomes the coin of the political realm with speakers and listeners convinced that they really understand such language. President Jimmy Carter could call the aborted raid to free the hostages in Tehran in 1980 an "incomplete success" and really believe that he had made a statement that clearly communicated with the American public. So, too, President Ronald Reagan could say in 1985 that "ultimately our security and our hopes for success at the arms reduction talks hinge on the determination that we show here to continue our program to rebuild and refortify our defenses" and really believe that greatly increasing the amount of money spent building new weapons will lead to a reduction in the number of weapons in the world.

The task of English teachers is to teach not just the effective use of language but respect for language as well. Those who use language to conceal or prevent or corrupt thought must be called to account. Only by teaching respect for and love of language can teachers of English instill in students the sense of outrage they should experience when they encounter doublespeak. But before students can experience that outrage, they must first learn to use language effectively, to understand its beauty and power. Only then will we begin to make headway in the fight against doublespeak, for only by using language well will we come to appreciate the perversion inherent in doublespeak.

In his book *The Miracle of Language,* Charlton Laird notes that

language is . . . the most important tool man ever devised. . . . Language is [man's] basic tool. It is the tool more than any other with which he makes his living, makes his home, makes his life. As man becomes more and more a social being, as the world becomes more and more a social community, communication grows ever more imperative. And language is the basis of communication. Language is also the instrument with which we think, and thinking is the rarest and most needed commodity in the world.[3]

In this opinion Laird echoes Orwell's comment that "if thought corrupts language, language can also corrupt thought."[4] Both men have given us a legacy of respect for language, a respect that should prompt us to cry "Enough!" when we encounter doublespeak. The greatest honor we can do Charlton Laird is to continue to have the greatest respect of language in all its manifestations, for, as Laird taught us, language is a miracle.

NOTES AND REFERENCES

1. Thucydides, *The Peloponnesian Way,* 3.82.
2. David Hess, "Reagan's Language on Benefits Confused, Angered Many," *Philadelphia Inquirer,* July 31, 1981, p. 6-A.
3. Charlton Laird, *The Miracle of Language* (New York: Fawcett, Premier Books, 1953), p. 224.
4. Orwell, *The Collected Essays,* 4:137.

Shakespeare in the Bush

Laura Bohannan

Laura Bohannan is a professor of anthropology at the University of Illinois, at Chicago.

Just before I left Oxford for the Tiv in West Africa, conversation turned to the season at Stratford. "You Americans," said a friend, "often have difficulty with Shakespeare. He was, after all, a very English poet, and one can easily misinterpret the universal by misunderstanding the particular."

I protested that human nature is pretty much the same the whole world over; at least the general plot and motivation of the greater tragedies would always be clear—everywhere—although some details of custom might have to be explained and difficulties of translation might produce other slight changes. To end an argument we could not conclude, my friend gave me a copy of *Hamlet* to study in the African bush: it would, he hoped, lift my mind above its primitive surroundings, and possibly I might, by prolonged meditation, achieve the grace of correct interpretation.

It was my second field trip to that African tribe, and I thought myself ready to live in one of its remote sections—an area difficult to cross even on foot. I eventually settled on the hillock of a very knowledgeable old man, the head of a homestead of some hundred and forty people, all of whom were either his close relatives or their wives and children. Like the other elders of the vicinity, the old man spent most of his time performing ceremonies seldom seen these days in the more accessible parts of the tribe. I was delighted. Soon there would be three months of enforced isolation and leisure, between the harvest that takes place just before the rising of the swamps and the clearing of new farms when the water goes down. Then, I thought, they would have even more time to perform ceremonies and explain them to me.

I was quite mistaken. Most of the ceremonies demanded the presence of elders from several homesteads. As the swamps rose, the old men found it too difficult to walk from one homestead to the next, and the ceremonies gradually ceased. As the swamps rose even higher, all activities but one came to an end. The women brewed beer from maize and millet. Men, women, and children sat on their hillocks and drank it.

People began to drink at dawn. By midmorning the whole homestead was singing, dancing, and drumming. When it rained, people had to sit inside their huts: there they drank and sang or they drank and told stories. In any case, by noon or before, I either had to join the party or retire to my own hut and my books. "One does not discuss serious matters when there is beer. Come, drink with us." Since I lacked their capacity for the thick native beer, I spent more and more time with *Hamlet*. Before the end of the second month, grace descended on me. I was quite sure that *Hamlet* had only one possible interpretation, and that one universally obvious.

Early every morning, in the hope of having some serious talk before the beer party, I used to call on the old man at his reception hut—a circle of posts supporting a thatched roof above a low mud wall to keep out wind and rain. One day I crawled through the low doorway and found most of the men of the homestead sitting huddled in their ragged cloths on stools, low plank beds, and reclining chairs, warming themselves against the chill of the rain around a smoky fire. In the center were three pots of beer. The party had started.

The old man greeted me cordially. "Sit down and drink." I accepted a large calabash full of beer, poured some into a small drinking gourd, and tossed it down. Then I poured some more into the same gourd for the man second in seniority to my host before I handed my calabash over to a young man for further distribution. Important people shouldn't ladle beer themselves.

 From *Natural History*, August/September 1966. Reprinted by permission of the author.

"It is better like this," the old man said, looking at me approvingly and plucking at the thatch that had caught in my hair. "You should sit and drink with us more often. Your servants tell me that when you are not with us, you sit inside your hut looking at a paper."

The old man was acquainted with four kinds of "papers": tax receipts, bride price receipts, court fee receipts, and letters. The messenger who brought him letters from the chief used them mainly as a badge of office, for he always knew what was in them and told the old man. Personal letters for the few who had relatives in the government or mission stations were kept until someone went to a large market where there was a letter writer and reader. Since my arrival, letters were brought to me to be read. A few men also brought me bride price receipts, privately, with requests to change the figures to a higher sum. I found moral arguments were of no avail, since in-laws are fair game, and the technical hazards of forgery difficult to explain to an illiterate people. I did not wish them to think me silly enough to look at any such papers for days on end, and I hastily explained that my "paper" was one of the "things of long ago" of my country.

"Ah," said the old man. "Tell us."

I protested that I was not a story-teller. Story telling is a skilled art among them; their standards are high, and the audiences critical—and vocal in their criticism. I protested in vain. This morning they wanted to hear a story while they drank. They threatened to tell me no more stories until I told them one of mine. Finally, the old man promised that no one would criticize my style "for we know you are struggling with our language." "But," put in one of the elders, "you must explain what we do not understand, as we do when we tell you our stories." Realizing that here was my chance to prove *Hamlet* universally intelligible, I agreed.

The old man handed me some more beer to help me on with my story-telling. Men filled their long wooden pipes and knocked coals from the fire to place in the pipe bowls; then, puffing contentedly, they sat back to listen. I began in the proper style, "Not yesterday, not yesterday, but long ago, a thing occurred. One night three men were keeping watch outside the homestead of the great chief, when suddenly they saw the former chief approach them."

"Why was he no longer their chief?"

"He was dead," I explained. "That is why they were troubled and afraid when they saw him."

"Impossible," began one of the elders, handing his pipe on to his neighbor, who interrupted, "Of course it wasn't the dead chief. It was an omen sent by a witch. Go on."

Slightly shaken, I continued. "One of these three was a man who knew things"—the closest translation for scholar, but unfortunately it also meant witch. The second elder looked triumphantly at the first. "So he spoke to the dead chief saying, 'Tell us what we must do so you may rest in your grave,' but the dead chief did not answer. He vanished, and they could see him no more. Then the man who knew things—his name was Horatio—said this event was the affair of the dead chief's son, Hamlet."

There was a general shaking of heads round the circle. "Had the dead chief no living brothers? Or was this son the chief?"

"No," I replied. "That is, he had one living brother who became the chief when the elder brother died."

The old men muttered: such omens were matters for chiefs and elders, not for youngsters; no good could come of going behind a chief's back; clearly Horatio was not a man who knew things.

"Yes, he was," I insisted, shooing a chicken away from my beer. "In our country the son is next to the father. The dead chief's younger brother had become the great chief. He had also married his elder brother's widow only about a month after the funeral."

"He did well," the old man beamed and announced to the others, "I told you that if we knew more about Europeans, we would find they really were very like us. In our country also," he added to me, "the younger brother marries the elder brother's widow and becomes the father of his children. Now, if your uncle, who married your widowed mother, is your father's full brother, then he will be a real father to you. Did Hamlet's father and uncle have one mother?"

His question barely penetrated my mind; I was too upset and thrown too far off balance by having one of the most important elements of *Hamlet* knocked straight out of the picture. Rather uncertainly I said that I thought they had the same mother, but I wasn't sure—the story didn't say. The old man told me severely that these genealogical details made all the difference and that when I got home I must ask the elders about it. He shouted out the door to one of his younger wives to bring his goatskin bag.

Determined to save what I could of the mother motif, I took a deep breath and began again. "The son Hamlet was very sad because his mother had married again so quickly. There was no need for her to do so, and it is our custom for a widow not to go to her next husband until she has mourned for two years."

"Two years is too long," objected the wife, who had appeared with the old man's battered goatskin bag. "Who will hoe your farms for you while you have no husband?"

"Hamlet," I retorted without thinking, "was old enough to hoe his mother's farms himself. There was no need for her to remarry." No one looked convinced. I gave up. "His mother and the great chief told Hamlet not to be sad, for the great chief himself would be a father to Hamlet. Furthermore, Hamlet would be the next chief: therefore he must stay to learn the things of a chief. Hamlet agreed to remain, and all the rest went off to drink beer."

While I paused, perplexed at how to render Hamlet's disgusted soliloquy to an audience convinced that Claudius and Gertrude had behaved in the best possible manner, one of the younger men asked me who had married the other wives of the dead chief.

"He had no other wives," I told him.

"But a chief must have many wives! How else can he brew beer and prepare food for all his guests?"

I said firmly that in our country even chiefs had only one wife, that they had servants to do their work, and that they paid them from tax money.

It was better, they returned, for a chief to have many wives and sons who would help him hoe his farms and feed his people; then everyone loved the chief who gave much and took nothing—taxes were a bad thing.

I agreed with the last comment, but for the rest fell back on their favorite way of fobbing off my questions: "That is the way it is done, so that is how we do it."

I decided to skip the soliloquy. Even if Claudius was here thought quite right to marry his brother's widow, there remained the poison motif, and I knew they would disapprove of fratricide. More hopefully I resumed, "That night Hamlet kept watch with the three who had seen his dead father. The dead chief again appeared, and although the others were afraid, Hamlet followed his dead father off to one side. When they were alone, Hamlet's dead father spoke."

"Omens can't talk!" The old man was emphatic.

"Hamlet's dead father wasn't an omen. Seeing him might have been an omen, but he was not." My audience looked as confused as I sounded. "It *was* Hamlet's dead father. It was a thing we call a 'ghost.'" I had to use the English word, for unlike many of the neighboring tribes, these people didn't believe in the survival after death of any individuating part of the personality.

"What is a 'ghost?' An omen?"

"No, a 'ghost' is someone who is dead but who walks around and can talk, and people can hear him and see him but not touch him."

They objected. "One can touch zombis."

"No, no! It was not a dead body the witches had animated to sacrifice and eat. No one else made Hamlet's dead father walk. He did it himself."

"Dead men can't walk," protested my audience as one man.

I was quite willing to compromise. "A 'ghost' is the dead man's shadow."

But again they objected. "Dead men cast no shadows."

"They do in my country," I snapped.

The old man quelled the babble of disbelief that arose immediately and told me with that insincere, but courteous, agreement one extends to the fancies of the young, ignorant, and superstitious, "No doubt in your country the dead can also walk without being zombis." From the depths of his bag he produced a withered fragment of kola nut, bit off one end to show it wasn't poisoned, and handed me the rest as a peace offering.

"Anyhow," I resumed, "Hamlet's dead father said that his own brother, the one who became chief, had poisoned him. He wanted Hamlet to avenge him. Hamlet believed this in his heart, for he did not like his father's brother." I took another swallow of beer. "In the country of the great chief, living in the same homestead, for it was a very large one, was an important elder who was often with the chief to advise and help him. His name was Polonius. Hamlet was courting his daughter, but her father and her brother . . .[I cast hastily about for some tribal analogy] warned her not to let Hamlet visit her when she was alone on her farm, for he would be a great chief and so could not marry her."

"Why not?" asked the wife, who had settled down on the edge of the old man's chair. He frowned at her for asking stupid questions and growled, "They lived in the same homestead."

"That was not the reason," I informed them. "Polonius was a stranger who lived in the homestead because he helped the chief, not because he was a relative."

"Then why couldn't Hamlet marry her?"

"He could have," I explained, "but Polonius didn't think he would. After all, Hamlet was a man of great importance who ought to marry a chief's daughter, for in his country a man could have only one wife. Polonius was afraid that if Hamlet made love to his daughter, then no one else would give a high price for her."

"That might be true," remarked one of the shrewder elders, "but a chief's son would give his mistress's father enough presents and patronage to more than make up the difference. Polonius sounds like a fool to me."

"Many people think he was," I agreed. "Meanwhile Polonius sent his son Laertes off to Paris to learn the things of that country, for it was the homestead of a very great chief indeed. Because he was afraid that Laertes might waste a lot of money on beer and women and gambling, or get into trouble by fighting, he sent one of his servants to Paris secretly, to spy out what Laertes was doing. One day Hamlet came upon Polonius's daughter Ophelia. He behaved so oddly he frightened her. Indeed"—I was fumbling for words to express the dubious quality of Hamlet's madness—"the chief and many others had also noticed that when Hamlet talked one could understand the words but not what they meant. Many people thought that he had become mad." My audience suddenly became much more attentive. "The great chief wanted to know what was wrong with Hamlet, so he sent for two of Hamlet's age mates [school friends would have taken long explanation] to talk to Hamlet and find out what troubled his heart. Hamlet, seeing that they had been bribed by the chief to betray him, told them nothing. Polonius, however, insisted that Hamlet was mad because he had been forbidden to see Ophelia, whom he loved."

"Why," inquired a bewildered voice, "should anyone bewitch Hamlet on that account?"

"Bewitch him?"

"Yes, only witchcraft can make anyone mad, unless, of course, one sees the beings that lurk in the forest."

I stopped being a storyteller, took out my notebook and demanded to be told more about these two causes of madness. Even while they spoke and I jotted notes, I tried to calculate the effect of this new factor on the plot. Hamlet had not been exposed to the beings that lurk in the forests. Only his relatives in the male line could bewitch him. Barring relatives not mentioned by Shakespeare, it had to be Claudius who was attempting to harm him. And, of course, it was.

For the moment I staved off questions by saying that the great chief also refused to believe that Hamlet was mad for the love of Ophelia and nothing else. "He was sure that something much more important was troubling Hamlet's heart."

"Now Hamlet's age mates," I continued, "had brought with them a famous storyteller. Hamlet decided to have this man tell the chief and all his homestead a story about a man who had poisoned his brother because he desired his brother's wife and wished to be chief himself. Hamlet was sure the great chief could not hear the story without making a sign if he was indeed guilty, and then he would discover whether his dead father had told him the truth."

The old man interrupted, with deep cunning, "Why should a father lie to his son?" he asked.

I hedged: "Hamlet wasn't sure that it really was his dead father." It was impossible to say anything, in that language, about devil-inspired visions.

"You mean," he said, "it actually was an omen, and he knew witches sometimes send false ones. Hamlet was a fool not to go to one skilled in reading omens and divining the truth in the first place. A man-who-sees-the-truth could have told him how his father died, if he really had been poisoned, and if there was witchcraft in it; then Hamlet could have called the elders to settle the matter."

The shrewd elder ventured to disagree. "Because his father's brother was a great chief, one-who-sees-the-truth might therefore have been afraid to tell it. I think it was for that reason that a friend of Hamlet's father—a witch and an elder—sent an omen so his friend's son would know. Was the omen true?"

"Yes," I said, abandoning ghosts and the devil; a witch-sent omen it would have to be. "It was true, for when the storyteller was telling his tale before all the homestead, the great chief rose in fear. Afraid that Hamlet knew his secret he planned to have him killed."

The stage set of the next bit presented some difficulties of translation. I began cautiously. "The great chief told Hamlet's mother to find out from her son what he knew. But because a woman's children are always first in her heart, he had the important elder Polonius hide behind a cloth that hung against the wall of Hamlet's mother's sleeping hut. Hamlet started to scold his mother for what she had done."

There was a shocked murmur from everyone. A man should never scold his mother.

"She called out in fear, and Polonius moved behind the cloth. Shouting, 'A rat!' Hamlet took his machete and slashed through the cloth." I paused for dramatic effect. "He had killed Polonius!"

The old men looked at each other in supreme disgust. "That Polonius truly was a fool and a man who knew nothing! What child would not know enough to shout, 'It's me!' " With a pang, I remembered that these people are ardent hunters, always armed with bow, arrow, and machete; at the first rustle in the grass an arrow is aimed and ready, and the hunter shouts "Game!" If no human voice answers immediately, the arrow speeds on its way. Like a good hunter Hamlet had shouted, "A rat!"

I rushed in to save Polonius's reputation. "Polonius did speak. Hamlet heard him. But he thought it was the chief and wished to kill him earlier that evening. . . ." I broke down, unable to describe to these pagans, who had no belief in individual afterlife, the difference between dying at one's prayers and dying "unhousel'd, disappointed, unaneled."

This time I had shocked my audience seriously. "For a man to raise his hand against his father's brother and and the one who has become his father—that is a terrible thing. The elders ought to let such a man be bewitched."

I nibbled at my kola nut in some perplexity, then pointed out that after all the man had killed Hamlet's father.

"No," pronounced the old man, speaking less to me than to the young men sitting behind the elders. "If your father's brother has killed your father, you must appeal to your father's age mates; *they* may avenge him. No man may use violence against his senior relatives." Another thought struck him. "But if his father's brother had indeed been wicked enough to bewitch Hamlet and make him mad that would be a good story indeed, for it would be his fault that Hamlet, being mad, no longer had any sense and thus was ready to kill his father's brother."

There was a murmur of applause. *Hamlet* was again a good story to them, but it no longer seemed quite the same story to me. As I thought over the coming complications of plot and motive, I lost courage and decided to skim over dangerous ground quickly.

"The great chief," I went on, "was not sorry that Hamlet had killed Polonius. It gave him a reason to send Hamlet away, with his two treacherous mates, with letters to a chief of a far country, saying that Hamlet should be killed. But Hamlet changed the writing on their papers, so that the chief killed his age mates instead." I encountered a reproachful glare from one of the men whom I had told undetectable forgery was not merely immoral but beyond human skill. I looked the other way.

"Before Hamlet could return, Laertes came back for his father's funeral. The great chief told him Hamlet had killed Polonius. Laertes swore to kill Hamlet because of this, and because his sister Ophelia, hearing her father had been killed by the man she loved, went mad and drowned in the river."

"Have you already forgotten what we told you?" The old man was reproachful. "One cannot take vengeance on a madman; Hamlet killed Polonius in his madness. As for the girl, she not only went mad, she was drowned. Only witches can make people drown. Water itself can't hurt anything. It is merely something one drinks and bathes in."

I began to get cross. "If you don't like the story, I'll stop."

The old man made soothing noises and himself poured me some more beer. "You tell the story well, and we are listening. But it is clear that the elders of your country have never told you what the story really means. No, don't interrupt! We believe you when you say your marriage customs are different, or your clothes and weapons. But people are the same everywhere; therefore, there are always witches and it is we, the elders, who know how witches work. We told you it was the great chief who wished to kill Hamlet, and now your own words have proved us right. Who were Ophelia's male relatives?"

"There were only her father and her brother." *Hamlet* was clearly out of my hands.

"There must have been many more; this also you must ask of your elders when you get back to your country. From what you tell us, since Polonius was dead, it must have been Laertes who killed Ophelia, although I do not see the reason for it."

We had emptied one pot of beer, and the old men argued the point with slightly tipsy interest. Finally one of them demanded of me, "What did the servant of Polonius say on his return?"

With difficulty I recollected Reynaldo and his mission. "I don't think he did return before Polonius was killed."

"Listen," said the elder, "and I will tell you how it was and how your story will go, then you may tell me if I am right. Polonius knew his son would get into trouble, and so he did. He had many fines to pay for fighting, and debts from gambling. But he had only two ways of getting money quickly. One was to marry off his sister at once, but it is difficult to find a man who will marry a woman desired by the son of a chief. For if the chief's heir commits adultery with your wife, what can you do? Only a fool calls a case against a man who will someday be his judge. Therefore Laertes had to take the second way: he killed his sister by witchcraft, drowning her so he could secretly sell her body to the witches."

I raised an objection. "They found her body and buried it. Indeed Laertes jumped into the grave to see his sister once more—so, you see, the body was truly there. Hamlet, who had just come back, jumped in after him."

"What did I tell you?" The elder appealed to the others. "Laertes was up to no good with his sister's body. Hamlet prevented him, because the chief's heir, like a chief, does not wish any other man to grow rich and powerful. Laertes would be angry, because he would have killed his sister without benefit to himself. In our country he would try to kill Hamlet for that reason. Is this not what happened?"

"More or less," I admitted. "When the great chief found Hamlet was still alive, he encouraged Laertes to try to kill Hamlet and arranged a fight with machetes between them. In the fight both the young men were wounded to death. Hamlet's mother drank the poisoned beer that the chief meant for Hamlet in case he won the fight. When he saw his mother die of poison, Hamlet, dying, managed to kill his father's brother with his machete."

"You see, I was right!" exclaimed the elder.

"That was a very good story," added the old man, "and you told it with very few mistakes. There was just one more error, at the very end. The poison Hamlet's mother drank was obviously meant for the survivor of the fight, whichever it was. If Laertes had won, the great chief would have poisoned him, for no one would know that he arranged Hamlet's death. Then, too, he need not fear Laertes' witchcraft; it takes a strong heart to kill one's only sister by witchcraft."

"Sometime," concluded the old man, gathering his ragged toga about him, "you must tell us some more stories of your country. We, who are elders, will instruct you in their true meaning, so that when you return to your own land your elders will see that you have not been sitting in the bush, but among those who know things and who have taught you wisdom."

A Cross-Cultural Experience: A Chinese Anthropologist in the United States

Huang Shu-min

Huang Shu-min is a professor of Anthropology at Iowa State University, where he has been teaching since 1975. Born and raised in China and Taiwan, Huang spent much of his research periods in these two regions. He received his B.A. in Anthropology from National Taiwan University (1967) and his M.A. and Ph.D. in Anthropology from Michigan State University (1973, 1977).

Using a variety of interesting and sometimes humorous encounters with Americans, Professor Huang Shu-min describes how these experiences can lead to a better understanding of one's own culture. He emphasizes that although these experiences can lead to greater awareness, it is difficult even for anthropologists to free themselves of the assumptions about their own culture.

Born and raised in many areas of China, including the Mainland, Hong Kong, and Taiwan, I have developed a deep appreciation for the enormous cultural variations in China. Ever since I can remember, I seemed to have been surrounded by people—including my own family members—who speak many languages and entertain various tastes in food and clothing that characterize regional differences in China.

However, despite my exposure to such a diverse way of life, I was probably brought up as a normal, average Chinese, taught to believe in the traditional Chinese values, manners, and beliefs characteristic of Confucian literati. A reverence for age and custom, a high motivation toward scholarly achievement, and a strong sense of responsibility toward society had all been incorporated into my thinking throughout the process of growth.

Contact with anthropology in my college years in Taiwan, however, brought about basic changes in my life. Anthropology claims that much of our behavior, customs, and even ways of thinking are molded by our culture, which is essentially a set of artificially designed symbols accumulated throughout human history. Accepting such a premise, I began to question the validity and rationale of all the values, beliefs, and even ways of thinking that I once had stood for and cherished. As a consequence, I was, to borrow a phrase from Muriel Dimen-Schein (1977), "drawn to its (anthropology's) moral emphasis that our culture was not the best or only way to live, and alternatives existed." My soul-searching along this line has not led to a total rejection of my culture; rather, I began to develop a habit of looking at my own behavior from an objective point of view and to be critical of things that I had taken for granted.

My career in anthropology has eventually brought me to study and to teach in the United States. Situated in an entirely different culture, I have been able not only to look at my own culture from this objective point of view but also to make a constant comparison between my own cultural practices and those of Americans. To bring my professional training into everyday situations, which involves explaining ordinary events against both the Chinese and American frames of thought, I have tried to explore the extent to which human beings are influenced by their specific cultures. The following incidents have occurred during my residence in the United States and form the foundation for some of my reflections.

INTRODUCTION TO AMERICA

My initiation into American culture was through my older sister, who had lived in San Francisco for some time before I arrived in 1970. Apparently aghast at my appearance when we met at the airport, especially my dandruff-ridden hair and unshaved face, she warned me that Americans are extremely sensitive about physical appearances. I should from then on use dandruff-proof shampoo and shave my face every day—even though there is not much to work on.

I was puzzled by her notions, for I had heard about the counterculture movement in the United States, especially on campuses across the country. My limited knowledge about the counterculture seemed to indicate the development of an alternative way of life, which also implied, to some extent, the rejection of American middle-class values. If that was the case, why bother with this physical appearance–laden life-style? I kept this question to myself, for I thought my sister was just old-fashioned and conservative, and so there was no point in arguing with her.

I stayed in San Francisco for a month, and during that period I made many sightseeing tours around the city. My specific interest was in the hippie ghettoes. As a novice in anthropology, I believed that the counterculture movement presented a unique opportunity to study how culture can be changed in a well-intentioned manner. Based on my superficial observations, these people appeared to be sincere about developing an alternative way of life in direct opposition to that of middle-class values: long and uncombed hair, bare feet, patched blue jeans and free-floating along the sidewalks, for example.

I was very much impressed by what I saw. But then I suddenly noticed that I had not seen anyone with dandruff. I brought up this question to an acquaintance who was very much involved in this particular way of life. "Oh, yes," he replied in a typically nonchalant manner, "dandruff is indeed a problem to many of us. But we use dandruff-proof shampoo."

Disappointed? No. It only confirmed an idea that I had but could not prove with evidence: While we may claim to reject our culture's values and moral standards en masse, in the deeper layer of the heart and mind, our thinking and behavior may still operate, even though unconsciously, under the same set of beliefs.

CULTURE AND HAIR COLOR

My graduate years at Michigan State University were some of the most interesting experiences during my time at school. We had a large student body—thirty-odd in my first-year class. A great number of my classmates were from different nations, and many of the other American students also had had personal experiences in other parts of the world. We formed a very close group, often having parties, picnics, and other activities together.

One day after class, we stayed in the classroom chatting about recent events. Suddenly, someone in the group mentioned the long absence of a female classmate: "Strange, I have not seen the little redhead for the past few days!"

Little redhead? The notion did not ring a bell at all. How could he refer to someone in such a strange way? Did this person really have red hair? Why had I never noticed this? I took a hard look around the classroom and realized that there were indeed different hair styles and colors among my classmates, something that I had never paid attention to!

The discovery that Americans frequently divide their hair into categories and use this taxonomical difference as a point of reference was something entirely new to me. Chinese would never refer to another person by describing his or her hair, for every Chinese has dark, straight hair, except the aged and bald. Because hair is an insignificant difference, Chinese probably do not have an acute conceptual system to categorize people on the basis of hair traits and, as a consequence, tend to neglect this physical characteristic entirely.

PRIMARY AND SECONDARY LANGUAGES

One incident that happened before I came to the States puzzled me for some time. In 1969, I was working with Professor and Mrs. Gallin in Taipei, studying rural migrants in the city. One day my father came to see me and also had a chat with Professor Gallin. Because my father does not speak English and his Mandarin has an accent that Professor Gallin could not quite follow, I had to serve as translator in the conversation. When my father spoke to me for the translation, I noticed that he used Taiwanese (or Min-nan), the native language in Taiwan, instead of the Mandarin or Cantonese that we normally use. Even though my father and I speak flawless Taiwanese, we never use it in our direct, personal conversation.

So, I mildly reminded my father that because Professor Gallin is not a Taiwanese, and because he was talking to him through me, there was no need to use this particular language. My suggestion was to no avail, and my father kept speaking to me in Taiwanese. After a few more protests, I decided to ignore it, thinking that my father was probably too excited by speaking to a "foreign barbarian."

When studying in Michigan, a similar incident occurred, which rekindled my old puzzlement. One day I was in the Gallins' house when another professor came for a visit and brought with him an Austrian friend. It was late in the afternoon, and we all decided to stay for dinner at the Gallins' invitation. Over the dinner table, Professor Gallin talked to this Austrian visitor about some general things, and suddenly he spoke in Chinese to this Austrian. He said, "Ch'ing-lai, puke-ch'i," which literally means, "Please help yourself; don't be polite." Unaware of this slip of the tongue, Professor Gallin continued the conversation in English.

These two incidents led me to theorize that cognition probably operates on several planes. The first and probably the most "instinctive" cognitive plane involves a person's primary language and the intimate way of life and cultural values in which one is brought up. Beyond this are the secondary and tertiary planes, which involve bodies of knowledge of foreign cultures. So when people encounter another person who does not belong to their primary cognitive community, they would probably immediately project their secondary or tertiary cognitive systems to this person, thinking that would fit the circumstance. If my hypothesis is correct, then there would be nothing unusual if we see a student majoring in Spanish who tries to communicate with a Japanese tourist in Spanish!

WHAT NOT TO SAY

It is a custom for Chinese to say something auspicious when two newly met friends part. Phrases like "Wish you make a fortune," or "Wish you success in your business" (or study, voyage, and so on) are appropriate on such occasions. Because in traditional China marriage was often arranged by parents, it was quite common for one to greet a couple in love with a phrase like "Wish you marry soon"—meaning that this couple would convince their parents to accept their own choice. This kind of greeting is still commonly used in Taiwan, and I suspect it is also true in Hong Kong, although to a lesser extent. But, used in a different cultural context, this kind of expression may cause some problems.

Once I was invited to a party in which the American host and hostess entertained a couple of their friends and some Chinese students. We were introduced to the host's younger sister and her boyfriend—both were college students and had lived together for some time. They professed their emotional attachment toward each other and also indicated their suspicion concerning the meaning of a formal marriage: "We prefer our current arrangement," said the young man. "If two persons really love each other, there is no need to bind them together with some kind of socially sanctioned contract."

It was a pleasant evening, and about the time we were to leave, a Chinese student approached the young lovers and inadvertently said, "Wish to see you marry soon!"

He probably did not literally mean what he had said nor even realize what he had said. But the reaction from this young couple was obvious. The young man was stunned and stood there with a stiffened mouth. Blushing, the young woman protested, "But we don't believe in marriage!"

FOOD

One aspect of American culture that I have not been able to develop full appreciation of is food. Brought up in a culture whose menu contains a wide range of food varieties and flavors, I consider American food rather plain. And, worst of all, when I have American meals, I often feel full rather quickly, sometimes after just the salad. But then in a short while, I will feel hungry.

Originally, I thought that this was a phenomenon peculiar to me, mainly because I do not have a taste for American food and hence cannot eat too much of it. Believing that Chinese dishes have a better taste than anything else, I never had the slightest idea that Americans could have the same problem when eating Chinese food.

One day, my wife and I invited a few colleagues of mine over for supper. Our conversation somehow had focused on food preparation in different cultures. I jokingly remarked that even though I am an anthropologist by training, my appetite does not really match my intellectual capacity. I told them of the peculiar problem I had in eating American meals and indicated the possible reason as I saw it. On hearing that, one of our guests burst into laughter. "This is exactly the same problem I have when I come to your house for dinner," he said. "Even though I am quite full now, I will be very hungry by the time I arrive home. And I used to think this was so because of the strange taste of Chinese food!" I was surprised to find that the same opinion was shared by others.

I was puzzled by this cross-cultural eating problem. Perhaps the differences in taste are not the cause of the problem. Comparing dietary differences between American and Chinese food from another angle, I began to realize that food variety and content is the main difference between them. Chinese food contains many starchy items, such as rice, bean products, and vegetables, while American food has more meat tissue. When eating meals, the human digestive system probably has certain expectations on the quantity of specific items habitually established in the culture. People may feel full when the quota for certain food items has been met but still feel hungry for the unmet ones. For that reason, we may all have problems eating a cross-cultural meal.

A COMPLEX PHENOMENON

Human culture is a complex phenomenon: It provides a way of life, cues for actions, and logic for reasoning for the members of a cultural community. Because we frequently all too strongly adhere to our own culture, we fail to understand or appreciate the alternative ways of life. It is not an easy task to eliminate the cultural bias that hinders a mutual understanding across cultural boundaries. Even among anthropologists, who claim to study human cultures objectively, the same kind of prejudices persist, for we are products of our unique cultures as are any other human beings. Anthropologists may be credited for providing a large amount of literature describing the "other cultures." But perhaps more is needed. Other cultures may serve as a mirror for us to look at our own practices as culture-bound human beings. We need to be as critical of our own ways of thinking, value standards, and behavior patterns as we are of the cultures that we study. It is hoped that, by such a consistent practice of self-examination, we may come to understand the deeper meaning of culture on a first-hand basis.

ACKNOWLEDGEMENT

I am grateful to Professor and Mrs. Bernard Gallin, both at Michigan State University, for introducing me to anthropology and American culture. Appreciations are also due to my colleagues and associates at Iowa State University, especially those who were involved in the course, "Cross-Cultural Exploration: Introduction to the Third World." Most of my ideas and reflections were discussed and developed in that class.

REFERENCE

Dimen-Schein, Muriel. 1977. The Anthropological Imagination. New York: McGraw-Hill.

The F Word

Valerie Steele

Valerie Steele teaches in the graduate division of the Fashion Institute of Technology (SUNY). She is the author of Fashion and Eroticism *(Oxford University Press, 1985), and* Paris Fashion: A Cultural History *(Oxford University Press, 1988), and is co-editor of* Men and Women: Dressing the Part *(Smithsonian Institution Press, 1989). Her book,* Women of Fashion, *is published by Rizzoli.*

Once, when I was a graduate student at Yale, a history professor asked me about my dissertation. "I'm writing about fashion," I said.

"That's interesting. Italian or German?"

It took me a couple of minutes, as thoughts of Armani flashed through my mind, but finally I realized what he meant. "Not *fascism*," I said. "*Fashion*. As in Paris."

"Oh." There was a long silence, and then, without another word, he turned and walked away.

The F-word still has the power to reduce many academics to embarrassed or indignant silence. Some of those to whom I spoke while preparing this article requested anonymity or even refused to address the subject; those who did talk explained that many of their colleagues found it "shameful to think about fashion." One professor explained the "denial" of fashion this way: "People say that they don't care about fashion, but that may be because they aren't self-conscious enough to envision a personal style. Style is what most academics don't have."

Academics may be the worst-dressed middle-class occupational group in the United States. But they do wear clothes. So I set out to discover what professors choose to wear (the clothes don't grow in their closets), what they think about fashion (even when they claim not to think about it), and, well, why they tend to dress so badly.

THE MIND-BODY PROBLEM

Obviously, a university is not like a law firm, where the rules governing appropriate attire are both narrow and explicit. Back in the 1950s some universities did have a coat-and-tie rule, but this has long since disappeared. Peter Baldwin, an assistant professor of history at UCLA, remarks that academics are "under no pressure to dress well." And Deborah Kaple, a lecturer in sociology at Princeton, observes that some academics regard it as "one of the perks" of the job that they "don't have to pay attention" to how they dress. But if everyone in academia is happily doing his or her own thing, why is it so often the same thing? (Just look around your department.)

"Theoretically, anything goes," says Susan Kaiser, author of *The Social-Psychology of Clothing: Symbolic Appearances in Context* and associate professor at UC Davis, "but in practice, within a small-group context, such as a department, a subtle kind of negotiation goes on. We influence one another."

Certain widely held (but little examined) philosophical and epistemological assumptions militate against on-campus sartorial nonconformity. In academic circles, many professors say, clothing is perceived as "material" (not intellectual) and, therefore, "beneath contempt." There is a sharp division between "the life of the mind and that of the body"—and as a result (one professorial source quips) academics tend to have "bad bodies, and no one dresses well."

According to John Brewer, a professor of history at UCLA, "To dress fashionably is to be labeled frivolous, to seem to care about the body and, therefore, by implication, to downplay the life of the mind. Most colleagues view sartorial interest and especially sartorial 'play' or facetiousness with a mixture of amusement, condescension, and fear. Dowdy is safe and serious; bad dressing, one of the last ways in which academics can project the illusion of otherworldliness."

Among leftists, fashion is also regarded as "bourgeois," and so they often "go out of their way to distance themselves" from it, observes Michael Solomon, editor of *The Psychology of Fashion* and chairman of the Department of Marketing in the business school of Rutgers University. Aging "'68 types" are often "aggressively informal," agrees Baldwin, and "deliberately dress down for class." But even conservative professors often look barely respectable. In fact, because so many academics implicitly believe that fashion is frivolous, vain, and politically incorrect, certain styles are, in effect, virtually compulsory, while others are practically taboo.

LE LOOK

When asked to characterize academic style, one Dartmouth professor immediately replied, "Tweedy and rumpled. But don't quote me." A woman at UC San Diego also summed up her male colleagues' sartorial style as "ratty tweed jackets and tight jeans." Please notice the modifiers "ratty" and "rumpled" (more later on "tight").

This state of neglect, which in the academic setting reads as a self-con-

 From *Lingua Franca*, April 1991, pp. 17-20. © 1991 by Lingua Franca, The Review of Academic Life, Mamaroneck, New York.

scious lack of interest, dates back at least to the 1950s and has Anglophile, even Anglican, antecedents. Gospel, according to the traditional upper-class Englishman, has it that a good Donegal tweed jacket lasts forever. If it gets a bit frayed, all the better. American academics have simply copied this shabby-genteel look, so today the tenured sons of Russian, Italian, Polish, and Irish immigrants all look like rural Church of England vicars.

In the modern American context, to wear jackets rather than suits is to adopt a lesser degree of formality compared, for example, with businessmen or, closer to home, college administrators. But to wear a sports jacket and tie imparts an impression of formality and authority.

As a result, there is something of a split between professors who wear ties and those who don't. Baldwin distinguishes between "the Harvard compulsion to cravats versus the California obligatory tieless look." But even aside from arty, upper-class cravats, there are ties and there are ties (*see* box).

MEN: THE SEMIOTICS OF DENIM

Beginning in the 1960s, when dress codes disappeared from American high schools, a new academic style also emerged among college professors. As British art historian Anita Brookner put it, "All degrees of seniority are obliterated in the desire to look as young [and] as carefree . . . as possible." Indeed, far from wanting to look like professionals or even working adults, professors "are dressed for play" (*London Review of Books*, April 15–May 5, 1982).

Blue jeans are the operative garment here. How better to assert solidarity with the young than to dress like them? And jeans have the added advantage of having (formerly) been associated with the proletariat. A professor might be the oldest, most powerful, and least hip person in the classroom, but his anti-establishment clothing signified that he was a free spirit opposed to pernicious hierarchical distinctions between the teacher and the taught.

Also, jeans tend to be worn tight. "Not to put too fine a point on it, his attire can be saying that he is ready to sleep with his students," wrote Jacob Epstein, an English professor at Northwestern University and author of "Reflections of an Academic Dandy," published in *Gentlemen's Quarterly* (October 1985). Surrounded by young people yet aging themselves, many professors succumbed to a type of arrested sartorial development. However, novelist Angela Carter is probably correct in suggesting that "jeans have lost their chic since the class of '68 took them into the senior common room. . . . They are now . . . a sign of grumpy middle age" (*New Society,* January 13, 1983). And one California professor reports that her students have said the professors should not wear jeans because they are "too old."

The sweater, either alone or under a jacket, is another garment frequently worn by male academics. Sweaters, of course, can be extremely beautiful, but in academic circles they almost invariably represent what one male professor ruefully calls another aesthetic "missed opportunity." As one woman scholar complains, the majority of professors seem to wear baggy, stretched-out sweaters in boring colors and cheap materials.

WOMEN: THE TYRANNY OF EARTH TONES

Women academics are "a disaster," insists one female professor in California, citing frumpy suits, sensible shoes, and outmoded haircuts. With their "asexual clothes and handbags [that] are satchels," with "no makeup and no jewelry," laments one woman professor at an Ivy League university, the "subconscious message" of her collegial sisters is: "If I could, I'd be male."

Certainly, femininity is out. So is anything too conspicuous or body-revealing. Like most female professionals, the majority of women in academia tend to minimize any sartorial eroticism while maximizing status signifiers. "Most female faculty look like bankers and lawyers, even when the men are in polo shirts," is the succinct assessment of a UC San Diego scholar.

Yet upon closer inspection, women academics do not really look like bankers, lawyers, or business executives. Sad to say, they lack marketplace flair. Skirts, for example, tend to be significantly longer than those of most professional women: to mid-calf, when the fashionable length is slightly above the knee. The jacket (the female executive's badge of authority) is seen less often in academia, where professors tend to wear separates.

Female academics almost never wear high heels, which are regarded as "politically retrograde." But most professional women do wear heels, and the highest-paid female executives frequently wear the highest heels. Academics eschew color (even as accents); instead, they favor "low-keyed earth tones" or "frumpy beige." Says one female professor, some are "literally slovenly"— a cardinal sin in the business world. And even when trying to look "nice," women academics tend to dress like teenagers: unsophisticated flower-print dress (Laura Ashley neo-Victoriana seems to appeal to historians) or simple skirts and blouses.

Thus, although professors self-consciously perform in classrooms and lecture halls, they tend to ignore sartorial strategies of self-presentation and seldom use clothing to "sell" themselves. The "cult of authenticity," says one Californian, means that you can't and shouldn't "disguise who you are."

What is responsible for this distaff fashion debacle? The problem, says Nancy Koehn, a lecturer in history and literature at Harvard, is that for women to be well dressed (not even fashionable, just well put together) can be "a double-edged sword." While students may actually prefer professors to dress with some flair (sophisticated post-sixties consumers, they do not share the fashion biases of their professors), says Koehn, there is always a question mark in her colleagues' minds: "Can we possibly take her seriously if she wears an Anne Klein skirt?"

Dressed to Thrill

It's just a skirt—albeit a skirt made out of men's ties, pointy ends drooping, joined at the waist. But ever since Jane Gallop first started wearing it on the lecture circuit, "The Skirt" has been the stuff of scholarly footnotes and lurid litcrit legend. Gallop collected ties, like limp trophies, from the guys she's slept with, goes one rumor. Or scalped them off her male colleagues at the MLA convention. "Oh, yeah, I've heard both of those, and they're both apocryphal," says Gallop, and English professor and the author of four books, including *The Daughter's Seduction: Feminism & Psychoanalysis* (1982) and *Thinking Through the Body* (1990). "The truth is that I bought the skirt when I was a graduate student at Yale. And for a while, I wore it whenever I gave talks about the phallus—there was a lecture I'd do called 'Phallus/Penis: Same Difference' and one that contained the line 'plunged into a network of complex ties.' It was the most eloquent dress-act I've ever been able to do. It was such an explicit comment on the phallic mode of dress, played with and transformed into the ultimate feminine form of dress." That skirt," she adds, "became famous before I did."

And it's not only the skirt. Gallop's dress-for-excess conference wear includes spike heels, seamed hose, a big black hat, and the kind of form-fitting black dress once favored by Joan Crawford and Rosalind Russell; a clingy, leopard-skin jersey dress, worn, pointedly, when Gallop was five months pregnant; black leather pants, wicked stiletto heels, a silk flower, tucked, Billie Holiday-style, behind her ear, crimson

metallic nail polish; a dress spattered with sequined stars, which she donned for a recent star turn as keynote speaker.

Gallop is the rare academic who thinks a lot about clothes and what they signify and, what's more, will cheerfully admit to the vice. Her sartorial style isn't fashion but costume; a way of manipulating, sometimes to the point of parody, certain conventions of femininity—a little like Madonna, a little like a drag queen. "When I was an undergraduate, I had a number of gay men friends . . . who saw feminine style not as some restrictive role but as something one could put on and take off as a kind of performance. It was made theatrical, put into quotation marks, because it was worn by men."

But women can project the same kind of irony when they adopt ultra-femme wear, Gallop believes, provided they do so in unexpected settings. Like the lecture hall. "I don't think you can pull it off at a cocktail party, or as a secretary or receptionist, when you're supposed to be advertising your sexuality. But in the academic world, because femininity is so deeply excluded—from the lectern, from the position of knowledge—that sort of dress operates in some kind of interesting tension with other expectations."

The thirty-eight-year-old Gallop, who now lives in Milwaukee and teaches at the University of Wisconsin, hopes her campy exhibitionism has challenged academics to think about the way they dress—to bring clothes out of the closet, as it were. She knows her hobble skirts and totter heels violate all

kinds of codes, and she's tickled that they do. Women in the academy tend to project a "gender-neutral" style, she says, while the understated tweeds worn by both men and women bespeak a certain elitism. "People have said that I dress like a bad girl but also like a poor girl. There's a class and an ethnic dimension to the way academics dress, as well as a gender dimension, because basically they're dressing like English landed gentry. When women wear sensible shoes and good tweeds, they're dressing like rich, WASP women. Drawing more attention to yourself is associated with non-WASP ethnic groups and non-rich people. And the way I dress is a refusal of some of these associations with the traditional academy."

Gallop's getups offer a running commentary on her work, a spotlight on the signifier, and an insistent reminder of the female body and its claims. "I see a strong analogy between how one dresses and how one writes," says Gallop, who has a background in deconstruction and has written on Barthes, Lacan, and de Sade. "Style is a good crossover word in this respect. You can either not think about your style and concentrate on your ideas—which tends toward disembodiment, and idealism—or you can think a lot about both." She always sits when she delivers a lecture so that "people can see my clothes and my body. Behind a lectern, people are seeing only a disembodied head." And what Gallop wants to announce is this: "Yes, I'm a mind—here are my ideas—but I'm also a body."

—M.T.

Sexually provocative dress is "definitely a big issue," according to a number of woman professors who report that both male and female students "always" comment on their appearance. The remarks are usually positive ("great dresser! so cool!") or innocuous ("She wore the same outfit twice in a row. I counted"). But not always.

"I can't concentrate on my work if I get a hard-on." A woman professor coming up for tenure at an Ivy League university is said to have received this comment on one of her student evaluations. She felt that is constituted sexual harassment and had it suppressed, but the issue is not so easily dismissed. Is your dress provocative to students?

How sexy are you allowed to look? These are questions, freighted with anxiety, that women academics of all political persuasions confront daily. One woman concludes that students tend to "take you more seriously if you wear a bra." A woman's colleagues may also be deeply hostile to the idea of feminine or provocative dress.

"I don't lecture to students wearing a codpiece," expostulated one male economist, as he angrily recalled that when he was teaching at MIT, a female colleague gave a lecture wearing a short skirt. "The students kept staring at her legs; it was very unprofessional. Women should dress to be one of the boys."

TENURE AND TASTE

Can a style of dress hurt one's professional career? True to form, most academics deny that it makes any difference whatsoever. But a few stories may indicate otherwise: When a gay male professor was denied tenure at an Ivy League university, some people felt that he was penalized, in part, for his dress. It was "not that he wore multiple earrings" or anything like that, but he did wear "beautiful, expensive, colorful clothes that stood out" on campus. At the design department on one of the campuses of the University of California system, a job applicant appeared for her interview wearing a navy blue suit. The style was perfect for most departments, of course, but in this case she was told—to her face—that she "didn't fit in, she didn't look arty enough."

Another bit of evidence that suggests dress is of career significance for academics is the fact that some universities (such as Harvard) now offer graduate students counseling on how to outfit themselves for job interviews. The tone apparently is patronizing ("You will need to think about an interview suit and a white blouse"), but the advice is perceived by the institution as necessary. Graduate students also talk to one another about what to wear to a thesis-defense interview. In fact, this is one of the few times when it is acceptable in academia to talk about one's clothing and appearance.

"My clothes are an expression of who I am," said one professor, "but I can't talk about it." Clothes, then, are a taboo subject, a forbidden realm of pleasure. Many of the very same professors who censoriously dismiss the pleasures of dress may well lavish time and money on couture cuisine, stereos, Volvos, computer gadgetry, skis, travel, and wine. But not clothes.

The Old School Ties

"There are no power ties at Berkeley, none that have opulent texture or fabulous fabrics. The men wear boring ties, a navy blue tie with a minuscule print of something or other or a brown with wimpy green stripes." At Dartmouth they wear "the power ties of three years ago, the yellow ones with amoebas." At Harvard they wear (what else?) Harvard ties. Also ties that "don't go with anything else the person is wearing," thus creating "a living version of 'What's wrong with this picture?'"

—V.S.

The Organization of Society and Culture

Human beings do not interact with one another or think about their world in random fashion. Instead, they engage in both structured and recurrent physical and mental activities. In this section, such patterns of behavior and thought—referred to here as the organization of society and culture—may be seen in a number of different contexts, from the hunter-collectors of the Arctic to the cattle-herding Masai of East Africa ("Mystique of the Masai") to the nomadic Travellers of modern Ireland ("An Unsettled People").

Of special importance are the ways in which people make a living—in other words, the production, distribution, and consumption of goods and services. It is only by knowing the basic subsistence systems that we can hope to gain insight into the other levels of social and cultural phenomena, for, as anthropologists have found, they are all inextricably bound together.

Noting the various aspects of a sociocultural system in harmonious balance, however, does not imply an anthropological seal of approval. To understand infanticide (killing of the newborn) in the manner that it is practiced among some peoples is neither to condone nor condemn it. Nevertheless, the adaptive patterns that have been in existence for a great length of time, such as many of the patterns of hunters and gatherers, probably owe their existence to their contributions to long-term human survival.

The articles in this section demonstrate that anthropologists are far more interested in problems than they are in place. "The Blood in Their Veins" conveys the hardships of living in the Arctic in such personal terms that the reader cannot help but understand the actions of Inuit (Eskimos) from their viewpoint. In fact, if it were not for the firsthand descriptions such as that provided by Richard Nelson in "Understanding Eskimo Science," the very notion that such people could have such a profound understanding of their environment would have been beyond belief.

Anthropologists, however, are not content with the data derived from individual experience. On the contrary, personal descriptions must become the basis for sound anthropological theory. Otherwise, they remain meaningless, isolated relics of culture in the manner of museum pieces. Thus, in "Too Many Bananas, Not Enough Pineapples, and No Watermelon at All" David Counts provides us with ground rules for reciprocity, derived from his own particular field experience and yet cross-culturally applicable. Then, "Life Without Chiefs" expresses that constant striving in anthropology to develop a general perspective from particular events by showing how shifts in technology may result in centralization of political power and marked changes in lifestyle.

While the articles in this section are to some extent descriptive, they also serve to challenge both academic and commonsense notions about why people behave and think as they do. They remind us that assumptions are never really safe. Any time anthropologists can be kept on their toes, the field as a whole is the better for it.

Looking Ahead: Challenge Questions

What traditional Inuit (Eskimo) practices do you find contrary to values professed in your society but important to Inuit survival under certain circumstances?

What can contemporary hunter-collector societies tell us about the quality of life in the prehistoric past?

In what ways can the Masai be seen as ecological conservationists?

Under what circumstances do social stratification and centralization of power appear in human societies?

What are the rules of reciprocity?

Is there a place for Travellers in modern Ireland?

Unit 3

Understanding Eskimo Science

Traditional hunters' insights into the natural world are worth rediscovering.

Richard Nelson

Just below the Arctic Circle in the boreal forest of interior Alaska; an amber afternoon in mid-November; the temperature -20°; the air adrift with frost crystals, presaging the onset of deeper cold.

Five men—Koyukon Indians—lean over the carcass of an exceptionally large black bear. For two days they've traversed the Koyukuk River valley, searching for bears that have recently entered hibernation dens. The animals are in prime condition at this season but extremely hard to find. Den entrances, hidden beneath 18 inches of powdery snow, are betrayed only by the subtlest of clues—patches where no grass protrudes from the surface because it's been clawed away for insulation, faint concavities hinting of footprint depressions in the moss below.

Earlier this morning the hunters took a yearling bear. In accordance with Koyukon tradition, they followed elaborate rules for the proper treatment of killed animals. For example, the bear's feet were removed first, to keep its spirit from wandering. Also, certain parts were to be eaten away from the village, at a kind of funeral feast. All the rest would be eaten either at home or at community events, as people here have done for countless generations.

Koyukon hunters know that an animal's life ebbs slowly, that it remains aware and sensitive to how people treat its body. This is especially true for the potent and demanding spirit of the bear.

The leader of the hunting group is Moses Sam, a man in his 60s who has trapped in this territory since childhood. He is known for his detailed knowledge of the land and for his extraordinary success as a bear hunter. "No one else has that kind of luck with bears," I've been told. "Some people are born with it. He always takes good care of his animals—respects them. That's how he keeps his luck."

Moses pulls a small knife from his pocket, kneels beside the bear's head, and carefully slits the clear domes of its eyes. "Now," he explains softly, "the bear won't see if one of us makes a mistake or does something wrong."

Contemporary Americans are likely to find this story exotic, but over the course of time episodes like this have been utterly commonplace, the essence of people's relationship to the natural world. After all, for 99 percent of human history we lived exclusively as hunter-gatherers; by comparison, agriculture has existed only for a moment and urban societies scarcely more than a blink.

From this perspective, much of human experience over the past several million years lies beyond our grasp. Probably no society has been so deeply alienated as ours from the community of nature, has viewed the natural world from a greater distance of mind, has lapsed into a murkier comprehension of its connections with the sustaining environment. Because of this, we have great difficulty understanding our rootedness to earth, our affinities with nonhuman life.

I believe it's essential that we learn from traditional societies, especially those whose livelihood depends on the harvest of a wild environment—hunters, fishers, trappers, and gatherers. These people have accumulated bodies of knowledge much like our own sciences. And they can give us vital insights about responsible membership in the community of life, insights founded on a wisdom we'd long forgotten and now are beginning to rediscover.

Since the mid-1960s I have worked as an ethnographer in Alaska, living intermittently in remote northern communities and recording native traditions centered around the natural world. I spent about two years in Koyukon Indian villages and just over a year with Inupiaq Eskimos on the Arctic coast—traveling by dog team and snowmobile, recording traditional knowledge, and learning the hunter's way.

Eskimos have long inhabited some of the harshest environments on earth, and they are among the most exquisitely adapted of all human groups. Because plant life is so scarce in their northern terrain, Eskimos depend more than any other people on hunting.

Eskimos are famous for the cleverness of their technology—kayaks, harpoons, skin clothing, snow houses, dog teams. But I believe their greatest genius, and the basis of their success, lies in the less tangible realm of the intellect—the nexus of mind and nature. For what repeatedly struck me above all else was their profound knowledge of the environment.

Several times, when my Inupiaq hunting companion did something especially clever, he'd point to his head

From *Audubon*, September/October 1993, pp. 102-109. © 1993 by Richard Nelson.

and declare: "You see—Eskimo scientist!" At first I took it as hyperbole, but as time went by I realized he was speaking the truth. Scientists had often come to his village, and he saw in them a familiar commitment to the empirical method.

Traditional Inupiaq hunters spend a lifetime acquiring knowledge—from others in the community and from their own observations. If they are to survive, they must have absolutely reliable information. When I first went to live with Inupiaq people, I doubted many things they told me. But the longer I stayed, the more I trusted their teachings.

The Inupiaq hunter possesses as much knowledge as a highly trained scientist in our own society.

For example, hunters say that ringed seals surfacing in open leads—wide cracks in the sea ice—can reliably forecast the weather. Because an unexpected gale might set people adrift on the pack ice, accurate prediction is a matter of life and death. When seals rise chest-high in the water, snout pointed skyward, not going anywhere in particular, it indicates stable weather, the Inupiaq say. But if they surface briefly, head low, snout parallel to the water, and show themselves only once or twice, watch for a sudden storm. And take special heed if you've also noticed the sled dogs howling incessantly, stars twinkling erratically, or the current running strong from the south. As time passed, my own experiences with seals and winter storms affirmed what the Eskimos said.

Like a young Inupiaq in training, I gradually grew less skeptical and started to apply what I was told. For example, had I ever been rushed by a polar bear, I would have jumped away to the animal's *right* side. Inupiaq elders say polar bears are left-handed, so you have a slightly better chance to

avoid their right paw, which is slower and less accurate. I'm pleased to say I never had the chance for a field test. But in judging assertions like this, remember that Eskimos have had close contact with polar bears for several thousand years.

During winter, ringed and bearded seals maintain tunnel-like breathing holes in ice that is many feet thick. These holes are often capped with an igloo-shaped dome created by water sloshing onto the surface when the animal enters from below. Inupiaq elders told me that polar bears are clever enough to excavate around the base of this dome, leaving it perfectly intact but weak enough that a hard swat will shatter the ice and smash the seal's skull. I couldn't help wondering if this were really true; but then a younger man told me he'd recently followed the tracks of a bear that had excavated one seal hole after another, exactly as the elders had described.

In the village where I lived, the most respected hunter was Igruk, a man in his 70s. He had an extraordinary sense of animals—a gift for understanding and predicting their behavior. Although he was no longer quick and strong, he joined a crew hunting bowhead whales during the spring migration, his main role being that of adviser. Each time Igruk spotted a whale coming from the south, he counted the number of blows, timed how long it stayed down, and noted the distance it traveled along the open lead, until it vanished toward the north. This way he learned to predict, with uncanny accuracy, where hunters could expect the whale to resurface.

I believe the expert Inupiaq hunter possesses as much knowledge as a highly trained scientist in our own society, although the information may be of a different sort. Volumes could be written on the behavior, ecology, and utilization of Arctic animals— polar bear, walrus, bowhead whale, beluga, bearded seal, ringed seal, caribou, musk ox, and others—based entirely on Eskimo knowledge.

Comparable bodies of knowledge existed in every Native American cul-

ture before the time of Columbus. Since then, even in the far north, Western education and cultural change have steadily eroded these traditions. Reflecting on a time before Europeans arrived, we can imagine the whole array of North American animal species—deer, elk, black bear, wolf, mountain lion, beaver, coyote, Canada goose, ruffed grouse, passenger pigeon, northern pike—each known in hundreds of different ways by tribal communities; the entire continent, sheathed in intricate webs of knowledge. Taken as a whole, this composed a vast intellectual legacy, born of intimacy with the natural world. Sadly, not more than a hint of it has ever been recorded.

Like other Native Americans, the Inupiaq acquired their knowledge through gradual accretion of naturalistic observations—year after year, lifetime after lifetime, generation after generation, century after century. Modern science often relies on other techniques—specialized full-time observation, controlled experiments, captive-animal studies, technological devises like radio collars—which can provide similar information much more quickly.

Yet Eskimo people have learned not only *about* animals but also *from* them. Polar bears hunt seals not only by waiting at their winter breathing holes, but also by stalking seals that crawl up on the ice to bask in the spring warmth. Both methods depend on being silent, staying downwind, keeping out of sight, and moving only when the seal is asleep or distracted. According to the elders, a stalking bear will even use one paw to cover its conspicuous black nose.

Inupiaq methods for hunting seals, both at breathing holes and atop the spring ice, are nearly identical to those of the polar bear. Is this a case of independent invention? Or did ancestral Eskimos learn the techniques by watching polar bears, who had perfected an adaptation to the sea-ice environment long before humans arrived in the Arctic?

The hunter's genius centers on knowing an animal's behavior so well he can turn it to his advantage. For instance, Igruk once saw a polar bear far off across flat ice, where he couldn't stalk it without being seen. But he knew an old technique of mimicking a seal. He lay down in plain sight, conspicuous in his dark parka and pants, then lifted and dropped his head like a seal, scratched the ice, and imitated flippers with his hands. The bear mistook his pursuer for prey. Each time Igruk lifted his head the animal kept still; whenever Igruk "slept" the bear crept closer. When it came near enough, a gunshot pierced the snowy silence. That night, polar bear meat was shared among the villagers.

"Each animal knows way more than you do," a Koyukon Indian elder was fond of telling me.

A traditional hunter like Igruk plumbs the depths of his intellect—his capacity to manipulate complex knowledge. But he also delves into his animal nature, drawing from intuitions of sense and body and heart: feeling the wind's touch, listening for the tick of moving ice, peering from crannies, hiding as if he himself were the hunted. He moves in a world of eyes, where everything watches—the bear, the seal, the wind, the moon and stars, the drifting ice, the silent waters below. He is beholden to powers we have long forgotten or ignored.

In Western society we rest comfortably on our own accepted truths about the nature of nature. We treat the environment as if it were numb to our presence and blind to our behavior. Yet despite our certainty on this matter, accounts of traditional people throughout the world reveal that most of humankind has concluded otherwise. Perhaps our scientific method really does follow the path to a single, absolute truth. But there may be wisdom in accepting other possibilities and opening ourselves to different views of the world.

I remember asking a Koyukon man about the behavior and temperament of the Canada goose. He described it as a gentle and good-natured animal, then added: "Even if [a goose] had the power to knock you over, I don't think it would do it."

For me, his words carried a deep metaphorical wisdom. They exemplified the Koyukon people's own restraint toward the world around them. And they offered a contrast to our culture, in which possessing the power to overwhelm the environment has long been sufficient justification for its use.

We often think of this continent as having been a pristine wilderness when the first Europeans arrived. Yet for at least 12,000 years, and possibly twice that long, Native American people had inhabited and intensively utilized the land; had gathered, hunted, fished, settled, and cultivated; had learned the terrain in all its details, infusing it with meaning and memory; and had shaped every aspect of their life around it. That humans could sustain membership in a natural community for such an enormous span of time without profoundly degrading it fairly staggers the imagination. And it gives strong testimony to the adaptation of mind—the braiding together of knowledge and ideology—that linked North America's indigenous people with their environment.

A Koyukon elder, who took it upon himself to be my teacher, was fond of telling me: "Each animal knows way more than you do." He spoke as if it summarized all that he understood and believed.

This statement epitomizes relationships to the natural world among many Native American people. And it goes far in explaining the diversity and fecundity of life on our continent when the first sailing ship approached these shores.

There's been much discussion in recent years about what biologist E. O. Wilson has termed "biophilia"—a deep, pervasive, ubiquitous, all-embracing affinity for nonhuman life. Evidence for this "instinct" may be elusive in Western cultures, but not among tradi-

tional societies. People like the Koyukon manifest biophilia in virtually all dimensions of their existence. Connectedness with nonhuman life infuses the whole spectrum of their thought, behavior, and belief.

It's often said that a fish might have no concept of water, never having left it. In the same way, traditional peoples might never stand far enough outside themselves to imagine a generalized concept of biophilia. Perhaps it would be impossible for people so intimately bound with the natural world, people who recognize that all nature is our own embracing community. Perhaps, to bring a word like *biophilia* into their language, they would first need to separate themselves from nature.

In April 1971 I was in a whaling camp several miles off the Arctic coast with a group of Inupiaq hunters, including Igruk, who understood animals so well he almost seemed to enter their minds.

Onshore winds had closed the lead that migrating whales usually follow, but one large opening remained, and here the Inupiaq men placed their camp. For a couple of days there had been no whales, so everyone stayed inside the warm tent, talking and relaxing. The old man rested on a soft bed of caribou skins with his eyes closed. Then, suddenly, he interrupted the conversation: "I think a whale is coming, and perhaps it will surface very close. . . ."

To my amazement everyone jumped into action, although none had seen or heard anything except Igruk's words. Only he stayed behind, while the others rushed for the water's edge. I was last to leave the tent. Seconds after I stepped outside, a broad, shining back cleaved the still water near the opposite side of the opening, accompanied by the burst of a whale's blow.

Later, when I asked how he'd known, Igruk said, "There was a ringing inside my ears." I have no explanation other than his; I can only report what I saw. None of the Inupiaq crew members even commented afterward, as if nothing out of the ordinary had happened.

The Blood in Their Veins

Farley Mowat

Barely visible from Gene Lushman's rickety dock at the mouth of Big River, Anoteelik stroked his kayak to seaward on the heaving brown waters of Hudson Bay. Vanishing, then reappearing on the long, slick swells, the kayak was so distant it might have been nothing more than an idle gull drifting aimlessly on the undulating waters.

I had helped Anoteelik prepare for that journey. Together we had carried the skin-wrapped packages of dress goods, food and tobacco down from Lushman's trading shack. Then the squat, heavy-bodied Eskimo, with his dreadfully scarred face, lashed the cargo to the afterdeck and departed. I watched him until the bright flashing of his double-bladed paddle was only a white flicker against the humped outlines of a group of rocky reefs lying three miles offshore.

This was the third time I had seen Anoteelik make his way out of the estuary to the farthest islet on the sombre rim of the sea but it was the first time I understood the real reason behind his yearly solitary voyage.

Gene Lushman, barrenland trapper and trader, had first drawn my attention to him three years earlier.

"See that old Husky there? Old Ano . . . tough old bugger . . . one of the inland people and queer like all of them. Twenty years now, every spring soon as the ice clears, Ano, he heads off out to the farthest rock, and every year he takes a hundred dollars of my best trade goods along. For why? Well, me son, that crazy old bastard is taking the stuff out there to his dead wife! That's

true, so help me God! He buried her there . . . far out to sea as there was a rock sticking up high enough to hold a grave!

"Father Debrie, he's tried maybe a half dozen times to make the old fellow quit his nonsense. It has a bad influence on the rest of the Huskies—they're supposed to be Christians, you know—but Ano, he just smiles and says: 'Yes, Father,' and every spring he turns in his fox skins to me and I sell him the same bill of goods, and he takes it and dumps it on that rock in the Bay."

It was the waste that bothered and puzzled Gene. Himself the product of a Newfoundland outport, he could not abide the waste . . . a hundred dollars every spring as good as dumped into the sea.

"Crazy old bastard!" he said, shaking his head in bewilderment.

Although he had traded with the Big River people for a good many years, Gene had never really bridged the gap between them and himself. He had learned only enough of their language for trade purposes and while he admired their ability to survive in their harsh land he had little interest in their inner lives, perhaps because he had never been able to stop thinking of them as a "lesser breed." Consequently, he never discovered the reason for Anoteelik's strange behaviour.

During my second year in the country, I became friendly with Itkut, old Anoteelik's son—indeed his only offspring. Itkut was a big, stocky man still in the full vigour of young manhood; a man who laughed a lot and liked making jokes. It was he who gave me my Eskimo name, *Kipmetna*, which translates as "noisy little dog." Itkut and I spent a lot of time together

that summer, including making a long boat trip north to Marble Island after walrus. A few days after our return, old Ano happened into Itkut's tent to find me struggling to learn the language under his son's somewhat less-than-patient guidance. For a while Ano listened to the garbled sounds I was making, then he chuckled. Until that moment the old man, with his hideously disfigured face, had seemed aloof and unapproachable, but now the warmth that lay hidden behind the mass of scar tissue was revealed.

"Itkut gave you a good name," he said smiling. "Indeed, the dog-spirit must live in your tongue. *Ayorama*—it doesn't matter. Let us see if we can drive it out."

With that he took over the task of instructing me, and by the time summer was over we had become friends.

One August night when the ice fog over the Bay was burning coldly in the long light of the late-setting sun, I went to a drum dance at Ano's tent. This was forbidden by the priest at Eskimo Point, who would send the R.C.M.P. constable down to Big River to smash the drums if he heard a dance was being held. The priest was a great believer in an ever-present Devil, and he was convinced the drums were the work of that Devil. In truth, these gatherings were song-feasts at which each man, woman or child took the drum in turn and sang a song. Sometimes it was an ancient song from far out of time, a voice from the shadowy distances of Innuit history; or perhaps it might be a comic song in which the singer made fun of himself. Often it was the story of a spectacular hunting incident; or it might be a song of tragic happenings and of the spirits of the land.

That night Itkut sang a song of the Hunting of Omingmuk, the muskox. As the story unwound, Ano's face came alight with pride—and with love.

Toward dawn people began to drift away and Ano suggested we walk to the shore and have a smoke. Flocks of plover, grey and ephemeral in the half light, fled shrilling before us, and out on the dim wastes of the sea spectral loons yapped at one another.

Ano's face was turned to the sea.

"I know you wonder at me, Kipmetna, yet you look at this torn face of mine and your questions are never heard. You watch as I make my spring journey out to the rock in the sea and your questions remain silent. That is the way also with my People. Tonight, perhaps because Itkut sang well and brought many memories to me from a long time ago, I would tell you a story."

Once there was a woman, and it was she who was my belly and my blood. Now she waits for me in that distant place where the deer are as many as the stars.

She was Kala, and she was of the Sea People, and not of my People who lived far from the sea on the great plains where no trees grow. But I loved her beyond all things in the sea or on the land. Some said I loved her too much, since I could never find the strength to share her, even with my song-cousin, Tanugeak. Most men respected my love and the *angeokok*, Mahuk, said that the sea-mother, Takanaluk Arnaluk, was pleased by the love I had for my wife.

My mother was Kunee and my father was Sagalik. I was born by the shore of Tulemaliguak, Lake of the Great Bones, far west of here, in the years when the camps of the inland people were almost emptied of life by the burning breath of the white man's sickness. My father died of it soon after my birth.

I was born in the late summer months, and Kunee, my mother, was dead before autumn. Then I was taken into the childless tent of Ungyala and his wife Aputna. They

were not young people. Once they had lived very far to the south but their camps too had been stricken by the sickness and they had fled north. They too had been burned by the flame in the lungs, and their sons and daughters had died.

Soon after they took me into their tent, Ungyala and Aputna made ready to flee again, for there were not enough people left in our camps even to bury the dead. So we three went west . . . far off to the west into a land where the Innuit had never lived for fear of the Indians who sometimes came out of the forests into the plains. The deer were plentiful in that place and we lived very well while I grew toward the age of a man and learned to hunt by myself and to drive the long sled over the hard-packed snow.

All the same, it was a lonely land we had come to. There were not even any Indians—perhaps they too, had been burned by the plague. We saw no *inukok*, little stone men set on the hills to tell us that other men of our race had travelled those long, rolling slopes. It was a good land but empty, and we hungered to hear other voices.

In the winter of the year when I became *angeutnak*, almost a man, the blizzards beat upon us for a very long time. Ungyala and I had made good kills of deer in the autumn so we three did not suffer; yet we longed for the coming of spring, the return of the deer and the birds. We yearned for the voices of life, for the voices we heard were of wind and, sometimes I thought, of those spirits who hide in the ground.

In the month when the wolves begin to make love there came a break in the storms. Then I, in the pride of my youth and filled with a hunger I could not yet name, decided to make a journey to the northwest. I said I hoped to kill muskox and bring fresh meat to the camp. Ungyala agreed to my going, though he was not very willing for he was afraid of the lands to the northwest. I took seven dogs and drove the komatik over the snow-hidden hills for three days, and saw no living thing. That land was dead, and my heart was chilled, and only

because I was stubborn and young did I go on.

On the fourth day I came to the lip of a valley, and as I began to descend my lead dog threw up her head. In a moment the dogs were plunging into soft snow, the traces all tangled, and all of them yelling like fiends. I stopped them and walked cautiously forward until I could look down into the flat run of a gulley that lay sheltered by walls of grey stone. There was movement down there. It was *kakwik*, the wolverine, digging with his slashing front claws into the top of what looked like a drift. I ran back to my team and tried to unleash a few of the dogs so they could chase him, but now they were fighting each other; and before I could free them, kakwik was gone, lumbering up the long slope and over the rocks.

I kicked at the dogs, jumped on the sled, and drove headlong into the gulley; but when I slowed past the place where kakwik had dug, my heart went out of the chase.

He had been digging into the top of a buried snowhouse.

Ungyala believed that no men lived to the west and north of our land, yet here was a house. The door tunnel was snowed in and drifts had almost buried the place. I took my snow probe and slid it into a crack between blocks in the roof. It went in so easily I could tell the inside was empty of snow.

I grew cautious and more than a little afraid. The thought came that this might be the home of an *Ino*, a dwarf with knives where his hands should be. Yet the thought that this might instead be the home of true men gave me courage.

With my snowknife I cut a hole in the dome . . . squeezed through it and dropped to the floor. As my eyes grew used to the gloom, I saw that this had been a shelter for men . . . only now it was a tomb for the dead.

There were many bones lying about and even in that dim light I could see that not all had belonged to deer or muskox. One was a skull with black hair hanging down over gleaming white bone where the flesh of the cheeks had been cut away with a knife.

I was about to leap up to the hole in the roof and drag myself out of that terrible place when I saw a shudder of movement under a pile of muskox robes at the back of the sleeping ledge. I was sure something terrible crouched there in the darkness and I raised my snowknife to strike, and fear was a sliver of ice in my belly.

But it was no devil that crawled painfully out from under that pile of rotting hides.

Once, I remember, I found the corpse of a fawn wedged in a deep crevice among some great rocks. It had been missed by the ravens, foxes and wolves and, because it was autumn, the maggots had not eaten the meat. It had dried into a bundle of bones bound around the skin.

The girl who lay helpless before me on the ledge of the snowhouse looked like that fawn. Only her eyes were alive.

Although I was young, and greatly afraid, I knew what I must do. There was a soapstone pot on the floor. I slid the blade of my knife into the flesh of my left arm and let the hot blood flow into the bowl.

Through the space of one day and night I fed the thing I had found with the blood from my veins. Drop by drop was she fed. In between feedings I held her close in my arms under a thick new robe I had fetched from my sled, and slowly the warmth from my body drove the chill from her bones.

Life came back to her but it was nearly three days before she could sit up at my side without aid. Yet she must have had hidden strength somewhere within her for later that day when I came back into the snowhouse after feeding my dogs, all the human bones on the floor, to the last fragment, had vanished. She had found strength, even though death still had his hands on her throat, to bury those things under the hard snow of the floor.

On the fifth day she was able to travel so I brought her back to Ungyala's camp and my parents-by-right took her in and were glad she had come. Neither one made any comment when I told how I had found her and what else I had found in the snowhouse. But later, when Ungyala and I were on a journey away from the camp picking up meat from an autumn cache, he spoke to me thus:

"Anoteelik, my son, this person has eaten the flesh of the dead . . . so much you know. Yet until you too have faced death in the way that he came to this girl, do not judge of her act. She has suffered enough. The spirits of those she has eaten will forgive her . . . the living must forgive her as well."

The girl quickly recovered her youth—she who had seemed beyond age—and as she grew fat she grew comely and often my heart speeded its beat when she was near. She spoke almost no words except to tell us her name was Kala and that her family, who were Sea People, had come inland from the north coast in the fall to hunt muskox.

It was not until the ravens returned that one day when we men were far from camp, she broke into speech to my mother-by-right. Then she told how the family dogs had died of the madness which is carried by foxes and wolves, and how, marooned in the heart of the dark frozen plains, her parents and brother had followed the Snow Walker. She told how she also had waited for death until hunger brought its own madness . . . and she began to eat the flesh of the dead. When she finished her tale she turned from my mother-by-right and cried, "I am unworthy to live!" She would have gone into the night and sought her own end had my mother not caught her and bound her and held her until we returned.

She was calmer by the next day, but she asked that we build her a snowhouse set apart from the camp, and we followed her wish. She lived alone there for many days. Aputna took food to her and talked to her, but we two men never saw her at all.

It was good that spring came so soon after, for spring is the time for forgetting the past. The deer streamed back into our land. The ptarmigan mated and called from the hills, and the male lemmings sought out the females deep in the moss.

The snowhouses softened under the sun and then Kala came back and lived with us in the big skin tent that we built. She seemed to have put out of mind the dark happenings of the winter, and she willingly helped with the work . . . but it was seldom she laughed.

My desire for the girl had become heavy and big during the days she had kept out of sight. It was more than the thrust of my loins; for I had known pity for her, and pity breeds passion in men.

One evening after the snow was all gone, I came and sat by her side on a ridge overlooking our camp where she had gone to watch the deer streaming by. I spoke awkwardly of my love. Kala turned her face from me, but one hand crept to my arm and touched the place where I had thrust the knife into my vein. That night, as we all lay together inside the big tent, she came into my arms and we became husband and wife.

Such was my finding of Kala—a finding that brought me the happiest days of my life, for she was a woman of women. Her sewing was gifted by spirits, and her cooking made even Ungyala grow fat. She could hunt nearly as well as a man. And she was avid for love, as one who has once nearly drowned is avid for air. We four lived a good life all that summer and it seemed as if Kala had brought many good things to our land. The deer were never so fat, the muskox never so many, the trout in the rivers never so large. Even our two bitch dogs, which had been fruitless for over two years, gave birth to big litters and raised eleven fine pups that became the best sled dogs I ever owned. So we believed the girl was forgiven . . . that the spirits wished her to suffer no more.

On a day of the following winter, Ungyala and I were sent out of the snowhouse and we sat and shivered in the lee of some rocks until we heard the voice of my mother-by-right singing birth songs to the Whispering Ones who flame in the sky.

3. THE ORGANIZATION OF SOCIETY AND CULTURE

After the birth of Itkut, our son, a restlessness seemed to come over us all. Kala yearned to return to the sea. Aputna was feeling her years, and longed once again to hear the voices and see the faces of people she had known long ago. As for me, I was anxious to visit some trader and buy the things Ungyala had told me about; especially guns, for I thought that hunting with spears, bows and arrows did not let me show what a fine hunter I had become. Only Ungyala thought that perhaps we should stay where we were. He remembered too well that he and Aputna had twice had to flee for their lives when the people in the camps where they were living were struck down by the new kind of dying that came from beyond the borders of the Innuit lands. Yet in his heart he too wished to see people again, so we decided to go.

We had two good teams and two sleds. We drove north and then east, making a broad detour around the now empty camps where I had been born. We saw no sign of living men until we finally came to Big River. There we met two families who spent their summers near Eskimo Point and their winters inland on the edge of the plains. We stayed with them for the rest of that winter, hearing much about the world Ungyala and Aputna had almost forgotten and that Kala and I had never known. In the spring, before the ice softened, we followed Big River down to the coast.

So we took up a new way of life. Every autumn we journeyed in a big canoe, with our dogs running free on the shore, up Big River to a lake near its head where the southbound deer crossed a narrows. Here Ungyala and I speared fat bucks in the water and shot more of them out on the bare, rocky plains with the rifles we had traded for at the coast. By the time the first snows drove the deer out of the land, we would have more than enough meat for the winter, plenty of fat for our lamps, and the best of hides for our clothing and robes.

In the late days of autumn, after the deer had passed and before we began trapping white foxes, there was little to do. Sometimes then I would sit and think and weigh up the worth of my life. It was good, but I understood that its goodness dwelt mainly in Kala. I loved her for the son she had borne, for the clothes that she made me, for the help that she gave me . . . but it went beyond that. I do not know how to explain it, but Kala held me in her soul. The love she gave me passed far beyond respect for a husband and entered that country of pleasure which we of the People do not often know. Such was our life as the child, Itkut, grew with the years.

Now I must tell how it was when we came to the coast. There we met the first white man we had ever seen. It was he who built the wood house at the mouth of Big River. He seemed a good man in some ways, but he was crazy for women. Before he had lived in the country a year, there were few women who had not spent a night in his house, for it was still our law then that a man might not refuse any gift that lay in his giving if another man asked. Kala never went to the house of the white man, though he asked me for her many times. He put shame upon me, for I was forced to refuse.

In the autumn of our fourth year in the new land, we had gone up the river as usual and made our camp at the lake of the Deer Crossing. Ours was the farthest camp from the sea, for we had come from the inland plains and they held no terrors for us. The coast dwellers did not care to go as far as we went. Our tent was pitched within sight of the ford and from the door we could look to see if the deer had arrived.

The time came when the forerunners of the big herd should have appeared, but the crossing remained empty of life. The darkening lichens on the bank were unmarked by the feet of the deer. The dwarf shrubs began to burn red in the first frosts. Ungyala and I walked many miles over the land, climbing the hills and staring out to the north. We saw none of the usual harbingers of the great herds—no ravens floating black in the pale sky, no wolves drifting white on the dark land.

Although we were worried, nothing was said. Kala and Aputna became very busy fishing for trout, suckers and char in the river. They caught little, for the autumn run was nearly over, yet they fished night and day. The dogs began to grow hungry and their howling became so loud we had to move them some miles from the camp in case they frightened the deer. Thinking back to those days I wonder if it was hunger alone that made them so distressed. Maybe they already knew what we would not believe could be true.

The morning came when snow blew in the air . . . only a thin mist of fine snow but enough to tell us that winter had come and it had not brought the deer.

But a few days afterwards the deer came. Ungyala and I went out with light hearts but only a few deer had come to the river. These few were so poor and lacking in fat that we knew they were not the forerunners of the great herds but stragglers that lagged behind, being either too weak or too sick to keep up. We knew then that the deer spirit had led the herds southward by some different path.

The next day there were no deer at the crossing and none to be seen anywhere upon the sweep of the plains and we had killed barely enough meat to feed ourselves and the dogs for two months.

The real snows came and we began the winter with hearts that were shaken by misgivings. We thought of abandoning our camp and trying to make our way to the coast but we could not do this until enough snow had fallen to make sled travel possible. So we stayed where we were, hoping we would find some of the solitary winter deer that sometimes remain in the land. Ungyala and I roamed with pack dogs over the country for many long miles. A few hares and ptarmigan fell to our guns, but these were no more than food for our hopes.

Before long we ran out of fat, then there was neither light nor heat in the snowhouse. One day Ungyala and I resolved to travel southeast on a journey to some distant islands of little trees where in times past deer used to winter. We took only one small team of dogs, but even these we could not feed and they soon weakened until after a few days they could go no farther. That night we camped in the lee of some cliffs and it was too cold to sleep so we sat and the old man talked of the days of his youth. He was very weak and his voice almost too low to hear. At last he dozed and I covered him with both our robes; but before the dawn he had ceased to breathe, and so I buried my father-by-right in the snow in a grave I cut with my snowknife.

I turned back, but before I reached the snowhouse I heard women's voices singing the song of the dead. Aputna had seen the death of Ungyala in the eye of her mind, and the two women were mourning.

A little time after the death of Ungyala, I wakened one night to the muted whispering of the women. I lay with my face turned to the wall and listened to what Kala was saying to my mother-by-right.

"My mother, the time is not yet come for you to take your old bones to sleep in the snow. Your rest will come after. Now comes a time when I have need of your help."

I knew then that Aputna had decided to take the way of release, and had been held from it by Kala. I did not understand why my wife had restrained her, for it is the right of the old ones that they be the first to die when starvation comes to a camp. But I had small time to wonder, for Kala moved over beside me and spoke softly in my ear, and she told me what I dreaded to hear—that now I must take the few dogs that were left and make my way eastward, down river, until I found a camp that had meat to spare.

I refused, and I called her a fool, for she knew the other camps could be no better off then we were. Kala had always been a woman of sense yet I could not make her see that such a trip would be useless. I knew, and she knew, I could not hope to find help until I reached the coast camps where people depended more on seal meat than on deer, and such a trip, there

and back with weak dogs, could not take less than a month. It would be better, I told her, if we killed and ate all the dogs, let my mother-by-right go to her rest, and wait where we were, eking out our lives by fishing for what little could be caught through holes in the ice. Then, if it came to the worst, we three, Kala and Itkut and I, would at least lie down for the last time together.

She would not heed what I said and I heard for the first time the hard edge of anger in her voice.

"You *will* go!" she whispered fiercely. "If you do not, I shall myself put the noose of release on your son when you are gone out of the snowhouse and so save him from the torments that were mine in a time you remember."

And . . . oh, Kipmetan . . . though I knew she was wrong, I could no longer refuse. No, and I did not, although I should have guessed at that which was hidden deep in her thoughts.

At parting next day only the old woman wept. There were no tears from Kala who knew what she knew, and none from young Itkut who was still too young to know what was afoot.

That was a journey! I walked eight days to the nearest camps of the people, for the dogs were too weak to do more than haul the empty sled along at a crawl. In that first camp I found it was as I had feared. Famine had got there before me. Things were nearly as bad all the way down the river. One by one I killed my dogs to keep me and their remaining brothers and sisters alive, and sometimes I shared a little of that lean, bitter meat with people in the camps that I passed.

I was almost in sight of the sea when I came to the camp of my song-cousin, Tanugeak. He and those with him were in good health for they had been living on the meat and the fat of seals Tanugeak had speared far out on the sea ice. They had none too much, though, for they had been helping feed many people who had already fled east from the inland camps. All the same, Tanugeak

proved his friendship. He gave me four seals and loaned me five of his own strong dogs, together with fish enough to feed them on the long journey home.

My strength was not much, but I began the up-river journey at once and I sang to the dogs as they ran strongly to the west. I had been away from my camp only two weeks, and now I hoped to return there in eight days at the most. So I sang as the sled ran smoothly over the hard river ice.

Two days up river and a few miles north of my track was a lake and by it two camps where I had stopped overnight on my way to the sea. In those camps I had been given soup made of old bones by people who were almost old bones themselves. Now, with much food on my sled, I did not turn off to give them at least a little of my meat and fat. I told myself I could spare neither the time nor the food if I was to save my own family from death . . . but I knew I did wrong. As my sled slipped into the darkening west I felt a foreboding and I almost turned back. If only I had . . . but such thoughts are useless, and they are a weakness in man; for he does what he does, and he must pay what he pays.

I decided to drive all that night, but when darkness came on it brought a blizzard that rose, full blown, right in my face. The thundering wind from the northwest lashed me with piercing arrows of snow until I could not tell where I was, and the dogs would face it no more. At last I made camp, turning the sled on its side and making a hole in a snowbank nearby for myself. I did not unharness the dogs but picketed them in their traces some way from the sled. Then I crawled into my robes, intending only to doze until the wind dropped. But I was more weary than I knew and I was soon so sound asleep that even the roar of the blizzard faded out of my mind.

All unknowing because of the storm, I had made my camp less than a mile upwind from another camp of the people. The surviving dogs of that camp were roaming about, a famished and half-mad pack. As I slept, they winded my load of seal meat.

I heard nothing until the damage was done. Only when the marauders attacked my own dogs did I awake. In my anguish and rage I flung myself on those beasts with only my small knife as a weapon. The dogs turned upon me and, though I killed some, the smell of fresh blood drove the remainder to fury. They tore the deerskin clothes from my body, savaged one arm until I dropped the knife, and slashed my face until the flesh hung down over my chin. They would have killed me if the fight with my own dogs had not drawn them off, leaving me to crawl back to my hole in the snow.

The morning broke clear and calm, as if no wind had ever blown. I could only manage to stand and shuffle about, and I went to the sled, but the meat was all gone. Nothing was left but some shreds of skin and some bones. Two of my own dogs had been killed and the remainder were hurt.

There was nothing to do. I began to look for my rifle in the debris near the sled but before I could find it I heard dogs howl in the distance and when I looked to the west I saw the domes of three snowhouses below the bank of the river. I turned and shuffled toward them.

I remember but little of the days I spent in that camp because my wounds festered and I was often unconscious. Those people were kind and they fed me with food they could

ill spare—though in truth it was partly my food, for it was the meat of the dogs who had eaten the seals. Before I could travel again, the sun had begun to grow warm and to rise higher up in the sky. Yet the warmth of the oncoming spring could not thaw the chill in my heart.

I made a light sled for the two dogs I had left and prepared to depart. Those in the camps tried to keep me with them for they said that by now there would be no life in my snowhouse that stood by the lake of the deer crossing, and I would only die there myself if I returned before spring brought the deer herds back to the land.

But I did not fear death anymore so I set out. Weak as we were, the dogs and I made the journey home in ten days. We had luck, for we found a deer cache that must have been lost by some hunter in the spring of the previous year. It was a foul mess of hair, bones, and long-rotted meat, but it gave us the strength to continue.

When we came in sight of the lake my belly grew sick and my legs weakened and I could hardly go on; yet when I neared the camp life pounded back through my veins . . . for the snowhouse still stood and snow had recently been dug away from the door!

I shouted until my lungs crackled in the bright, cold air and when none answered, I began to run. I reached the passage and scrambled inside.

Abruptly Anoteelik ceased speaking. He sat staring out over the lightening waters of the Bay . . . out toward the islands that were still no more than grey wraiths on the shifting horizon. Tears were running down his disfigured cheeks . . . running like rain. Then with his head bowed forward over his knees, very quietly he finished the tale.

I was greeted by Aputna, my mother-by-right, and by Itkut. The old woman had shrunk to a miserable rag of a thing that should have been gone long ago; but Itkut seemed strong and his body was firm to the touch when I took him up in my arms.

I looked over his shoulder, and asked, "Where is Kala?" though I knew what the answer would be.

Aputna's reply was no louder than the whisper of wind on the hills.

"What was done . . . was done as she wished. As for me, I will not go away from this place, yet I only did what she said must be done . . . and Itkut still lives . . . Where is Kala? Hold your son close in your arms, love him well for the blood in his veins. Hold him close, oh, my son, for you hold your wife too in your arms."

When the ice left the river, Itkut and I came back down to the coast. Kala was of the Sea People, so I took her bones out to that island which lies far from the shore. While I live I shall take gifts to her spirit each spring . . . in the spring, when the birds make love on the slopes and the does come back to our land, their bellies heavy with fawn.

Mystique of the Masai

Pastoral as well as warlike, they have persisted in maintaining their unique way of life

Ettagale Blauer

Ettagale Blauer is a New York-based writer who has studied the Masai culture extensively in numerous trips to Africa and who specializes in writing about Africa and jewelry.

The noble bearing, self-assurance, and great beauty of the Masai of East Africa have been remarked upon from the time the first Europeans encountered them on the plains of what are now Kenya and Tanzania. (The word 'Masai' derives from their spoken language, Maa.) Historically, the Masai have lived among the wild animals on the rolling plains of the Rift Valley, one of the most beautiful parts of Africa. Here, the last great herds still roam freely across the plains in their semiannual migrations.

Although the appearance of people usually marks the decline of the game, it is precisely the presence of the Masai

that has guaranteed the existence of these vast herds. Elsewhere in Kenya and Tanzania, and certainly throughout the rest of Africa, the herds that once roamed the lands have been decimated. But the Masai are not hunters, whom they call *iltorrobo*—poor men—because they don't have cattle. The Masai do not crave animal trophies, they do not value rhinoceros horns for aphrodisiacs, meat is not part of their usual diet, and they don't farm the land, believing it to be a sacrilege to break the earth. Traditionally, where Masai live, the game is unmolested.

In contrast to their peaceful and harmonious relationship to the wildlife, however, the Masai are warlike in relationship to the neighboring tribes, conducting cattle raids where they take women as well as cattle for their prizes, and they have been fiercely independent in resisting the attempts of colonial

governments to change or subdue them. Although less numerous than the neighboring Kikuyu, the Masai have a strong feeling of being "chosen" people, and have been stubborn in maintaining their tribal identity.

However, that traditional tribal way of life is threatened by the exploding populations of Kenya and Tanzania (41 million people), who covet the vast open spaces of Masai Mara, Masai Amboseli, and the Serengeti Plain. Today, more than half of the Masai live in Kenya, with a style of life that requires extensive territory for cattle herds to roam in search of water and pastureland, and the freedom to hold ceremonies that mark the passage from one stage of life to the next. The Masai's need for land for their huge herds of cattle is not appreciated by people who value the land more for agriculture than for pasturage and for herds of wild animals.

3. THE ORGANIZATION OF SOCIETY AND CULTURE

The Masai live in countries that are attractive to tourists and whose leaders have embraced the values and life-style of the Western world. These two facts make it increasingly difficult for the Masai to live according to traditional patterns. The pressure to change in Kenya comes in part from their proximity to urban centers, especially the capital city of Nairobi, whose name is a Masai word meaning cool water.

Still, many Masai live in traditional homes and dress in wraps of bright cloth or leather, decorated with beaded jewelry, their cattle nearby. But the essence of the Masai culture—the creation of age-sets whose roles in life are clearly delineated—is under constant attack. In both Kenya and Tanzania, the governments continually try to "civilize" the Masai, to stop cattle raiding, and especially to put an end to the *morani*—the warriors—who are seen as the most disruptive of the age-sets.

TRADITIONAL LIFE

Masai legends trace the culture back some 300 years, and are recited according to age-groups, allowing fifteen years for each group. But anthropologists believe they arrived in the region some 1,000 years ago, having migrated from southern Ethiopia. As a racial group, they are considered a Nilo-Hamitic mix. Although deep brown in color, their features are not negroid. (Their extensive use of ochre may give their skin the look of American Indians but that is purely cosmetic.)

Traditional Masai people are governed by one guiding principle: that all the cattle on earth are theirs, that they were put there for them by *Ngai*, who is the god of both heaven and earth, existing also in the rains which bring the precious grass to feed the cattle. Any cattle they do not presently own are only temporarily out of their care, and must be recaptured. The Masai do not steal material objects; theft for them is a separate matter from raiding cattle, which is seen as the *return* of cattle to their rightful owners. From this basic belief, an entire culture has grown. The

grass that feeds the cattle and the ground on which it grows are sacred; to the Masai, it is sacrilege to break the ground for any reason, whether to grow food or to dig for water, or even to bury the dead.

Cattle provide their sole sustenance: milk and blood to drink, and the meat feast when permitted. Meat eating is restricted to ceremonial occasions, or when it is needed for gaining strength, such as when a woman gives birth or someone is recovering from an illness. When they do eat meat at a ceremony they consume their own oxen, which are sacrificed for a particular reason and in the approved way. Hunting and killing for meat are not Masai activities. It is this total dependence on their cattle, and their disdain for the meat of game

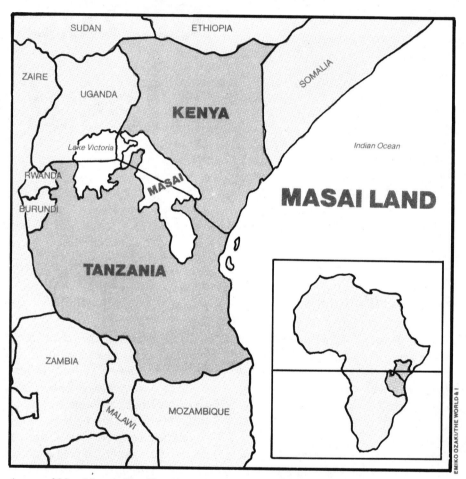

A map of Masai Land. The Masai's traditional territory exists within the two countries of Kenya and Tanzania.

animals, that permits them to coexist with the game, and which, in turn, has kept intact the great herds of the Masai Mara and the Serengeti Plain. Their extraordinary diet of milk, blood, and occasionally, meat, keeps them sleek and fit, and Westerners have often noted their physical condition with admiration.

In 1925 Norman Leys wrote, "Physically they are among the handsomest of mankind, with slender bones, narrow hips and shoulders and most beautifully rounded muscles and limbs." That same description holds today. The Masai live on about 1,300 calories a day, as opposed to our consumption of nearly 3,000. They are invariably lean.

Traditional nomadic life of the Masai, however, was ferocious and warlike in relation to other tribes. The warriors (*morani*) built *manyattas,* a type of shelter, throughout the lands and used each for a few months at a time, then moved to another area when the grazing was used up. As the seasons changed, they would return to those manyattas. They often went out raiding cattle from neighboring tribes whom they terrorized with their great ferocity.

A large part of that aggressiveness is now attributed to drugs; the morani worked themselves into a frenzy as they prepared for a raid, using the leaves and barks of certain trees known to create such moods. A soup was made of fat, water, and the bark of two trees, *il kitos-loswa* and *il kiluretti.* From the description, these seem to act as hallucinogens. As early as the 1840s, Europeans understood that the morani's extremely aggressive behavior derived from drug use. Drugs were used for endurance and for strength throughout warriorhood. During a meat feast, which could last a month, they took stimulants throughout, raising them to a virtual frenzy. This, combined with the natural excitement attendant to crowd behavior, made them formidable foes.

Having gained this supernatural energy and courage, they were ready to go cattle raiding among other tribes. To capture the cattle, the men of the other tribe had to be killed. Women were never touched in battle, but were taken to Masailand to become Masai wives. The rate of intermarriage was great during these years. Today, intermarriage is less frequent and the result mostly of chance meetings with other people. It is likely that intermarriage has actually prolonged the life of the Masai as a people; many observers from the early 1900s remarked upon the high rate of syphilis among the Masai, attributable to their habit of taking multiple sexual partners. Their birthrate is notably lower than the explosive population growth of the other peoples of Kenya and Tanzania. Still, they have increased from about 25,000 people at the turn of the century to the estimated 300,000-400,000 they are said to number today.

While the ceaseless cycle of their nomadic life has been sharply curtailed, many still cross the border between the two countries as they have for hundreds of years, leading their cattle to water and grazing lands according to the demands of the wet and dry seasons. They are in tune with the animals that migrate from the Serengeti Plain in Tanzania to Masai Mara in Kenya, and back again.

MALE AGE-SETS

The life of a traditional Masai male follows a well-ordered progression through a series of life stages.

Masai children enjoy their early years as coddled and adored love objects. They are raised communally, with great affection. Children are a great blessing in Africa. Among the Masai, with the lack of emphasis on paternity, and with a woman's prestige tied to her children, natural love for children is enhanced by their desirability in the society. Children are also desired because they bring additional cattle to a family, either as bride-price in the case of girls or by raiding in the case of boys.

During their early years, children play and imitate the actions of the elders, a natural school in which they learn the rituals and daily life practices of their people. Learning how to be a Masai is the lifework of every one in the community. Infant mortality in Africa remains high; catastrophic diseases introduced by Europeans, such as smallpox, nearly wiped them out. That memory is alive in their oral traditions; having children is a protection against the loss of the entire culture, which they know from experience could easily happen. Africans believe that you must live to see your face reflected in that of a child; given the high infant mortality rate, the only way to protect that human chain is by having as many children as possible.

For boys, each stage of life embraces an age-group created at an elaborate ceremony, the highlight of their lives being the elevation to moran. Once initiated, they learn their age-group's specific duties and privileges. Males pass through four stages: childhood, boyhood, warriorhood, and elderhood. Warriors, divided into junior and senior, form one generation, or age-set.

Four major ceremonies mark the passage from one group to another: boys who are going to be circumcised participate in the *Alamal Lenkapaata* ceremony, preparation for circumcision; *Emorata* is followed by initiation into warriorhood—status of moran; the passage from warrior to elderhood is marked by the *Eunoto* ceremony; and total elderhood is confirmed by the *Oln-gesherr.* All ceremonies have in common ritual head shaving, continual blessings, slaughter of an animal, ceremonial painting of face or body, singing, dancing, and feasting. *Laibons*—spiritual advisers—must be present at all ceremonies, and the entire tribe devotes itself to these preparations.

Circumcision is a rite of passage and more for teenage boys. It determines the role the boy will play throughout his life, as leader or follower. How he conducts himself during circumcision is keenly observed by all; a boy who cries out during the painful operation is branded a coward and shunned for a long time; his mother is disgraced. A boy who is brave, and who had led an exemplary life, becomes the leader of his age-group.

It takes months of work to prepare for these ceremonies so the exact date of such an event is rarely known until the last minute. Westerners, with contacts into the Masai community, often stay ready for weeks, hoping to be on hand when such a ceremony is about to take place. Each such ceremony may well be the last, it is thought.

Before they can be circumcised, boys must prove themselves ready. They tend the cattle—the Masai's only wealth—and guard them from predators whose tracks they learn to recognize. They know their cattle individually, the way we know people. Each animal has a name and is treated as a personality. When they feel they are ready, the boys approach the junior elders and ask them to open a new circumcision period. If this is approved, they begin a series of rituals, among them the Alamal Lenkapaata, the last step before the formal

Masai ceremony of the Alamal Lenkapaata which is part of the Morani (warrior) coming of age for young Masai men.

Young Masai Morani (warriors) dancing traditionally with their hair caked with red ochre mud and their legs in an abstract pattern in a traditional Masai Manyatta with long mud huts in the Rift Valley, Kenya.

Under a tree, elders from many areas gathered together and their discussion was very intense. John Galaty, professor of anthropology from McGill University in Montreal, who has studied the Masai extensively, flew in specifically to attend this ceremony. He is fluent in Masai and translated the elders' talk. "We are lucky," they said, "to be able to have this ceremony. The government does not want us to have it. We have to be very careful. The young men have to be warned that there should be no cattle raiding." And there wasn't any.

An ox was slaughtered, for meat eating is a vital element of this ceremony. The boys who were taking part cut off hunks of meat which they cooked over an open fire. Though there was a hut set aside for them, the boys spent little time sleeping. The next day, all the elders gathered to receive gifts of sugar and salt from John Keen, a member of Kenya's parliament, and himself a Masai. (Kenya has many Masai in government, including the Minister of Finance, George Saitoti.) The dancing, the meat eating, all the elements of the ceremony continued for several days. If this had been a wealthy group, they might have kept up the celebration for as long as a month.

Once this ceremony is concluded, the boys are allowed to hold councils and to discuss important matters. They choose one from their own group to be their representative. The Alamal Lenkapaata ceremony includes every boy of suitable age, preparing him for circumcision and then warriorhood. The circumcisions will take place over the next few years, beginning with the older boys in this group. The age difference may be considerable in any age-group since these ceremonies are held infrequently; once a circumcision period ends, though, it may not be opened again for many years.

THE MORAN

The Masai who exemplifies his tribe is the moran. This is the time of life that

initiation. The boys must have a laibon, a leader with the power to predict the future, to guide them in their decisions. He creates a name for this new generation. The boys decorate themselves with chalky paint, and spend the night out in the open. The elders sing and celebrate and dance through the night to honor the boys.

An Alamal Lenkapaata held in 1983 was probably the most recent to mark the opening of a new age-set. Ceremonies were held in Ewaso Ngiro, in the Rift Valley. As boys joined into groups and danced, they raised a cloud of dust around themselves. All day long, groups would form and dance, then break apart and later start again.

expresses the essence of the Masai—bravery, willingness to defend their people and their cattle against all threats, confidence to go out on cattle raids to increase their own herds, and ability to stand up to threats even from Europeans, whose superior weapons subdued the Masai but never subjugated them. The Masai moran is the essence of that almost mythical being, the noble savage, a description invented by Europeans but here actually lived out. With his spear, his elaborately braided and reddened hair, his bountiful beaded jewelry, his beautiful body and proud bearing, the moran is the symbol of everything that is attractive about the Masai. When a young man becomes a moran, his entire culture looks upon him with reverence.

The life a moran enjoys as his birthright is centered on cattle raiding, enhancing his appearance, and sex. The need to perform actual work, such as building fences, rescuing a cow that has gone astray, and standing ready to defend their homeland—Masailand—is only occasionally required. Much of his time is devoted to the glorification of his appearance. His body is a living showcase of Masai art.

From the moment a boy undergoes the circumcision ceremony, he looks ahead to the time when he will be a moran. He grows his hair long so it can be braided into myriad tiny plaits, thickened with ochre and fat. The age-mates spend hours at this, the whole outdoors being their salon. As they work, they chat, always building the bonds between them. Their beaded jewelry is made by their girlfriends. Their bare legs are ever-changing canvases on which they trace patterns, using white chalk and ochre. Though nearly naked, they are a medley of patterns and colors.

After being circumcised, the young men "float" in society for up to two years, traveling in loose groups and living in temporary shelters called *inkangitie*. After that time they can build a manyatta. Before fully becoming a moran, however, they must enter a "holy house" at a special ceremony. Only a young man who has not slept with a circumcised woman can enter the holy house. The fear of violating this taboo is very strong, and young men who do not enter the house are beaten by their parents and carry the disrespect of the tribe all their lives.

The dancing of the morani celebrates everything that they consider beautiful and strong: morani dance competitively by jumping straight into the air, knees straight, over and over again, each leap trying to go higher than the last, as they sing and chant and encourage each other. The morani also dance with their young girlfriends. Each couple performs sinuous motions repeatedly, then breaks off and another couple takes their place. A hypnotic rhythm develops as they follow the chanting and hand clapping of their mates.

Although they are now forbidden by the governments of Kenya and Tanzania to kill a lion—a traditional test of manhood—or to go cattle raiding, they retain all the trappings of a warrior, without the possibility of practicing their skill. They occasionally manage a cattle raid, but even without it, they still live with pride and dignity. Masai remain morani for about fifteen years, building up unusually strong relationships among their age-mates with whom they live during that time. Hundreds of boys may become morani at one time.

Traditionally, every fifteen years saw the advent of a new generation of warriors. Now, both colonial governments and independent black-ruled governments have tampered with this social process, and have been successful in reducing the time men spend as warriors. By forcing this change, the governments hope to mold the Masai male into a more tractable citizen, especially by forbidding such disruptive activities as lion killing and cattle raiding. But tinkering with the Masai system can have unforeseen and undesirable consequences. It takes a certain number of years before a moran is ready to take on the duties of that age-group. They need time to build up herds of cattle to be used for bride-price and to learn to perform the decision-making tasks expected. This change also leaves the younger boys without warriors to keep them in check, and to guide them through the years leading up to the circumcision ceremony.

More significantly, since 1978 it has been illegal to build a manyatta, and warriors from that time have been left with no place to live. Their mothers cannot live with them, they cannot tend their cattle or increase their herds, they have no wives or jobs. Since, once they become warriors, they are not allowed to enter another person's house to eat, they are forced to steal other peoples' cattle and live off the land.

Circumcision exists for women as well as for men. From the age of nine until puberty, young girls live with the morani as sexual partners; it is an accepted part of Masai life that girls do not reach puberty as virgins. It is because of this practice that syphilis causes the most serious problems for the Masai. The girls, unfamiliar with their bodies, contract the disease and leave it untreated until sterility results. This sexual activity changes dramatically when a girl reaches puberty. At that time, she is circumcised and forbidden to stay with the warriors. This is to prevent her from becoming pregnant before she is married. As soon as she recovers from the circumcision, or clitoridectomy, an operation that destroys her ability to experience orgasm, she is considered ready for marriage. Circumcision is seen as a means of equalizing men and women. By removing any vestige of the appearance of the organs of the opposite sex, it purifies the gender. Although female circumcision has long been banned by the Kenyan government, few girls manage to escape the operation.

While the entire tribe devotes itself to the rituals that perpetuate the male age-set system, girls travel individually through life in their roles as lovers, wives, and child bearers, in all instances subservient to the boys and men. They have no comparable age-set system and hence do not develop the intensely felt friendships of the men who move through life together in groups, and who, during the period of senior warriorhood live together, away from their families.

It is during this period that the mothers move away from their homes. They build manyattas in which they live with their sons who have achieved the status of senior morani, along with their sons' girlfriends, and away from their own small children. The husbands, other wives, and the other women of the tribe, take care of these children.

The male-female relationship is dictated according to the male age-sets. When a newly circumcised girl marries, she joins the household of her husband's family, and likely will be one among several of his wives. Her role is to milk the cows, to build the house, and to bear children, especially male children. Only through childbirth can she achieve high status; all men, on the other hand, achieve status simply by graduating from one age-set to the next.

A childless Masai woman is virtually without a role in her society. One of the rarest ceremonies among the Masai is a blessing for women who have not given birth and for women who want more children. While the women play a peripheral role in the men's ceremonies, the men are vital to the women's, for it is a man who blesses the women. To prepare for the ritual, the women brew great quantities of beer and offer beer and lambs to the men who are to bless them.

In their preparation for this ceremony, and in conducting matters that pertain to their lives, the women talk things out democratically, as do the men. They gather in the fields and each woman presents her views. Not until all who want to speak have done so does the group move toward a consensus. As with the men, a good speaker is highly valued and her views are listened to attentively. But these sessions are restricted to women's issues; the men have the final say over all matters relating to the tribe. Boys may gather in councils as soon as they have completed the Alamal Lenkapaata; girls don't have similar opportunities. They follow their lovers, the morani, devotedly, yet as soon as they reach the age when they can marry, they are wrenched out of this love relation-

ship and given in marriage to much older men, men who have cattle for bride-price.

Because morani do not marry until they are elevated to elderhood, girls must accept husbands who are easily twice their age. But just as the husband has more than one wife, she will have lovers, who are permitted as long as they are members of her husband's circumcision group, not the age group for whom she was a girlfriend. This is often the cause of tension among the Masai. All the children she bears are considered to be her husband's even though they may not be his biologically. While incest taboos are clearly observed and various other taboos also pertain, multiple partners are expected. Polygamy in Masailand (and anywhere it prevails) dictates that some men will not marry at all. These men are likely to be those without cattle, men who cannot bring bride-price. For the less traditional, the payment of bride-price is sometimes made in cash, rather than in cattle, and to earn money, men go to the cities to seek work. Masai tend to find jobs that permit them to be outside and free; for this reason, many of the night watchmen in the capital city of Nairobi are Masai. They sit around fires at night, chatting, in an urban version of their life in the countryside. . . .

RAIDING, THEFT, AND THE LAW

Though now subject to national laws, the Masai do not turn to official bodies or courts for redress. They settle their own disputes democratically, each man giving his opinion until the matter at hand is settled. Men decide all matters for the tribe (women do not take part in these discussions), and they operate virtually without chiefs. The overriding concern is to be fair in the resolution of problems because kinship ties the Masai together in every aspect of their lives. Once a decision is made, punishment is always levied in the form of a fine. The Masai have no jails, nor do they inflict physical punishment. For a people who value cattle as much as they do, there is no greater sacrifice

than to give up some of their animals.

The introduction of schools is another encroachment upon traditional life which was opposed by the Masai. While most African societies resisted sending their children to school, the Masai reacted with particular intensity. They compared school to death or enslavement; if children did go to school, they would be lost to the Masai community. They would forget how to survive on the land, how to identify animals by their tracks, and how to protect the cattle. All of these things are learned by example and by experience.

David Read is a white Kenyan, fluent in Masai who said that, as a boy: "I may not have been able to read or write, but I knew how to live in the bush. I could hunt my dinner if I had to."

The first school in their territory was opened in 1919 at Narok but few children attended. The Masai scorned the other tribes, such as the Kikuyu, who later embraced Western culture and soon filled the offices of the government's bureaucracies. The distance between the Masai and the other tribes became even greater. The Masai were seen as a painful reminder of the primitivism that Europeans as well as Africans had worked so hard to erase. Today, however, many Masai families will keep one son at home to maintain traditional life, and send another one to school. In this way, they experience the benefits of literacy, opportunities for employment, money, connections to the government, and new knowledge, especially veterinary practices, while keeping their traditions intact. Masai who go to school tend to succeed, many of them graduating from college with science degrees. Some take up the study of animal diseases, and bring this knowledge back to help their communities improve the health of their cattle. The entire Masai herd was once nearly wiped out during the rinderpest epidemic in the late nineteenth century. Today, the cattle are threatened by tsetse flies. But where the Masai were able to rebuild their herds in the past, today, they would face tremendous pressure to give up cattle raising entirely.

LIVING CONDITIONS

While the Masai are admired for their great beauty, their living conditions are breeding grounds for disease. Since they keep their small livestock (sheep and goats) in the huts where they live, they are continually exposed to the animals' excrement. The cattle are just outside, in an open enclosure, and their excrement is added to the mix. Flies abound wherever cattle are kept, but with the animals living right next to the huts, they are ever-present. Like many tribal groups living in relative isolation, the Masai are highly vulnerable to diseases brought in by others. In the 1890s, when the rinderpest hit their cattle, the Masai were attacked by smallpox which, coupled with drought, reduced their numbers almost to the vanishing point.

For the most part, the Masai rely on the remedies of their traditional medicine and are renowned for their extensive knowledge and use of natural plants to treat illnesses and diseases of both people and cattle. Since they live in an area that had hardly any permanent sources of water, the Masai have learned to live without washing. They are said to have one bath at birth, another at marriage. Flies are pervasive; there is scarcely a picture of a Masai taken in their home environment that does not show flies alit on them.

Their rounded huts, looking like mushrooms growing from the ground, are built by the women. On a frame of wooden twigs, they begin to plaster mud and cow dung. Layers and layers of this are added until the roof reaches the desired thickness. Each day, cracks and holes are repaired, especially after the rains, using the readily available dung. Within the homes, they use animal hides. Everything they need can be made from the materials at hand. There are a few items such as sugar, tea, and cloth that they buy from the *dukas,* or Indian shops, in Narok, Kajiado, and other nearby towns, but money is readily obtained by selling beaded jewelry, or simply one's own image. Long ago, the Masai discovered their photogenic qualities. If they cannot survive as warriors by raiding, they will survive as icons of warriors, permitting tourists to take their pictures for a fee, and that fee is determined by hard bargaining. One does not simply take a picture of a Masai without payment; that is theft.

Their nomadic patterns have been greatly reduced; now they move only the cattle as the seasons change. During the dry season, the Masai stay on the higher parts of the escarpment and use the pastures there which they call *osukupo.* This offers a richer savannah with more trees. When the rains come, they move down to the pastures of the Rift Valley to the plains called *okpurkel.*

Their kraals are built a few miles from the water supply. The cattle drink on one day only, then are grazed the next, so they can conserve the grazing by using a larger area than they would be able to if they watered the cattle every day. But their great love of cattle has inevitably brought them to the point of overstocking. As the cattle trample their way to and from the waterhole, they destroy all vegetation near it, and the soil washes away. Scientists studying Masai land use have concluded that with the change from a totally nomadic way of life, the natural environmental resistance of this system was destroyed; there is no self-regulating mechanism left. Some Masai have permitted wheat farming on their land for the exploding Kenyan population, taking away the marginal lands that traditionally provided further grazing for their cattle.

PRESSURE TO CHANGE

In June 1901, Sir Charles Eliot, colonial governor of Kenya, said, "I regard the Masai as the most important and dangerous of the tribes with whom we have to deal in East Africa and I think it will be long necessary to maintain an adequate military force in the districts which they inhabit."

The traditional Masai way of life has been under attack ever since. The colonial British governments of Kenya and Tanzania (then Tanganyika) outlawed Masai cattle raiding and tried to stifle the initiation ceremony; the black governments that took over upon independence in the 1960s continued the process. The Masai resisted these edicts, ignored them, and did their best to circumvent them throughout the century. In some areas, they gave in entirely—cattle raiding, the principal activity of the morani—rarely occurs, but their ceremonies, the vital processes by which a boy becomes a moran and a moran becomes an elder, remain intact, although they have been banned over and over again. Stopping these ceremonies is more difficult than just proclaiming them to be over, as the Kenyan government did in 1985.

Some laws restrict the very essence of a Masai's readiness to assume the position of moran. Hunting was banned entirely in Kenya and nearly so in Tanzania (except for expensive permits issued to tourists, and restricted to designated hunting blocks), making it illegal for a moran to kill a lion to demonstrate his bravery and hunting skills. Although the Masai ignore the government whenever possible, at times such as this, conflict is unavoidable. Lions are killed occasionally, but stealthily; some modern Masai boys say, "Who needs to kill a lion? It doesn't prove anything."

The Kenyan governments requirement that Masai children go to school has also affected the traditional roles of girls and women, who traditionally married at age twelve or thirteen and left school. Now the government will send fathers and husbands to jail for taking these girls out of school. There was a case in Kenya in 1986 of a girl who wrote to the government protesting the fact that her father had removed her from school to prepare for marriage. Her mother carried the letter to the appropriate government officials, the father was tried, and the girl was allowed to return to school.

Sometimes there is cooperation between governmental policy and traditional life-style. Ceremonies are scheduled to take place in school holidays, and while government policies continue to erode traditional customs, the educated and traditional groups within the

Masai community try to support each other.

TRADITION IN THE FACE OF CHANGE

Although the Masai in both countries are descended from the same people, national policies have pushed the Kenyan Masai further away from their traditions. The Tanzanian Masai, for example, still dress occasionally in animal skins, decorated with beading. The Kenyan Masai dress almost entirely in cloth, reserving skins for ceremonial occasions.

In 1977, Kenya and Tanzania closed their common border, greatly isolating the Tanzanian Masai from Western contact. Though the border has been re-opened, the impact on the Masai is clear. The Kenyan Masai became one of the sights of the tourist route while the Tanzanian Masai were kept from such interaction. This has further accelerated change among the Kenyan Masai. Tepilit Ole Saitoti sees a real difference in character between the Masai of Kenya and Tanzania. "Tem-peramentally," he says, "the Tanzanian Masai tend to be calmer and slower than those in Kenya."

Tribal people throughout Africa are in a constant state of change, some totally urbanized, their traditions nearly forgotten; others are caught in the middle, part of the tribe living traditionally, some moving to the city and adopting Western ways. The Masai have retained their culture, their unique and distinctive way of life, longer than virtually all the other tribes of East Africa, and they have done so while living in the very middle of the tourist traffic. Rather than disappear into the bush, the Masai use their attractiveness and mystique to their own benefit. Masai Mara and Amboseli, two reserves set aside for them, are run by them for their own profit.

Few tribes in Africa still put such a clear cultural stamp on an area; few have so successfully resisted enormous efforts to change them, to modernize and "civilize" them, to make them fit into the larger society. We leave it to Tepilit Ole Saitoti to predict the future of his own people: "Through their long and difficult history, the Masai have fought to maintain their traditional way of life. Today, however, they can no longer resist the pressures of the modern world. The survival of Masai culture has ceased to be a question; in truth, it is rapidly disappearing."

BIBLIOGRAPHY

Bleeker, Sonia, *The Masai, Herders of East Africa,* 1963.

Fedders, Andrew, *Peoples and Cultures of Kenya,* TransAfrica Books, Nairobi, 1979.

Fisher, Angela, *Africa Adorned,* Harry N. Abrams Inc., New York, 1984.

Kinde, S.H., *Last of the Masai,* London, 1901.

Kipkorir, B., *Kenya's People, People of the Rift Valley,* Evans Bros. Ltd., London, 1978

Lamb, David, *The Africans,* Vintage Books, New York, 1984.

Moravia, Alberto, *Which Tribe Do You Belong To?,* Farrar, Straus & Firous, New York, 1974.

Read, David, *Barefoot Over the Serengeti,* Read, Nairobi, 1979.

Ole Saitoti, Tepilit, *Masai,* Barry N. Abrams, Inc., New York 1980.

—,*The Worlds of a Masai Warrior,* Random House, New York, 1986.

Ricciardi, Mirella, *Vanishing Africa,* Holt, Rinehard Winston, 1971.

Sankan, S.S., *The Masai,* Kenya Literature Bureau, Nairobi, 1971.

Thomson, Joseph, *Through Masai Land,* Sampson Low, Marston & Co., London 1885.

Tignor, Robert, *The Colonial Transformation of Kenya, The Kamba, Kikuyu and Masai from 1900 to 1939,* Princeton, NJ 1976.

Too Many Bananas, Not Enough Pineapples, and No Watermelon at All: Three Object Lessons in Living with Reciprocity

David Counts

McMaster University

NO WATERMELON AT ALL

The woman came all the way through the village, walking between the two rows of houses facing each other between the beach and the bush, to the very last house standing on a little spit of land at the mouth of the Kaini River. She was carrying a watermelon on her head, and the house she came to was the government "rest house," maintained by the villagers for the occasional use of visiting officials. Though my wife and I were graduate students, not officials, and had asked for permission to stay in the village for the coming year, we were living in the rest house while the debate went on about where a house would be built for us. When the woman offered to sell us the watermelon for two shillings, we happily agreed, and the kids were delighted at the prospect of watermelon after yet another meal of rice and bully beef. The money changed hands and the

seller left to return to her village, a couple of miles along the coast to the east.

It seemed only seconds later that the woman was back, reluctantly accompanying Kolia, the man who had already made it clear to us that he was the leader of the village. Kolia had no English, and at that time, three or four days into our first stay in Kandoka Village on the island of New Britain in Papua New Guinea, we had very little Tok Pisin. Language difficulties notwithstanding, Kolia managed to make his message clear: The woman had been outrageously wrong to sell us the watermelon for two shillings and we were to return it to her and reclaim our money immediately. When we tried to explain that we thought the price to be fair and were happy with the bargain, Kolia explained again and finally made it clear that we had missed the point. The problem wasn't that we had paid too much; it was that we had paid at all. Here he was, a leader, responsible for us while we were living in his village, and we had shamed him. How would it look if he let guests in his village *buy* food? If we wanted watermelons, or bananas, or anything else,

all that was necessary was to let him know. He told us that it would be all right for us to give little gifts to people who brought food to us (and they surely would), but *no one* was to sell food to us. If anyone were to try—like this woman from Lauvore—then we should refuse. There would be plenty of watermelons without us buying them.

The woman left with her watermelon, disgruntled, and we were left with our two shillings. But we had learned the first lesson of many about living in Kandoka. We didn't pay money for food again that whole year, and we did get lots of food brought to us . . . but we never got another watermelon. That one was the last of the season.

LESSON 1: *In a society where food is shared or gifted as part of social life, you may not buy it with money.*

TOO MANY BANANAS

In the couple of months that followed the watermelon incident, we managed to become at least marginally competent in Tok Pisin, to negotiate the construction of a house on what we hoped was neutral ground, and to settle into the routine of our fieldwork. As our village leader had predicted, plenty of food was brought to us. Indeed, seldom did a day pass without something coming in—some sweet potatoes, a few taro, a papaya, the occasional pineapple, or some bananas—lots of bananas.

We had learned our lesson about the money, though, so we never even offered to buy the things that were brought, but instead made gifts, usually of tobacco to the adults or chewing gum to the children. Nor were we so gauche as to haggle with a giver over how much of a return gift was appropriate, though the two of us sometimes conferred as to whether what had been brought was a "two-stick" or a "three-stick" stalk, bundle, or whatever. A "stick" of tobacco was a single large leaf, soaked in rum and then twisted into a ropelike form. This, wrapped in half a sheet of newsprint (torn for use as cigarette paper), sold in the local trade stores for a shilling. Nearly all of the adults in the village smoked a great deal, and they seldom had much cash, so our stocks of twist tobacco and stacks of the Sydney *Morning Herald* (all, unfortunately, the same day's issue) were seen as a real boon to those who preferred "stick" to the locally grown product.

We had established a pattern with respect to the gifts of food. When a donor appeared at our veranda we would offer our thanks and talk with them for a few minutes (usually about our children, who seemed to hold a real fascination for the villagers and for whom most of the gifts were intended) and then we would inquire whether they could use some tobacco. It was almost never refused, though occasionally a small bottle of kerosene, a box of matches, some laundry soap, a cup of rice, or a tin of meat would be requested instead of (or even in addition to) the tobacco. Everyone, even Kolia, seemed to think this arrangement had worked out well.

Now, what must be kept in mind is that while we were following their rules—or seemed to be—we were *re-ally still buying food.* In fact we kept a running account of what came in and what we "paid" for it. Tobacco as currency got a little complicated, but since the exchange rate was one stick to one shilling, it was not too much trouble as long as everyone was happy, and meanwhile we could account for the expenditure of "informant fees" and "household expenses." Another thing to keep in mind is that not only did we continue to think in terms of our buying the food that was brought, we thought of them as *selling it.* While it was true they never quoted us a price, they also never asked us if we needed or wanted whatever they had brought. It seemed clear to us that when an adult needed a stick of tobacco, or a child wanted some chewing gum (we had enormous quantities of small packets of Wrigley's for just such eventualities) they would find something surplus to their own needs and bring it along to our "store" and get what they wanted.

By late November 1966, just before the rainy reason set in, the bananas were coming into flush, and whereas earlier we had received banana gifts by the "hand" (six or eight bananas in a cluster cut from the stalk), donors now began to bring bananas, "for the children," by the *stalk!* The Kaliai among whom we were living are not exactly specialists in banana cultivation—they only recognize about thirty varieties, while some of their neighbors have more than twice that many—but the kinds they produce differ considerably from each other in size, shape, and taste, so we were not dismayed when we had more than one stalk hanging on our veranda. The stalks ripen a bit at the time, and having some variety was nice. Still, by the time our accumulation had reached *four* complete stalks, the delights of variety had begun to pale a bit. The fruits were ripening progressively and it was clear that even if we and the kids ate nothing but bananas for the next week, some would still fall from the stalk onto the floor in a state of gross overripeness. This was the situation as, late one afternoon, a woman came bringing yet another stalk of bananas up the steps of the house.

Several factors determined our reaction to her approach: one was that there was literally no way we could possibly use the bananas. We hadn't quite reached the point of being crowded off our veranda by the stalks of fruit, but it was close. Another factor was that we were tired of playing the gift game. We had acquiesced in playing it—no one was permitted to sell us anything, and in turn we only gave things away, refusing under any circumstances to sell tobacco (or anything else) for money. But there had to be a limit. From our perspective what was at issue was that the woman wanted something and she had come to trade for it. Further, what she had brought to trade was something we neither wanted nor could use, and it should have been obvious to her. So we decided to bite the bullet.

The woman, Rogi, climbed the stairs to the veranda, took the stalk from where it was balanced on top of her head, and laid it on the floor with the word, "Here are some bananas for the children." Dorothy and I sat near her on the floor and thanked her for her thought but explained, "You know, we really have too many bananas—we can't use these; maybe you ought to give them to someone else. . . ." The woman looked mystified, then brightened and explained that she didn't want anything for them, she wasn't short of tobacco or anything. They were just a gift for the kids. Then she just sat there, and we sat there, and the bananas sat there, and we tried again. "Look," I said, pointing up to them and counting, "we've got four stalks already hanging here on the veranda—there are too many for us to eat now. Some are rotting already. Even if we eat only bananas, we can't keep up with what's here!"

Rogi's only response was to insist that these were a gift, and that she didn't want anything for them, so we tried yet another tack: "Don't *your* children like bananas?" When she admitted that they did, and that she had none at her house, we suggested that she should take them there. Finally, still puzzled, but convinced we weren't going to keep the bananas, she replaced them on her head, went down the stairs, and made her way back through the village toward her house.

As before, it seemed only moments before Kolia was making his way up the stairs, but this time he hadn't brought the woman in tow. "What was wrong with those bananas? Were they no good?" he demanded. We explained that there was nothing wrong with the bananas at all, but that we simply couldn't use them and it seemed foolish to take them when we had so many and Rogi's own children had none. We obviously didn't make ourselves clear because Kolia then took up the same refrain that Rogi had—he insisted that we shouldn't be worried about taking the bananas, because they were a gift for the children and Rogi hadn't wanted anything for them. There was no reason, he added, to send her away with them—she would be ashamed. I'm afraid we must have seemed as if we were hard of hearing or thought he was, for our only response was to repeat our reasons. We went through it again—there they hung, one, two, three, *four* stalks of bananas, rapidly ripening and already far beyond our capacity to eat—we just weren't ready to accept any more and let them rot (and, we added to ourselves, pay for them with tobacco, to boot).

Kolia finally realized that we were neither hard of hearing nor intentionally offensive, but merely ignorant. He stared at us for a few minutes, thinking, and then asked: "Don't you frequently have visitors during the day and evening?" We nodded. Then he asked, "Don't you usually offer them cigarettes and coffee or milo?" Again, we nodded. "Did it ever occur to you to suppose," he said, "that your visitors might be hungry?" It was at this point in the conversation, as we recall, that we began to see the depth of the pit we had dug for ourselves. We nodded, hesitantly. His last words to us before he went down the stairs and stalked away were just what we were by that time afraid they might be. "When your guests are hungry, *feed them bananas!*"

LESSON 2: *Never refuse a gift, and never fail to return a gift. If you cannot*

use it, you can always give it away to someone else—there is no such thing as too much—there are never too many bananas.*

NOT ENOUGH PINEAPPLES

During the fifteen years between that first visit in 1966 and our residence there in 1981 we had returned to live in Kandoka village twice during the 1970s, and though there were a great many changes in the village, and indeed for all of Papua New Guinea during that time, we continued to live according to the lessons of reciprocity learned during those first months in the field. We bought no food for money and refused no gifts, but shared our surplus. As our family grew, we continued to be accompanied by our younger children. Our place in the village came to be something like that of educated Kaliai who worked far away in New Guinea. Our friends expected us to come "home" when we had leave, but knew that our work kept us away for long periods of time. They also credited us with knowing much more about the rules of their way of life than was our due. And we sometimes shared the delusion that we understood life in the village, but even fifteen years was not long enough to relieve the need for lessons in learning to live within the rules of gift exchange.

In the last paragraph I used the word *friends* to describe the villagers intentionally, but of course they were not all our friends. Over the years some really had become friends, others were acquaintances, others remained consultants or informants to whom we turned when we needed information. Still others, unfortunately, we did not like at all. We tried never to make an issue of these distinctions, of course, and to be evenhanded and generous to all, as they were to us. Although we almost never actually refused requests that were made of us, over the long term our reciprocity in the village was balanced. More was given to those who helped us the most, while we gave assistance or donations of small items even to those who were not close or helpful.

One elderly woman in particular was a trial for us. Sara was the eldest of a group of siblings and her younger brother and sister were both generous, informative, and delightful persons. Her younger sister, Makila, was a particularly close friend and consultant, and in deference to that friendship we felt awkward in dealing with the elder sister.

Sara was neither a friend nor an informant, but she had been, since she returned to live in the village at the time of our second trip in 1971, a constant (if minor) drain on our resources. She never asked for much at a time. A bar of soap, a box of matches, a bottle of kerosene, a cup of rice, some onions, a stick or two of tobacco, or some other small item was usually all that was at issue, but whenever she came around it was always to ask for something—or to let us know that when we left, we should give her some of the furnishings from the house. Too, unlike almost everyone else in the village, when she came, she was always empty-handed. We ate no taro from her gardens, and the kids chewed none of her sugarcane. In short, she was, as far as we could tell, a really grasping, selfish old woman—and we were not the only victims of her greed.

Having long before learned the lesson of the bananas, one day we had a stalk that was ripening so fast we couldn't keep up with it, so I pulled a few for our own use (we only had one stalk at the time) and walked down through the village to Ben's house, where his five children were playing. I sat down on his steps to talk, telling him that I intended to give the fruit to his kids. They never got them. Sara saw us from across the open plaza of the village and came rushing over, shouting, "My bananas!" Then she grabbed the stalk and went off gorging herself with them. Ben and I just looked at each other.

Finally it got to the point where it seemed to us that we had to do something. Ten years of being used was long enough. So there came the afternoon when Sara showed up to get some tobacco—again. But this time, when we gave her the two sticks she had demanded, we confronted her.

3. THE ORGANIZATION OF SOCIETY AND CULTURE

First, we noted the many times she had come to get things. We didn't mind sharing things, we explained. After all, we had plenty of tobacco and soap and rice and such, and most of it was there so that we could help our friends as they helped us, with folktales, information, or even gifts of food. The problem was that she kept coming to get things, but never came to talk, or to tell stories, or to bring some little something that the kids might like. Sara didn't argue—she agreed. "Look," we suggested, "it doesn't have to be much, and we don't mind giving you things—but you can help us. The kids like pineapples, and we don't have any—the next time you need something, bring something—like maybe a pineapple." Obviously somewhat embarrassed, she took her tobacco and left, saying that she would bring something soon. We were really pleased with ourselves. It had been a very difficult thing to do, but it was done, and we were convinced that either she would start bringing things or not

come. It was as if a burden had lifted from our shoulders.

It worked. Only a couple of days passed before Sara was back, bringing her bottle to get it filled with kerosene. But this time, she came carrying the biggest, most beautiful pineapple we had seen the entire time we had been there. We had a friendly talk, filled her kerosene container, and hung the pineapple up on the veranda to ripen just a little further. A few days later we cut and ate it, and whether the satisfaction it gave came from the fruit or from its source would be hard to say, but it was delicious. That, we assumed, was the end of that irritant.

We were wrong, of course. The next afternoon, Mary, one of our best friends for years (and no relation to Sara), dropped by for a visit. As we talked, her eyes scanned the veranda. Finally she asked whether we hadn't had a pineapple there yesterday. We said we had, but that we had already eaten it. She commented that it had been a really nice-looking one, and we

told her that it had been the best we had eaten in months. Then, after a pause, she asked, "Who brought it to you?" We smiled as we said, "Sara!" because Mary would appreciate our coup—she had commented many times in the past on the fact that Sara only *got* from us and never gave. She was silent for a moment, and then she said, "Well, I'm glad you enjoyed it—my father was waiting until it was fully ripe to harvest it for you, but when it went missing I thought maybe it was the one you had here. I'm glad to see you got it. I thought maybe a thief had eaten it in the bush."

LESSON 3: *Where reciprocity is the rule and gifts are the idiom, you cannot demand a gift, just as you cannot refuse a request.*

It says a great deal about the kindness and patience of the Kaliai people that they have been willing to be our hosts for all these years despite our blunders and lack of good manners. They have taught us a lot, and these three lessons are certainly not the least important things we learned.

Life Without Chiefs

Are we forever condemned to a world of haves and have-nots, rulers and ruled?
Maybe not, argues a noted anthropologist—if we can relearn some ancient lessons.

Marvin Harris

Marvin Harris is a graduate research professor of anthropology at the University of Florida and chair of the general anthropology division of the American Anthropological Association. His seventeen books include Cows, Pigs, Wars and Witches *and* Cannibals and Kings.

Can humans exist without some people ruling and others being ruled? To look at the modern world, you wouldn't think so. Democratic states may have done away with emperors and kings, but they have hardly dispensed with gross inequalities in wealth, rank, and power.

However, humanity hasn't always lived this way. For about 98 percent of our existence as a species (and for four million years before then), our ancestors lived in small, largely nomadic hunting-and-gathering bands containing about 30 to 50 people apiece. It was in this social context that human nature evolved. It has been only about ten thousand years since people began to settle down into villages, some of which eventually grew into cities. And it has been only in the last two thousand years that the majority of people in the world have not lived in hunting-and-gathering societies. This brief period of time is not nearly sufficient for noticeable evolution to have taken place. Thus, the few remaining foraging societies are the closest analogues

we have to the "natural" state of humanity.

To judge from surviving examples of hunting-and-gathering bands and villages, our kind got along quite well for the greater part of prehistory without so much as a paramount chief. In fact, for tens of thousands of years, life went on without kings, queens, prime ministers, presidents, parliaments, congresses, cabinets, governors, and mayors—not to mention the police officers, sheriffs, marshals, generals, lawyers, bailiffs, judges, district attorneys, court clerks, patrol cars, paddy wagons, jails, and penitentiaries that help keep them in power. How in the world did our ancestors ever manage to leave home without them?

Small populations provide part of the answer. With 50 people per band or 150 per village, everybody knew everybody else intimately. People gave with the expectation of taking and took with the expectation of giving. Because chance played a great role in the capture of animals, collection of wild foodstuffs, and success of rudimentary forms of agriculture, the individuals who had the luck of the catch on one day needed a handout on the next. So the best way for them to provide for their inevitable rainy day was to be generous. As expressed by anthropologist Richard Gould, "The greater the amount of risk, the greater the extent of sharing." Reciprocity is a small society's bank.

In reciprocal exchange, people do not specify how much or exactly what they expect to get back or when they expect to get it. That would besmirch the quality of that transaction and make it similar to mere barter or to buying and selling. The distinction lingers on in societies dominated by other forms of exchange, even capitalist ones. For we do carry out a give-and-take among close kin and friends that is informal, uncalculating, and imbued with a spirit of generosity. Teen-agers do not pay cash for their meals at home or for the use of the family car, wives do not bill their husbands for cooking a meal, and friends give each other birthday gifts and Christmas presents. But much of this is marred by the expectation that our generosity will be acknowledged with expression of thanks.

Where reciprocity really prevails in daily life, etiquette requires that generosity be taken for granted. As Robert Dentan discovered during his fieldwork among the Semai of Central Malaysia, no one ever says "thank you" for the meat received from another hunter. Having struggled all day to lug the carcass of a pig home through the jungle heat, the hunter allows his prize to be cut up into exactly equal portions, which he then gives away to the entire group. Dentan explains that to express gratitude for the portion received indicates that you are the kind of ungenerous person who calculates how much you give and take: "In this con-

From *New Age Journal,* November/December 1989, pp. 42-45, 205-209. Excerpts from *Our Kind* by Marvin Harris. © 1989 by Marvin Harris. Reprinted by permission of HarperCollins Publishers.

text, saying 'thank you' is very rude, for it suggests, first, that one has calculated the amount of a gift and, second, that one did not expect the donor to be so generous." To call attention to one's generosity is to indicate that others are in debt to you and that you expect them to repay you. It is repugnant to egalitarian peoples even to suggest that they have been treated generously.

Canadian anthropologist Richard Lee tells how, through a revealing incident, he learned about this aspect of reciprocity. To please the !Kung, the "bushmen" of the Kalahari desert, he decided to buy a large ox and have it slaughtered as a present. After days of searching Bantu agricultural villages for the largest and fattest ox in the region, he acquired what appeared to be a perfect specimen. But his friends took him aside and assured him that he had been duped into buying an absolutely worthless animal. "Of course, we will eat it," they said, "but it won't fill us up—we will eat and go home to bed with stomachs rumbling." Yet, when Lee's ox was slaughtered, it turned out to be covered with a thick layer of fat. Later, his friends explained why they had said his gift was valueless, even though they knew better than he what lay under the animal's skin:

"Yes, when a young man kills much meat he comes to think of himself as a chief or a big man, and he thinks of the rest of us as his servants or inferiors. We can't accept this, we refuse one who boasts, for someday his pride will make him kill somebody. So we always speak of his meat as worthless. This way we cool his heart and make him gentle."

Lee watched small groups of men and women returning home every evening with the animals and wild fruits and plants that they had killed or collected. They shared everything equally, even with campmates who had stayed behind and spent the day sleeping or taking care of their tools and weapons.

"Not only do families pool that day's production, but the entire camp—residents and visitors alike—shares equally in the total quantity of food available," Lee observed. "The evening meal of any one family is made up of portions of food from each of the other families resident. There is a constant flow of nuts, berries, roots, and melons from one family fireplace to another, until each person has received an equitable portion. The following morning a different combination of foragers moves out of camp, and when they return late in the day, the distribution of foodstuffs is repeated."

In small, prestate societies, it was in everybody's best interest to maintain each other's freedom of access to the natural habitat. Suppose a !Kung with a lust for power were to get up and tell his campmates, "From now on, all this land and everything on it belongs to me. I'll let you use it but only with my permission and on the condition that I get first choice of anything you capture, collect, or grow." His campmates, thinking that he had certainly gone crazy, would pack up their few belongings, take a long walk, make a new camp, and resume their usual life of egalitarian reciprocity. The man who would be king would be left by himself to exercise a useless sovereignty.

THE HEADMAN: LEADERSHIP, NOT POWER

To the extent that political leadership exists at all among band-and-village societies, it is exercised by individuals called headmen. These headmen, however, lack the power to compel others to obey their orders. How can a leader be powerful and still lead?

The political power of genuine rulers depends on their ability to expel or exterminate disobedient individuals and groups. When a headman gives a command, however, he has no certain physical means of punishing those who disobey. So, if he wants to stay in "office," he gives few commands. Among the Eskimo, for instance, a group will follow an outstanding hunter and defer to his opinion with respect to choice of hunting spots. But in all other matters, the leader's opinion carries no more weight than any other man's. Similarly, among the !Kung, each band has its recognized leaders, most of whom are males. These men speak out more than others and are listened to

with a bit more deference. But they have no formal authority and can only persuade, never command. When Lee asked the !Kung whether they had headmen—meaning powerful chiefs—they told him, "Of course we have headmen! In fact, we are all headmen. Each one of us is headman over himself."

Headmanship can be a frustrating and irksome job. Among Indian groups such as the Mehinacu of Brazil's Zingu National Park, headmen behave something like zealous scoutmasters on overnight cookouts. The first one up in the morning, the headman tries to rouse his companions by standing in the middle of the village plaza and shouting to them. If something needs to be done, it is the headman who starts doing it, and it is the headman who works harder than anyone else. He sets an example not only for hard work but also for generosity: After a fishing or hunting expedition, he gives away more of his catch than anyone else does. In trading with other groups, he must be careful not to keep the best items for himself.

In the evening, the headman stands in the center of the plaza and exhorts his people to be good. He calls upon them to control their sexual appetites, work hard in their gardens, and take frequent baths in the river. He tells them not to sleep during the day or bear grudges against each other.

COPING WITH FREELOADERS

During the reign of reciprocal exchange and egalitarian headmen, no individual, family, or group smaller than the band or village itself could control access to natural resources. Rivers, lakes, beaches, oceans, plants and animals, the soil and subsoil were all communal property.

Among the !Kung, a core of people born in a particular territory say that they "own" the water holes and hunting rights, but this has no effect on the people who happen to be visiting and living with them at any given time. Since !Kung from neighboring bands are related through marriage, they often visit each other for months at a time and have free use of whatever resources they need without having to ask permission. Though people from distant bands must make a request to use another band's territory, the "owners" seldom refuse them.

The absence of private possession in land and other vital resources means that a form of communism probably existed among prehistoric hunting and collecting bands and small villages. Perhaps I should emphasize that this did not rule out the existence of private property. People in simple band-and-village societies own personal effects such as weapons, clothing, containers, ornaments, and tools. But why should anyone want to steal such objects? People who have a bush camp and move about a lot have no use for extra possessions. And since the group is small enough that everybody knows everybody else, stolen items cannot be used anonymously. If you want something, better to ask for it openly, since by the rules of reciprocity such requests cannot be denied.

I don't want to create the impression that life within egalitarian band-and-village societies unfolded entirely without disputes over possessions. As in every social group, nonconformists and malcontents tried to use the system for their own advantage. Inevitably there were freeloaders, individuals who consistently took more than they gave and lay back in their hammocks while others did the work. Despite the absence of a criminal justice system, such behavior eventually was punished. A widespread belief among band-and-village peoples attributes death and misfortune to the malevolent conspiracy of sorcerers. The task of identifying these evildoers falls to a group's shamans, who remain responsive to public opinion during their divinatory trances. Well-liked individuals who enjoy strong support from their families need not fear the shaman. But quarrelsome, stingy people who do not give as well as take had better watch out.

FROM HEADMAN TO BIG MAN

Reciprocity was not the only form of exchange practiced by egalitarian band-and-village peoples. Our kind long ago found other ways to give and take. Among them the form of exchange known as redistribution played a crucial role in creating distinctions of rank during the evolution of chiefdoms and states.

Redistribution occurs when people turn over food and other valuables to a prestigious figure such as a headman, to be pooled, divided into separate portions, and given out again. The primordial form of redistribution was probably keyed to seasonal hunts and harvests, when more food than usual became available.

True to their calling, headmen-redistributors not only work harder than their followers but also give more generously and reserve smaller and less desirable portions for themselves than for anyone else. Initially, therefore, redistribution strictly reinforced the political and economic equality associated with reciprocal exchange. The redistributors were compensated purely with admiration and in proportion to their success in giving bigger feasts, in personally contributing more than anybody else, and in asking little or nothing for their effort, all of which initially seemed an innocent extension of the basic principle of reciprocity.

But how little our ancestors understood what they were getting themselves into! For if it is a good thing to have a headman give feasts, why not have several headmen give feasts? Or, better yet, why not let success in organizing and giving feasts be the measure of one's legitimacy as a headman? Soon, where conditions permit, there are several would-be headmen vying with each other to hold the most lavish feasts and redistribute the most food and other valuables. In this fashion there evolved the nemesis that Richard Lee's !Kung informants had warned about: the youth who wants to be a "big man."

A classic anthropological study of big men was carried out by Douglas Oliver among the Siuai, a village people who live on the South Pacific island of Bougainville, in the Solomon Islands. In the Siuai language, big men were known as *mumis*. Every Siuai boy's highest ambition was to become a mumi. He began by getting married, working hard, and restricting his own consumption of meats and coconuts. His wife and parents, impressed with the seriousness of his intentions, vowed to help him prepare for his first feast. Soon his circle of supporters widened and he began to construct a clubhouse in which his male followers could lounge about and guests could be entertained and fed. He gave a feast at the consecration of the clubhouse; if this was a success, the circle of people willing to work for him grew larger still, and he began to hear himself spoken of as a mumi. Larger and larger feasts meant that the mumi's demands on his supporters became more irksome. Although they grumbled about how hard they had to work, they remained loyal as long as their mumi continued to maintain and increase his renown as a "great provider."

Finally the time came for the new mumi to challenge the older ones. He did this at a *muminai* feast, where both sides kept a tally of all the pigs, coconut pies, and sago-almond puddings given away by the host mumi and his followers to the guest mumi and his followers. If the guests could not reciprocate with a feast as lavish as that of the challengers, their mumi suffered a great social humiliation, and his fall from mumihood was immediate.

At the end of a successful feast, the greatest of mumis still faced a lifetime of personal toil and dependence on the moods and inclinations of his followers. Mumihood did not confer the power to coerce others into doing one's bidding, nor did it elevate one's standard of living above anyone else's. In fact, because giving things away was the essence of mumihood, great mumis consumed less meat and other delicacies than ordinary men. Among the Kaoka, another Solomon Islands group, there is the saying, "The giver of the feast takes the bones and the stale cakes; the meat and the fat go to the others." At one great feast attended by 1,100 people, the host mumi, whose name was Soni, gave away thirty-two pigs and a large quantity of sago-almond puddings. Soni himself and some of his closest followers went hungry. "We shall eat Soni's renown," they said.

FROM BIG MAN TO CHIEF

The slide (or ascent?) toward social stratification gained momentum wherever extra food produced by the inspired diligence of redistributors could be stored while awaiting muminai feasts, potlatches, and other occasions of redistribution. The more concentrated and abundant the harvest and the less perishable the crop, the greater its potential for endowing the big man with power. Though others would possess some stored-up foods of their own, the redistributor's stores would be the largest. In times of scarcity, people would come to him, expecting to be fed; in return, he could call upon those who had special skills to make cloth, pots, canoes, or a fine house for his own use. Eventually, the redistributor no longer needed to work in the fields to gain and surpass big-man status. Management of the harvest surpluses, a portion of which continued to be given to him for use in communal feasts and other communal projects (such as trading expeditions and warfare), was sufficient to validate his status. And, increasingly, people viewed this status as an office, a sacred trust, passed on from one generation to the next according to the rules of hereditary succession. His dominion was no longer a small, autonomous village but a large political community. The big man had become a chief.

Returning to the South Pacific and the Trobriand Islands, one can catch a glimpse of how these pieces of encroaching stratification fell into place. The Trobrianders had hereditary chiefs who held sway over more than a dozen villages containing several thousand people. Only chiefs could wear certain shell ornaments as the insignia of high rank, and it was forbidden for commoners to stand or sit in a position that put a chief's head at a lower elevation. British anthropologist Bronislaw Malinowski tells of seeing all the people present in the village of Bwoytalu drop from their verandas "as if blown down by a hurricane" at the sound of a drawn-out cry warning that an important chief was approaching.

Yams were the Trobrianders' staff of life; the chiefs validated their status by storing and redistributing copious quantities of them acquired through donations from their brothers-in-law at harvest time. Similar "gifts" were received by husbands who were commoners, but chiefs were polygymous and, having as many as a dozen wives, received many more yams than anyone else. Chiefs placed their yam supply on display racks specifically built for this purpose next to their houses. Commoners did the same, but a chief's yam racks towered over all the others.

This same pattern recurs, with minor variations, on several continents. Striking parallels were seen, for example, twelve thousand miles away from the Trobrianders, among chiefdoms that flourished throughout the southeastern region of the United States—specifically among the Cherokee, former inhabitants of Tennessee, as described by the eighteenth-century naturalist William Bartram.

At the center of the principal Cherokee settlements stood a large circular house where a council of chiefs discussed issues involving their villages and where redistributive feasts were held. The council of chiefs had a paramount who was the principal figure in the Cherokee redistributive network. At the harvest time a large crib, identified as the "chief's granary," was erected in each field. "To this," explained Bartram, "each family carries and deposits a certain quantity according to his ability or inclination, or none at all if he so chooses." The chief's granaries functioned as a public treasury in case of crop failure, a source of food for strangers or travelers, and as military store. Although every citizen enjoyed free access to the store, commoners had to acknowledge that it really belonged to the supreme chief, who had "an exclusive right and ability . . . to distribute comfort and blessings to the necessitous."

Supported by voluntary donations, chiefs could now enjoy lifestyles that set them increasingly apart from their followers. They could build bigger and finer houses for themselves, eat and dress more sumptuously, and enjoy the sexual favors and personal services of several wives. Despite these harbingers, people in chiefdoms voluntarily invested unprecedented amounts of labor on behalf of communal projects. They dug moats, threw up defensive earthen embankments, and erected great log palisades around their villages. They heaped up small mountains of rubble and soil to form platforms and mounds on top of which they built temples and big houses for their chief. Working in teams and using nothing but levers and rollers, they moved rocks weighing fifty tons or more and set them in precise lines and perfect circles, forming sacred precincts for communal rituals marking the change of seasons.

If this seems remarkable, remember that donated labor created the megalithic alignments of Stonehenge and Carnac, put up the great statues on Easter Island, shaped the huge stone heads of the Olmec in Vera Cruz, dotted Polynesia with ritual precincts set on great stone platforms, and filled the Ohio, Tennessee, and Mississippi valleys with hundreds of large mounds. Not until it was too late did people realize that their beautiful chiefs were about to keep the meat and fat for themselves while giving nothing but bones and stale cakes to their followers.

IN THE END

As we know, chiefdoms would eventually evolve into states, states into empires. From peaceful origins, humans created and mounted a wild beast that ate continents. Now that beast has taken us to the brink of global annihilation.

Will nature's experiment with mind and culture end in nuclear war? No one knows the answer. But I believe it is essential that we understand our past before we can create the best possible future. Once we are clear about the roots of human nature, for example, we can refute, once and for all, the notion that it is a biological imperative for our kind to form hierarchical groups. An observer viewing human life shortly after cultural takeoff would easily have concluded that our species was destined to be irredeemably egalitarian except for distinctions of sex and age. That someday the world would be divided into aristocrats and commoners, masters and slaves, billionaires and homeless beggars would have seemed wholly contrary to human nature as evidenced in the affairs of every human society then on Earth.

Of course, we can no more reverse the course of thousands of years of cultural evolution than our egalitarian ancestors could have designed and built the space shuttle. Yet, in striving for the preservation of mind and culture on Earth, it is vital that we recognize the significance of cultural takeoff and the great difference between biological and cultural evolution. We must rid ourselves of the notion that we are an innately aggressive species for whom war is inevitable. We must reject as unscientific claims that there are superior and inferior races and that the hierarchical divisions within and between societies are the consequences of natural selection rather than of a long process of cultural evolution. We must struggle to gain control over cultural selection through objective studies of the human condition and the recurrent process of history. Not only a more just society, but our very survival as a species may depend on it.

From peaceful origins, humans created and mounted a wild beast that ate continents. Now that beast has taken us to the brink of global annihilation.

An Unsettled People

Rural Nomads Seek a Place in Modern Ireland

Written and photographed by Amy Seidman

Amy Seidman is a free-lance photographer. This article was developed in field research conducted in 1989, 1990, and 1992.

They are Ireland's unrecognized minority—homeless and ostracized. Despite public disapproval, their family groups wander the Irish countryside. Other than a limited number of official halting sites they have no place to stop. Most live by the side of the road. They bathe, eat, and sleep in public. They live without electricity or permanent running water, bathing facilities, or toilets. Their child-mortality rate is similar to those in Third World countries, and there is a 98 percent illiteracy rate among adults. According to the Economic and Social Research Institute's 1985 report, "The circumstances of the Irish Travelling People are intolerable. No humane and decent society once made aware of such circumstances could permit them to persist."

But although local political groups and organizations have expressed the need to create permanent housing for the Travellers (most commonly described as "gypsies" or "tinkers"), the settled community prefers what Traveller Nell McDonaugh calls an

On the road again: Traveller Patty Donovan explains why his group moves on following another eviction.

"unspoken segregation." Travellers are evicted from areas not designated as official halting sites, and grassy lanes that Traveller groups have frequented for years are blocked and barred. Most official halting sites are located in undesirable, often industrial, areas.

Most settled people want nothing to do with Travellers. Popular belief has it that Travellers draw the dole (welfare) in more than one county at a time, are troublemakers, and leave piles of garbage in their wake. Many local people are opposed to having halting sites in their vicinity. Why should "respectable" people support itinerants?

But these "homeless" outcasts have filled a social niche in Ireland for centuries. Theirs may be a distinct lifestyle, and their traditions are unlike those of other Irish, but they are, nonetheless, Irish. In a traditionally rural society, Travellers served acceptable social purposes as itinerant farm workers, metal craftsmen, lace makers, and storytellers. But in today's settled, urban society, this integrated group of nomads are a people displaced by and at odds with contemporary expectations. They are a community without a place in its own homeland and a cultural group in danger of losing its identity.

TRADITIONAL CRAFTSMEN

Before automobiles, television, telephones, and mass production, Travellers provided essential goods and services to isolated communities. George and Sharon Gmelsh described the Travellers in their 1988 article "Nomads in Cities": "Gypsies were rural people who lived in the countryside for at least eight months of the year harvesting fruits and vegetables, producing tinware and handicrafts, selling small household wares, performing odd jobs, entertaining the populace, and dealing with farm animals."

Today, there is no longer a demand for storytellers or tinkers. In just a few decades, telephones replaced the need for news carriers, mass-produced household products replaced metal containers, automobiles replaced horses, and farm machines replaced manual labor. As a result, Travellers are neither economically nor socially capable of carrying out their traditional ways, and they maintain a marginal, sometimes desperate, existence.

The nickname tinker derives from their ability to work metal. Travellers repaired leaking metal buckets and jugs and created beautiful ornamental housewares out of copper and brass. Using simple hand tools to precisely shape metal, patient craftsmen pounded, cut, and stamped sheet metal into containers reputed to be watertight. Only about ten aging tinsmiths remain. They occasionally demonstrate their traditional craft at local youth centers where metal- and wood-working classes are held.

These Travellers still make ornamental containers to sell to tourists and other Travellers. Unfortunately, tourist demand for authentic metal containers is not sufficient to support the thousands of Travellers in Ireland today,

While her children play, a Traveller mother describes their home life.

giving little reason for their traditional trade to continue. Few of the elders have passed their knowledge to their children.

To earn money, Travellers have adapted their metalworking skills and now scrounge dump sites for scrap. Being called a tinker has become an insult, a reminder of their struggle to live in the modern world. Quite a few Travellers are apathetic about their future. Unemployed and with little to do, they draw the dole. Their lack of work adds to their increasingly low self-esteem, and, with little hope of changing their lives for the better, many turn to alcohol.

PRESERVING THEIR HERITAGE

In addition to transience and economic disparity, one more significant cultural difference separates Travellers from other Irish. This is their unique language, Cant, also known as Gammon or Shelta. "It was used by Travellers as a secret language when they felt they were in danger," Michael McDonaugh explains. (McDonaugh, the only college-educated Traveller in Ireland, was interviewed for this article in November 1992.)

Travellers still may use a few Cant words for secrecy while bargaining, to warn one another in the presence of authority, and in everyday conversation. Today, many young Travellers have little knowledge of their native tongue, but a knowledgeable person might know one hundred words, according to Sharon Gmelsh. Educated Travellers like McDonaugh believe in Cant as an important means of preserving their heritage. Their persistent admonitions to learn the language are causing its resurgence among young Travellers.

Knowing their heritage is becoming increasingly important. McDonaugh says, "Rebirth in the pride of our identity is the light at the end of the tunnel." Travellers insist their nomadic ancestors roamed Ireland for hundreds of years, a claim supported by linguistic ties between Cant to ancient Celtic and historical records that say Travellers were in Ireland during the twelfth century. Genetic studies comparing blood samples, conducted by physical anthropologists in the early 1970s, also demonstrated that Travellers are indigenous Irish people and not Romani.

Travellers live in mobile homes, caravans, or trailers. They stop wherever they find shelter and jobs and move on

Left: Adding the finishing touches to a new metal bucket, a Traveller metalworker practices a fast-disappearing skill. *Right:* A younger man with a knack for tinkering salvages metal from junkyards.

once they've depleted an area of casual work. McDonaugh reveals that the importance of mobility goes far beyond economic need and encompasses every part of the Travellers' lives. In his unpublished paper "The Functions of Nomadism," he states that travel is carried out in small groups of closely related nuclear families:

> When we travel, we meet up with other family members, often focusing on a social occasion such as a wedding or funeral. Even families who are sedentary most of the year feel a lot of joy and happiness when setting out on a journey, although it may only be a short one.

The Traveller's very identity requires "keeping in touch," and this in turn requires travel. Just as traveling gives an opportunity of meeting up with people, it also makes it possible to avoid people. This is of major importance to Travellers. When arguments arise, being able to move on means keeping the conflict from becoming too serious.

Keeping in touch through travel also means keeping tabs on a wide range of potential marriage partners. But keeping tabs on family members applies to everyone. When people meet, they pass on news, including scandal. Travellers live their lives balanced on a thin line, their every move watched by the whole family. If they do anything that brings them close to crossing it, they'll be let know about it in dozens of ways by dozens of people. And if they cross that line, it will be very, very hard to get back on the right side of it.

Mobility and the deliberate contact between families provide the cement that holds the Travellers' identity in place. Strong family values will be their cultural savior. Yet this close-knit community serves as a double-edged sword in relationships with settled people. Though most Travellers are quiet, decent people, all are considered likely vagrants or criminals. The group is condemned for mistakes made by a few. The individual Traveller who is

caught stealing or whose drunken stint ends in a barroom brawl rarely is singled out. Such actions are seen by the settled community as a reflection on all Travellers. As a result, Travellers commonly are refused service in bars and stores. Settled people fear that they may wreck the place or steal, or that regular customers won't return if Travellers frequent a place of business. As a result of this constant harassment, Travellers are wary of outsiders. One finds it impossible to enter the Travellers' world without an invitation.

MATCHMAKING AND MARRIAGE

One cannot become a Traveller by choice; it is a matter of birthright. Marriage plays a significant role in Traveller culture but also contributes to the people's social isolation. Marriages are arranged by parents. To avoid po-

Traveller youngsters visit with friends at their carts or wagons. Some homes, like this one, are richly hand-painted.

house affair to which all family members are welcome. Formal invitations are not needed, as word spreads by the grapevine. Celebrations tend to be wild and festive. They continue for days on end, giving a chance for relatives to catch up on news and for other matches to be arranged. Immediately after the wedding, a Traveller bride and groom go home to their separate families until they are ready to begin life together.

When they eventually move into their own caravan, it usually is parked close to Mum and Dad's. They are considered to be a separate nuclear family, however.

Family responsibilities are strictly defined. Traditionally, the woman cleans the home and minds the children, while the man goes out to make money. Although the husband has ultimate authority in the family, the wife makes all

tential health defects caused by inbreeding, matches are carefully made with distant family members. Marriage or integration with settled people (those "not of the family") is almost nonexistent.

Once a young person reaches puberty, the parents begin a long arrangement process during which the dowry is agreed on, usually in the form of a gold ring. This custom is an insurance policy. If all else fails, the portable wealth can be sold to feed the young people, no matter where they are. Parents also purchase a caravan for the couple and pay for an elaborate wedding celebration. The cost of a marriage can exceed fifteen thousand dollars or more, requiring the average, poverty-stricken Traveller family to save for this event over many years. This is the most important obligation Traveller parents have, and it is one in which they take great pride.

A wedding is the most celebrated event in their culture. It is an open-

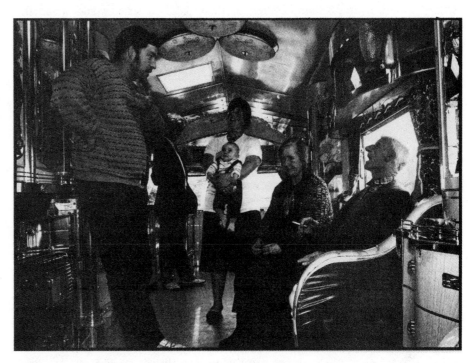

Above: *Michael McDonaugh (left) socializes with relatives inside a shiny metal home on wheels, a tinsmith's masterpiece.* Below: *Like all Travellers, cousins Teresa, Bridget, and Winnie Stokes, and Tina Reilly revere their heritage, holding pictures of their grandfathers.*

the decisions on how the household is run and is respectfully given free rein to do so.

Since they commonly marry cousins, couples often share the same grandparents. Most Travellers can trace their relations through an intricate web of siblings, cousins, aunts, and uncles. Although it is virtually taboo to marry outside the family, marriage with outsiders is given slightly more thought today than before. A Traveller's extended family averages one hundred individual yet related subgroups, each with about eight children. Over 2,850 Traveller families were identified in 1986, and the numbers are increasing. Explains McDonaugh, "We understand our family membership in terms of a vast extended family."

Although marriages are arranged, individuals are given the opportunity to reject a match should they despise proposed mates. Commonly, parents will review potential choices, deciding for their children who would make the

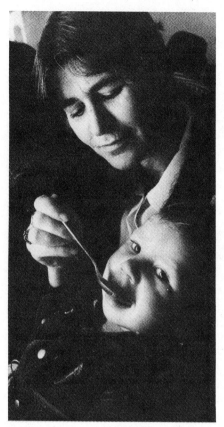

Adults have to worry about where the next meal is coming from, but children only need Mom.

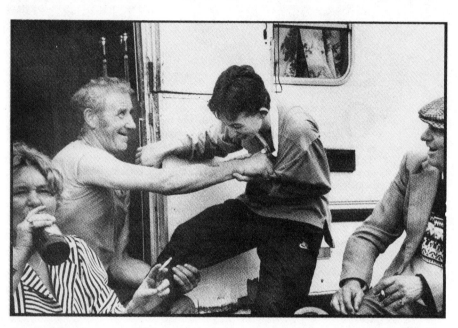

Above: *Larry Donovan and his young cousin have some fun.* Below: *Seemingly enjoying the work, two Traveller lads prepare a pony for the next move.*

most suitable mate. The would-be pair is then consulted. If no serious objections exist, the engagement, usually lasting two years or more, is arranged between the two sets of parents. The potential couple meets briefly under the strict supervision of several chaperons but never dates. When McDonaugh was seventeen, his parents matched him with his cousin Nell. Recalls Nell: "Neither Michael nor I had ever been out together before our marriage. In fact, I was three days married before I spoke to him!"

Falling in love before marriage is scarcely a consideration. In rare cases, a young man who fancies a girl from afar may hint to his or her parents about a match. Actually asking for a match is even rarer and considered very modern. When considering a potential match, Travellers usually base their decision on the marriage's effect on other family members. At times Traveller families have been known to feud, making matches between family groups with conflicting views undesirable. Because Travellers' lives revolve around family ties, considering a new union in regard to its effect on extended relations is far more important than romantic love.

SETTLEMENT DEPRESSION

The Irish nomad holds contempt for the idea of settling permanently. McDonaugh claims, "In some cases, Travellers have become physically sick and very depressed when they move into houses and never adjust psychologically to living in the one place permanently. Many Travellers have left houses for these reasons."

Indeed, the Travellers' personal and cultural identities may be completely at odds with the concepts of settled life. A recent government report, *School Provision for Gypsy and Traveller Children,* states that

a Traveller is someone who remains detached from his surroundings, who is able to pick up and move whenever it is useful or necessary to do so. . . . There is an important difference between the objective reality of travelling (the fact of moving from one place to another) and the subjective reality: feeling oneself to be a Traveller. . . . Nomadism is as much a state of mind as a state of fact.

When faced with settlement, most reassure themselves that the move into a house will be temporary. Travellers are actively lobbying for permanent housing schemes and halting sites that take into account their psychological and cultural need to be mobile. "Whether living on a halting site or in a house, accommodation is always seen as temporary," explains McDonaugh, adding that sedentary families are seen by others as having "lost their identity as Travellers."

The McDonaughs live "illegally," in an unofficial halting site outside the town of Navan. There are about 150 families with forty trailers at the site. Water must be fetched from a spring two miles away. Both Michael and Nell are active in programs to aid other Travellers. They are well read and extremely bright. Recently, Nell went back to school to get her degree. Michael is active in developmental youth programs.

Currently employed as a social worker with the Navan Travellers Association, McDonaugh previously was employed by the Committee to Monitor the Implementation of Government Policy on Travelling People. He visited most of the nomadic families across Ireland, assessing their living standards. His work gave him personal insight on how to help his people help themselves. When asked his opinion on current issues, McDonaugh states emphatically, "Some would curse the day settled people began interfering with Travellers. Through [receiving] Christian giving we have lost our resourcefulness and become dependent upon the settled agencies."

Most of the agencies, communities, and other groups representing Irish Travellers are composed of settled people. McDonaugh feels strongly that his people should be allowed to make decisions about their future for themselves. "Trying to accelerate change does damage to us," he says. "If Travellers were allowed to change as a society and culture, without interference, the change would be natural to our people. Many settled people speak on our behalf but don't ask for our opinion. Then on bended knees they expect us to thank them for damaging us.

"Inferiority complexes and identity crises exist among Travellers who promote settled ways of life. Their goal is equality. They want us to be like settled people, because all their lives they were told that they were no good."

"Yet when settled people interfere, saying, 'We are all the same,' they are actually damaging because we are *not* all the same. Subtle differences exist between us in many ways, and the people who provide to [try to help] us only provide with settled ways. There is an inevitable [cultural] clash, after which settled people say Travellers are ungrateful."

Because Travellers now are recognized by scientists as a distinct and separate people, they are seeking political rights as an indigenous Irish minority to escape the influences of the settled community. A glimmer of hope exists for them. The standard Irish education does not provide programs and facilities suitable for Travellers, but some Traveller children are able to attend special schools designed to accommodate their unusual life-style. Nowadays, 35–50 percent of children are literate, thus boosting their future ability to make decisions for themselves in a modern society.

Michael and Nell hope to help other Travellers realize that they are equal to settled people, to enhance their lives without compromising the traditional life-style. The McDonaughs want to be recognized as being Travellers, and to know that being one is acceptable. In the words of a poem by Theresa McInerney:

I would never deny I am a Traveller,
no matter where I go . . .
We will let them talk about us
and say what they want . . .
For they are not our kind of people
and will never know our ways.

Other Families, Other Ways

Since most people in small-scale societies of the past spent their whole lives within a local area, it is understandable that their primary interactions—economic, religious, and otherwise—were with their relatives. As shown in "Memories of a !Kung Girlhood," every age group, from children to the very old, played an active and indispensable role in the survival of the collective unit. It also makes sense that, through marriage customs, they strengthened those kinship relationships that clearly defined their mutual rights and obligations. Indeed, the resulting family structure may be surprisingly flexible and adaptive, as witnessed in "When Brothers Share a Wife," by Melvyn Goldstein, in "Family Planning, Amazon Style," by Warren Hern, and in "Arranging a Marriage in India," by Serena Nanda. It is for these reasons that anthropologists have looked upon family and kinship as the key mechanisms through which culture is transmitted from one generation to the next. Since social changes take place slowly, and as social horizons have widened accordingly, family relationships and community alliances are increasingly based upon new sets of principles. There is no question that kinship networks have diminished in size and strength as we have increasingly become involved with others as co-workers in a market economy. Our associations depend more and more upon factors such as personal aptitudes, educational backgrounds, and job opportunities. Yet, the family is still there. It is smaller, but it still functions in its age-old nurturing and protective role, even under conditions of extreme poverty and a high infant mortality rate (see "Death Without Weeping" by Nancy Scheper-Hughes). Beyond the immediate family, the situation is still in a state of flux. Certain ethnic groups, especially those living in poverty, still have a need for a broader network, and in some ways they seem to be reformulating those ties.

Where the changes described in this section will lead us and which ones will ultimately prevail, we do not know. One thing is certain: anthropologists will be there to document the trends, for the discipline of anthropology has had to change as well. One important feature of the articles in this section is the growing interest of anthropologists in the study of complex societies, where old theoretical perspectives are increasingly inadequate.

Current trends do not necessarily mean the eclipse of the kinship unit, however, as "Young Traders of Northern Nigeria" illustrates. The message is that the large family network is still the best guarantee of individual survival and well-being in an urban setting.

Looking Ahead: Challenge Questions

In what ways is !Kung childhood similar to childhood in American culture?

What can contemporary hunter-collector societies tell us about the quality of life in the prehistoric past?

Why is "fraternal polyandry" socially acceptable in Tibet but not in our society?

Why is polygyny practiced among the Shipibo?

What are the implications of Western education for the ability of Hausa women to earn an income?

How do differences in child care relate to economic circumstances?

What are the pros and cons of arranged marriages versus freedom of choice?

Unit 4

Memories of a !Kung Girlhood

A woman of the hunter-gatherers recalls her childhood; the differences in her way of life fade in the face of basic human similarities.

Marjorie Shostak

Marjorie Shostak is a writer and photographer who first became interested in the !Kung while working with her husband, an anthropologist. For two years, from 1969 to 1971, she lived and worked among the !Kung San of Botswana as a research assistant to Irven DeVore, an anthropologist at Harvard University. After developing fluency in the !Kung language, Shostak began to tape interviews with !Kung women. In 1975 she returned to Botswana for six months to complete the life histories of several women and to correct ambiguous translations. At the same time she collaborated with four other researchers in a study of hormone level and mood fluctuations in relation to menstrual cycles.

I remember when my mother was pregnant with Kumsa. I was still small (about four years old) and I asked, "Mommy, that baby inside you . . . when that baby is born, will it come out from your bellybutton?" She said, "No, it won't come out from there. When you give birth, a baby comes from here." And she pointed to her genitals.

When she gave birth to Kumsa, I wanted the milk she had in her breasts,

and when she nursed him, my eyes watched as the milk spilled out. I cried all night . . . cried and cried.

Once when my mother was with him and they were lying down asleep, I took him away from her and put him down on the other side of the hut. Then I lay down beside her. While she slept I squeezed some milk and started to nurse, and nursed and nursed and nursed. Maybe she thought it was him. When she woke and saw me she cried, "Where . . . tell me . . . what did you do with Kumsa? Where is he?"

I told her he was lying down inside the hut. She grabbed me and pushed me hard away from her. I lay there and cried. She took Kumsa, put him down beside her, and insulted me by cursing my genitals.

"Are you crazy? Nisa-Big Genitals, what's the matter with you? What craziness grabbed you that you took a baby, dropped him somewhere else, and then lay down beside me and nursed? I thought it was Kumsa."

When my father came home, she told him, "Do you see what kind of mind your daughter has? Hit her! She almost killed Kumsa. This little baby, this little thing here, she took from my side and dropped him somewhere else.

I was lying here holding him and fell asleep. She came and took him away, left him by himself, then lay down where he had been and nursed. Now, hit her!"

I said, "You're lying! Me . . . daddy, I didn't nurse. Really I didn't. I don't even want her milk anymore."

He said, "If I ever hear of this again, I'll hit you. Now, don't ever do that again!"

I said, "Yes, he's my little brother, isn't he? My little baby brother and I *love* him. I won't do that again. He can nurse all by himself. Daddy, even if you're not here, I won't try to steal Mommy's breasts. They belong to my brother."

We lived and lived, and as I kept growing, I started to carry Kumsa around on my shoulders. My heart was happy and I started to love him. I carried him everywhere. I would play with him for a while, and whenever he started to cry, I'd take him over to mother to nurse. Then I'd take him back with me and we'd play together again.

That was when Kumsa was still little. But once he was older and started to talk and then to run around, that's when we were mean to each other all

From *Human Nature,* June 1978, pp. 80, 82-88. For permission to photocopy this selection, please contact Harvard University Press. Reprinted by permission of the publishers from *Kalahari Hunter-Gatherers: Studies of The !Kung San and Their Neighbors,* edited by Richard Lee and Irven DeVore. Cambridge, MA: Harvard University Press. © 1976 by the President and Fellows of Harvard College.

the time. Sometimes we hit each other. Other times I grabbed him and bit him and said, "Ooooh . . . what is this thing that has such a horrible face and no brains and is so mean? Why is it so mean to me when I'm not doing anything to it?" Then he said, "I'm going to *hit* you!" And I said, "You're just a *baby!* I, *I* am the one who's going to hit *you.* Why are you so miserable to me?" I insulted him and he insulted me and then I insulted him back. We just stayed together and played like that.

Once, when our father came back carrying meat, we both called out, "Ho, ho, Daddy! Ho, ho, Daddy!" But when I heard him say, "Daddy, Daddy," I yelled, "Why are you greeting my father? He's *my* father, isn't he? You can only say, 'Oh, hello Father.' " But he called out, "Ho, ho . . . Daddy!" I said, "Be quiet! Only *I* will greet him. Is he your father? I'm going to hit you!"

We fought and argued until Mother finally stopped us. Then we just sat around while she cooked the meat.

This was also when I used to take food. It happened over all kinds of food—sweet *nin* berries or *klaru* bulbs . . . other times it was mongongo nuts. Sometimes before my mother left to go gathering, she'd leave food inside a leather pouch and hang it high on one of the branches inside the hut.

But as soon as she was gone, I'd take some of whatever food was left in the bag. If it was *klaru,* I'd find the biggest bulbs and take them. I'd hang the bag back on the branch and go sit somewhere to eat them.

One time I sat down in the shade of a tree while my parents gathered food nearby. As soon as they had moved away from me, I climbed the tree where they had left a pouch hanging, full of *klaru,* and took the bulbs.

I had my own little pouch, the one my father had made me, and I took the bulbs and put them in the pouch. Then I climbed down and sat waiting for my parents to return.

They came back. "Nisa, you ate the *klaru!*" What do you have to say for yourself?" I said, "Uhn uh, I didn't eat them."

I started to cry. Mother hit me and yelled, "Don't take things. You can't seem to understand! I tell you but you

don't listen. Don't your ears hear when I talk to you?"

I said, "Uhn uh. Mommy's been making me feel bad for too long now. She keeps saying I steal things and hits me so that my skin hurts. I'm going to stay with Grandma!"

But when I went to my grandmother, she said, "No, I can't take care of you now. If I try you will be hungry. I am old and just go gathering one day at a time. In the morning I just rest. We would sit together and hunger would kill you. Now go back and sit beside your mother and father."

I said, "No, Daddy will hit me. Mommy will hit me. I want to stay with you."

So I stayed with her. Then one day she said, "I'm going to bring you back to your mother and father." She took me to them, saying, "Today I'm giving Nisa back to you. But isn't there someone here who will take good care of

---

About the !Kung

Nisa is a 50-year-old !Kung woman, one of an estimated 13,000 !Kung San living on the northern fringe of the Kalahari Desert in southern Africa. Much of her life—as daughter, sister, wife, mother, and lover—has been spent in the semi-nomadic pursuit of food and water in the arid savanna.

Like many !Kung, Nisa is a practiced storyteller. The !Kung have no written language with which to record their experiences, and people sit around their fires for hours recounting recent events and those long past. Voices rise and fall, hands move in dramatic gestures, and bird and animal sounds are imitated as stories are told and retold, usually with much exaggeration.

I collected stories of Nisa's life as part of my anthropological effort to record the lives of !Kung women in their own words. Nisa enjoyed working with the machine that "grabs your voice" and the interviews with her produced 25 hours of tape and 425 pages of transcription. The excerpts included here are faithful to her narrative except where awkward or discontinuous passages have been modified or deleted, and where long passages have been shortened.

Although most of Nisa's memories are typical of !Kung life, her early memories, like those of most people, are probably idiosyncratic mixtures of fact and fantasy. Her memories of being hit for taking food are probably not accurate. The !Kung tend to be lenient and indulgent with their children, and researchers have rarely

observed any physical punishment or the withholding of food.

Strong feelings of sibling rivalry, like those that Nisa describes, are common. !Kung women wean their children as soon as they find they are pregnant again because they believe the milk belongs to the fetus. Children are not usually weaned until they are three or four years old, which tends to make them resent their younger siblings. Nisa's complaints about being given too little food probably stem from her jealousy of her little brother.

Despite the lack of privacy, !Kung parents are generally discreet in their sexual activity. As children become aware of it, they engage each other in sexual play. Parents say they do not approve of this play but do little to stop it.

Many !Kung girls first marry in their early teens, but these relationships are not consummated until the girls begin menstruating around the age of 16. Early marriages are relatively unstable. Nisa was betrothed twice before marrying Tashay.

The exclamation point at the beginning of !Kung represents one of the many click sounds in the !Kung language. Clicks are made by the tongue breaking air pockets in different parts of the mouth; but the notation for clicks has been eliminated from the translation in all cases except for the name of the !Kung people. Nisa, for instance, should be written as N≠isa.

Marjorie Shostak

her? You don't just hit a child like this one. She likes food and likes to eat. All of you are lazy and you've just left her so she hasn't grown well. You've killed this child with hunger. Look at her now, how small she still is."

Oh, but my heart was happy! Grandmother was scolding Mother! I had so much happiness in my heart that I laughed and laughed. But then, when Grandmother went home and left me there, I cried and cried.

My father started to yell at me. He didn't hit me. His anger usually came out only from his mouth. "You're so senseless! Don't you realize that after you left, everything felt less important? We wanted you to be with us. Yes, even your mother wanted you and missed you. Today, everything will be all right when you stay with us. Your mother will take you where she goes; the two of you will do things together and go gathering together."

Then when my father dug *klaru* bulbs, I ate them, and when he dug *chon* bulbs, I ate them. I ate everything they gave me, and I wasn't yelled at any more.

Mother and I often went to the bush together. The two of us would walk until we arrived at a place where she collected food. She'd set me down in the shade of a tree and dig roots or gather nuts nearby.

Once I left the tree and went to play in the shade of another tree. I saw a tiny steenbok, one that had just been born, hidden in the grass and among the leaves. It was lying there, its little eye just looking out at me.

I thought, "What should I do?" I shouted, *"Mommy!"* I just stood there and it just lay there looking at me.

Suddenly I knew what to do—I ran at it, trying to grab it. But it jumped up and ran away and I started to chase it. It was running and I was running and it was crying as it ran. Finally, I got very close and put my foot in its way, and it fell down. I grabbed its legs and started to carry it back. It was crying, "Ehn . . . ehn . . . ehn. . . ."

Its mother had been close by and when she heard it call, she came running. As soon as I saw her, I started to run again. I wouldn't give it back to its mother!

I called out, "Mommy! Come! Help me with this steenbok! Mommy! The steenbok's mother is coming for me! Run! Come! Take this steenbok from me."

But soon the mother steenbok was no longer following, so I took the baby, held its feet together, and banged it hard against the sand until I killed it. It was no longer crying; it was dead. I felt wonderfully happy. My mother came running and I gave it to her to carry.

The two of us spent the rest of the day walking in the bush. While my mother was gathering, I sat in the shade of a tree, waiting and playing with the dead steenbok. I picked it up. I tried to make it sit up, to open its eyes. I looked at them. After mother had dug enough *sha* roots, we left and returned home.

My father had been out hunting that day and had shot a large steenbok with his arrows. He had skinned it and brought it back hanging on a branch.

"Ho, ho. Daddy killed a steenbok!" I said. "Mommy! Daddy! I'm not going to let anyone have any of *my* steenbok. Now *don't* give it to anyone else. After you cook it, just my little brother and I will eat it, just the two of us."

I remember another time when we were traveling from one place to another and the sun was burning. It was the hot, dry season and there was no water anywhere. The sun was burning! Kumsa had already been born and I was still small.

After we had been walking a long time, my older brother Dau spotted a beehive. We stopped while he and my father chopped open the tree. All of us helped take out the honey. I filled my own little container until it was completely full.

We stayed there, eating the honey, and I found myself getting very thirsty. Then we left and continued to walk, I carrying my honey and my digging stick. Soon the heat began killing us and we were all dying of thirst. I started to cry because I wanted water so badly.

After a while, we stopped and sat down in the shade of a baobab tree. There was still no water anywhere. We just sat in the shade like that.

Finally my father said, "Dau, the rest of the family will stay here under this baobab. But you, take the water

containers and get us some water. There's a well not too far away."

Dau collected the empty ostrich eggshell containers and the large clay pot and left. I lay there, already dead from thirst and thought, "If I stay with Mommy and Daddy, I'll surely die of thirst. Why don't I follow my big brother and go drink water with him?"

With that I jumped up and ran after him, crying out, calling to him, following his tracks. But he didn't hear me. I kept running . . . crying and calling out.

Finally, he heard something and turned to see. There I was. "Oh, no!" he said. "Nisa's followed me. What can I do with her now that she's here?" He just stood there and waited for me to catch up. He picked me up and carried me high up on his shoulder, and along we went. He really liked me!

The two of us went on together. We walked and walked and walked and walked. Finally, we reached the well. I ran to the water and drank, and soon my heart was happy again. We filled the water containers, put them in a twine mesh sack, and my brother carried it on his back. Then he took me and put me on his shoulder again.

We walked the long way back until we arrived at the baobab where our parents were sitting. They drank the water. Then they said, "How well our children have done, bringing us this water! We are alive once again!"

We just stayed in the shade of the baobab. Later we left and traveled to another water hole where we settled for a while. My heart was happy . . . eating honey and just living.

We lived there, and after some time passed, we saw the first rain clouds. One came near but just hung in the sky. More rain clouds came over and they too just stood there. Then the rain started to spill itself and it came pouring down.

The rainy season had finally come. The sun rose and set, and the rain spilled itself and fell and kept falling. It fell without ceasing. Soon the water pans were full. And my heart! My heart within me was happy and we lived and ate meat and mongongo nuts. There was more meat and it was all delicious.

And there were caterpillars to eat, those little things that crawl along going "mmm . . . mmmmm . . . mmmmm. . . ." People dug roots and collected nuts and berries and brought home more and more food. There was plenty to eat, and people kept bringing meat back on sticks and hanging it in the trees.

My heart was bursting. I ate lots of food and my tail was wagging, always wagging about like a little dog. I'd laugh with my little tail, laugh with a little donkey's laugh, a tiny thing that is. I'd throw my tail one way and the other, shouting, "Today I'm going to eat caterpillars . . . *cat-er-pillars!*" Some people gave me meat broth to drink, and others prepared the skins of caterpillars and roasted them for me to eat, and I ate and ate and ate. Then I went to sleep.

But that night, after everyone was dead asleep, I peed right in my sleeping place. In the morning, when everyone got up, I just lay there. The sun rose and had set itself high in the sky, and I was still lying there. I was afraid of people shaming me. Mother said, "Why is Nisa acting like this and refusing to leave her blankets when the sun is sitting up in the sky? Oh . . . she has probably wet herself."

When I did get up, my heart felt miserable. I thought, "I've peed on myself and now everyone's going to laugh at me." I asked one of my friends, "How come, after I ate all those caterpillars, when I went to sleep I peed in my bed?" Then I thought, "Tonight, when this day is over, I'm going to lie down separate from the others. If I pee in my bed again, won't mother and father hit me?"

When a child sleeps beside her mother, in front, and her father sleeps behind and makes love to her mother, the child watches. Her parents don't fear her, a small child, because even if the child sees, even if she hears, she is unaware of what it is her parents are doing. She is still young and without sense. Perhaps this is the way the child learns. The child is still senseless, without intelligence, and just watches.

If the child is a little boy, when he plays with other children, he plays sex with them and teaches it to himself, just like a baby rooster teaches itself. The little girls also learn it by themselves.

Little boys are the first ones to know its sweetness. Yes, a young girl, while she is still a child, her thoughts don't know it. A boy has a penis, and maybe, while he is still inside his mother's belly, he already knows about sex.

When you are a child you play at nothing things. You build little huts and play. Then you come back to the village and continue to play. If people bother you, you get up and play somewhere else.

Once we left a pool of rain water where we had been playing and went to the little huts we had made. We stayed there and played at being hunters. We went out tracking animals, and when we saw one, we struck it with our make-believe arrows. We took some leaves and hung them over a stick and pretended it was meat. Then we carried it back to our village. When we got back, we stayed there and ate the meat and then the meat was gone. We went out again, found another animal, and killed it.

Sometimes the boys asked if we wanted to play a game with our genitals and the girls said no. We said we didn't want to play that game, but would like to play other games. The boys told us that playing sex was what playing was all about. That's the way we grew up.

When adults talked to me I listened. Once they told me that when a young woman grows up, she takes a husband. When they first talked to me about it, I said: "What? What kind of thing am I that I should take a husband? Me, when I grow up, I won't marry. I'll just lie by myself. If I married a man, what would I think I would be doing it for?"

My father said: "Nisa, I am old. I am your father and I am old; your mother's old, too. When you get married, you will gather food and give it to your husband to eat. He also will do things for you and give you things you can wear. But if you refuse to take a husband, who will give you food to eat? Who will give you things to have? Who will give you things to wear?"

I said to my father and mother, "No. There's no question in my mind—I refuse a husband. I won't take one. Why should I? As I am now, I am still a child and won't marry."

Then I said to Mother, "Why don't you marry the man you want for me and sit him down beside Father? Then you'll have two husbands."

Mother said: "Stop talking nonsense. I'm not going to marry him; you'll marry him. A husband is what I want to give you. Yet you say I should marry him. Why are playing with me with this talk?"

We just continued to live after that, kept on living and more time passed. One time we went to the village where Old Kantla and his son Tashay were living. My friend Nhuka and I had gone to the water well to get water, and Tashay and his family were there, having just come back from the bush. When Tashay saw me, he decided he wanted to marry me. He called Nhuka over and said, "Nhuka, that young woman, that beautiful young woman . . . what is her name?"

Nhuka told him my name was Nisa, and he said, "That young woman . . . I'm going to tell Mother and Father about her. I'm going to ask them if I can marry her."

The next evening there was a dance at our village, and Tashay and his parents came. We sang and danced into the night. Later his father said, "We have come here, and now that the dancing is finished, I want to speak to you. Give me your child, the child you gave birth to. Give her to me, and I will give her to my son. Yesterday, while we were at the well, he saw your child. When he returned he told me in the name of what he felt that I should come and ask for her today so I could give her to him."

My mother said, "Yes . . . but I didn't give birth to a woman, I bore a child. She doesn't think about marriage, she just doesn't think about the inside of her marriage hut."

Then my father said, "Yes, I also conceived that child, and it is true: She just doesn't think about marriage. When she marries a man, she leaves him and marries another man and leaves him and gets up and marries another man and leaves him. She refuses men completely. There are two men whom she has already refused. So when I look at Nisa today, I say she is not a woman."

Then Tashay's father said, "Yes, I have listened to what you have said.

That, of course, is the way of a child; it is a child's custom to do that. She gets married many times until one day she likes one man. Then they stay together. That is a child's way."

They talked about the marriage and agreed to it. In the morning Tashay's parents went back to their camp, and we went to sleep. When the morning was late in the sky, his relatives came back. They stayed around and his parents told my aunt and my mother that they should all start building the marriage hut. They began building it together, and everyone was talking and talking. There were a lot of people there. Then all the young men went and brought Tashay to the hut. They stayed around together near the fire. I was at Mother's hut. They told two of my friends to get me. But I said to myself, "Ooooh . . . I'll just run away."

When they came, they couldn't find me. I was already out in the bush, and I just sat there by the base of a tree. Soon I heard Nhuka call out, "Nisa . . . Nisa . . . my friend . . . there are things there that will bite and kill you. Now leave there and come back here."

They came and brought me back. Then they laid me down inside the hut. I cried and cried, and people told me: "A man is not something that kills you; he is someone who marries you, and becomes like your father or your older brother. He kills animals and gives you things to eat. Even tomorrow he would do that. But because you are crying, when he kills an animal, he will eat it himself and won't give you any. Beads, too. He will get some beads, but he won't give them to you. Why are you afraid of your husband and why are you crying?"

I listened and was quiet. Later Tashay lay down by the mouth of the hut, near the fire, and I was inside. He came in only after he thought I was asleep. Then he lay down and slept. I woke while it was still dark and thought,

"How am I going to jump over him? How can I get out and go to Mother's hut?" Then I thought, "This person has married me . . . yes." And, I just lay there. Soon the rain came and beat down and it fell until dawn broke.

In the morning, he got up first and sat by the fire. I was frightened. I was so afraid of him, I just lay there and waited for him to go away before I got up.

We lived together a long time and began to learn to like one another before he slept with me. The first time I didn't refuse. I agreed just a little and he lay with me. But the next morning my insides hurt. I took some leaves and wound them around my waist, but it continued to hurt. Later that day I went with the women to gather mongongo nuts. The whole time I thought "Ooooh . . . what has he done to my insides that they feel this way."

That evening we lay down again. But this time I took a leather strap, held my skin apron tightly against me, tied up my genitals with it, and then tied the strap to the hut's frame. I didn't want him to take me again. The two of us lay there and after a while he started to touch me. When he reached my stomach, he felt the leather strap. He felt around to see what it was. He said, "What is this woman doing? Yesterday she lay with me so nicely when I came to her. Why has she tied up her genitals this way?

He sat me up and said, "Nisa . . . Nisa . . . what happened? Why are you doing this?" I didn't answer him.

"What are you so afraid of that you tied your genitals?"

I said, "I'm not afraid of anything."

He said, "No, now tell me what you are afraid of. In the name of what you did, I am asking you."

I said, "I refuse because yesterday when you touched me my insides hurt."

He said, "Do you see me as someone who kills people? Am I going to eat you? I am not going to kill you. I have

married you and I want to make love to you. Have you seen any man who has married a woman and who just lives with her and doesn't have sex with her?"

I said, "No, I still refuse it! I refuse sex. Yesterday my insides hurt, that's why."

He said, "Mmm. Today you will lie there by yourself. But tomorrow I will take you."

The next day I said to him, "Today I'm going to lie here, and if you take me by force, you will have me. You will have me because today I'm just going to lie here. You are obviously looking for some 'food,' but I don't know if the food I have is food at all, because even if you have some, you won't be full."

I just lay there and he did his work.

We lived and lived, and soon I started to like him. After that I was a grown person and said to myself, "Yes, without doubt, a man sleeps with you. I thought maybe he didn't."

We lived on, and then I loved him and he loved me, and I kept on loving him. When he wanted me I didn't refuse and he just slept with me. I thought, "Why have I been so concerned about my genitals? They are, after all, not so important. So why was I refusing them?"

I thought that and gave myself to him and gave and gave. We lay with one another, and my breasts had grown very large. I had become a woman.

FOR FURTHER INFORMATION:

Lee, Richard, B., and Irven DeVore, eds. *Kalahari Hunter-Gatherers: Studies of the !Kung San and Their Neighbors.* Harvard University Press, 1976.

Lee, Richard B., and Irven DeVore, eds. *Man the Hunter.* Aldine, 1968.

Marshall, Lorna. *The !Kung of Nyae Nyae.* Harvard University Press, 1976.

Shostak, Marjorie. "Life before Horticulture: An African Gathering and Hunting Society." *Horticulture*, Vol. 55, No. 2, 1977.

When Brothers Share a Wife

Among Tibetans, the good life relegates many women to spinsterhood

Melvyn C. Goldstein

Melvyn C. Goldstein, now a professor of anthropology at Case Western Reserve University in Cleveland, has been interested in the Tibetan practice of fraternal polyandry (several brothers marrying one wife) since he was a graduate student in the 1960s.

Eager to reach home, Dorje drives his yaks hard over the 17,000-foot mountain pass, stopping only once to rest. He and his two older brothers, Pema and Sonam, are jointly marrying a woman from the next village in a few weeks, and he has to help with the preparations.

Dorje, Pema, and Sonam are Tibetans living in Limi, a 200-square-mile area in the northwest corner of Nepal, across the border from Tibet. The form of marriage they are about to enter—fraternal polyandry in anthropological parlance—is one of the world's rarest forms of marriage but is not uncommon in Tibetan society, where it has been practiced from time immemorial. For many Tibetan social strata, it traditionally represented the ideal form of marriage and family.

The mechanics of fraternal polyandry are simple. Two, three, four, or more brothers jointly take a wife, who leaves her home to come and live with them. Traditionally, marriage was arranged by parents, with children, particularly females, having little or no say. This is changing somewhat nowadays, but it is still unusual for children to marry without their parents' consent. Marriage ceremonies vary by income and region and range from all the brothers sitting together as grooms to only the eldest one formally doing so. The age of the brothers plays an important role in determining this: very young brothers almost never participate in actual marriage ceremonies, although they typically join the marriage when they reach their midteens.

The eldest brother is normally dominant in terms of authority, that is, in managing the household, but all the brothers share the work and participate as sexual partners. Tibetan males and females do not find the sexual aspect of sharing a spouse the least bit unusual, repulsive, or scandalous, and the norm is for the wife to treat all the brothers the same.

Offspring are treated similarly. There is no attempt to link children biologically to particular brothers, and a brother shows no favoritism toward his child even if he knows he is the real father because, for example, his other brothers were away at the time the wife became pregnant. The children, in turn, consider all of the brothers as their fathers and treat them equally, even if they also know who is their real father. In some regions children use the term "father" for the eldest brother and "father's brother" for the others, while in other areas they call all the brothers by one term, modifying this by the use of "elder" and "younger."

Unlike our own society, where monogamy is the only form of marriage permitted, Tibetan society allows a variety of marriage types, including monogamy, fraternal polyandry, and polygyny. Fraternal polyandry and monogamy are the most common forms of marriage, while polygyny typically occurs in cases where the first wife is barren. The widespread practice of fraternal polyandry, therefore, is not the outcome of a law requiring brothers to marry jointly. There is choice, and in fact, divorce traditionally was relatively simple in Tibetan society. If a brother in a polyandrous marriage became dissatisfied and wanted to separate, he simply left the main house and set up his own household. In such cases, all the children stayed in the main household with the remaining brother(s), even if the departing brother was known to be the real father of one or more of the children.

The Tibetans' own explanation for choosing fraternal polyandry is materialistic. For example, when I asked Dorje why he decided to marry with his two brothers rather than take his own wife, he thought for a moment, then said it prevented the division of his family's farm (and animals) and thus facilitated all of them achieving a higher standard of living. And when I later asked Dorje's bride whether it wasn't difficult for her to cope with three brothers as husbands, she laughed and echoed the rationale of avoiding fragmentation of the family and land, ad-

Reprinted with permission from *Natural History,* Vol. 96, No. 3, March 1987, pp. 39-48. © 1987 by The American Museum of Natural History.

ding that she expected to be better off economically, since she would have three husbands working for her and her children.

Exotic as it may seem to Westerners, Tibetan fraternal polyandry is thus in many ways analogous to the way primogeniture functioned in nineteenth-century England. Primogeniture dictated that the eldest son inherited the family estate, while younger sons had to leave home and seek their own employment—for example, in the military or the clergy. Primogeniture maintained family estates intact over generations by permitting only one heir per generation. Fraternal polyandry also accomplishes this but does so by keeping all the brothers together with just one wife so that there is only one *set* of heirs per generation.

While Tibetans believe that in this way fraternal polyandry reduces the risk of family fission, monogamous marriages among brothers need not necessarily precipitate the division of the family estate: brothers could continue to live together, and the family land could continue to be worked jointly. When I asked Tibetans about this, however, they invariably responded that such joint families are unstable because each wife is primarily oriented to her own children and interested in their success and well-being over that of the children of the other wives. For example, if the youngest brother's wife had three sons while the eldest brother's wife had only one daughter, the wife of the youngest brother might begin to demand more resources for her children since, as males, they represent the future of the family. Thus, the children from different wives in the same generation are competing sets of heirs, and this makes such families inherently unstable. Tibetans perceive that conflict will spread from the wives to their husbands and consider this likely to cause family fission. Consequently, it is almost never done.

Although Tibetans see an economic advantage to fraternal polyandry, they do not value the sharing of a wife as an end in itself. On the contrary, they articulate a number of problems inherent in the practice. For example, because authority is customarily exercised by the eldest brother, his younger male siblings have

Family Planning in Tibet

An economic rationale for fraternal polyandry is outlined in the diagram below, which emphasizes only the male offspring in each generation. If every wife is assumed to bear three sons, a family splitting up into monogamous households would rapidly multiply and fragment the family land. In this case, a rule of inheritance, such as primogeniture, could retain the family land intact, but only at the cost of creating many landless male offspring. In contrast, the family practicing fraternal polyandry maintains a steady ratio of persons to land.
Joe LeMonnier

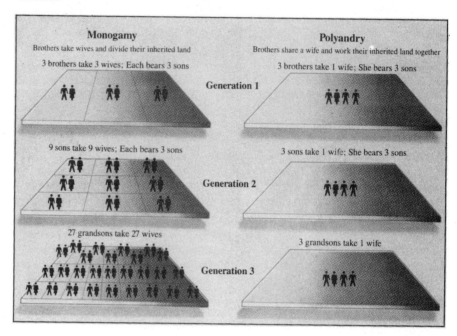

Monogamy — Brothers take wives and divide their inherited land

3 brothers take 3 wives; Each bears 3 sons — Generation 1

9 sons take 9 wives; Each bears 3 sons — Generation 2

27 grandsons take 27 wives — Generation 3

Polyandry — Brothers share a wife and work their inherited land together

3 brothers take 1 wife; She bears 3 sons

3 sons take 1 wife; She bears 3 sons

3 grandsons take 1 wife

to subordinate themselves with little hope of changing their status within the family. When these younger brothers are aggressive and individualistic, tensions and difficulties often occur despite there being only one set of heirs.

In addition, tension and conflict may arise in polyandrous families because of sexual favoritism. The bride normally sleeps with the eldest brother, and the two have the responsibility to see to it that the other males have opportunities for sexual access. Since the Tibetan subsistence economy requires males to travel a lot, the temporary absence of one or more brothers facilitates this, but there are also other rotation practices. The cultural ideal unambiguously calls for the wife to show equal affection and sexuality to each of the brothers (and vice versa), but deviations from this ideal occur, especially when there is a sizable difference in age between the partners in the marriage.

Dorje's family represents just such a

potential situation. He is fifteen years old and his two older brothers are twenty-five and twenty-two years old. The new bride is twenty-three years old, eight years Dorje's senior. Sometimes such a bride finds the youngest husband immature and adolescent and does not treat him with equal affection; alternatively, she may find his youth attractive and lavish special attention on him. Apart from that consideration, when a younger male like Dorje grows up, he may consider his wife "ancient" and prefer the company of a woman his own age or younger. Consequently, although men and women do not find the idea of sharing a bride or a bridegroom repulsive, individual likes and dislikes can cause familial discord.

Two reasons have commonly been offered for the perpetuation of fraternal polyandry in Tibet: that Tibetans practice female infanticide and therefore have to marry polyandrously, owing to a shortage of females; and that Tibet, lying at extremely high altitudes, is so barren and bleak that Tibetans would starve without resort to this mechanism. A Jesuit who lived in Tibet during the eighteenth century articulated this second view: "One reason for this most odious custom is the sterility of the soil, and the small amount of land that can be cultivated owing to the lack of water. The crops may suffice if the brothers all live together, but if they form separate families they would be reduced to beggary."

Both explanations are wrong, however. Not only has there never been institutionalized female infanticide in Tibet, but Tibetan society gives females considerable rights, including inheriting the family estate in the absence of brothers. In such cases, the woman takes a bridegroom who comes to live in her family and adopts her family's name and identity. Moreover, there is no demographic evidence of a shortage of females. In Limi, for example, there were (in 1974) sixty females and fifty-three males in the fifteen- to thirty-five-year age category, and many adult females were unmarried.

The second reason is also incorrect. The climate in Tibet is extremely harsh, and ecological factors do play a major role perpetuating polyandry, but polyandry is not a means of preventing starvation. It is characteristic, not of the poorest segments of the society, but rather of the peasant landowning families.

In the old society, the landless poor could not realistically aspire to prosperity, but they did not fear starvation. There was a persistent labor shortage throughout Tibet, and very poor families with little or no land and few animals could subsist through agricultural labor, tenant farming, craft occupations such as carpentry, or by working as servants. Although the per person family income could increase somewhat if brothers married polyandrously and pooled their wages, in the absence of inheritable land, the advantage of fraternal polyandry was not generally sufficient to prevent them from setting up their own households. A more skilled or energetic younger brother could do as well or better alone, since he would completely control his income and would not have to share it with his siblings. Consequently, while there was and is some polyandry among the poor, it is much less frequent and more prone

to result in divorce and family fission.

An alternative reason for the persistence of fraternal polyandry is that it reduces population growth (and thereby reduces the pressure on resources) by relegating some females to lifetime spinsterhood. Fraternal polyandrous marriages in Limi (in 1974) averaged 2.35 men per woman, and not surprisingly, 31 percent of the females of child-bearing age (twenty to forty-nine) were unmarried. These spinsters either continued to live at home, set up their own households, or worked as servants for other families. They could also become Buddhist nuns. Being unmarried is not synonymous with exclusion from the reproductive pool. Discreet extramarital relationships are tolerated, and actually half of the adult unmarried women in Limi had one or more children. They raised these children as single mothers, working for wages or weaving cloth and blankets for sale. As a group, however, the unmarried woman had far fewer offspring than the married women, averaging only 0.7 children per woman, compared with 3.3 for married women, whether polyandrous, monogamous, or polygynous. While polyandry helps regulate population, this function of polyandry is not consciously perceived by Tibetans and is not the reason they consistently choose it.

If neither a shortage of females nor the fear of starvation perpetuates fraternal polyandry, what motivates brothers, particularly younger brothers, to opt for this system of marriage? From the perspective of the younger brother in a landholding family, the main incentive is the attainment or maintenance of the good life. With polyandry, he can expect a more secure and higher standard of living, with access not only to this family's land and animals but also to its inherited collection of clothes, jewelry, rugs, saddles, and horses. In addition, he will experience less work pressure and much greater security because all responsibility does not fall on one "father." For Tibetan brothers, the question is whether to trade off the greater personal freedom inherent in monogamy for the real or potential economic security, affluence, and social prestige associated with life in a larger, labor-rich polyandrous family.

A brother thinking of separating from his polyandrous marriage and taking his own wife would face various disadvantages. Although in the majority of Tibetan regions all brothers theoretically have rights to their family's estate, in reality Tibetans are reluctant to divide their land into small fragments. Generally, a younger brother who insists on leaving the family will receive only a small plot of land, if that. Because of its power and wealth, the rest of the family usually can block any attempt of the younger brother to increase his share of land through litigation. Moreover, a younger brother may not even get a house and cannot expect to receive much above the minimum in terms of movable possessions, such as furniture, pots, and pans. Thus, a brother contemplating going it on his own must plan on achieving economic security and the good life not through inheritance but through his own work.

The obvious solution for younger brothers—creating new fields from virgin land—is generally not a feasible option. Most Tibetan populations live at high altitudes (above 12,000 feet), where arable land is extremely scarce. For example, in Dorje's village, agriculture ranges only from about 12,900 feet, the lowest point in the area, to 13,300 feet. Above that altitude, early frost and snow destroy the staple barley crop. Furthermore, because of the low rainfall caused by the Himalayan rain shadow, many areas in Tibet and northern Nepal that are within the appropriate altitude range for agriculture have no reliable sources of irrigation. In the end, although there is plenty of unused land in such areas, most of it is either too high or too arid.

Even where unused land capable of being farmed exists, clearing the land and building the substantial terraces necessary for irrigation constitute a great undertaking. Each plot has to be completely dug out to a depth of two to two and half feet so that the large rocks and boulders can be removed. At best, a man might be able to bring a few new fields under cultivation in the first years after separating from his brothers, but he could not expect to acquire substantial amounts of arable land this way.

In addition, because of the limited farmland, the Tibetan subsistence economy characteristically includes a strong emphasis on animal husbandry. Tibetan farmers regularly maintain cattle, yaks, goats, and sheep, grazing them in the areas too high for agriculture. These herds produce wool, milk, cheese, butter, meat, and skins. To obtain these resources, however, shepherds must accompany the animals on a daily basis. When first setting up a monogamous household, a younger brother like Dorje would find it difficult to both farm and manage animals.

In traditional Tibetan society, there was an even more critical factor that operated to perpetuate fraternal polyandry—a form of hereditary servitude somewhat analogous to serfdom in Europe. Peasants were tied to large estates held by aristocrats, monasteries, and the Lhasa government. They were allowed the use of some farmland to produce their own subsistence but were required to provide taxes in kind and corvée (free labor) to their lords. The corvée was a substantial hardship, since a peasant household was in many cases required to furnish the lord with one laborer daily for most of the year and more on specific occasions such as the harvest. This enforced labor, along with the lack of new land and ecological pressure to pursue both agriculture and animal husbandry, made polyandrous families particularly beneficial. The polyandrous family allowed an internal division of adult labor, maximizing economic advantage. For example, while the wife worked the family fields, one brother could perform the lord's corvée, another could look after the animals, and a third could engage in trade.

Although social scientists often discount other people's explanations of why they do things, in the case of Tibetan fraternal polyandry, such explanations are very close to the truth. The custom, however, is very sensitive to changes in its political and economic milieu and, not surprisingly, is in decline in most Tibetan areas. Made less important by the elimination of the traditional serf-based economy, it is disparaged by the dominant non-Tibetan leaders of India, China, and Nepal. New opportunities for economic and social mobility in these countries, such as the tourist trade and government employment, are also eroding the rationale for polyandry, and so it may vanish within the next generation.

Young Traders of Northern Nigeria

Enid Schildkrout

Thirty years ago, Erik Erikson wrote that "the fashionable insistence on dramatizing the dependence of children on adults often blinds us to the dependence of the older generation on the younger one." As a psychoanalyst, Erikson was referring mainly to the emotional bonds between parents and children, but his observation is a reminder that in many parts of the world, adults depend on children in quite concrete ways. In northern Nigeria, children with trays balanced on their heads, carrying and selling a variety of goods for their mothers or themselves, are a common sight in villages and towns. Among the Muslim Hausa, aside from being a useful educational experience, this children's trade, as well as children's performance of household chores and errands, complements the activity of adults and is socially and emotionally significant.

Children's services are especially important to married Hausa women, who, in accordance with Islamic practices, live in purdah, or seclusion. In Nigeria, purdah is represented not so much by the wearing of the veil but by the mud-brick walls surrounding every house or compound and by the absence of women in the markets and the streets. Women could not carry out their domestic responsibilities, not to mention their many income-earning enterprises, without the help of children, who are free from the rigid sexual segregation that so restricts adults.

Except for elderly women, only children can move in and out of their own and other people's houses without violating the rules of purdah. Even children under three years of age are sent on short errands, for example, to buy things for their mothers.

Hausa-speaking people are found throughout West Africa and constitute the largest ethnic group in northern Nigeria, where they number over eighteen million. Their adherence to Islam is a legacy of the centuries during which Arabs came from the north to trade goods of North African and European manufacture. The majority of the Hausa are farmers, but markets and large commercial cities have existed in northern Nigeria since long before the period of British colonial rule. The city of Kano, for example, which was a major emporium for the trans-Saharan caravan trade, dates back to the eighth century. Today it has a population of about one million.

Binta is an eleven-year-old girl who lives in Kano, in a mud-brick house that has piped water, but no electricity. The household includes her father and mother, her three brothers, her father's second wife and her three children, and a foster child, who is the daughter of one of Binta's cousins. By Kano standards, it is a middle-income family. Binta's father sells shoes, and her mother cooks and sells bean cakes and *tuwo*, the stiff porridge made of guinea corn (*Shorghum vulgare*), which is the Hausa's staple. Binta described for me one day's round of activities, which

began very early when she arose to start trading.

"After I woke up, I said my prayers and ate breakfast. Then I went outside the house to sell the bean cakes my mother makes every morning. Soon my mother called me in and asked me to take more bean cakes around town to sell; she spoke to me about making an effort to sell as much as I usually do. I sold forty-eight bean cakes at one kobo each [one kobo is worth one and a half cents]. After I returned home, some people came to buy more cakes from me. Then I went out for a second round of trading before setting out for Arabic school. I study the Koran there every morning from eight to nine.

"When school was over, I washed and prepared to sell *tuwo*. First my mother sent me to another neighborhood to gather the customers' empty bowls. I also collected the money from our regular customers. My mother put the *tuwo* in the bowls and told me the amount of money to collect for each. Then I delivered them to the customers.

"On my way home, a man in the street, whom I know, sent me on an errand to buy him fifteen kobo worth of food; he gave me a reward of one kobo. I then sold some more *tuwo* outside our house by standing there and shouting for customers. When the *tuwo* was finished, I was sent to another house to buy some guinea corn, and one of the women there asked me to bring her one of my mother's big pots. The pot was too heavy for me to carry,

Reprinted with permission from *Natural History*, Vol. 90, No. 6, June 1981. © 1981 by The American Museum of Natural History.

but finally one of my brothers helped me take it to her.

"When I returned, my mother was busy pounding some grain, and she sent me out to have some locust beans pounded. She then sent me to pick up three bowls of pounded guinea corn, and she gave me money to take to the woman who had pounded it. The woman told me to remind my mother that she still owed money from the day before.

"When I came home I was sent out to trade again, this time with salt, bouillon cubes, and laundry detergent in small packets. Afterward I prepared some pancakes using ingredients I bought myself—ten kobo worth of flour, one kobo worth of salt, five kobo worth of palm oil, and ten kobo worth of firewood. I took this food outside to sell it to children.

"My mother then gave me a calabash of guinea corn to take for grinding; my younger sister also gave me two calabashes of corn to take. The man who ran the grinding machine advised me that I should not carry so large a load, so I made two trips on the way back. He gave me and my younger brothers, who accompanied me, one kobo each.

"I was then told to take a bath, which I did. After that I was sent to visit a sick relative who was in the hospital. On the way I met a friend, and we took the bus together. I also bought some cheese at the market for five kobo. I met another friend on the way home, and she bought some fish near the market for ten kobo and gave me some. I played on the way to the hospital. When I got home, I found the women of the house preparing a meal. One of them was already eating, and I was invited to eat with her.

"After nightfall, I was sent to take some spices for pounding, and I wasted a lot of time there. The other children and I went to a place where some fruits and vegetables are sold along the street. We bought vegetables for soup for fifty kobo, as my mother had asked me to do. By the time I got home it was late, so I went to sleep."

Binta's many responsibilities are typical for a girl her age. Like many women, Binta's mother relies upon her children in carrying out an occupation

at home. Although purdah implies that a woman will be supported by her husband and need not work, most Hausa women do work, keeping their incomes distinct from the household budget. Women usually cook one main meal a day and purchase their other meals from other women. In this way they are able to use their time earning a living instead of performing only unpaid domestic labor.

Among the Hausa, men and women spend relatively little time together, eating separately and, except in certain ritual contexts, rarely doing the same things. Differences in gender are not as important among children, however. In fact, it is precisely because children's activities are not rigidly defined by sex that they are able to move between the world of women, centered in the inner courtyard of the house, and the world of men, whose activities take place mainly outside the home. Children of both sexes care for younger children, go to the market, and help their mothers cook.

Both boys and girls do trading, although it is more common for girls. From the age of about five until marriage, which is very often at about age twelve for girls, many children like Binta spend part of every day selling such things as fruits, vegetables, and nuts; bouillon cubes, bread, and small packages of detergent, sugar, or salt; and bowls of steaming rice or *tuwo*. If a woman embroiders, children buy the thread and later take the finished product to the client or to an agent who sells it.

Women in purdah frequently change their occupations depending on the availability of child helpers. In Kano, women often trade in small commodities that can be sold in small quantities, such as various kinds of cooked food. Sewing, embroidery, mat weaving, and other craft activities (including, until recently, spinning) are less remunerative occupations, and women pursue them when they have fewer children around to help. Unlike the situation common in the United States, where children tend to hamper a woman's ability to earn money, the Hausa woman finds it difficult to earn income without children's help. Often, if a

woman has no children of her own, a relative's child will come to live with her.

Child care is another service children perform that benefits women. It enables mothers to devote themselves to their young infants, whom they carry on their backs until the age of weaning, between one and two. Even though women are always at home, they specifically delegate the care of young children to older ones. The toddler moves from the mother's back into a group of older children, who take the responsibility very seriously. Until they are old enough, children do not pick up infants or very young children, but by the age of nine, both boys and girls bathe young children, play with them, and take them on errands. The older children do a great deal of direct and indirect teaching of younger ones. As soon as they can walk, younger children accompany their older siblings to Arabic school. There the children sit with their age-mates, and the teacher gives them lessons according to their ability.

Much of a child's activity is directed toward helping his or her parents, but other relatives—grandparents, aunts, uncles, and stepmothers—and adults living in the same house as servants or tenants may call on a child for limited tasks without asking permission of the parents. Like other Muslims, Hausa men may have up to four wives, and these women freely call on each other's children to perform household chores. Even strangers in the street sometimes ask a child to do an errand, such as delivering a message, particularly if the chore requires entering a house to which the adult does not have access. The child will be rewarded with a small amount of money or food.

Adults other than parents also reprimand children, who are taught very early to obey the orders of grownups. Without ever directly refusing to obey a command, however, children do devise numerous strategies of non-compliance, such as claiming that another adult has already co-opted their time or simply leaving the scene and ignoring the command. Given children's greater mobility, there is little an adult can do to enforce compliance.

Besides working on behalf of adults, children also participate in a "children's economy." Children have their own money—from school allowances given to them daily for the purchase of snacks, from gifts, from work they may have done, and even from their own investments. For example, boys make toys for sale, and they rent out valued property, such as slide viewers or bicycles. Just as women distinguish their own enterprises from the labor they do as wives, children regard the work they do for themselves differently from the work they do on behalf of their mothers. When Binta cooks food for sale, using materials she has purchased with her own money, the profits are entirely her own, although she may hand the money over to her mother for safekeeping.

Many girls begin to practice cooking by the age of ten. They do not actually prepare the family meals, for this heavy and tedious work is primarily the wives' responsibility. But they do carry out related chores, such as taking vegetables out for grinding, sifting flour, and washing bowls. Many also cook food for sale on their own. With initial help from their mothers or other adult female relatives, who may given them a cooking pot, charcoal, or a small stove, children purchase small amounts of ingredients and prepare various snacks. Since they sell their products for less than the adult women do, and since the quantities are very small, their customers are mainly children. Child entrepreneurs even extend credit to other children.

Aisha is a ten-year-old girl who was notoriously unsuccessful as a trader. She disliked trading and regularly lost her mother's investment. Disgusted, her mother finally gave her a bit of charcoal, some flour and oil, and a small pot. Aisha set up a little stove outside her house and began making small pancakes, which she sold to very young children. In three months she managed to make enough to buy a new dress, and in a year she bought a pair of shoes. She had clearly chosen her occupation after some unhappy trials at street trading.

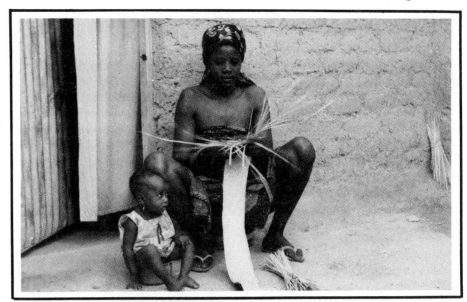

Hausa women usually engage in some form of enterprise; most of their profits are invested in their children's marriage expenses. Working at home, a woman weaves a mat for sale.

In the poorest families, as in Aisha's, the profit from children's work goes toward living expenses. This may occur in households that are headed by divorced or widowed women. It is also true for the *almajirai*, or Arabic students, who often live with their teachers. The proceeds of most children's economic activity, however, go to the expenses of marriage. The income contributes to a girl's dowry and to a boy's bridewealth, both of which are considerable investments.

The girl's dowry includes many brightly painted enamel, brass, and glass bowls, collected years before marriage. These utensils are known as *kayan daki*, or "things of the room." After the wedding they are stacked in a large cupboard beside the girl's bed. Very few of them are used, but they are always proudly displayed, except during the mourning period if the husband dies. *Kayan daki* are not simply for conspicuous display, however. They remain the property of the woman unless she sells them or gives them away. In the case of divorce or financial need, they can provide her most important and immediate source of economic security.

Kayan daki traditionally consisted of brass bowls and beautifully carved calabashes. Today the most common form is painted enamel bowls manufactured in Nigeria or abroad. The styles and designs change frequently, and the cost is continually rising.

Among the wealthier urban women and the Western-educated women, other forms of modern household equipment, including electric appliances and china tea sets, are becoming part of the dowry.

The money a young girl earns on her own, as well as the profits she brings home through her trading, are invested by her mother or guardian in *kayan daki* in anticipation of her marriage. Most women put the major part of their income into their daughters' *kayan daki* as well as helping their sons with marriage expenses. When a woman has many children, the burden can be considerable.

For girls, marriage, which ideally coincides with puberty, marks the transition to adult status. If a girl marries as early as age ten, she does not cook for her husband or have sexual relations with him for some time, but she enters purdah and loses the freedom of childhood. Most girls are married by age fifteen, and for many the transition is a difficult one.

Boys usually do not marry until they are over twenty and are able to support a family. They also need to have raised most of the money to cover the cost of getting married. Between the ages of eight and ten, however, they gradually begin to move away from the confines of the house and to regard it as a female domain. They begin taking their food outside and eating it with friends, and they roam much farther than girls in their play activities. By the onset of puberty, boys have begun to observe the rules of purdah by refraining from entering the houses of all but their closest relatives. In general, especially if they have sisters, older boys spend less time than girls doing chores and errands and more time playing and, in recent years, going to school. Traditionally, many boys left home to live and study with an Arabic teacher. Today many also pursue Western education, sometimes in boarding school. Although the transition to adulthood is less abrupt for boys, childhood for both sexes ends by age twelve to fourteen.

As each generation assumes the responsibilities of adulthood and the restrictions of sexual separation, it must rely on the younger members of society who can work around the purdah system. Recently, however, the introduction of Western education has begun to threaten this traditional arrangement, in part just by altering the pattern of children's lives.

The Nigerian government is now engaged in a massive program to provide Western education to all school-age children. This program has been undertaken for sound economic and political reasons. During the colonial period, which ended in the early 1960s, the British had a "hands-off"

policy regarding education in northern Nigeria. They ruled through the Islamic political and judicial hierarchy and supported the many Arabic schools, where the Koran and Islamic law, history, and religion were taught. The British discouraged the introduction of Christian mission schools in the north and spent little on government schools.

The pattern in the rest of Nigeria was very different. In the non-Muslim areas of the country, mission and government schools grew rapidly during the colonial period. The result of this differential policy was the development of vast regional imbalances in the extent and level of Western education in the country. This affected the types of occupational choices open to Nigerians from different regions. Despite a longer tradition of literacy in Arabic in the north, few northerners were eligible for those civil service jobs that required literacy in English, the language of government business. This was one of the many issues in the tragic civil war that tore Nigeria apart in the 1960s. The current goal of enrolling all northern children in public schools, which offer training in English and secular subjects, has, therefore, a strong and valid political rationale.

Western education has met a mixed reception in northern Nigeria. While

it has been increasingly accepted for boys—as an addition to, not a substitute for, Islamic education—many parents are reluctant to enroll their daughters in primary school. Nevertheless, there are already more children waiting to get into school than there are classrooms and teachers to accommodate them. If the trend continues, it will almost certainly have important, if unintended, consequences for purdah and the system of child enterprise that supports it.

Children who attend Western school continue to attend Arabic school, and thus are removed from the household for much of the day. For many women this causes considerable difficulty in doing daily housework. It means increased isolation and a curtailment of income-producing activity. It creates a new concern about where to obtain the income for children's marriages. As a result of these practical pressures, the institution of purdah will inevitably be challenged. Also, the schoolgirl of today may develop new skills and new expectations of her role as a woman that conflict with the traditional ways. As Western education takes hold, today's young traders may witness a dramatic change in Hausa family life— for themselves as adults and for their children.

Family Planning, Amazon Style

Amid cultural change, high fertility imposes new hardships on an Indian people

Text and photographs by Warren M. Hern

Warren M. Hern earned his B.A. and M.D. from the University of Colorado in the 1960s. Hern went on to get a masters degree in public health and a Ph.D. in epidemiology and is now an associate professor adjunct in anthropology at the University of Colorado, Boulder. He continues to divide his time between a medical practice in Boulder and his continuing studies of the health effects of cultural and ecological change among the Shipibo Indians in Peru.

"When you come back, don't forget to bring *toötimarau*," Chomoshico called to me. I was leaving the Shipibo Indian village of Manco Capac, on the banks of the Pisqui River in the Peruvian Amazon, where I had been doing medical research. Chomoshico was nearing the end of her eleventh pregnancy. She already had seven living children. Neither she nor her husband wants more. "Enough. Clothes cost," they told me. "I'm tired of having children," she said. "I almost died with the last one." Her husband has tuberculosis.

Toötimarau means "medicine to keep from being pregnant"—birth control. I knew I could promise Chomoshico worm medicine for her children's parasites, and I might be able to bring her vitamins and iron for her pregnancy, even medicine for tuberculosis. But while I could informally provide other kinds of medical care, I could not arrange to bring her birth control without risking reprisals from politicians who are against it. The Shipibo have been asking me for *toötimarau* for more than twenty-five years, but I haven't been able to arrange any yet. I can only refer them to a Peruvian doctor in Pucallpa, many days away by canoe. Most can never get there. The men even pull me aside to ask if I know about an operation to "fix" men—vasectomy—and, again, I tell them the name of my medical colleague in Pucallpa.

In the same village, a few weeks before, a young girl had died on her thirteenth birthday trying to give birth to twins. And in that girl's natal village, just up the river, I had just seen my first case of frank starvation among the Shipibo Indians, with whom I had worked as a physician and scientist since 1964. The starving man had tuberculosis. His family, which would normally have taken care of someone so ill, was away working for a logging company.

Chomoshico's desperate request for birth control, the death of the thirteen-year-old girl, and the plight of the starving man are all related. The Shipibo's own high fertility, uncontrolled by any effective means, is compounding the problem of the population pressure created by an influx of outsiders, who are moving into Shipibo territory and destroying the natural resources.

The Shipibo Indians who live along the Ucayali River and its tributaries, such as the Pisqui, notice that the fish are getting smaller and harder to find, and that the game animals they rely on during the rainy season—when fish are almost impossible to catch—are more elusive than in the past. Palm leaves for thatching roofs seem scarcer, and people have to trek long distances, sometimes a mile or more, to gather firewood, once available a few steps away. People are aware that their own village is growing, that they do not know all its inhabitants, that the village school is crowded. Sometimes they have to go all day without eating fish. The Shipibo word for fish, *piti*, is also their word for food: a Shipibo without fish is truly poor.

In this crisis, the Shipibo are not alone. The Peruvian government has urged desperate people from the crowded coastal cities and Andean communities to settle and live in the jungle "paradise." They have. Pucallpa, the major port on the Ucayali, the "highway" river that becomes the Amazon, was probably an aboriginal Shipibo settlement (its Shipibo name means "red earth"). In the 1940s, just before the trans-Andes highway was put through to Pucallpa from Lima, the settlement's population was about 2,500. When I first visited Pucallpa in 1964, the population had grown to about 25,000. It was a raw, dusty, frontier town with dirt streets and Saturday night gunfights. More than

4. OTHER FAMILIES, OTHER WAYS

250,000 people live there now—a hundredfold increase in fifty years.

With the local waters already depleted, fishing boats from Pucallpa speed downstream more than 150 miles, where they take all fish more than two inches long with drift nets, pack the fish in ice, and start back up the river. The smaller fish are discarded to rot. There is not much left for the Shipibo, for the mestizo colonists from elsewhere in Peru, for the large fish, for the alligators, or for the wading birds that used to line the shores of the Ucayali. Areas around Pucallpa that were covered by canopy rain forest in 1964 now look like Oklahoma. The hundreds of bird species that enlivened the forest have been replaced by emaciated cows. Swamps filled with fish are replaced by causeways carrying buses and motorcycles. Twenty years ago, a traveler camped on the beach of the Ucayali River could not sleep for the sounds of fish splashing and alligators hunting them. There aren't enough fish to keep one awake now; the traveler is kept awake by the whine of fishermen's outboard motors.

Instead of living by subsistence fishing and horticulture, as the Shipibo principally do, their new neighbors exploit the environment to make money. First come the timber cutters, followed by cattle ranchers, commercial fishermen, and the farmers of bananas, rice, and other cash crops. The resultant deforestation and flooding have eliminated some crops and game animals that were sources of food for the Shipibo in the rainy season. The Shipibo themselves are drawn into the money economy and sometimes sell products from scarce animals (such as water turtle eggs) in order to get cash.

The Shipibo painfully admit that, although they work much harder than before, they don't have enough money for clothes (which they used to make by hand from woven cloth) and schoolbooks for their children (not a factor thirty years ago). They now have to buy food at times, even though it was previously plentiful.

The Shipibo (and the closely related Conibo) are the dominant indigenous people of the upper Peruvian Amazon.

A Shipibo man skins a fifty-six-pound armored catfish, one of many catfish species found in the Ucayali. In recent years, however, such catches are exceptional. The human population along the river has been growing explosively, and the Shipibo report that fish—their traditional staple food—are smaller and harder to find.

They have survived there for about a thousand years, but only by battling fiercely with other tribes and exhibiting a pragmatic tenacity in the face of colonization. Before the European conquest, they may have numbered more than 50,000. By the early twentieth century, fewer than 3,000 remained. Somehow they escaped the further decimation or complete extinction that befell many other Amazon tribes exposed to European diseases, enslavement, intertribal warfare sponsored by rubber tappers, and other openly genocidal attempts to rid the Amazon of its native inhabitants. Their population is now about 30,000 and growing.

The last smallpox epidemic was in 1964. But now, in addition to the modern plagues of tuberculosis and cholera, the Shipibo have a new health problem: high fertility, which places pressure on resources and takes a heavy toll among Shipibo women.

In the past the Shipibo controlled their birth rate and population growth in a variety of ways: by sexual abstinence, by abortion (using pressure on the uterus), by infanticide, and by the use of herbal contraceptives. Knowledge of these contraceptives was passed down through the generations from mother to daughter, from grandmother to granddaughter. But several things happened to interrupt this tradition. The horrifying epidemics that wiped out whole villages following European contact prompted shamans in related tribes to forbid the practices of infanticide and abortion. The Shipibo shamans may also have taken this step, but more likely, Christian missionaries played a role in disrupting the cultural traditions that controlled fertility. In 1697, the Shipibo massacred a group of Franciscans who were insisting that the Shipibo give up polygyny (multiple wives). Today, the custom remains strong in some parts of the Shipibo culture area but is declining in villages close to centers of Western influence.

Even though polygyny allows some men to have more offspring than others, it permits women to have fewer children with longer intervals between births. This arrangement has several important effects: it allows women to recover from each pregnancy; it allows children to gain maturity before being weaned and placed on a diet of all solid foods; and it reduces the total number of children borne by individual women. The result for the group is that women have a better chance of recovering from pregnancy and therefore of living longer, and child survival is better.

These advantages of polygyny are often cited by members of traditional societies, whose strategy is, not to have as many children as possible, but to have as many as possible that survive to adulthood. A final result of polygyny, paradoxically, is that community fertility could be restrained.

My acquaintance with Shipibo methods of controlling fertility began in 1964, when I was a third-year medical student from the University of Colorado. I had just finished working intensively for several months at the Hospital Amazonico "Albert Schweitzer" near Pucallpa, and had traveled to the Shipibo village of Paococha to learn about native ideas concerning the nature, treatment, and control of disease. A Shipibo friend who was helping me, Ambrosio, came to me one day to tell me that his wife was bleeding to death: she had just had a baby. Ambrosio asked me to see her, and I treated his wife for retained membranes and postpartum uterine atony (relaxation of the uterus). She recovered, and he asked me what he could do for me. I told him I would like to learn about medicines that women use to control pregnancy. His aunt Julia was the local expert.

From Julia I learned that Shipibo women have several such herbal preparations. One of the most common is called *toötimahuaste* (*toöti* means "pregnancy," *ma* means "not," and *huaste* means "herb"). Taken as a tea during three successive menstrual periods, it is supposed to cause sterility.

A Shipibo health worker administers intravenous solution to rehydrate a cholera victim in the Pisqui village of Nuevo Eden, in July 1991. The girl recovered, but that year's cholera epidemic killed about twenty Shipibo in the area.

In 1969, for my master of public health thesis, I returned to the village to conduct a more formal census and collect the inhabitants' reproductive histories. I asked the Shipibo women in my survey if they knew about these medicines and if they used them. They roared with laughter at the idea of a male gringo asking these intimate questions in their language. Then they usually told me that they knew about them; many had used them. Some of the women had seriously harmed themselves by using highly toxic natural substances in a desperate attempt to control fertility.

At first I was puzzled to find that women who had used the herbal contraceptives had more children, on the average, than those who hadn't. This turned out to be because older women, who had already had many children, were more likely to have used the herbal contraceptives. But my doubts about the effectiveness of the traditional contraceptives were renewed when I analyzed the results of my two population studies in 1964 and 1969. The Shipibo in Paococha turned out to have the highest fertility ever recorded for a human group, with a woman having an average of ten births during her reproductive life.

Moreover, their rate of population growth was nearly 4.9 percent per year, with the population doubling every 14.5 years. Such a population explosion had to be fairly recent, for if such a rate had been in effect for very long the population would have been huge. The phenomenon could not be completely explained by better medical care (some of which I had provided) and a declining death rate. Either the herbal contraceptives didn't work, or I wasn't getting all the information.

There were two other factors. By 1969, a large extended family from down the Ucayali river, at the periphery of the Shipibo territory, moved into Paococha. Several of the men had multiple wives. (The local, "downtown" Shipibo assured me that, unlike themselves, the new family was composed of *salvajes*—savages—and that they practiced the old ways, including polygyny.) Because missionaries and schoolteachers discouraged it, this family structure was becoming rare.

The second factor was suggested to me when I remembered that the Shipibo always observed certain taboos, including "dieting," when taking medications of any kind. I asked the women what they did when they took *toötimahuaste*. They replied that one cannot eat salt, honey from the forest or other sweets, ripe bananas, and certain kinds of fish. And a woman taking *toötimahuaste* may not have sex. This would mean an abstinence of three months or more. Right away, I suspected what epidemiologists call a "secondary noncausal association" between the use of herbal contraceptives and fewer pregnancies.

Postpartum sexual abstinence is often linked with polygyny in tribal societies. The woman who has just given birth may not sleep with her husband for a period of time, which may be from three months to three years. During that time her husband sleeps with one of the other wives. In Shipibo tradition, it is not uncommon for a man to have two or three wives. Because women in polygynous marriages might be better able to observe the sexual abstinence associated with herbal contraceptives, and because this might help these women have longer birth intervals, I speculated that a decline in the practice of polygyny could be contributing to the community's high fertility.

To be sure of this, I had to determine that, on average, the birth intervals were indeed longer for women in polygynous marriages than for women in monogamous marriages and that fertility was actually lower for the former than for the latter. Further, I wanted to determine if the rates of polygyny differed among the villages, and if so, whether less polygyny is associated with lower or higher community fertility. By studying Shipibo villages that were separated by long distances and had different levels of cultural contact with Western society, I could compare the relationship between polygyny and fertility.

Up on the Pisqui River, Shipibo lives are more traditional than in the Shipibo villages lining the Ucayali. The Pisqui is much smaller and fluctuates more quickly than the Ucayali. It contains fewer fish and other edible wildlife. The Pisqui Shipibo live more by hunting and gathering than their Ucayali brethren. They are more isolated from outside influences, and have been since at least early colonial times.

In 1983 and 1984, I studied eight Shipibo villages in different states of cultural transition. Six of the villages were as much as sixty miles up the Pisqui. The results of the study showed that polygyny is generally more common on the Pisqui, and that longer birth intervals occur in the polygynous unions there. In some Pisqui villages, 45 percent of the women were in polygynous marriages, whereas in Paoyhän, a new Shipibo village on the Ucayali, only about 5 percent of the women were in this kind of union.

Comparing the birth interval lengths and fertility of all women, regardless of their villages, I found that, on average, the birth intervals for women in polygynous marriages were thirty-four months—four months longer than those of women in monogamous marriages. And most significant, women in monogamous marriages had 1.3 more children during their reproductive lives than women in polygynous marriages. Accordingly, in villages where polygyny was more common, the average intervals between births were longer and community fertility rates were lower.

The most acute health problem for the Shipibo, as both they and I see it, is epidemic disease—tuberculosis, cholera, and influenza, to mention a few. These diseases carry off the older people who know the cultural traditions, and they carry off many children. But the long-term problem is high fertility, which is placing pressure on the diminishing resources. Weakened by increasingly poor nutrition, the Shipibo are more vulnerable to epidemics. In their case, population growth means poverty and disease.

For Shipibo women, high fertility means sickness and death. They have an extremely high rate of cervical cancer, which is probably related, among other things, to early childbearing and many pregnancies. I estimate that the maternal mortality ratio—the proportion of women who die from pregnancy and childbirth—is roughly one for every hundred live births, one hundred times higher than in the United States.

A larger question raised by studies such as mine is whether we really understand how fast the world's popu-

The influence of outside cultures on traditional life styles has driven Shipibo fertility higher, but at a great cost to maternal health and survival.

lation is growing and will grow in the future. The Shipibo are essentially not counted in the Peruvian census, and neither are their mestizo and other Shipibo neighbors. Numbers sent to the government offices are highly inaccurate (but then I, for one, never received a U.S. census form in 1990).

From my experiences in Latin America, I would speculate that official census counts are missing at least one in ten people and perhaps every fourth person. Some of those groups excluded appear to have population growth rates of more than 3.5 percent. If this is true—and if it is similarly true in other parts of the developing world—world population growth rates may not only be higher than official estimates but may also grow higher as traditional societies like the Shipibo experience rapid cultural change.

Human population growth is not new. But there was a time, long past, when it took 100,000 years for world population to double. Soon after agriculture was invented, the doubling time dropped to 700 years. Now our population is doubling every 35 to 40 years. What happened?

While there are many answers, one emerges from this study and others like it: many human societies that controlled their fertility in the past have lost the tradition of doing so in the frenzy of modern cultural change. The old methods that reduced births have not yet been replaced by the new technologies of fertility control. The result is chaos, suffering, more cultural change, and in some cases, even more rapid population growth. Where will it stop?

For the Shipibo it stops when the beloved *yoshanshico* (grandmother) dies of tuberculosis and takes with her the ancient Amazon traditions of pottery making and weaving and knowledge of the plants and seasons. It stops with the loss of half the village's children to a measles epidemic. It stops with the death of a beautiful thirteen-year-old girl in childbirth. It stops when the village chief, a vigorous and intelligent young man, dies of cholera. It stops when the legendary hunter of *piache,* a giant fish once commonly found in Amazon lakes, returns after three days in the bush with his canoe empty and his harpoon unused. His family gets by on another meal of banana porridge.

It stops when the bright but superfluous young men and women of the village leave for the city, where they can get low-level jobs and survive. Their village education, which kept them from the forest and from learning their environment and own culture, has given them only minimal skills for life in town, where they sometimes conceal their cultural identity to get jobs.

It stopped for Ambrosio's wife when she died, exhausted, trying to give birth the next time, at the end of her twelfth pregnancy. The previous child proved to be mentally retarded, probably the result of a two-day labor and difficult delivery. For Ambrosio, a friendly man with a mischievous smile and quick wit, it stopped when he died from tetanus two years later. For Julia, who became one of my dearest friends in life, a woman who had outlived two husbands and thrown out several others, who was fiercely independent and could hunt and fish with the men, who

was a skilled artist and walking library of Shipibo culture, it stopped when she started coughing blood and bled to death in a few minutes in front of her horrified family. The Shipibo are being forced to choose between buying tuberculosis medicine for people like Julia and building schools for their children.

For me, there are few things as delightful as the sound of Shipibo children laughing. The Shipibo love their children, and it shows. But what is ahead for people like Chomoshico and her husband and children? The inexorable arithmetic of population growth is upon them, and the consequences for their environment and families are plain to see. As a public health physician, I cannot help noticing that the Shipibo's fertility problems are inseparable from their other health problems and the changes going on around them. I also cannot help noticing that each family, with few exceptions, wants to limit its fertility but has no safe, effective means of doing so. That is not a scientific issue, but a political problem that neither I nor the Shipibo can solve.

Death Without Weeping

Has poverty ravaged mother love in the shantytowns of Brazil?

Nancy Scheper-Hughes

Nancy Scheper-Hughes is a professor in the Department of Anthropology at the University of California, Berkeley. She has written Death Without Weeping: Violence of Everyday Life in Brazil *(1992).*

I have seen death without weeping
The destiny of the Northeast is death
Cattle they kill
To the people they do something worse
—Anonymous Brazilian singer (1965)

"Why do the church bells ring so often?" I asked Nailza de Arruda soon after I moved into a corner of her tiny mud-walled hut near the top of the shantytown called the Alto do Cruzeiro (Crucifix Hill). I was then a Peace Corps volunteer and a community development/health worker. It was the dry and blazing hot summer of 1965, the months following the military coup in Brazil, and save for the rusty, clanging bells of N. S. das Dores Church, an eerie quiet had settled over the market town that I call Bom Jesus da Mata. Beneath the quiet, however, there was chaos and panic. "It's nothing," replied Nailza, "just another little angel gone to heaven."

Nailza had sent more than her share of little angels to heaven, and sometimes at night I could hear her engaged in a muffled but passionate discourse with one of them, two-year-old Joana. Joana's photograph, taken as she lay propped up in her tiny cardboard coffin, her eyes open, hung on a wall next to one of Nailza and Ze Antonio taken on the day they eloped.

Nailza could barely remember the other infants and babies who came and went in close succession. Most had died unnamed and were hastily baptized in their coffins. Few lived more than a month or two. Only Joana, properly baptized in church at the close of her first year and placed under the protection of a powerful saint, Joan of Arc, had been expected to live. And Nailza had dangerously allowed herself to love the little girl.

In addressing the dead child, Nailza's voice would range from tearful imploring to angry recrimination: "Why did you leave me? Was your patron saint so greedy that she could not allow me one child on this earth?" Ze Antonio advised me to ignore Nailza's odd behavior, which he understood as a kind of madness that, like the birth and death of children, came and went. Indeed, the premature birth of a stillborn son some months later "cured" Nailza of her "inappropriate" grief, and the day came when she removed Joana's photo and carefully packed it away.

More than fifteen years elapsed before I returned to the Alto do Cruzeiro, and it was anthropology that provided the vehicle of my return. Since 1982 I have returned several times in order to pursue a problem that first attracted my attention in the 1960s. My involvement with the people of the Alto do Cruzeiro now spans a quarter of a century and three generations of parenting in a community where mothers and daughters are often simultaneously pregnant.

The Alto do Cruzeiro is one of three shantytowns surrounding the large market town of Bom Jesus in the sugar plantation zone of Pernambuco in Northeast Brazil, one of the many zones of neglect that have emerged in the shadow of the now tarnished economic miracle of Brazil. For the women and children of the Alto do Cruzeiro the only miracle is that some of them have managed to stay alive at all.

The Northeast is a region of vast proportions (approximately twice the size of Texas) and of equally vast social and developmental problems. The nine states that make up the region are the poorest in the country and are representative of the Third World within a dynamic and rapidly industrializing nation. Despite waves of migrations from the interior to the teeming shantytowns of coastal cities, the majority still live in rural areas on farms and ranches, sugar plantations and mills.

Life expectancy in the Northeast is only forty years, largely because of the appallingly high rate of infant and child mortality. Approximately one million children in Brazil under the age of five die each year. The children of the Northeast, especially those born in shantytowns on the periphery of urban life, are at a very high risk of death. In these areas, children are born without the traditional protection of breast-feeding, subsistence gardens, stable marriages, and multiple adult caretakers that exists in the interior. In the hillside shantytowns that spring up around cities or, in this case, interior market towns, marriages are brittle, single parenting is the norm, and women are

 From *Natural History,* October 1989, pp. 8, 10, 12, 14, 16. © 1989 by Nancy Scheper-Hughes. Reprinted by permission of the author.

frequently forced into the shadow economy of domestic work in the homes of the rich or into unprotected and oftentimes "scab" wage labor on the surrounding sugar plantations, where they clear land for planting and weed for a pittance, sometimes less than a dollar a day. The women of the Alto may not bring their babies with them into the homes of the wealthy, where the often-sick infants are considered sources of contamination, and they cannot carry the little ones to the riverbanks where they wash clothes because the river is heavily infested with schistosomes and other deadly parasites. Nor can they carry their young children to the plantations, which are often several miles away. At wages of a dollar a day, the women of the Alto cannot hire baby sitters. Older children who are not in school will sometimes serve as somewhat indifferent caretakers. But any child not in school is also expected to find wage work. In most cases, babies are simply left at home alone, the door securely fastened. And so many also die alone and unattended.

Bom Jesus da Mata, centrally located in the plantation zone of Pernambuco, is within commuting distance of several sugar plantations and mills. Consequently, Bom Jesus has been a magnet for rural workers forced off their small subsistence plots by large landowners wanting to use every available piece of land for sugar cultivation. Initially, the rural migrants to Bom Jesus were squatters who were given tacit approval by the mayor to put up temporary straw huts on each of the three hills overlooking the town. The Alto do Cruzeiro is the oldest, the largest, and the poorest of the shantytowns. Over the past three decades many of the original migrants have become permanent residents, and the primitive and temporary straw huts have been replaced by small homes (usually of two rooms) made of wattle and daub, sometimes covered with plaster. The more affluent residents use bricks and tiles. In most Alto homes, dangerous kerosene lamps have been replaced by light bulbs. The once tattered rural garb, often fashioned from used sugar sacking, has likewise been replaced by store-bought clothes, often castoffs from a wealthy *patrão* (boss). The trappings are modern, but the hunger, sickness, and death that they conceal are traditional, deeply rooted in a history of feudalism, exploitation, and institutionalized dependency.

My research agenda never wavered. The questions I addressed first crystallized during a veritable "die-off" of Alto babies during a severe drought in 1965. The food and water shortages and the political and economic chaos occasioned by the military coup were reflected in the handwritten entries of births and deaths in the dusty, yellowed pages of the ledger books kept at the public registry office in Bom Jesus. More than 350 babies died in the Alto during 1965 alone—this from a shantytown population of little more than 5,000. But that wasn't what surprised me. There were reasons enough for the deaths in the miserable conditions of shantytown life. What puzzled me was the seeming indifference of Alto women to the death of their infants, and their willingness to attribute to their own tiny offspring an aversion to life that made their death seem wholly natural, indeed all but anticipated.

Although I found that it was possible, and hardly difficult, to rescue infants and toddlers from death by diarrhea and dehydration with a simple sugar, salt, and water solution (even bottled Coca-Cola worked fine), it was more difficult to enlist a mother herself in the rescue of a child she perceived as ill-fated for life or better off dead, or to convince her to take back into her threatened and besieged home a baby she had already come to think of as an angel rather than as a son or daughter.

I learned that the high expectancy of death, and the ability to face child death with stoicism and equanimity, produced patterns of nurturing that differentiated between those infants thought of as thrivers and survivors and those thought of as born already "wanting to die." The survivors were nurtured, while stigmatized, doomed infants were left to die, as mothers say, *a mingua*, "of neglect." Mothers stepped back and allowed nature to take its course. This pattern, which I call mortal selective neglect, is called passive infanticide by anthropologist Marvin Harris. The Alto situation, although culturally specific in the form that it takes, is not unique to Third World shantytown communities and may have its correlates in our own impoverished urban communities in some cases of "failure to thrive" infants.

I use as an example the story of Zezinho, the thirteen-month-old toddler of one of my neighbors, Lourdes. I became involved with Zezinho when I was called in to help Lourdes in the delivery of another child, this one a fair and robust little tyke with a lusty cry. I noted that while Lourdes showed great interest in the newborn, she totally ignored Zezinho who, wasted and severely malnourished, was curled up in a fetal position on a piece of urine- and feces-soaked cardboard placed under his mother's hammock. Eyes open and vacant, mouth slack, the little boy seemed doomed.

When I carried Zezinho up to the community day-care center at the top of the hill, the Alto women who took turns caring for one another's children (in order to free themselves for part-time work in the cane fields or washing clothes) laughed at my efforts to save Ze, agreeing with Lourdes that here was a baby without a ghost of a chance. Leave him alone, they cautioned. It makes no sense to fight with death. But I did do battle with Ze, and after several weeks of force-feeding (malnourished babies lose their interest in food), Ze began to succumb to my ministrations. He acquired some flesh across his taut chest bones, learned to sit up, and even tried to smile. When he seemed well enough, I returned him to Lourdes in her miserable scrap-material lean-to, but not without guilt about what I had done. I wondered whether returning Ze was at all fair to Lourdes and to his little brother. But I was busy and washed my hands of the matter. And Lourdes did seem more interested in Ze now that he was looking more human.

When I returned in 1982, there was Lourdes among the women who formed my sample of Alto mothers—still struggling to put together some semblance of life for a now grown Ze and her five other surviving children. Much was made of my reunion with Ze in 1982, and everyone enjoyed retelling the story of Ze's rescue and of how his mother had given him up for dead. Ze would laugh the loudest when told how I had had to force-feed him like a fiesta turkey. There was no hint of guilt on the part of Lourdes and no resentment on the part of Ze. In fact, when questioned in private as to who was the best friend he ever had in life, Ze took a long drag on his cigarette and answered without a trace of irony, "Why my mother, of course." "But of course," I replied.

Part of learning how to mother in the Alto do Cruzeiro is learning when to let go of a child who shows that it "wants" to die or that it has no "knack" or no "taste" for life. Another part is learning when it is safe to let oneself love a child. Frequent child death remains a powerful shaper of maternal thinking and practice. In the absence of firm expectation that a child will survive, mother love as we conceptualize it (whether in popular terms or in the psychobiological notion of maternal bonding) is attenuated and delayed with consequences for infant survival. In an environment already precarious to young life, the emotional detachment of mothers toward some of their babies contributes even further to the spiral of high mortality—high fertility in a kind of macabre lock-step dance of death.

The average woman of the Alto experiences 9.5 pregnancies, 3.5 child deaths, and 1.5 stillbirths. Seventy percent of all child deaths in the Alto occur in the first six months of life, and 82 percent by the end of the first year. Of all deaths in the community each year, about 45 percent are of children under the age of five.

Women of the Alto distinguish between child deaths understood as natural (caused by diarrhea and communicable diseases) and those resulting from sorcery, the evil eye, or other magical or supernatural afflictions. They also recognize a large category of infant deaths seen as fated and inevitable. These hopeless cases are classified by mothers under the folk terminology "child sickness" or "child attack." Women say that there are at least fourteen different types of hopeless child sickness, but most can be subsumed under two categories—chronic and acute. The chronic cases refer to infants who are born small and wasted. They are deathly pale, mothers say, as well as weak and passive. They demonstrate no vital force, no liveliness. They do not suck vigorously; they hardly cry. Such babies can be this way at birth or they can be born sound but soon show no resistance, no "fight" against the common crises of infancy: diarrhea, respiratory infections, tropical fevers.

The acute cases are those doomed infants who die suddenly and violently. They are taken by stealth overnight, often following convulsions that bring on head banging, shaking, grimacing, and shrieking. Women say it is horrible to look at such a baby. If the infant begins to foam at the mouth or gnash its teeth or go rigid with its eyes turned back inside its head, there is absolutely no hope. The infant is "put aside"— left alone—often on the floor in a back room, and allowed to die. These symptoms (which accompany high fevers, dehydration, third-stage malnutrition, and encephalitis) are equated by Alto women with madness, epilepsy, and worst of all, rabies, which is greatly feared and highly stigmatized.

Most of the infants presented to me as suffering from chronic child sickness were tiny, wasted famine victims, while those labeled as victims of acute child attack seemed to be infants suffering from the deliriums of high fever or the convulsions that can accompany electrolyte imbalance in dehydrated babies.

Local midwives and traditional healers, praying women, as they are called, advise Alto women on when to allow a baby to die. One midwife explained: "If I can see that a baby was born unfortuitously, I tell the mother that she need not wash the infant or give it a cleansing tea. I tell her just to dust the infant with baby powder and wait for it to die." Allowing nature to take its course is not seen as sinful by these often very devout Catholic women. Rather, it is understood as cooperating with God's plan.

Often I have been asked how consciously women of the Alto behave in this regard. I would have to say that consciousness is always shifting between allowed and disallowed levels of awareness. For example, I was awakened early one morning in 1987 by two neighborhood children who had been sent to fetch me to a hastily organized wake for a two-month-old infant whose mother I had unsuccessfully urged to breast-feed. The infant was being sustained on sugar water, which the mother referred to as *soro* (serum), using a medical term for the infant's starvation regime in light of his chronic diarrhea. I had cautioned the mother that an infant could not live on *soro* forever.

The two girls urged me to console the young mother by telling her that it was "too bad" that her infant was so weak that Jesus had to take him. They were coaching me in proper Alto etiquette. I agreed, of course, but asked, "And what do *you* think?" Xoxa, the eleven-year-old, looked down at her dusty flip-flops and blurted out, "Oh, Dona Nanci, that baby never got enough to eat, but you must never say that!" And so the death of hungry babies remains one of the best kept secrets of life in Bom Jesus da Mata.

Most victims are waked quickly and with a minimum of ceremony. No tears are shed, and the neighborhood children form a tiny procession, carrying the baby to the town graveyard where it will join a multitude of others. Although a few fresh flowers may be scattered over the tiny grave, no stone or wooden cross will mark the place, and the same spot will be reused within a few months' time. The mother will never visit the grave, which soon becomes an anonymous one.

What, then, can be said of these women? What emotions, what sentiments motivate them? How are they able to do what, in fact, must be done? What does mother love mean in this inhospitable context? Are grief, mourning, and melancholia present, although deeply repressed? If so, where shall we look for them? And if not, how are we to understand the moral visions and moral sensibilities that guide their actions?

I have been criticized more than once for presenting an unflattering portrait of poor Brazilian women, women who are, after all, themselves the victims of severe social and institutional neglect. I have described these women as allowing some of their children to die, as if this were an unnatural and inhuman act rather than, as I would assert, the way any one of us might act, reasonably and rationally, under similarly desperate conditions. Perhaps I have not emphasized enough the real pathogens in this environment of high risk: poverty, deprivation, sexism, chronic hunger, and economic exploitation. If mother love is, as many psychologists and some feminists believe, a seemingly natural and universal maternal script, what does it mean to women for whom scarcity, loss, sickness, and deprivation have made that love frantic and robbed them of their grief, seeming to turn their hearts to stone?

Throughout much of human history—as in a great deal of the impoverished Third World today—women have had to give birth and to nurture children under ecological conditions and social arrangements hostile to child survival, as well as to their own well-being. Under circumstances of high childhood mortality, patterns of selective neglect and passive infanticide may be seen as active survival strategies.

They also seem to be fairly common practices historically and across cultures. In societies characterized by high childhood mortality and by a correspondingly high (replacement) fertility, cultural practices of infant and child care tend to be organized primarily around survival goals. But what this means is a pragmatic recognition that not all of one's children can be expected to live. The nervousness about child survival in areas of northeast Brazil, northern India, or Bangladesh, where a 30 percent or 40 percent mortality rate in the first years of life is common, can lead to forms of delayed attachment and a casual or benign neglect that serves to weed out the worst

bets so as to enhance the life chances of healthier siblings, including those yet to be born. Practices similar to those that I am describing have been recorded for parts of Africa, India, and Central America.

Life in the Alto do Cruzeiro resembles nothing so much as a battlefield or an emergency room in an overcrowded inner-city public hospital. Consequently, morality is guided by a kind of "lifeboat ethics," the morality of triage. The seemingly studied indifference toward the suffering of some of their infants, conveyed in such sayings as "little critters have no feelings," is understandable in light of these women's obligation to carry on with their reproductive and nurturing lives.

In their slowness to anthropomorphize and personalize their infants, everything is mobilized so as to prevent maternal overattachment and, therefore, grief at death. The bereaved mother is told not to cry, that her tears will dampen the wings of her little angel so that she cannot fly up to her heavenly home. Grief at the death of an angel is not only inappropriate, it is a symptom of madness and of a profound lack of faith.

Infant death becomes routine in an environment in which death is anticipated and bets are hedged. While the routinization of death in the context of shantytown life is not hard to understand, and quite possible to empathize with, its routinization in the formal institutions of public life in Bom Jesus is not as easy to accept uncritically. Here the social production of indifference takes on a different, even a malevolent, cast.

In a society where triplicates of every form are required for the most banal events (registering a car, for example), the registration of infant and child death is informal, incomplete, and rapid. It requires no documentation, takes less than five minutes, and demands no witnesses other than office clerks. No questions are asked concerning the circumstances of the death, and the cause of death is left blank, unquestioned and unexamined. A neighbor, grandmother, older sibling, or common-law husband may register the

death. Since most infants die at home, there is no question of a medical record.

From the registry office, the parent proceeds to the town hall, where the mayor will give him or her a voucher for a free baby coffin. The full-time municipal coffinmaker cannot tell you exactly how many baby coffins are dispatched each week. It varies, he says, with the seasons. There are more needed during the drought months and during the big festivals of Carnaval and Christmas and São Joao's Day because people are too busy, he supposes, to take their babies to the clinic. Record keeping is sloppy.

Similarly, there is a failure on the part of city-employed doctors working at two free clinics to recognize the malnutrition of babies who are weighed, measured, and immunized without comment and as if they were not, in fact, anemic, stunted, fussy, and irritated starvation babies. At best the mothers are told to pick up free vitamins or a health "tonic" at the municipal chambers. At worst, clinic personnel will give tranquilizers and sleeping pills to quiet the hungry cries of "sick-to-death" Alto babies.

The church, too, contributes to the routinization of, and indifference toward, child death. Traditionally, the local Catholic church taught patience and resignation to domestic tragedies that were said to reveal the imponderable workings of God's will. If an infant died suddenly, it was because a particular saint had claimed the child. The infant would be an angel in the service of his or her heavenly patron. It would be wrong, a sign of a lack of faith, to weep for a child with such good fortune. The infant funeral was, in the past, an event celebrated with joy. Today, however, under the new regime of "liberation theology," the bells of N. S. das Dores parish church no longer peal for the death of Alto babies, and no priest accompanies the procession of angels to the cemetery where their bodies are disposed of casually and without ceremony. Children bury children in Bom Jesus da Mata. In this most Catholic of communities, the coffin is handed to the disabled and irritable municipal gravedigger, who often chides the children for one reason or another. It may be that the coffin is larger than expected and the gravedigger can find no appropriate space. The children do not wait for the gravedigger to complete his task. No prayers are recited and no sign of the cross made as the tiny coffin goes into its shallow grave.

When I asked the local priest, Padre Marcos, about the lack of church ceremony surrounding infant and childhood death today in Bom Jesus, he replied: "In the old days, child death was richly celebrated. But those were the baroque customs of a conservative church that wallowed in death and misery. The new church is a church of hope and joy. We no longer celebrate the death of child angels. We try to tell mothers that Jesus doesn't want all the dead babies they send him." Similarly, the new church has changed its baptismal customs, now often refusing to baptize dying babies brought to the back door of a church or rectory. The mothers are scolded by the church attendants and told to go home and take care of their sick babies. Baptism, they are told, is for the living; it is not to be confused with the sacrament of extreme unction, which is the anointing of the dying. And so it appears to the women of the Alto that even the

church has turned away from them, denying the traditional comfort of folk Catholicism.

The contemporary Catholic church is caught in the clutches of a double bind. The new theology of liberation imagines a kingdom of God on earth based on justice and equality, a world without hunger, sickness, or childhood mortality. At the same time, the church has not changed its official position on sexuality and reproduction, including its sanctions against birth control, abortion, and sterilization. The padre of Bom Jesus da Mata recognizes this contradiction intuitively, although he shies away from discussions on the topic, saying that he prefers to leave questions of family planning to the discretion and the "good consciences" of his impoverished parishioners. But this, of course, sidesteps the extent to which those good consciences have been shaped by traditional church teachings in Bom Jesus, especially by his recent predecessors. Hence, we can begin to see that the seeming indifference of Alto mothers toward the death of some of their infants is but a pale reflection of the official indifference of church and state to the plight of poor women and children.

Nonetheless, the women of Bom Jesus are survivors. One woman, Biu, told me her life history, returning again

and again to the themes of child death, her first husband's suicide, abandonment by her father and later by her second husband, and all the other losses and disappointments she had suffered in her long forty-five years. She concluded with great force, reflecting on the days of Carnaval '88 that were fast approaching:

No, Dona Nanci, I won't cry, and I won't waste my life thinking about it from morning to night. . . . Can I argue with God for the state that I'm in? No! And so I'll dance and I'll jump and I'll play Carnaval! And yes, I'll laugh and people will wonder at a *pobre* like me who can have such a good time.

And no one did blame Biu for dancing in the streets during the four days of Carnaval—not even on Ash Wednesday, the day following Carnaval '88 when we all assembled hurriedly to assist in the burial of Mercea, Biu's beloved *casula,* her last-born daughter who had died at home of pneumonia during the festivities. The rest of the family barely had time to change out of their costumes. Severino, the child's uncle and godfather, sprinkled holy water over the little angel while he prayed: "Mercea, I don't know whether you were called, taken, or thrown out of this world. But look down at us from your heavenly home with tenderness, with pity, and with mercy." So be it.

Arranging a Marriage in India

Serena Nanda

John Jay College of Criminal Justice

Sister and doctor brother-in-law invite correspondence from North Indian professionals only, for a beautiful, talented, sophisticated, intelligent sister, 5′ 3″, slim, M.A. in textile design, father a senior civil officer. Would prefer immigrant doctors, between 26–29 years. Reply with full details and returnable photo.

A well-settled uncle invites matrimonial correspondence from slim, fair, educated South Indian girl, for his nephew, 25 years, smart, M.B.A., green card holder, 5′ 6″. Full particulars with returnable photo appreciated.

Matrimonial Advertisements,
India Abroad

In India, almost all marriages are arranged. Even among the educated middle classes in modern, urban India, marriage is as much a concern of the families as it is of the individuals. So customary is the practice of arranged marriage that there is a special name for a marriage which is not arranged: It is called a "love match."

On my first field trip to India, I met many young men and women whose parents were in the process of "getting them married." In many cases, the bride and groom would not meet each other before the marriage. At most they might meet for a brief conversation, and this meeting would take place only after their parents had decided that the match was suitable. Parents do not compel their children to marry a person who either marriage partner finds objectionable. But only after one match is refused will another be sought.

As a young American woman in India for the first time, I found this custom of arranged marriage oppressive. How could any intelligent young person agree to such a marriage without great reluctance? It was contrary to everything I believed about the importance of romantic love as the only basis of a happy marriage. It also clashed with my strongly held notions that the choice of such an intimate and permanent relationship could be made only by the individuals involved. Had anyone tried to arrange my marriage, I would have been defiant and rebellious!

At the first opportunity, I began, with more curiosity than tact, to question the young people I met on how they felt about this practice. Sita, one of my young informants, was a college graduate with a degree in political science. She had been waiting for over a year while her parents were arranging a match for her. I found it difficult to accept the docile manner in which this well-educated young woman awaited the outcome of a process that would result in her spending the rest of her life with a man she hardly knew, a virtual stranger, picked out by her parents.

"How can you go along with this?" I asked her, in frustration and distress. "Don't you care who you marry?"

"Of course I care," she answered. "This is why I must let my parents choose a boy for me. My marriage is too important to be arranged by such an inexperienced person as myself. In such matters, it is better to have my parents' guidance."

I had learned that young men and women in India do not date and have very little social life involving members of the opposite sex. Although I could not disagree with Sita's reasoning, I continued to pursue the subject.

"But how can you marry the first man you have ever met? Not only have you missed the fun of meeting a lot of different people, but you have not given yourself the chance to know who is the right man for you."

"Meeting with a lot of different people doesn't sound like any fun at all," Sita answered. "One hears that in America the girls are spending all their

From *The Naked Anthropologist*, Wadsworth, 1992, pp. 34–45. © 1992 by Serena Nanda. Reprinted by permission.

time worrying about whether they will meet a man and get married. Here we have the chance to enjoy our life and let our parents do this work and worrying for us."

She had me there. The high anxiety of the competition to "be popular" with the opposite sex certainly was the most prominent feature of life as an American teenager in the late fifties. The endless worrying about the rules that governed our behavior and about our popularity ratings sapped both our self-esteem and our enjoyment of adolescence. I reflected that absence of this competition in India most certainly may have contributed to the self-confidence and natural charm of so many of the young women I met.

And yet, the idea of marrying a perfect stranger, whom one did not know and did not "love," so offended my American ideas of individualism and romanticism, that I persisted with my objections.

"I still can't imagine it," I said. "How can you agree to marry a man you hardly know?"

"But of course he will be known. My parents would never arrange a marriage for me without knowing all about the boy's family background. Naturally we will not rely only on what the family tells us. We will check the particulars out ourselves. No one will want their daughter to marry into a family that is not good. All these things we will know beforehand."

Impatiently, I responded, "Sita, I don't mean know the family, I mean, know the man. How can you marry someone you don't know personally and don't love? How can you think of spending your life with someone you may not even like?"

"If he is a good man, why should I not like him?" she said. "With you people, you know the boy so well before you marry, where will be the fun to get married? There will be no mystery and no romance. Here we have the whole of our married life to get to know and love our husband. This way is better, is it not?"

Her response made further sense, and I began to have second thoughts on the matter. Indeed, during months of meeting many intelligent young Indian people, both male and female, who had the same ideas as Sita, I saw arranged marriages in a different light. I also saw the importance of the family in Indian life and realized that a couple who took their marriage into their own hands was taking a big risk, particularly if their families were irreconcilably opposed to the match. In a country where every important resource in life—a job, a house, a social circle—is gained through family connections, it seemed foolhardy to cut oneself off from a supportive social network and depend solely on one person for happiness and success.

Six years later I returned to India to again do fieldwork, this time among the middle class in Bombay, a modern, sophisticated city. From the experience of my earlier visit, I decided to include a study of arranged marriages in my project. By this time I had met many Indian couples whose marriages had been arranged and who seemed very happy. Particularly in contrast to the fate of many of my married friends in the United States who were already in the process of divorce, the positive aspects of arranged marriages appeared to me to outweigh the negatives. In fact, I thought I might even participate in arranging a marriage myself. I had been fairly successful in the United States in "fixing up" many of my friends, and I was confident that my matchmaking skills could be easily applied to this new situation, once I learned the basic rules. "After all," I thought, "how complicated can it be? People want pretty much the same things in a marriage whether it is in India or America."

An opportunity presented itself almost immediately. A friend from my previous Indian trip was in the process of arranging for the marriage of her eldest son. In India there is a perceived shortage of "good boys," and since my friend's family was eminently respectable and the boy himself personable, well educated, and nice looking, I was sure that by the end of my year's fieldwork, we would have found a match.

The basic rule seems to be that a family's reputation is most important.

It is understood that matches would be arranged only within the same caste and general social class, although some crossing of subcastes is permissible if the class positions of the bride's and groom's families are similar. Although dowry is now prohibited by law in India, extensive gift exchanges took place with every marriage. Even when the boy's family do not "make demands," every girl's family nevertheless feels the obligation to give the traditional gifts, to the girl, to the boy, and to the boy's family. Particularly when the couple would be living in the joint family—that is, with the boy's parents and his married brothers and their families, as well as with unmarried siblings—which is still very common even among the urban, upper-middle class in India, the girl's parents are anxious to establish smooth relations between their family and that of the boy. Offering the proper gifts, even when not called "dowry," is often an important factor in influencing the relationship between the bride's and groom's families and perhaps, also, the treatment of the bride in her new home.

In a society where divorce is still a scandal and where, in fact, the divorce rate is exceedingly low, an arranged marriage is the beginning of a lifetime relationship not just between the bride and groom but between their families as well. Thus, while a girl's looks are important, her character is even more so, for she is being judged as a prospective daughter-in-law as much as a prospective bride. Where she would be living in a joint family, as was the case with my friend, the girl's ability to get along harmoniously in a family is perhaps the single most important quality in assessing her suitability.

My friend is a highly esteemed wife, mother, and daughter-in-law. She is religious, soft-spoken, modest, and deferential. She rarely gossips and never quarrels, two qualities highly desirable in a woman. A family that has the reputation for gossip and conflict among its womenfolk will not find it easy to get good wives for their sons. Parents will not want to send their daughter to a house in which there is conflict.

My friend's family were originally from North India. They had lived in Bombay, where her husband owned a business, for forty years. The family had delayed in seeking a match for their eldest son because he had been an Air Force pilot for several years, stationed in such remote places that it had seemed fruitless to try to find a girl who would be willing to accompany him. In their social class, a military career, despite its economic security, has little prestige and is considered a drawback in finding a suitable bride. Many families would not allow their daughters to marry a man in an occupation so potentially dangerous and which requires so much moving around.

The son had recently left the military and joined his father's business. Since he was a college graduate, modern, and well traveled, from such a good family, and, I thought, quite handsome, it seemed to me that he, or rather his family, was in a position to pick and choose. I said as much to my friend.

While she agreed that there were many advantages on their side, she also said, "We must keep in mind that my son is both short and dark; these are drawbacks in finding the right match." While the boy's height had not escaped my notice, "dark" seemed to me inaccurate; I would have called him "wheat" colored perhaps, and in any case, I did not realize that color would be a consideration. I discovered, however, that while a boy's skin color is a less important consideration than a girl's, it is still a factor.

An important source of contacts in trying to arrange her son's marriage was my friend's social club in Bombay. Many of the women had daughters of the right age, and some had already expressed an interest in my friend's son. I was most enthusiastic about the possibilities of one particular family who had five daughters, all of whom were pretty, demure, and well educated. Their mother had told my friend, "You can have your pick for your son, whichever one of my daughters appeals to you most."

I saw a match in sight. "Surely," I said to my friend, "we will find one there. Let's go visit and make our choice." But my friend held back; she did not seem to share my enthusiasm, for reasons I could not then fathom.

When I kept pressing for an explanation of her reluctance, she admitted, "See, Serena, here is the problem. The family has so many daughters, how will they be able to provide nicely for any of them? We are not making any demands, but still, with so many daughters to marry off, one wonders whether she will even be able to make a proper wedding. Since this is our eldest son, it's best if we marry him to a girl who is the only daughter, then the wedding will truly be a gala affair."

Even today, almost all marriages in India are arranged. It is believed that parents are much more effective at deciding who their daughters should marry.

4. OTHER FAMILIES, OTHER WAYS

I argued that surely the quality of the girls themselves made up for any deficiency in the elaborateness of the wedding. My friend admitted this point but still seemed reluctant to proceed.

"Is there something else," I asked her, "some factor I have missed?" "Well," she finally said, "there is one other thing. They have one daughter already married and living in Bombay. The mother is always complaining to me that the girl's in-laws don't let her visit her own family often enough. So it makes me wonder, will she be that kind of mother who always wants her daughter at her own home? This will prevent the girl from adjusting to our house. It is not a good thing." And so, this family of five daughters was dropped as a possibility.

Somewhat disappointed, I nevertheless respected my friend's reasoning and geared up for the next prospect. This was also the daughter of a woman in my friend's social club. There was clear interest in this family and I could see why. The family's reputation was excellent; in fact, they came from a subcaste slightly higher than my friend's own. The girl, who was an only daughter, was pretty and well educated and had a brother studying in the United States. Yet, after expressing an interest to me in this family, all talk of them suddenly died down and the search began elsewhere.

"What happened to that girl as a prospect?" I asked one day. "You never mention her any more. She is so pretty and so educated, what did you find wrong?"

"She is too educated. We've decided against it. My husband's father saw the girl on the bus the other day and thought her forward. A girl who 'roams about' the city by herself is not the girl for our family." My disappointment this time was even greater, as I thought the son would have liked the girl very much. But then I thought, my friend is right, a girl who is going to live in a joint family cannot be too independent or she will make life miserable for everyone. I also learned that if the family of the girl has even a slightly higher social status than the family of the boy, the bride may think herself too good

for them, and this too will cause problems. Later my friend admitted to me that this had been an important factor in her decision not to pursue the match.

The next candidate was the daughter of a client of my friend's husband. When the client learned that the family was looking for a match for their son, he said, "Look no further, we have a daughter." This man then invited my friends to dinner to see the girl. He had already seen their son at the office and decided that "he liked the boy." We all went together for tea, rather than dinner—it was less of a commitment—and while we were there, the girl's mother showed us around the house. The girl was studying for her exams and was briefly introduced to us.

After we left, I was anxious to hear my friend's opinion. While her husband liked the family very much and was impressed with his client's business accomplishments and reputation, the wife didn't like the girl's looks. "She is short, no doubt, which is an important plus point, but she is also fat and wears glasses." My friend obviously thought she could do better for her son and asked her husband to make his excuses to his client by saying that they had decided to postpone the boy's marriage indefinitely.

By this time almost six months had passed and I was becoming impatient. What I had thought would be an easy matter to arrange was turning out to be quite complicated. I began to believe that between my friend's desire for a girl who was modest enough to fit into her joint family, yet attractive and educated enough to be an acceptable partner for her son, she would not find anyone suitable. My friend laughed at my impatience: "Don't be so much in a hurry," she said. "You Americans want everything done so quickly. You get married quickly and then just as quickly get divorced. Here we take marriage more seriously. We must take all the factors into account. It is not enough for us to learn by our mistakes. This is too serious a business. If a mistake is made we have not only ruined the life of our son or daughter, but we have spoiled the reputation of our family as well. And that will make

it much harder for their brothers and sisters to get married. So we must be very careful."

What she said was true and I promised myself to be more patient, though it was not easy. I had really hoped and expected that the match would be made before my year in India was up. But it was not to be. When I left India my friend seemed no further along in finding a suitable match for her son than when I had arrived.

Two years later, I returned to India and still my friend had not found a girl for her son. By this time, he was close to thirty, and I think she was a little worried. Since she knew I had friends all over India, and I was going to be there for a year, she asked me to "help her in this work" and keep an eye out for someone suitable. I was flattered that my judgment was respected, but knowing now how complicated the process was, I had lost my earlier confidence as a matchmaker. Nevertheless, I promised that I would try.

It was almost at the end of my year's stay in India that I met a family with a marriageable daughter whom I felt might be a good possibility for my friend's son. The girl's father was related to a good friend of mine and by coincidence came from the same village as my friend's husband. This new family had a successful business in a medium-sized city in central India and were from the same subcaste as my friend. The daughter was pretty and chic; in fact, she had studied fashion design in college. Her parents would not allow her to go off by herself to any of the major cities in India where she could make a career, but they had compromised with her wish to work by allowing her to run a small dress-making boutique from their home. In spite of her desire to have a career, the daughter was both modest and home-loving and had had a traditional, sheltered upbringing. She had only one other sister, already married, and a brother who was in his father's business.

I mentioned the possibility of a match with my friend's son. The girl's parents were most interested. Although their daughter was not eager to marry just yet, the idea of living in

Bombay—a sophisticated, extremely fashion-conscious city where she could continue her education in clothing design—was a great inducement. I gave the girl's father my friend's address and suggested that when they went to Bombay on some business or whatever, they look up the boy's family.

Returning to Bombay on my way to New York, I told my friend of this newly discovered possibility. She seemed to feel there was potential but, in spite of my urging, would not make any moves herself. She rather preferred to wait for the girl's family to call upon them. I hoped something would come of this introduction, though by now I had learned to rein in my optimism.

A year later I received a letter from my friend. The family had indeed come to visit Bombay, and their daughter and my friend's daughter, who were near in age, had become very good friends. During that year, the two girls had frequently visited each other. I thought things looked promising.

Last week I received an invitation to a wedding: My friend's son and the girl were getting married. Since I had found the match, my presence was particularly requested at the wedding. I was thrilled. Success at last! As I prepared to leave for India, I began thinking, "Now, my friend's younger son, who do I know who has a nice girl for him . . .?"

Sex Roles and Statuses

The feminist movement in the United States has had a significant impact on the development of anthropology. Feminists have rightly charged that anthropologists have tended to gloss over the lives of women in studies of society and culture. In part, this is because, up until recent times, most anthropologists have been men. The result has been an undue emphasis upon male activities as well as male perspectives in descriptions of particular societies.

These charges, however, have proven to be a firm corrective. In the last few years, anthropologists have begun to study women and, more particularly, the sexual division of labor and its relation to biology (see "Why Don't We Act Like the Opposite Sex?" by Anthony Layng) as well as to social and political status. In addition, these changes in emphasis have been accompanied by an increase in the number of women in the field.

Feminist anthropologists have begun to critically attack many of the established anthropological truths. They have shown, for example, that field studies of nonhuman primates, which were often used to demonstrate the evolutionary basis of male dominance, distorted the actual evolutionary record by focusing primarily on baboons. (Male baboons are especially dominant and aggressive.) Other, less-quoted primate studies show how dominance and aggression are highly situational phenomena, sensitive to ecological variation. Feminist anthropologists have also shown that the subsistence contribution of women has likewise been ignored by anthropologists. A classic case is that of the !Kung, a hunting and gathering people in Southern Africa, where women provide the bulk of the foodstuffs, including most of the available protein, and who, not coincidentally, enjoy a more egalitarian relationship with men.

The most common occurrence, at least in recent history, has been male domination over women, even in situations where daughters are favored over sons, as detailed in "Parental Favoritism Toward Daughters" by Lee Cronk. Recent studies have concerned themselves with why there has been such gender inequality. Although the subordination of women can be extreme (as seen in "The Little Emperors" by Daniela Deane), Ernestine Friedl, in "Society and Sex Roles," explains that the sex that controls the valued goods of exchange in a society is the dominant gender and, since this is a matter of cultural variation, male authority is not biologically predetermined. Even so, Lori Heise ("The Global War Against Women") points out that sexual equality is still far from being a reality in many parts of the world, and Maxine Margolis ("Blaming the Victim") shows how ideology is still a very effective force in keeping women subordinate, even in modern America.

Looking Ahead: Challenge Questions

What is it about foraging societies that encourages an egalitarian relationship between the sexes?

What kinds of shifts in the social relations of production are necessary for women to achieve equality with men?

To what extent are the different behaviors of men and women inherited?

What have been the unforeseen consequences of China's one-child policy?

Does China's one-child policy represent the wave of the future for the world?

What kinds of personal dilemmas do women face in a changing society?

What kinds of historical, religious, and legal legacies have contributed to violence against women around the world?

How may a culture's ideology serve to justify sex role differences?

How does the "blaming the victim" rationale help to keep women subordinate?

Society and Sex Roles

Ernestine Friedl

Ernestine Friedl is a professor of anthropology at Duke University; a former president of the American Anthropological Association, a fellow of the American Academy of Arts and Sciences, and an advisory editor to Human Nature. *She received her Ph.D. from Columbia University in 1950. Until recently, Friedl was a firm believer in the relative equality of women in the field of anthropology and had little interest in the anthropological study of women. None of her field work among the Pomo and Chippewa Indians of North America, or in rural and urban Greece was concerned with women's issues.*

In the early 1970s, while serving on the American Anthropological Association Committee on the Status of Women, Friedl became convinced that women were discriminated against as much in anthropology as in the other academic disciplines. Since that time, she has devoted her efforts to the cross-cultural study of sex roles and has written one book on the topic, Women and Men: An Anthropologist's View. *Friedl now accounts for her own success in part by the fact that she attended an all-women's college and taught for many years at the City University of New York, a university system that included a women's college.*

"Women must respond quickly to the demands of their husbands," says anthropologist Napoleon Chagnon describing the horticultural Yanomamo Indians of Venezuela. When a man returns from a hunting trip, "the woman, no matter what she is doing, hurries home and quietly but rapidly prepares a meal for her husband. Should the wife be slow in doing this, the husband is within his rights to beat her. Most reprimands...take the form of blows with the hand or with a piece of firewood. . . .Some of them chop their wives with the sharp edge of a machete or axe, or shoot them with a barbed arrow in some nonvital area, such as the buttocks or leg."

Among the Semai agriculturalists of central Malaya, when one person refuses the request of another, the offended party suffers *punan,* a mixture of emotional pain and frustration. "Enduring *punan* is commonest when a girl has refused the victim her sexual favors," reports Robert Dentan. "The jilted man's 'heart becomes sad.' He loses his energy and his appetite. Much of the time he sleeps, dreaming of his lost love. In this state, he is in fact very likely to injure himself 'accidentally.' " The Semai are afraid of violence; a man would never strike a woman.

The social relationship between men and women has emerged as one of the principal disputes occupying the attention of scholars and the public in recent years. Athough the discord is sharpest in the United States, the controversy has spread throughout the world. Numerous national and international conferences, including one in Mexico sponsored by the United Nations, have drawn together delegates from all walks of life to discuss such questions as the social and political rights of each sex, and even the basic nature of males and females.

Whatever their position, partisans often invoke examples from other cultures to support their ideas about the proper role of each sex. Because women are clearly subservient to men in many societies, like the Yanomamo, some experts conclude that the natural pattern is for men to dominate. But among the Semai no one has the right to command others, and in West Africa women are often chiefs. The place of women in these societies supports the argument of those who believe that sex roles are not fixed, that if there is a natural order, it allows for many different arrangements.

The argument will never be settled as long as the opposing sides toss examples from the world's cultures at each other like intellectual stones. But the effect of biological differences on male and female behavior can be clarified by looking at known examples of the earliest forms of human society and examining the relationship between technology, social organization, environment, and sex roles. The problem is to determine the conditions in which different degrees of male dominance are found, to try to discover the social and cultural arrangements that give rise to equality or inequality between the sexes, and to attempt to apply this knowledge to our understanding of the changes taking place in modern industrial society.

As Western history and the anthropological record have told us, equality between the sexes is rare; in most known societies females are subordinate. Male dominance is so widespread that it is virtually a human universal; societies in which women are consistently dominant do not exist and have never existed.

Evidence of a society in which women control all strategic resources like food and water, and in which women's activities are the most prestigious has never been found. The Iroquois of North America and the Lovedu of Africa came closest. Among the Iroquois, women raised food, controlled its distribution, and helped to choose male political leaders. Lovedu women ruled as queens, exchanged valuable cattle, led ceremonies, and controlled their own sex lives. But among both the Iroquois and the Lovedu, men owned the land and held other positions of power and prestige. Women were equal to men; they did not have ultimate authority over them. Neither culture was a true matriarchy.

Patriarchies are prevalent, and they appear to be strongest in societies in which men control significant goods that are exchanged with people outside the family. Regardless of who produces food, the person who gives it to others creates the obligations and alliances that are at the center of all political relations. The greater the male monopoly on the distribution of scarce items, the stronger their control of women seems to be. This is most obvious in relatively simple hunter-gatherer societies.

Hunter-gatherers, or foragers, subsist on wild plants, small land animals, and small river or sea creatures gathered by hand; large land animals and sea mammals hunted with spears, bows and arrows, and blow guns; and fish caught with hooks and nets. The 300,000 hunter-gatherers alive in the world today include the Eskimos, the Australian aborigines, and the Pygmies of Central Africa.

Foraging has endured for two million years and was replaced by farming and animal husbandry only 10,000 years ago; it covers more than 99 percent of human history. Our foraging ancestry is not far behind us and provides a clue to our understanding of the human condition.

Hunter-gatherers are people whose ways of life are technologically simple and socially and politically egalitarian. They live in small groups of 50 to 200 and have neither kings, nor priests, nor social classes. These conditions permit anthropologists to observe the essential bases for inequalities between the sexes without the distortions induced by the complexities of contemporary industrial society.

The source of male power among hunter-gatherers lies in their control of a scarce, hard to acquire, but necessary nutrient—animal protein. When men in a hunter-gatherer society return to camp with game, they divide the meat in some customary way. Among the !Kung San of Africa, certain parts of the animal are given to the owner of the arrow that killed the beast, to the first hunter to sight the game, to the one who threw the first spear and to all men in the hunting party. After the meat has been divided, each hunter distributes his share to his blood relatives and his in-laws, who in turn share it with others. If an animal is large enough, every member of the band will receive some meat.

Vegetable foods, in contrast, are not distributed beyond the immediate household. Women give food to their children, to their husbands, to other members of the household, and rarely, to the occasional visitor. No one outside the family regularly eats any of the wild fruits and vegetables that are gathered by the women.

The meat distributed by the men is a public gift. Its source is widely known, and the donor expects a reciprocal gift when other men return from a successful hunt. He gains honor as a supplier of a scarce item and simultaneously obligates others to him.

These obligations constitute a form of power or control over others, both men and women. The opinions of hunters play an important part in decisions to move the village; good hunters attract the most desirable women; people in other groups join camps with good hunters; and hunters, because they already participate in an internal system of exchange, control exchange with other groups for flint, salt, and steel axes. The male monopoly on hunting unites men in a system of exchange and gives them power; gathering vegetable food does not give women equal power even among foragers who live in the tropics, where the food collected by women provides more than half the hunter-gatherer diet.

If dominance arises from a monopoly on big-game hunting, why has the male monopoly remained unchallenged? Some women are strong enough to participate in the hunt and their endurance is certainly equal to that of men. Dobe San women of the Kalahari Desert in Africa walk an average of 10 miles a day carrying from 15 to 33 pounds of food plus a baby.

Women do not hunt, I believe, because of four interrelated factors: variability in the supply of game; the different skills required for hunting and gathering; the incompatibility between carrying burdens and hunting; and the small size of semi-nomadic foraging populations.

Because the meat supply is unstable, foragers must make frequent expeditions to provide the band with gathered food. Environmental factors such as seasonal and annual variation in rainful often affect the size of the wildlife population. Hunters cannot always find game, and when they do encounter animals, they are not always successful in killing their prey. In northern latitudes, where meat is the primary food, periods of starvation are known in every generation. The irregularity of the game supply leads hunter-gatherers in areas where plant foods are available to depend on these predictable foods a good part of the time. Someone must gather the fruits, nuts, and roots and carry them back to camp to feed unsuccessful hunters, children, the elderly, and anyone who might not have gone foraging that day.

Foraging falls to the women because hunting and gathering cannot be combined on the same expedition. Although gatherers sometimes notice signs of game as they work, the skills required to track game are not the same as those required to find edible roots or plants. Hunters scan the horizon and the land for traces of large game; gatherers keep their eyes to the ground, studying the distribution of plants and the texture of the soil for hidden roots and animal holes. Even if a woman who was collecting plants came across the track of an antelope, she could not follow it; it is impossible to carry a load and hunt at the same time. Running with a heavy load is difficult, and should the animal be sighted, the hunter would be off balance and could neither shoot an arrow nor throw a spear accurately.

Pregnancy and child care would also present difficulties for a hunter. An unborn child affects a woman's body balance, as does a child in her arms, on her back, or slung at her side. Until they are two years old, many hunter-gatherer children are carried at all times, and until they are four, they are carried some of the time.

An observer might wonder why young women do not hunt until they become pregnant, or why mature women and men do not hunt and gather on alternate days, with some women staying in camp to act as wet nurses for the young. Apart from the effects hunting might have on a mother's milk production, there are two reasons. First, young girls begin to bear children as soon as they are physically mature and strong enough to hunt, and second, hunter-gatherer bands are so small that there are unlikely to be enough lactating

women to serve as wet nurses. No hunter-gatherer group could afford to maintain a specialized female hunting force.

Because game is not always available, because hunting and gathering are specialized skills, because women carrying heavy loads cannot hunt, and because women in hunter-gatherer societies are usually either pregnant or caring for young children, for most of the last two million years of human history men have hunted and women have gathered.

If male dominance depends on controlling the supply of meat, then the degree of male dominance in a society should vary with the amount of meat available and the amount supplied by the men. Some regions, like the East African grasslands and the North American woodlands, abounded with species of large mammals; other zones, like tropical forests and semi-deserts, are thinly populated with prey. Many elements affect the supply of game, but theoretically, the less meat provided exclusively by the men, the more egalitarian the society.

All known hunter-gatherer societies fit into four basic types; those in which men and women work together in communal hunts and as teams gathering edible plants, as did the Washo Indians of North America; those in which men and women each collect their own plant foods although the men supply some meat to the group, as do the Hadza of Tanzania; those in which male hunters and female gatherers work apart but return to camp each evening to share their acquisitions, as do the Tiwi of North Australia; and those in which the men provide all the food by hunting large game, as do the Eskimo. In each case the extent of male dominance increases directly with the proportion of meat supplied by individual men and small hunting parties.

Among the most egalitarian of hunter-gatherer societies are the Washo Indians, who inhabited the valleys of the Sierra Nevada in what is now southern California and Nevada. In the spring they moved north to Lake Tahoe for the large fish runs of sucker and native trout.

Everyone—men, women, and children—participated in the fishing. Women spent the summer gathering edible berries and seeds while the men continued to fish. In the fall some men hunted deer but the most important source of animal protein was the jack rabbit, which was captured in communal hunts. Men and women together drove the rabbits into nets tied end to end. To provide food for the winter, husbands and wives worked as teams in the late fall to collect pine nuts.

Since everyone participated in most food-gathering activities, there were no individual distributors of food and relatively little difference in male and female rights. Men and women were not segregated from each other in daily activities; both were free to take lovers after marriage; both had the right to separate whenever they chose; menstruating women were not isolated from the rest of the group; and one of the two major Washo rituals celebrated hunting while the other celebrated gathering. Men were accorded more prestige if they had killed a deer, and men directed decisions about the seasonal movement of the group. But if no male leader stepped forward, women were permitted to lead. The distinctive feature of groups such as the Washo is the relative equality of the sexes.

The sexes are also relatively equal among the Hadza of Tanzania but this near-equality arises because men and women tend to work alone to feed themselves. They exchange little food. The Hadza lead a leisurely life in the seemingly barren environment of the East African Rift Gorge that is, in fact, rich in edible berries, roots, and small game. As a result of this abundance, from the time they are 10 years old, Hadza men and women gather much of their own food. Women take their young children with them into the bush, eating as they forage, and collect only enough food for a light family meal in the evening. The men eat berries and roots as they hunt for small game, and should they bring down a rabbit or a hyrax, they eat the meat on the spot. Meat is

In the maritime Inuit (Eskimo) societies, inequality between the sexes is matched by the ability to supply food for the group. The men hunt for meat and control the economy. Women perform all the other duties that support life in the community, and are virtually treated as objects. (Photo credit: American Museum of Natural History—Dr. F. Rainey)

carried back to the camp and shared with the rest of the group only on those rare occasions when a poisoned arrow brings down a large animal—an impala, a zebra, an eland, or a giraffe.

Because Hadza men distribute little meat, their status is only slightly higher than that of the women. People flock to the camp of a good hunter and the camp might take on his name because of his popularity, but he is in no sense a leader of the group. A Hadza man and a woman have an equal right to divorce and each can repudiate a marriage simply by living apart for a few weeks. Couples tend to live in the same camp as the wife's mother but they sometimes make long visits to the camp of the husband's mother. Although a man may take more than one wife, most Hadza males cannot afford to

indulge in this luxury. In order to maintain a marriage, a man must supply both his wife and his mother-in-law with some meat and trade goods, such as beads and cloth, and the Hadza economy gives few men the wealth to provide for more than one wife and mother-in-law. Washo equality is based on cooperation; Hadza equality is based on independence.

In contrast to both these groups, among the Tiwi of Melville and Bathurst Islands off the northern coast of Australia, male hunters dominate female gatherers. The Tiwi are representative of the most common form of foraging society, in which the men supply large quantities of meat, although less than half the food consumed by the group. Each morning Tiwi women, most with babies on

their backs, scatter in different directions in search of vegetables, grubs, worms, and small game such as bandicoots, lizards, and opossums. To track the game, they use hunting dogs. On most days women return to camp with some meat and with baskets full of *korka*, the nut of a native palm, which is soaked and mashed to make a porridge-like dish. The Tiwi men do not hunt small game and do not hunt every day, but when they do they often return with kangaroo, large lizards, fish, and game birds.

The porridge is cooked separately by each household and rarely shared outside the family, but the meat is prepared by a volunteer cook, who can be male or female. After the cook takes one of the parts of the animal traditionally reserved for him or her, the animal's "boss," the one who caught it, distributes the rest to all near kin and then to all others residing with the band. Although the small game supplied by the women is distributed in the same way as the big game supplied by the men, Tiwi men are dominant because the game they kill provides most of the meat.

The power of the Tiwi men is clearest in their betrothal practices. Among the Tiwi, a woman must always be married. To ensure this, female infants are betrothed at birth and widows are remarried at the gravesides of their late husbands. Men form alliances by exchanging daughters, sisters, and mothers in marriage and some collect as many as 25 wives. Tiwi men value the quantity and quality of the food many wives can collect and the many children they can produce.

The dominance of the men is offset somewhat by the influence of adult women in selecting their next husbands. Many women are active strategists in the political careers of their male relatives, but to the exasperation of some sons attempting to promote their own futures, widowed mothers sometimes insist on selecting their own partners. Women also influence the marriages of their daughters and granddaughters, especially when the selected husband dies before the bestowed child moves to his camp.

Among the Eskimo, representative of the rarest type of forager society, inequality between the sexes is matched by inequality in supplying the group with food. Inland Eskimo men hunt caribou throughout the year to provision the entire society, and maritime Eskimo men depend on whaling, fishing, and some hunting to feed their extended families. The women process the carcasses, cut and sew skins to make clothing, cook, and care for the young; but they collect no food of their own and depend on the men to supply all the raw materials for their work. Since men provide all the meat, they also control the trade in hides, whale oil, seal oil, and other items that move between the maritime and inland Eskimos.

Eskimo women are treated almost exclusively as objects to be used, abused, and traded by men. After puberty all Eskimo girls are fair game for any interested male. A man shows his intentions by grabbing the belt of a woman and if she protests, he cuts off her trousers and forces himself upon her. These encounters are considered unimportant by the rest of the group. Men offer their wives' sexual services to establish alliances with trading partners and members of hunting and whaling parties.

Despite the consistent pattern of some degree of male dominance among foragers, most of these societies are egalitarian compared with agricultural and industrial societies. No forager has any significant opportunity for political leadership. Foragers, as a rule, do not like to give or take orders, and assume leadership only with reluctance. Shamans (those who are thought to be possessed by spirits) may be either male or female. Public rituals conducted by women in order to celebrate the first menstruation of girls are common, and the symbolism in these rituals is similar to that in the ceremonies that follow a boy's first kill.

In any society, status goes to those who control the distribution of valued goods and services outside the family. Equality arises when both sexes work side by side in food production, as do the Washo, and the products are simply distributed among the workers. In such circumstances, no person or sex has greater access to valued items than do others. But when women make no contribution to the food supply, as in the case of the Eskimo, they are completely subordinate.

When we attempt to apply these generalizations to contemporary industrial society, we can predict that as long as women spend their discretionary income from jobs on domestic needs, they will gain little social recognition and power. To be an effective source of power, money must be exchanged in ways that require returns and create obligations. In other words, it must be invested.

Jobs that do not give women control over valued resources will do little to advance their general status. Only as managers, executives, and professionals are women in a position to trade goods and services, to do others favors, and therefore to obligate others to them. Only as controllers of valued resources can women achieve prestige, power, and equality.

Within the household, women who bring in income from jobs are able to function on a more nearly equal basis with their husbands. Women who contribute services to their husbands and children without pay, as do some middle-class Western housewives, are especially vulnerable to dominance. Like Eskimo women, as long as their services are limited to domestic distribution they have little power relative to their husbands and none with respect to the outside world.

As for the limits imposed on women by their procreative functions in hunter-gatherer societies, child-bearing and child care are organized around work as much as work is organized around reproduction. Some foraging groups space their children three to four years apart and have an average of only four to six children, far fewer than many women in other cultures. Hunter-gatherers nurse their infants for extended periods, sometimes for as long as four years. This custom suppresses ovulation and limits the size of their families. Sometimes, although rarely, they practice infanticide. By limiting reproduction, a woman who is gathering food has only one child to carry.

Different societies can and do adjust the frequency of birth and the care of children to accommodate whatever productive activities women customarily engage in. In horticultural societies, where women work long hours in gardens that may be far from home, infants get food to supplement their mothers' milk, older children take care of younger children, and pregnancies are widely spaced. Throughout the world, if a society requires a woman's labor, it finds ways to care for her children.

In the United States, as in some other industrial societies, the accelerated entry of women with preschool children into the labor force has resulted in the development of a variety of child-care arrangements. Individual women have called on friends, relatives, and neighbors. Public and private child-care centers are growing. We should realize that the declining birth rate, the increasing acceptance of childless or single-child families, and a de-emphasis on motherhood are adaptations to a sexual division of labor reminiscent of the system of production found in hunter-gatherer societies.

In many countries where women no longer devote most of their productive years to childbearing, they are beginning to demand a change in the social relationship of the sexes. As women gain access to positions that control the exchange of resources, male dominance may become archaic, and industrial societies may one day become as egalitarian as the Washo.

REFERENCES

Friedl, Ernestine, *Women and Men: An Anthropologist's View,* Holt, Rinehart and Winston, 1975.

Martin, M. Kay, and Barbara Voorhies, eds., *Female of the Species,* Columbia University Press, 1977.

Murphy, Yolanda, and Robert Murphy, *Women of the Forest,* Columbia University Press, 1974.

Reiter, Rayna, ed., *Toward an Anthropology of Women,* Monthly Review Press, 1975.

Rosaldo, M.Z., and Louise Lamphere, eds., *Women, Culture, and Society,* Stanford University Press, 1974.

Schlegel, Alice, ed., *Sexual Stratification; A Cross-Cultural View,* Columbia University Press, 1977.

Strathern, Marilyn, *Women in Between: Female Roles in a Male World,* Academic Press, 1972.

Why Don't We Act Like The Opposite Sex?

The new field of sociobiology prompts arguments as to whether different behavior by men and women is inherited or learned.

Anthony Layng

Dr. Layng is professor of anthropology, Elmira (N.Y.) College

Social scientists long have been aware of the distinctive sex roles characteristic of tribal societies around the world, but many are reluctant to conclude that this is anything other than learned behavior. Most American cultural anthropologists have assumed that sex roles are largely arbitrary. This is illustrated by citing examples characteristic of males in one population and females in another—as in the American Southwest, where Navajo weavers are women and Hopi weavers are men.

To suggest that female roles are determined to any significant degree by biological factors invites an implication that the lower social status of women found in most societies also might be attributed to innate differences between the sexes, that "anatomy is destiny." American anthropologists have been influenced by social liberalism to such an extent that any scholarly proponent of biological determinism (racism, sexism, etc.) is likely to be challenged immediately. Their arguments against racism have pointed out that there is no reliable correlation

between race and social behavior; people of the same race may have sharply contrasting cultures; and a given population can alter its culture dramatically without, presumably, altering its genes. For instance, the Aztecs and Apache were of the same race, but the former evolved a complex state civilization while the latter remained primitive nomads. The post–World War II Japanese have shown us how much a homogeneous racial population can change its culture in a very short time.

When it comes to sexism—the belief that the distinctive behavior of females and males is influenced significantly by their differing physiology—ethnographic challenges are less convincing. One major difficulty is the fact that there are no societies where men and women act alike. Even where conscious attempts have been made to eliminate behavioral differences between the sexes, distinctions remain. A study of American communes in the 1970s found that none have "come anywhere near succeeding in abolishing sex-role distinctions, although a number . . . have made this their highest ideological priority."

Another reason why cross-cultural comparisons have been relatively ineffectual in undermining sexist thinking is that, regardless of the great vari-

ability of sex roles from one society to another, there are certain behavior patterns and attitudes that appear to be the same in both traditional and modern societies. For example:

- Women generally prefer older men as mates, while most males prefer younger females.
- In courtship and mating behavior, most men are more sexually aggressive and most women are more coy.
- Males are more inclined to delay marriage.
- Men are more likely to seek a variety of mates.
- Women tend to be more tolerant of adulterous mates.
- Females are more likely to be domestic and nurturing.

In some societies, women prefer men who are considerably older than themselves; in others, the age discrepancy is slight. What is constant is that, on average, the male in each couple is older. Unlike bands of apes, where females are the usual initiators of copulation, "presenting" themselves to males, it is far more common for men to initiate sex, while women are more likely to take a relatively passive role beyond flirtation. Nearly everywhere, shyness or coquettishness is associated strongly with female sexual behavior.

Although some males may have to sell the idea of marriage to their mates, it is far more usual for women to be in the position of favoring such a binding relationship and men to be reluctant to commit themselves. However, males are less reticent about participating in purely sexual relationships, often doing so with more than one partner concurrently. Females seem far more inclined to restrict themselves to one mate, or at least to one at a time. These behavioral differences often are reflected in the "double standard"—the attitude that female infidelity is a far more serious moral breech than male unfaithfulness. Typically, both men and women are more inclined to condemn the adultress. This is not to say that wives do not disapprove strongly of spouses who cheat on them. The point is that a woman far more often will put up with such a husband. Men, on the other hand, are more likely to leave,

severely beat, or even kill an unfaithful mate.

Finally, men are far less inclined toward "nesting" and nurturing. It is the women in all societies who are the most domestic and more adept at nursing the sick and comforting those who are troubled. Both sexes generally agree that it is a woman's nature that makes her so well suited to these activities.

If women and men naturally are inclined to view each other in programmed ways regardless of their class or culture and naturally are predisposed to act toward each other in similarly uniform ways, it might seem reasonable to conclude that female human nature is clearly distinct from that of males and that an Equal Rights Amendment goes against nature. As an active proponent of the ERA and an opponent to all sexism, I am troubled by such a conclusion, but unable simply to dismiss it.

In light of such global uniformity in behavior and attitudes, it is difficult to account for these patterns solely in terms of socialization. Cultures differ dramatically from one to another, and religious beliefs, kinship systems, social structures, political traditions, and subsistence systems vary. So why do men in such contrasting societies all behave so aggressively in the pursuit of sex? Why do male hunters, farmers, and warriors tend to show such interest in seducing new sex partners? Why do Latin American and Asian women put up with adulterous husbands? Why do females in primitive tribes and industrial societies usually prefer older men? Why do peasant women and debutantes tend to want marriage before their male counterparts do? Why are both American and African men relatively disinterested in domestic chores? If it is all a matter of learning, of cultural conditioning, why are there not some societies where most men and women do not conform to these patterns?

Are these traits determined to some extent by the biological peculiarities of the different sexes? If so, it is distressing to consider the social and political implications of such a finding. If human nature (and not only nurture) leads females to behave in a distinctive way, is it therefore not suitable that they be treated in a discriminating fashion? If chasing women only is doing what comes naturally to men, then promiscuous females should have less excuse for their infidelities. Should husbands, even of working wives, be excused from house cleaning and child care? Clearly, one need not be a militant feminist to be made very uncomfortable by such questions.

It is further disturbing to liberals to learn about the findings of sociobiology, a new discipline which suggests some rather startling explanations for behavior traits such as those cited above. According to many sociobiologists, mating practices are the result of an evolutionary process favoring genes that most successfully replicate themselves. This theory states that those most successful in this regard give rise to behavior and attitudes maximizing reproductive success.

Supposedly, genetically inherited behavior that causes people to have the most offspring eventually results, through natural selection, in such action becoming more and more common. Genes which induce people to behave otherwise, by the same selective process, are weeded out since people who behave this way have fewer children—that is, they do not produce as many carriers of their genes. Over time, as the result of this process, genes which most successfully cause men and women to produce carriers of these genes become more and more prevalent.

The most convincing illustrations of sociobiological explanations have been provided by studies of animal populations. For example, when a male langur monkey takes over a harem from an older male, he proceeds to kill all the infants of nursing mothers in the troop. From the perspective of Darwin's Theory of Evolution (survival of the fittest), this makes no sense at all, for it destroys healthy and fit infants as well as any others. From a sociobiological perspective, however, this wholesale infanticide is a sound reproductive strategy because it ensures that the genes of this newly dominant male soon will be replicated and in maximum numbers. Were he to wait until each female weaned her infant and ceased to lactate—a prerequisite to coming back into heat—it would be that much longer before he could impregnate them. By killing all the infants carrying some other male's genes, he speeds up the process whereby his genes begin to predominate. Also, he does not waste any energy protecting infants not carrying his genes.

The females of any species, goes this theory, are likely to develop very different kinds of reproductive strategies given the fact that they produce fewer offspring than do males. The genes of males, in competition with those of other males, induce behavior that results in the greatest number of offspring. Females, who are not able to produce nearly as many offspring as are males, compete for quality, rather than quantity, behaving so as to ensure that each child produced will be likely to survive and reproduce. In these ways, males and females alike are directed by their genes to see to it that they reproduce them as successfully as possible.

REPRODUCTIVE STRATEGIES

Among human beings, the fact that men prefer younger wives is fully consistent with their desire to have children since young women are highly fertile and the most likely to bear full-term healthy offspring. A young wife may devote her entire reproductive potential to producing children fathered by her husband. Since the reproductive strategy of women stresses *quality* of offspring, they are inclined to seek established and mature men as providers and protectors of their children. Male sexual aggressiveness serves to spread male genes. Female coyness helps to assure a potential mate that pregnancy has not occurred already. Her fidelity helps to convince him to stay around to protect what he therefore can assume to be his own offspring. (The sexual aggressiveness of female apes would be inappropriate in a human population, but not for them since male apes are not providers. Given the human sexual division of labor, men and women are economically dependent on each other; apes are not.)

By delaying marriage, a man is free to impregnate more women who will bear his children (his genes) without obligating him to care for them. A woman seeks marriage to monopolize not a man's sexuality, but, rather, his political and economic resources, to ensure that her children (her genes) will be well provided for. She may worry about her husband's infidelities, but only because this can siphon off resources she wants for her children. He, on the other hand, is far more concerned about sexually monopolizing her. He wants assurance that he is the father of any child she gives birth to; otherwise, he will be providing for those who do not carry his genes. Moreover, if she becomes pregnant by another man, it will be many months before she can produce a fetus carrying her husband's genes. With or without her husband's faithfulness, she can get pregnant and produce the maximum number of children carrying her genes. Thus, a wife's affair is less tolerable to her husband for, according to the sociobiological perspective, it threatens to diminish the number of offspring he can produce by her.

The domesticity of women and the wanderings of men also are consistent with the differential reproductive strategies each sex has evolved. In stressing the quality of her offspring, since she can have relatively few, a woman provides a comfortable domicile for her children and stays home to nurture them, to better ensure their survivability so they are most likely to mature and further reproduce her genes. Meanwhile, the man is off chasing women, producing as many children as possible and being far less concerned with sticking around to guarantee their welfare. If he were to limit himself sexually to one woman, he greatly would diminish the number of children he potentially could propagate. In short, from a sociobiological perspective, she "succeeds" by being faithful to her husband since this helps to ensure that he will provide for her children; he does so not only by monopolizing her as a producer of his offspring, but by having children with other women as well.

By this point, you probably are thinking of people who exemplify sociobiologically sound traits of lecherous males and the women who put up with them. Certainly, we all are familiar with this behavior. Even though it often runs counter to accepted moral standards, we frequently hear people say, "That's the way men (or women)

are." Sociobiologists seem to be offering theoretical confirmation of this folk wisdom.

Is human social behavior influenced by our genes? Whether further research will confirm or refute sociobiological theory as it applies to human behavior, we shall have to wait until far more information is available. No matter what the effect on our behavior, we should keep in mind that learning plays an important role. Consequently, social policy should not be based on any assumption that biological determinants of human behavior and attitudes are more instrumental than learning, for cultural factors can counteract human genetic predispositions. Our early ancestors were subject to natural selection. Since the time of the Neanderthals, though, human populations have adapted to environmental change almost entirely by altering their learned behavior and attitudes—their culture, not their genes. There are individuals whose behavior conforms to sociobiological generalizations, but, especially among the educated, one finds many contrasting examples—men who do not chase young women, females who are sexually aggressive and/or disinterested in marriage, and couples who choose to have no children at all.

If traditional social inequality be-

tween men and women somewhat is perpetuated by genetically determined and sexually specific reproductive strategies, why are contraceptives and abortions so popular in modern society? Even most modern women may seem to conform to sociobiologically correct behavior (being attracted to older men, tolerating unfaithful spouses, accepting primary responsibility for domestic duties, etc.). Since most males still earn more than females do and since society continues to socialize boys and girls quite differently (encouraging girls to play with infant dolls, rewarding boys for being physically aggressive, etc.), the continuation of such behavior may be more a matter of cultural inertia than genetic compulsion.

So, even if inborn factors influence male and female human sexual behavior, the extent to which they do so clearly is limited and subordinate to learning and conditioning. Consequently, we neither need fear intellectually the findings of sociobiologists nor allow them significantly to influence interpersonal behavior and social attitudes regarding gender-specific behavior. If men and women continue to behave differently (and it seems there is no clear trend away from this pattern), we may yet learn just why we do not act like the opposite sex.

The Global War Against Women

Lori Heise

Lori Heise is a senior researcher at the Worldwatch Institute. She prepared a recent report on this subject for World Watch *magazine.*

Violence against women—including assault, mutilation, murder, infanticide, rape and cruel neglect—is perhaps the most pervasive yet least recognized human-rights issue in the world. It is also a profound health problem sapping women's physical and emotional vitality and undermining their confidence—both vital to achieving widely held goals for human progress, especially in the Third World.

Despite its invisibility, the dimensions of the problem are vast. In Bangkok, Thailand, a reported 50 percent of married women are beaten regularly by their husbands. In the barrios of Quito, Ecuador, 80 percent of women are said to have been physically abused. And in Nicaragua, 44 percent of men admit to beating their wives or girlfriends. Equally shocking statistics can be found in the industrial world.

Then there are the less recognized forms of violence. In Nepal, female babies die from neglect because parents value sons over daughters; in Sudan, girls' genitals are mutilated to ensure virginity until marriage; and in India, young brides are murdered by their husbands when parents fail to provide enough dowry.

In all these instances, women are targets of violence because of their sex. This is not random violence. The risk factor is being female.

Most of these abuses have been reported in one or another country, at one or another time. But is only when you begin to amass statistics and reports from international organizations and countries around the world that the horrifying dimensions of this global war on women come into focus. For me the revelation came only recently after talking with scores of village women throughout the world.

I never intended to investigate violence; I was researching maternal and child health issues overseas. But I would commonly begin my interviews with a simple question: What is your biggest problem? With unnerving frequency, the answer came back: "My husband beats me."

These are women who daily have to walk four hours to gather enough wood for the evening meal, whose children commonly die of treatable illnesses, whose security can be wiped out with one failed rain. Yet when defining their own concerns, they see violence as their greatest dilemma. Those dedicated to helping Third World women would do well to listen.

More than simply a "women's issue," violence could thwart other widely held goals for human progress in the Third World. Study after study has shown that maternal education is the single most effective way to reduce child mortality—not because it imparts new knowledge or skills related to health, but because it erodes fatalism, improves self-confidence and changes the power balance within the family.

In effect, these studies say that women's sense of self is critical to reducing infant mortality. Yet acts of violence and society's tacit acceptance of them stand as constant reminders to women of their low worth. Where women's status is critical to achieving a development goal—such as controlling fertility and improving child survival—violence will remain a powerful obstacle to progress.

Measured by its human costs alone, female-focused violence is worthy of international attention and action. But it has seldom been raised at that level, much less addressed. Millions of dollars are spent each year to protect the human rights of fetuses. It is time to stand up for the human rights of women.

The Indian subcontinent is home to one of the most pernicious forms of wife abuse, known locally as "bride-burning" or "dowry deaths." Decades ago dowry referred to the gifts that a woman received from her parents upon marriage. Now dowry has become an important part of premarital negotiations and refers to the wealth that the bride's parents must pay the groom as part of the marriage settlement.

Once a gesture of love, ever-escalating dowry now represents a real financial burden to the parents of unwed

From *The Washington Post*, April 9, 1989, pp. B1, B4. © 1989 by Lori Heise. Reprinted by permission.

daughters. Increasingly, dowry is being seen as a "get rich quick" scheme by prospective husbands, with young brides suffering severe abuse if promised money or goods do not materialize. In its most severe form, dowry harassment ends in suicide or murder, freeing the husband to pursue a more lucrative arrangement.

Dowry deaths are notoriously undercounted, largely because the husband and his relatives frequently try to disguise the murder as a suicide or an accident and the police are loathe to get involved. A frequent scam is to set the women alight with kerosene, and then claim she died in a kitchen accident—hence the term "bride-burning." In 1987 the police official recorded 1,786 dowry deaths in all of India, but the Ahmedabad Women's Action Group estimates that 1,000 women may have been burned alive that year in Gujurat State alone.

A quick look at mortality data from India reveals the reasonableness of this claim. In both urban Maharashtra and greater Bombay, 19 percent of all deaths among women 15 to 44 years old are due to "accidental burns." In other Third World countries, such as Guatemala, Ecuador and Chile, the same statistic is less [than] 1 percent.

Elsewhere in the world, the marriage transaction is reversed, with prospective husbands paying "bridewealth" to secure a woman's hand in marriage. In many cultures—especially in Africa—the exchange has become so commercialized that inflated bridewealth leaves the man with the distinct impression that he has "purchased" his wife.

The notion that bridewealth confers ownership was clearly depicted during recent parliamentary debates in Papua New Guinea over whether wife-beating should be made illegal. Transcripts show that most ministers were violently against the idea of parliament interfering in "traditional family life." Minister William Wi of North Waghi argued that wife-beating "is an accepted custom and we are wasting our time debating the issue." Another parliamentarian added: "I paid for my wife, so she should not overrule my decisions, because I am the head of the family."

It is this unequal power balance—institutionalized in the structure of the patriarchal family—that is at the root of wife-beating. As Cheryl Bernard, director of Austria's Ludwig Boltzmann Institute of Politics, notes: "Violence against women in the family takes place because the perpetrators feel, and their environment encourages them to feel, that this is an acceptable exercise of male prerogative, a legitimate and appropriate way to relieve their own tension in conditions of stress, to sanction female behavior . . . or just to enjoy a feeling of supremacy."

While stress and alcohol may increase the likelihood of violence, they do not "cause" it. Rather, it is the belief that violence is an acceptable way to resolve conflict, and that women are "appropriate" and "safe" targets for abuse, that leads to battering.

Today's cultures have strong historical, religious and legal legacies that reinforce the legitimacy of wife-beating. Under English common law, for example, a husband had the legal right to discipline his wife—subject to a "rule of thumb" that barred him from using a stick broader than his thumb. Judicial decisions in England and the United States upheld this right until well into the 19th century. Only last week, a New York judge let off with only five years' probation a Chinese immigrant who admitted bludgeoning his wife to death. The judge justified the light sentence partly by reference to traditional Chinese attitudes toward female adultery.

While less overt, the preference for male offspring in many cultures can be as damaging and potentially fatal to females as rape or assault. The same sentiment that once motivated infanticide is now expressed in the systematic neglect of daughters—a neglect so severe in some countries that girls aged 2 to 4 die at nearly twice the rate of boys.

"Let it be late, but let it be a son," goes a saying in Nepal, a country that shares its strong preference for male children with the rest of the Indian subcontinent, as well as China, South Korea and Taiwan. In these cultures and others, sons are highly valued because only they can perpetuate the family line and perform certain religious rituals. Even more important, sons represent an economic asset to the family and a source of security for parents in their old age.

Studies confirm that where the preference for sons is strong, girls receive inferior medical care and education, and less food. In Punjab, India, for example, parents spend more than twice as much on medical care for boy infants as for girls.

In fact, the pressure to bear sons is so great in India and China that women have begun using amniocentesis as a sex identification test to selectively abort female fetuses. Until protests forced them to stop, Indian sex detection clinics boldly advertised it was better to spend $38 now on terminating a girl than $3,800 later on her dowry. Of 8,000 fetuses examined at six abortion clinics in Bombay, 7,999 were found to be female.

In parts of Africa and the Middle East, young girls suffer another form of violence, euphemistically known as female circumcision. More accurately, this operation—which removes all or part of the external female genitalia, including the clitoris—is a life-threatening form of mutilation. According to the World Health Organization, more than 80 million women have undergone sexual surgery in Africa alone.

While female circumcision has its origin in the male desire to control female sexuality, today a host of other superstitions and beliefs sustains the practice. Some Moslem groups mistakenly believe that it is demanded by the Islamic faith, although it has no basis in the Koran. Others believe the operation will increase fertility, affirm femininity or prevent still births. Yet ultimately what drives the tradition is that men will not marry uncircumcised women, believing them to be promiscuous, unclean and sexually untrustworthy.

The medical complications of circumcision are severe. Immediate risks include hemorrhage, tetanus and blood poisoning from unsterile and often primitive cutting implements (knife, razor blade or broken glass), and shock from the pain of the operation, which is carried out without anesthesia. Not uncommonly, these complications result in death.

The long-term effects, in addition to loss of all sexual feeling, include chronic urinary tract infections, pelvic infections that can lead to infertility, painful intercourse and severe scarring that can cause tearing of tissue and hemorrhage during childbirth. In fact, women who are infibulated—the most severe form of circumcision—must be cut open on their wedding night to make intercourse possible, and more cuts are necessary for delivery of a child.

Despite these horrific death effects, many still oppose the eradication of this practice. As late as June 1988, Muslim religious scholars in Somalia argued that milder forms of circumcision should be maintained to temper female sexuality. Others defend circumcision as an "important African tradition." But as the Kenyan women's magazine *Via* observes: "There is nothing 'African' about injustice or violence, whether it takes the form of mistreated wives and mothers, or slums or circumcision. Often the very men who . . . excuse injustice to women with the phrase 'it is African' are wearing three-piece pin-striped suits and shiny shoes."

Fortunately, women have not sat idle in the face of such abuse. Around the world they are organizing shelters, lobbying for legal reform and fighting the sexism that underlies violence.

Most industrial countries and at least a dozen developing nations now have shelter movements to provide refuge for abused women and their children. Brazil has established almost 30 all-female police stations for victims of rape, battering and incest. And in Africa, women are organizing education campaigns to combat sexual surgery.

Elsewhere women have organized in their own defense. In San Juan de Miraflores, a shantytown of Lima, Peru, women carry whistles that they use to summon other women in case of attack.

Yet it will take more than the dedicated action of a few women to end crimes of gender. Most important is for women worldwide to recognize their common oppression. Violence against women cuts across all cultures and all socioeconomic groups. Indeed, we in America live in our own glass house: In the United States a woman is beaten every 15 seconds, and each day four women are killed by their batterers.

Such statistics are as important as they are shocking. Violence persists in part because it is hidden. If governments and women's groups can expose violence through surveys and better documentation, then ignorance will no longer be an excuse for inaction.

Also critical is challenging the legal framework that undergirds male violence, such as unequal inheritance, discriminatory family laws and a husband's right to chastise. Especially important are the social inequities and cultural beliefs that leave women economically dependent on men. As long as women must marry to survive, they will do whatever they must to secure a husband—including tolerating abuse and submitting themselves and their daughters to sexual surgery.

Action against violence, however, must proceed from the international community down as well as from the grass roots up. Where governments tacitly condone violence through their silence, or worse yet, legitimize it through discriminatory laws and customs, international pressure can be an important impetus for reform. Putting violence against women high on the world agenda is not appeasing a "special interest" group. It is restoring the birthright of half of humanity.

The Little Emperors

A generation of spoiled brats, a tidal wave of abortions and thousands of missing girls—these are some of the unintended consequences of China's revolutionary one-child policy

Daniela Deane

Daniela Deane, who has two sons and lives in Hong Kong, is a free-lance writer who contributes to the Washington Post *and* Newsweek. *Her last article for this magazine was "The Vanishing Border," about the growing integration of southern China and Hong Kong.*

XU MING SITS ON THE WORN SOFA WITH his short, chubby arms and legs splayed, forced open by fat and the layers of padded clothing worn in northern China to ward off the relentless chill. To reach the floor, the tubby 8-year-old rocks back and forth on his big bottom, inching forward slowly, eventually ending upright. Xu Ming finds it hard to move.

"He got fat when he was about 3," says his father, Xu Jianguo, holding the boy's bloated, dimpled hand. "We were living with my parents and they were very good to him. He's the only grandson. It's a tradition in China that boys are very loved. They love him very much, and so they feed him a lot. They give him everything he wants."

Xu Ming weighs 135 pounds, about twice what he should at his age. He's one of hundreds of children who have sought help in the past few years at the Beijing Children's Hospital, which recently began the first American-style fat farm for obese children in what was once the land of skin and bones.

"We used to get a lot of cases of malnutrition," says Dr. Ni Guichen, director of endocrinology at the hospi-

tal and founder of the weight-reduction classes. "But in the last 10 years, the problem has become obese children. The number of fat children in China is growing very fast. The main reason is the one-child policy," she says, speaking in a drab waiting room. "Because parents can only have one child, the families take extra good care of that one child, which means feeding him too much."

Bulging waistlines are one result of China's tough campaign to curb its population. The one-child campaign, a strict national directive that seeks to limit each Chinese couple to a single son or daughter, has other dramatic consequences: millions of abortions, fewer girls and a generation of spoiled children.

The 10-day weight-reduction sessions—a combination of exercise, nutritional guidance and psychological counseling—are very popular. Hundreds of children—some so fat they can hardly walk—are turned away for each class.

According to Ni, about 5% of children in China's cities are obese, with two obese boys for every overweight girl, the traditional preference toward boys being reflected in the amount of attention lavished on the child. "Part of the course is also centered on the parents. We try to teach them how to bring their children up properly, not just by spoiling them," Ni says.

Ming's father is proud that his son, after two sessions at the fat farm, has managed to halve his intake of *jiaozi*,

the stodgy meat-filled dumplings that are Ming's particular weakness, from 30 to 15 at a sitting. "Even if he's not full, that's all he gets," he says. "In the beginning, it was very difficult. He would put his arms around our necks and beg us for more food. We couldn't bear it, so we'd give him a little more."

Ming lost a few pounds but hasn't been able to keep the weight off. He's a bit slimmer now, but only because he's taller. "I want to lose weight," says Ming, who spends his afternoons snacking at his grandparents' house and his evenings plopped in front of the television set at home. "The kids make fun of me, they call me a fat pig. I hate the nicknames. In sports class, I can't do what the teacher says. I can run a little bit, but after a while I have to sit down. The teacher puts me at the front of the class where all the other kids can see me. They all laugh and make fun of me."

The many fat children visible on China's city streets are just the most obvious example of 13 years of the country's one-child policy. In the vast countryside, the policy has meant shadowy lives as second-class citizens for thousands of girls, or, worse, death. It has made abortion a way of life and a couple's sexual intimacy the government's concern. Even women's menstrual cycles are monitored. Under the directive, couples literally have to line up for permission to procreate. Second children are sometimes possible, but only on payment of a heavy fine.

The policy is an unparalleled intrusion into the private lives of a nation's citizens, an experiment on a scale never attempted elsewhere in the world. But no expert will argue that China—by far the world's most populous country with 1.16 billion people—could continue without strict curbs on its population.

China's communist government adopted the one-child policy in 1979 in response to the staggering doubling of the country's population during Mao Tse-tung's rule. Mao, who died in 1976, was convinced that the country's masses were a strategic asset and vigorously encouraged the Chinese to produce even-larger families.

But large families are now out for the Chinese—20% of the world's population living on just 7% of the arable land. "China has to have a population policy," says Huang Baoshan, deputy director of the State Family Planning Commission. With the numbers ever growing, "how can we feed these people, clothe them, house them?"

DINNER TIME FOR ONE 5-YEAR-OLD GIRL consists of granddad chasing her through the house, bowl and spoon in hand, barking like a dog or mewing like a cat. If he performs authentically enough, she rewards him by accepting a mouthful of food. No problem, insists granddad, "it's good exercise for her."

An 11-year-old boy never gets up to go to the toilet during the night. That's because his mother, summoned by a shout, gets up instead and positions a bottle under the covers for him. "We wouldn't want him to have to get up in the night," his mother says.

Another mother wanted her 16-year-old to eat some fruit, but the teen-ager was engrossed in a video game. Not wanting him to get his fingers sticky or daring to interrupt, she peeled several grapes and popped one after another into his mouth. "Not so fast," he snapped. "Can't you see I have to spit out the seeds?"

Stories like these are routinely published in China's newspapers, evidence that the government-imposed birth-control policy has produced an emerging generation of spoiled, lazy, selfish, self-centered and overweight children. There are about 40 million only chil-

dren in China. Dubbed the country's "Little Emperors," their behavior toward their elders is likened to that of the young emperor Pu Yi, who heaped indignities on his eunuch servants while making them cater to his whims, as chronicled in Bernardo Bertolucci's film "The Last Emperor."

Many studies on China's only children have been done. One such study confirmed that only children generally are not well liked. The study, conducted by a team of Chinese psychologists, asked a group of 360 Chinese children, half who have siblings and half who don't, to rate each other's behavior. The only children were, without fail, the least popular, regardless of age or social background. Peers rated them more uncooperative and selfish than children with brothers and sisters. They bragged more, were less helpful in group activities and more apt to follow their own selfish interests. And they wouldn't share their toys.

The Chinese lay a lot of blame on what they call the "4-2-1" syndrome—four doting grandparents, two overindulgent parents, all pinning their hopes and ambitions on one child.

Besides stuffing them with food, Chinese parents have very high expectations of their one *bao bei,* or treasured object. Some have their still-in-strollers babies tested for IQ levels. Others try to teach toddlers Tang Dynasty poetry. Many shell out months of their hard-earned salaries for music lessons and instruments for children who have no talent or interest in playing. They fill their kids' lives with lessons in piano, English, gymnastics and typing.

The one-child parents, most of them from traditionally large Chinese families, grew up during the chaotic, 10-year Cultural Revolution, when many of the country's cultural treasures were destroyed and schools were closed for long periods of time. Because many of that generation spent years toiling in the fields rather than studying, they demand—and put all their hopes into—academic achievement for their children.

"We've already invested a lot of money in his intellectual development," Wang Zhouzhi told me in her Spartan home in a tiny village of Changping

county outside Beijing, discussing her son, Chenqian, an only child. "I don't care how much money we spend on him. We've bought him an organ and we push him hard. Unfortunately, he's only a mediocre student," she says, looking toward the 10-year-old boy. Chenqian, dressed in a child-sized Chinese army uniform, ate 10 pieces of candy during the half-hour interview and repeatedly fired off his toy pistol, all without a word of reproach from his mother.

Would Chenqian have liked a sibling to play with? "No," he answers loudly, firing a rapid, jarring succession of shots. His mother breaks in: "If he had a little brother or sister, he wouldn't get everything he wants. Of course he doesn't want one. With only one child, I give my full care and concern to him."

But how will these children, now entering their teen-age years and moving quickly toward adulthood, become the collectivist-minded citizens China's hard-line communist leadership demands? Some think they never will. Ironically, it may be just these overindulged children who will change Chinese society. After growing up doing as they wished, ruling their immediate families, they're not likely to obey a central government that tells them to fall in line. This new generation of egotists, who haven't been taught to take even their parents into consideration, simply may not be able to think of the society as a whole—the basic principle of communism.

THE NEED FOR FAMILY PLANNING IS OBvious in the cities, where living space is limited and the one-child policy is strictly enforced and largely successful. City dwellers are slowly beginning to accept the notion that smaller families are better for the country, although most would certainly want two children if they could have them. However, in the countryside, where three of every four Chinese live—nearly 900 million people—the goal of limiting each couple to only one child has proved largely elusive.

In the hinterlands, the policy has become a confusing patchwork of special cases and exceptions. Provincial authorities can decide which couples can have a second child. In the southern province of Guangdong, China's richest, two children are allowed and many couples can afford to pay the fine to have even a third or fourth child. The amounts of the fines vary across the country, the highest in populous Sichuan province, where the fine for a second child can be as much as 25% of a family's income over four years. Special treatment has been given to China's cultural minorities such as the Mongolians and the Tibetans because of their low numbers. Many of them are permitted three or four children without penalty, although some Chinese social scientists have begun to question the privilege.

"It's really become a two-child policy in the countryside," says a Western diplomat. "Because of the traditional views on labor supply, the traditional bias toward the male child, it's been impossible for them to enforce a one-child policy outside the cities. In the countryside, they're really trying to stop that third child."

Thirteen years of strict family planning have created one of the great mysteries of the vast and remote Chinese countryside: Where have all the little girls gone? A Swedish study of sex ratios in China, published in 1990, and based on China's own census data, concluded that several million little girls are "missing"—up to half a million a year in the years 1985 to 1987—since the policy was introduced in late 1979.

In the study, and in demographic research worldwide, sex ratio at birth in humans is shown to be very stable, between 105 and 106 boys for every 100 girls. The imbalance is thought to be nature's way of compensating for the higher rates of miscarriage, stillbirth and infant mortality among boys.

In China, the ratio climbed consistently during the 1980s, and it now rests at more than 110 boys to 100 girls. "The imbalance is evident in some areas of the country," says Stirling Scruggs, director of the United Nations Population Fund in China. "I don't think the reason is widespread

infanticide. They're adopting out girls to try for a boy, they're hiding their girls, they're not registering them. Throughout Chinese history, in times of famine, and now as well, people have been forced to make choices between boys and girls, and for many reasons, boys always win out."

With the dismantling of collectives, families must, once again, farm their own small plots and sons are considered necessary to do the work. Additionally, girls traditionally "marry out" of their families, transferring their filial responsibilities to their in-laws. Boys carry on the family name and are entrusted with the care of their parents as they age. In the absence of a social security system, having a son is the difference between starving and eating when one is old. To combat the problem, some innovative villages have begun issuing so-called "girl insurance," an old-age insurance policy for couples who have given birth to a daughter and are prepared to stop at that.

"People are scared to death to be childless and penniless in their old age," says William Hinton, an American author of seven books chronicling modern China. "So if they don't have a son, they immediately try for another. When the woman is pregnant, they'll have a sex test to see if it's a boy or a girl. They'll abort a girl, or go in hiding with the girl, or pay the fine, or bribe the official or leave home. Anything. It's a game of wits."

Shen Shufen, a sturdy, round-faced peasant woman of 33, has two children—an 8-year-old girl and a 3-year-old boy—and lives in Sihe, a dusty, one-road, mud-brick, village in the countryside outside Beijing. Her husband is a truck driver. "When we had our girl, we knew we had to have another child somehow. We saved for years to pay the fine. It was hard giving them that money, 3,000 yuan ($550 in U.S. dollars), in one night. That's what my husband makes in three years. I was so happy when our second child was a boy."

The government seems aware of the pressure its policies put on expectant parents, and the painful results, but has not shown any flexibility. For instance,

Beijing in 1990 passed a law forbidding doctors to tell a couple the results of ultrasound tests that disclose the sex of their unborn child. The reason: Too many female embryos were being aborted.

And meanwhile, several hundred thousand women—called "guerrilla moms"—go into hiding every year to have their babies. They become part of China's 40-million-strong floating population that wanders the country, mostly in search of work, sleeping under bridges and in front of railway stations. Tens of thousands of female children are simply abandoned in rural hospitals.

And although most experts say female infanticide is not widespread, it does exist. "I found a dead baby girl," says Hinton. "We stopped for lunch at this mountain ravine in Shaanxi province. We saw her lying there, at the bottom of the creek bed. She was all bundled up, with one arm sticking out. She had been there a while, you could tell, because she had a little line of mold growing across her mouth and nostrils."

Death comes in another form, too: neglect. "It's female neglect, more than female infanticide, neglect to the point of death for little girls," says Scruggs of the U.N. Population Fund. "If you have a sick child, and it's a girl," he says, "you might buy only half the dose of medicine she needs to get better."

Hundreds of thousands of unregistered little girls—called "black children"—live on the edge of the law, unable to get food rations, immunizations or places in school. Many reports are grim. The government-run China News Service reported last year that the drowning of baby girls had revived to such an extent in Guangxi province that at least 1 million boys will be unable to find wives in 20 years. And partly because of the gender imbalance, the feudalistic practice of selling women has been revived.

The alarming growth of the flesh trade prompted authorities to enact a law in January that imposes jail sentences of up to 10 years and heavy fines for people caught trafficking. The government also recently began broadcasting a television dramatization to warn women against the practice. The public-service message shows two women, told that they would be given high-paying jobs, being lured to a suburban home. Instead, they are locked in a small, dark room, and soon realize that they have been sold.

LI WANGPING IS NERVOUS. SHE KEEPS looking at the air vents at the bottom of the office door, to see if anyone is walking by or, worse still, standing there listening. She rubs her hands together over and over. She speaks in a whisper. "I'm afraid to get into trouble talking to you," Li confides. She says nothing for a few minutes.

"After my son was born, I desperately wanted another baby," the 42-year-old woman finally begins. "I just wanted to have more children, you understand? Anyway, I got pregnant three times, because I wasn't using any birth control. I didn't want to use any. So, I had to have three abortions, one right after the other. I didn't want to at all. It was terrible killing the babies I wanted so much. But I had to."

By Chinese standards, Li (not her real name) has a lot to lose if she chooses to follow her maternal yearnings. As an office worker at government-owned CITIC, a successful and dynamic conglomerate, she has one of the best jobs in Beijing. Just being a city-dweller already puts her ahead of most of the population.

"One of my colleagues had just gotten fired for having a second child. I couldn't afford to be fired," continues Li, speaking in a meeting room at CITIC headquarters. "I had to keep everything secret from the family-planning official at CITIC, from everyone at the office. Of course, I'm supposed to be using birth control. I had to lie. It was hard lying, because I felt so bad about everything."

She rubs her hands furiously and moves toward the door, staring continuously at the air slats. "I have to go now. There's more to say, but I'm afraid to tell you. They could find me."

China's family-planning officials wield awesome powers, enforcing the policy through a combination of incentives and deterrents. For those who comply, there are job promotions and small cash awards. For those who resist, they suffer stiff fines and loss of job and status within the country's tightly knit and heavily regulated communities. The State Family Planning Commission is the government ministry entrusted with the tough task of curbing the growth of the world's most populous country, where 28 children are born every minute. It employs about 200,000 full-time officials and uses more than a million volunteers to check the fertility of hundreds of millions of Chinese women.

"Every village or enterprise has at least one family-planning official," says Zhang Xizhi, a birth-control official in Changping county outside Beijing. "Our main job is propaganda work to raise people's consciousness. We educate people and tell them their options for birth control. We go down to every household to talk to people. We encourage them to have only one child, to marry late, to have their child later."

China's population police frequently keep records of the menstrual cycles of women of childbearing age, on the type of birth control they use and the pending applications to have children. If they slip up, street committees—half-governmental, half-civilian organizations that have sprung up since the 1949 Communist takeover—take up the slack. The street committees, made up mostly of retired volunteers, act as the central government's ear to the ground, snooping, spying and reporting on citizens to the authorities.

When a couple wants to have a child—even their first, allotted one—they must apply to the family-planning office in their township or workplace, literally lining up to procreate. "If a woman gets pregnant without permission, she and her husband will get fined, even if it's their first," Zhang says. "It is fair to fine her, because she creates a burden on the whole society by jumping her place in line."

If a woman in Nanshao township, where Zhang works, becomes pregnant with a second child, she must terminate her pregnancy unless she or her husband or their first child is disabled or if both parents are only children. Her local family-planning official will repeatedly visit her at home to pressure her to comply. "Sometimes I have to go to people's homes five or six times to explain everything to them over and over to get them to have an abortion," says Zhang Cuiqing, the family-planning official for Sihe village, where there are 2,900 married women of childbearing age, of which 2,700 use some sort of birth control. Of those, 570 are sterilized and 1,100 have IUDs. Zhang recites the figures proudly, adding, "If they refuse, they will be fined between 20,000 and 50,000 yuan (U.S. $3,700 to $9,500)." The average yearly wage in Sihe is 1,500 yuan ($285).

The lack of early sexual education and unreliable IUDs are combining to make abortion—which is free, as are condoms and IUDs—a cornerstone of the one-child policy. Local officials are told not to use force, but rather education and persuasion, to meet their targets. However, the desire to fulfill their quotas, coupled with pressure from their bosses in Beijing, can lead to abuses by overzealous officials.

"Some local family-planning officials are running amok, because of the targets they have to reach," a Western health specialist says, "and there are a bunch of people willing to turn a blind eye to abuses because the target is so important."

The official Shanghai Legal Daily last year reported on a family-planning committee in central Sichuan province that ordered the flogging of the husbands of 10 pregnant women who refused to have abortions. According to the newspaper, the family-planning workers marched the husbands one by one into an empty room, ordered them to strip and lie on the floor and then beat them with a stick, once for every day their wives were pregnant.

"In some places, yes, things do happen," concedes Huang of the State Family Planning Commission. "Sometimes, family-planning officials do carry it too far."

THE YOUNG WOMAN LIES STILL ON THE narrow table with her eyes shut and her legs spread while the doctor quickly performs a suction abortion. A few moments, and the fetus is removed. The woman lets out a short, sharp yell. "OK, next," the doctor says.

She gets off the table and, holding a piece of cloth between her legs to catch the blood and clutching her swollen womb, hobbles over to a bed and collapses. The next patient gets up and walks toward the abortion table. No one notices a visitor watching. "It's very quick, it only takes about five minutes per abortion," says Dr. Huang Xiaomiao, chief physician at Beijing's Maternity Hospital. "No anesthetic. We don't use anesthetic for abortions or births here. Only for Cesarean sections, we use acupuncture."

Down the hall, 32-year-old Wu Guobin waits to be taken into the operating room to have her Fallopian tubes untied—a reversal of an earlier sterilization. "After my son was killed in an accident last year, the authorities in my province said I could try for another." In the bed next to Wu's, a dour-faced woman looks ready to cry. "She's getting sterilized," the nurse explains. "Her husband doesn't want her to, but her first child has mental problems."

Although it's a maternity hospital, the Family Planning Unit—where abortions, sterilizations, IUD insertions and the like are carried out—is the busiest department. "We do more abortions than births," says Dr. Fan Huimin, head of the unit. "Between 10 and 20 a day."

Abortions are a way of life in China, where about 10.5 million pregnancies are terminated each year. (In the United States, 1.6 million abortions are performed a year, but China's population is four to five times greater than the United States'.) One fetus is aborted for about every two children born and Chinese women often have several abortions. Usually, abortions are performed during the first trimester. But because some women resist, only to cave in under mental bullying further into their terms, abortions are also done in the later months of pregnancy, sometimes up till the eighth month.

Because of their population problem, the Chinese have become pioneers in contraceptive research. China will soon launch its own version of the controversial French abortion pill RU-486, which induces a miscarriage. They have perfected a non-scalpel procedure for male sterilization, with no suture required, allowing the man to "ride his bicycle home within five minutes." This year, the government plans to spend more than the $34 million it spent last year on contraception. The state will also buy some 961 million condoms to be distributed throughout the country, 11% more than in 1991.

But even with a family-planning policy that sends a chill down a Westerner's spine and touches every Chinese citizen's life, 64,000 babies are born every day in China and overpopulation continues to be a paramount national problem. Officials have warned that 24 million children will be born in 1992—a number just slightly less than the population of Canada. "The numbers are staggering," says Scruggs, the U.N. Population Fund official, noting that "170 million people will be added in the 1990s, which is the current population of England, France and Italy combined. There are places in China where the land can't feed that many more people as it is."

China estimates that it has prevented 200 million births since the one-child policy was introduced. Women now are having an average of 2.4 children as compared to six in the late '60s. But the individual sacrifice demanded from every Chinese is immense.

Large billboards bombard the population with images of happy families with only one child. The government is desperately trying to convince the masses that producing only one child leads to a wealthier, healthier and happier life. But foreigners in China tell a different story, that the people aren't convinced. They tell of being routinely approached—on the markets, on the streets, on the railways—and asked about the contraceptive policies of their countries. Expatriate women in Beijing all tell stories of Chinese women enviously asking them how many sons they have and how many children they plan to have. They explain that they only have one child because the government allows them only one.

"When I'm out with my three children on the weekend," says a young American father who lives in Beijing, "people are always asking me why am I allowed to have three children. You can feel when they ask you that there is envy there. There's a natural disappointment among the people. They just want to have more children. But there's a resigned understanding, an acceptance that they just can't."

Parental Favoritism toward Daughters

Why do the parents of some cultures invest more in the offspring of one sex than the other? A case study of the Kenyan Mukogodo offers an evolutionary explanation

Lee Cronk

Lee Cronk is assistant professor of anthropology at Texas A&M University. He received his Ph.D. in anthropology in 1989 from Northwestern University. He has received a Fulbright grant to spend this summer continuing his research among the Mukogodo, where he will be looking in detail at the effects of variations in parental behavior on children's health, nutritional status and development. Address: Department of Anthropology, Texas A&M University, College Station, TX 77843-4352.

The birth of a healthy child is greeted with great fanfare in almost every part of the world. But not every birth inspires a celebration. In many cultures, the birth of a girl is merely shrugged off by a couple hoping to produce a son. In others, the favoritism toward boys is so strong that parents may resort to infanticide, refusing to invest energy and affection in a daughter. The question this behavior raises has always been an intriguing one for anthropologists. Why would parents show such strong bias toward children of one sex?

Although there have been many studies of cultures that favor boy children, the question of sex-biased parental favoritism arose in a different way, and unexpectedly, in my own research

a few years ago. My wife and I had been studying cultural change among the Mukogodo people of central Kenya. Because the Mukogodo had recently shifted from hunting and gathering to sheep and goat herding, the people had experienced a drastic change in their life-style. It seemed to be a perfect opportunity to study the adaptive responses of a small society during a rapid economic transition.

While we were conducting a census of the population, however, we discovered a curious statistic: A survey of Mukogodo births in the previous year showed that 32 girls had been born, but only 13 boys! Intriguingly, the biased sex ratio persisted for children under four years of age. As of 1986 there were 98 girls and only 66 boys less than five years old. Whereas most cultures around the world have roughly equal or slightly male-biased childhood sex ratios, the Mukogodo had veered in the opposite direction in a very big way. Could parental favoritism account for the Mukogodo's lopsided sex ratios? If so, why did they favor girls?

The anomalous sex ratio of the Mukogodo instigated a course of research that I have pursued to the present day. In the course of my investigation, I discovered that female-biased parental favoritism is very rare. A few instances are known, however, in such disparate countries as Pakistan, New

Guinea, and the United States. In recent years these and other cases of sex-biased parental investment have become the focus of a great deal of research, especially from an evolutionary point of view. There is in fact a body of evolutionary theory that offers a biological explanation for the lopsided sex ratio among the Mukogodo, even though the same explanation may not hold true for other examples of unequal treatment of daughters and sons in human society. The theory asks the question: Could the tendency to favor daughters or sons in particular circumstances be the product of our species' history of natural selection?

PARENTAL INVESTMENT

The mix of males and females among newborns in a sexually reproducing population tends to be roughly 50–50. There are species, however, that exhibit different sex ratios, and evolutionary biologists have attempted to explain these differences. One way that parents might modify the sex ratios of their offspring is to invest different amounts of energy in activities that promote an offspring's survival.

At first glance, favoring or neglecting some offspring would seem to be a nonadaptive response. Shouldn't a parent want to produce as many offspring

From *American Scientist*, May/June 1993, pp. 272-279. Reprinted by permission of the *American Scientist*, journal of Sigma Xi, The Scientific Research Society.

Figure 1. Among the Mukogodo people of Kenya, girls and boys receive an unequal amount of attention from their parents. Young girls appear to receive greater medical care and appear to be better nourished than their male siblings. According to the author, Mukogodo parents unknowingly provide more care for their daughters because of an adaptive response to the greater reproductive success of women in their society. (Photograph courtesy of the author.)

as possible, of either sex? As with so many important issues in evolutionary theory, Charles Darwin was the first to attempt an explanation of sex-biased parental investment and the closely related problem of offspring sex ratios. In this case, however, Darwin soon decided that "the whole problem is so intricate that it is safer to leave its solution for the future."

The British biostatistician Sir Ronald A. Fisher offered the first convincing explanation of sex-biased parental investment. Fisher began with the observation that because every individual in a sexually reproducing diploid (duplicate chromosome) species gets half of its genetic material from its father and half from its mother, selec-

tion should favor parents who invest equally in sons and daughters. In this view a single unit of investment in an individual of one sex will have the same effect on a parent's fitness (measured in terms of grandchildren) as a unit invested in the other sex. If daughters and sons cost the same to rear to adulthood (and provide an equal payoff in terms of grandchildren), then this would lead to equal numbers of sons and daughters.

On the other hand, if daughters and sons do not cost the same, selection should favor greater production of the cheaper sex so that the overall parental investment in the sexes is equal. For example, if sons cost half as much to rear as daughters, then the equilibrium

sex ratio for the population would be two males for every female. Although an average male would leave only half as many offspring as an average female, males also cost only half as much to produce. So one unit of investment in a male yields the same number of grandchildren as one unit of investment in a female.

This idea, called "Fisher's principle of the sex ratio," assumes that all offspring of all parents have essentially the same reproductive prospects as other members of their sex. But what if the reproductive prospects vary among offspring of the same sex? This question was posed by evolutionary biologist Robert Trivers and mathematician Dan Willard in 1973. Trivers and Wil-

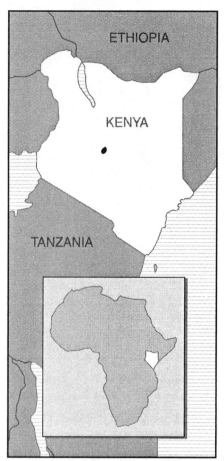

Figure 2. Mukogodo territory (*black*) is located in a region of central Kenya that is inhabited by pastoralist Maasai-speaking peoples. The Mukogodo (*right*) have recently shifted from a hunting and gathering subsistence to a sheep- and goat-herding economy. In the process they have adopted the culture and language of their Maasai-speaking neighbors. Because the hunter-gatherer life-style is disparaged by Maasai society, the Mukogodo have been relegated to the bottom of the social hierarchy in their newfound culture. (Photograpy courtesy of the author.)

Figure 3. A Mukogodo girl—here milking a family goat—will ultimately provide more livestock for her parents when her prospective husband pays a bridewealth to her family in exchange for the privilege of marrying her. In this respect, a daughter is more valuable than a son to a Mukogodo family. (Photograph courtesy of the author.)

lard pointed out that in many species, male reproductive success is both more variable than that of females and more likely to be influenced by environmental conditions during the period of parental investment. When conditions are good, both male and female offspring are likely to benefit reproductively, but males benefit more because of their greater reproductive potential. When conditions are bad, both male and female offspring are likely to suffer reproductively, but males usually suffer more. Given those conditions, parents who find themselves in good condition while raising their offspring would do best to favor their sons, whereas those who find themselves in poor condition should focus their energies on their daughters in order to have the most grandchildren.

Evidence for the Trivers-Willard hypothesis was thin and easily criticized until the 1980s, when a series of studies seemed to confirm the hypothesis among certain species. It was found that a large South American rodent, the coypu or nutria, adjusted its offspring sex ratio in a way that fit Trivers and Willard's predictions. In particular, when conditions are good, a fat, healthy female coypu selectively aborts small, mostly female litters but keeps small, mostly male litters. Since small litters produce large offspring, and a large body size is probably more important for male reproductive success, it behooves the parents to invest more in male than in female offspring.

Steven Austad of Harvard University and Melvin Sunquist of the University of Florida observed a similar pattern when they experimented with the diets of female opossums. They found that female opossums receiving food supplements produced about 40 percent more male offspring than female offspring. In contrast, female opossums that were maintained on a normal diet produced equal numbers of male and female offspring.

Some of the best evidence for the Trivers-Willard effect among primates comes from studies of spider monkeys. Because male spider monkeys stay in the social group in which they are born, whereas female spider monkeys leave their natal troops, the reproductive success of a male is highly dependent on his mother's rank in the social hierarchy. Accordingly, low-ranking mothers produce all daughters, whereas high-ranking mothers have a balanced sex ratio. High-ranking spider monkey mothers also put more effort into raising their sons by carrying their sons for a longer period than their daughters and by waiting longer to get pregnant after the birth of a son than the birth of a daughter.

Trivers and Willard suggested that their model might also be fruitfully applied to the human species, with socioeconomic class replacing maternal conditions. In human beings, as in many other species, the variance in male reproductive success is typically greater than that of females. The reproductive success of a male is usually more affected by socioeconomic status than is the reproductive success of a

female. This is especially true in societies where men are able to have more than one wife and where they must pay a bridewealth to the wife's family in order to marry. These conditions serve to enhance the advantages of being wealthy, powerful and prestigious.

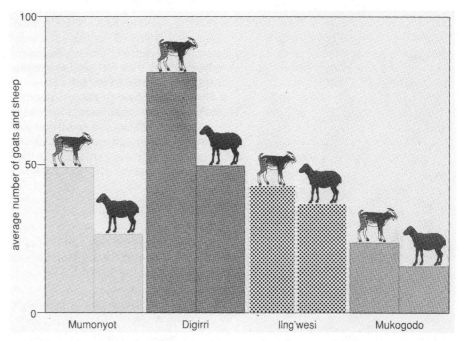

Figure 4. Relative wealth (measured in numbers of goats and sheep) of the Mukogodo and their neighbors finds the Mukogodo at the bottom of an economic hierarchy. Because of their economic status, Mukogodo men have difficulty accumulating the bridewealth necessary to arrange a marriage.

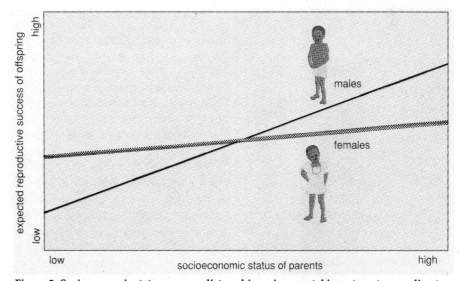

Figure 5. Socioeconomic status may predict sex biases in parental investment, according to a model first proposed by Robert Trivers and Dan Willard in the early 1970s. Male offspring (*black*) typically have greater reproductive success than female offspring (*gray*) when their parents have high socioeconomic status. In contrast, female offspring are typically more reproductively successful than male offspring when their parents have low socioeconomic status. The Trivers-Willard model predicts that parents will favor the sex of offspring with the best reproductive prospects. The Mukogodo, who are at the bottom of a socioeconomic hierarchy, are predicted to favor daughters over sons.

THE MUKOGODO

The Mukogodo are neither wealthy, powerful nor prestigious. Until the early part of this century they were foragers and beekeepers, living in caves within the forest that bears their

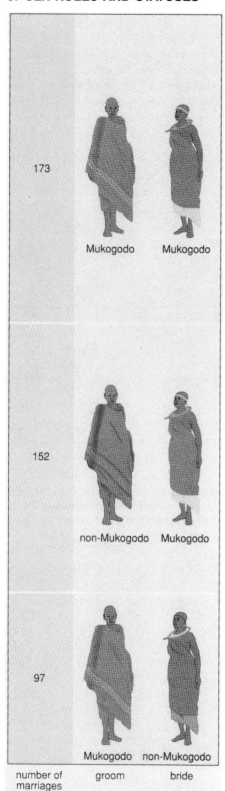

number of marriages | groom | bride

Figure 6. Inter-ethnic marriages occur most often between a Mukogodo bride and a non-Mukogodo groom. In contrast, Mukogodo men marry non-Mukogodo women much less frequently. The highest proportion of marriages consists of a Mukogodo bride and groom. Ultimately, it is easier for a Mukogodo woman to marry than it is for a Mukogodo man because the bridewealth for a Mukogodo woman is relatively low, and Mukogodo men have difficulty acquiring the livestock required to marry a woman of higher status.

name. One British colonial settler described them as "a miserable tribe living in clefts in the rocks and subsisting on wild yams and honey and the chase."

Within a few years, however, the Mukogodo acquired cattle, sheep and goats—mostly as bridewealth when their daughters married men from neighboring herding groups. These groups—the Mumonyot, Ilng'wesi, Digirri and Samburu—speak the same language and have a culture similar to the better-known Maasai of southern Kenya and northern Tanzania. The Mukogodo moved out of their caves, which were inconvenient for maintaining livestock, and adopted the language and most of the other customs of their neighbors.

One result of the change was to put the Mukogodo firmly at the bottom of a regional hierarchy of wealth, prestige and, ultimately, marital and reproductive opportunities. A livestock census conducted by the British in the early 1930s clearly shows that the Mukogodo were the poorest people in the area at that time. A recent survey (in the 1980s) of the most economically important stock (goats and sheep) shows that the Mukogodo are still on the bottom rung of the socioeconomic ladder.

The Mukogodo also carry a stigma due to their history of hunting and gathering, an activity that the Maasai and other local groups consider appropriate for wild animals, not civilized people. Maasai-speakers refer to the Mukogodo as *il-torrobo* (anglicized as Dorobo), which translates roughly as "poor scum." Maasai-speakers associate Dorobo with all manner of negative characteristics—cowardice, envy, selfishness—and even with their version of the original fall from grace. In their mythology, a Dorobo is said to have shot an arrow that severed a cord by which God had been sending cattle from heaven to earth. The fact that the Mukogodo once spoke a different, now nearly extinct language makes them even more alien and suspect to their neighbors. Many of the Maasai-speakers falsely believe that the Mukogodo secretly speak their old language in private, mysterious ceremonies.

For Mukogodo men the consequence

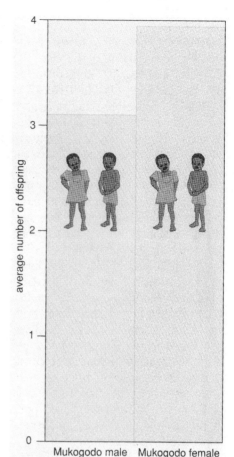

Figure 7. Fertility of the average Mukogodo woman (*right*) is greater than that of the average Mukogodo man (*left*). The greater reproductive success of Mukogodo women means that Mukogodo parents can produce a greater number of grandchildren by having more daughters than sons.

of their socioeconomic status is simple: It is harder for them to find wives than it is for other men in the area. Their lack of livestock means they do not have the bridewealth needed to pay for a wife, and the stigma attached to their Dorobo status means that the women of the other ethnic groups do not find them desirable. The situation is exacerbated because Mukogodo men must pay a higher bridewealth when they marry women from other groups in comparison to men from other groups who marry Mukogodo women. This may be due to the difficult bargaining position of the Mukogodo and the taint of their Dorobo label.

Women in the Mukogodo area, in contrast, are always in short supply since men can have as many wives as they can afford. As a result, Mukogodo women all find husbands—often among their wealthier, higher-status neighbors—despite their Dorobo origins. In the end, the average Mukogodo woman has more children than the average Mukogodo man.

FAVORED DAUGHTER

The Mukogodo situation clearly fits the preconditions set by Trivers and Willard for sex-biased parental investment. But what is it that the Mukogodo do, if anything, to produce such a female-biased sex ratio among their children?

Given the imbalance in births during the year of our fieldwork, it would be tempting to say that something physiological is taking place. Perhaps there are more female conceptions or more

male miscarriages than normal. Unfortunately, the data to test this idea are simply not available (partly because the Mukogodo women are reluctant to talk about the details of reproduction). The data we do have suggests that the sex ratio at birth is just about normal, with slightly more males than females at birth. (The sex ratio of births during 1986 may be a statistical anomaly.)

That leaves the time after the babies

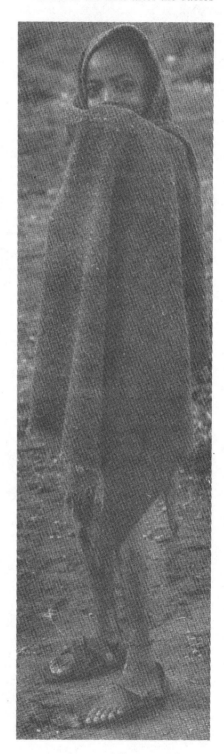

Figure 8. Mukogodo boys *(right)* are more likely than girls *(left)* to be neglected by their parents. Mukogodo parents take their sons to a medical clinic less often than they take their daughters, and a Mukogodo mother typically breastfeeds a son for a shorter period of time than a daughter. As a result, there are more undernourished and sickly young Mukogodo boys than girls. (Photographs courtesy of the author.)

are born. One possibility, seen in many other parts of the world, is infanticide: Mukogodo mothers could be killing their sons. But there is no evidence of this. The Mukogodo have no tradition of infanticide, they do not admit having practiced it, and there is no physical evidence of it. Mukogodo parents are also not overtly abusive of their children, and corporal punishment is rare.

It is more likely that their sons are dying at a higher rate than normal because of a broad tendency to favor daughters over sons. The best evidence for this comes from the records of health facilities run by a local Roman Catholic mission. Mukogodo parents show a clear and statistically significant tendency to take their daughters more often than their sons for treatment at a dispensary. Mukogodo parents also enroll their daughters more frequently in the mission's monthly traveling baby clinic, which provides mothers with some food and child-care lessons.

In contrast, the non-Mukogodo people in the region show no bias toward sons or daughters when they take them to the dispensary or clinic. Since the Mukogodo and their neighbors share the same views about children and childrearing, it seems unlikely that the Mukogodo's female bias could be due to a belief that girls are more sickly than boys.

For the Mukogodo, taking a child to the dispensary or the clinic is a major investment. The dispensary charges a fee of five Kenyan shillings (equivalent to 30 U.S. cents in 1986) for every visit. The fee is intended to discourage frivolous visits, but in combination with the time it takes to travel to the dispensary (from half a day to three days) it amounts to a substantial bother and expense to take a child to see the doctor. The clinic is also relatively expensive, charging a monthly fee of 22 Kenyan shillings (about $1.38), and requires nearly a full day of travel.

Mukogodo mothers also tend to breastfeed their daughters longer than their sons. In one instance a two-and-one-half-year-old girl was still being nursed. Nearly 84 percent of all girls, but only 70 percent of all boys less than

Figure 9. Nomadic Kanjar family of Pakistan reverses the sex roles typical in southwest Asia. A Kanjar woman dominates the public and private affairs of the family and provides most of the income—by singing, dancing, selling toys and engaging in prostitution. A Kanjar family may also receive a large bridewealth when a daughter is married. Because of the greater economic value of a Kanjar woman to her family, the birth of a girl is more highly desired than the birth of a boy. (Courtesy of Joseph Berland, Henderson, Kentucky.)

Figure 10. Industrial revolution in 19th-century America provided many job opportunities for young women and made them more valuable than sons to urban families. In rural areas, however, a young man was more valuable to his family because of the farm work he could do. The life expectancies of girls and boys during this period suggest that parents invested more effort in daughters in urban areas, but directed more effort toward their sons in rural areas. Parents appear to invest more in the offspring that provides greater economic or reproductive success. Here a young woman works at a loom in the burgeoning textile industry of New England circa 1850. (Daguerreotype courtesy of the Museum of American Textile History.)

two-and-one half years old were being nursed.

Although Mukogodo standards of child-care are different from our own, there were three clear cases of child neglect, all of which involved boys. One little boy was made miserable for months by a chronic eye infection because his mother refused to take him to the dispensary. Another infant boy was visibly underdeveloped, listless and easily frightened, whereas his older sister was bright, healthy and well fed. A physician had diagnosed the boy's problem as malnutrition. In the third instance, a five-year-old boy had a large, festering wound behind one ear for the entire year we were among the Mukogodo because his parents refused to take him for medical treatment. (Although we tried to bandage the wound several times, it did not heal until it was treated by a health worker from the Catholic mission who was passing through the village.)

OTHER SOCIETIES

In my perusal of the literature, I have discovered the existence of other societies in which the sex ratios of the population did not follow the standard bias in favor of boys. In an attempt to understand these aberrant societies, I have tried to interpret their circumstances in the light of the Trivers-Willard model.

The Cheyenne Indians of the 19th century offer a striking example. These people were divided into two groups, lower-status "war bands," led by "war chiefs," and upper-status "peace bands," led by "peace chiefs." Peace chiefs naturally tended to survive longer than war chiefs, they tended to have more wives, and their bands were generally wealthier than those of the war chiefs. Interestingly, a census from 1892 shows that the childhood sex ratios in the peace bands were about even, with 97 boys for every 100 girls, whereas the ratio in the war bands was about 69 boys for every 100 girls.

In other instances where parents favor their daughters over their sons, the Trivers-Willard model does not apply since girls do not have better reproductive prospects than their brothers. In such cases, it appears that in one way or another girls are either cheaper to raise than boys or provide more benefits to their families than boys do. In rural areas of 19th-century America, sons were more valuable to their families than daughters because of the important farm work they were called upon to do. In more urban areas, in contrast, the economic value of girls was higher since they could get jobs in the many new industries that were arising. Demographic data suggest that parents directed more investment toward the economically more productive sex. In non-urbanized regions, there were more boys than girls in the United States between 1800 and 1860, whereas in urbanized regions such as New England there were more girls than boys. The life expectancy was higher for girls in towns of 10,000 people or more, but higher for boys in towns with fewer than 10,000 people.

A more colorful example is provided by the Kanjar of Pakistan and northern India who travel from town to town selling ceramic and papier-mâché toys, dancing, begging and occasionally offering carnival rides and engaging in prostitution. Almost all of these activities are the realm of girls and women, who provide more than half of the income of most Kanjar families. As a result, Kanjar society presents one of the clearest recorded examples of a reversal of the usual sex roles in human societies. Kanjar men are passive, cooperative and subordinate to females, whereas Kanjar women dominate public and private affairs and are socialized to be aggressive and independent.

Kanjar girls also help their brothers get married. Bridewealth payments are very high for the Kanjar, sometimes amounting to ten times a family's annual income. To reduce their costs, two families will often exchange daughters. As one Kanjar woman explained, "The only way I can avoid paying a fortune for my son's bride is to arrange his marriage with my brother's daughter and to give my daughter to my brother's son. We call this *wady de shadi,* or exchange marriage."

When Kanjar girls do marry for bridewealth, they bring a great deal of wealth to their parents. It is not surprising, then, that the Kanjar buck the general trend in South Asia of favoritism toward sons. This is best seen in their response to the birth of a child. A newborn girl is greeted with celebrations, but the birth of a boy is received with no fanfare.

One of the strangest examples of female-biased parental investment was provided by Margaret Mead and Reo Fortune in their study of the Mundugumor of New Guinea in the 1930s. According to Mead and Fortune, Mundugumor mothers and fathers had different opinions about the value of sons and daughters, with fathers tending to favor daughters and mothers favoring sons. Father-daughter relationships were reportedly very close; fathers tried to favor their daughters in inheritance and tried to allocate more property to them. Mundugumor mothers, in contrast, were closer to their sons and tried to give them more of the family's property.

The explanation for this may lie in the Mundugumor marriage system, which involved the exchange of women between families and pitted fathers against sons for access to brides. Traditionally, daughters were to be used as currency to obtain wives for their brothers. However, since men were allowed to have multiple wives, they could also use their daughters to obtain more wives. Sons had to be vigilant to ensure that their fathers did not cheat them. As a consequence, father-son relationships were stiff and formal.

CONCLUSION

Although many human societies show a disturbing amount of favoritism toward their sons, this is by no means a universal human pattern. Societies in which daughters are favored clearly exist. Moreover, it is also possible to identify some of the reasons for the parents' bias.

In all of these examples, I have

focused on the *behavior* of the parents when they favor their daughters or sons. Another approach to studying biases in parental investment is to note the parents' *opinions* in response to questions about the number of sons and daughters they would like to have. Although the survey approach is commonly used by demographers, the statements of the Mukogodo parents suggest that there is a problem with it. Despite their behavior, most Mukogodo mothers claim to prefer sons rather than daughters. The discrepancy makes sense only in the light of the pervasiveness of the Maasai-speaking culture, which is extremely male-biased.

Since the Mukogodos' statements clearly do not reflect their behavior, it may be that the Mukogodo parents are not aware of their favoritism toward daughters. Whether or not the Mukogodo are aware of the contrast between their statements and their actions, research on the psychology of sex-biased parental investment could provide some fascinating insights into the phenomenon. It also stands as a caveat to the demographer's practice of using a parent's statements as a substitute for observations of the parent's behavior.

In the future I intend to return to the Mukogodo to understand whether subtle variations in parental behavior can affect a child's health. For example, is there any measurable relationship between the amount of time spent holding and nursing a child and the child's health, nutritional status or cognitive development? Through continued research on the causes and consequences of sex biases in parental behavior, we should be able to determine which children are likely to be at risk and how we might be able to help them and their parents cope with their situation.

BIBLIOGRAPHY

Austad, S., and M. E. Sunquist. 1986. Sex-ratio manipulation in the common opossum. *Nature* 324:58–60.

Austad, S., and M. E. Sunquist. 1988. More sons for plump possums. *Natural History* 97(4):74–75.

Berland, J. C. 1982. *No Five Fingers Are Alike: Cognitive Amplifiers in Social Context.* Cambridge: Harvard University Press.

Berland, J. C. 1987. Kanjar Social Organization. In *The Other Nomads: Peripatetic Minorities in Cross-Cultural Perspective,* ed. A. Rao, pp. 247–265. Köln: Böhlau Verlag.

Cronk, L. 1989. Low socioeconomic status and female-biased parental investment: The Mukogodo example. *American Anthropologist* 91:414–429.

Cronk, L. 1991a. Intention vs. behaviour in parental sex preferences among the Mukogodo of Kenya. *Journal of Biosocial Science* 23:229–240.

Cronk, L. 1991b. Preferential parental investment in daughters over sons. *Human Nature* 2(4):387–417.

Fisher, R. A. 1958. *The Genetical Theory of Natural Selection.* 2nd ed. Oxford: Clarendon.

Gosling, L. M. 1986. Selective abortion of entire litters in the coypu: Adaptive control of offspring production in relation to quality and sex. *American Naturalist* 127:772–795.

Hammel, E. A., S. R. Johansson and C. A. Ginsberg. 1983. The value of children during industrialization: Sex ratios in childhood in nineteenth-century America. *Journal of Family History* 8:346–366.

Hrdy, S. B. 1987. Sex-biased parental investment among primates and other mammals: A critical evaluation of the Trivers-Willard hypothesis. In *Child Abuse and Neglect: Biosocial Dimensions,* ed. R. J. Gelles and J. B. Lancaster, pp. 97–147. New York: Aldine De Gruyter.

Hrdy, S. B. 1988. Daughters or sons. *Natural History* 97(4):63–83.

McDowell, N. 1991. *The Mundugumor: From the Field Notes of Margaret Mead and Reo Fortune.* Washington, DC: Smithsonian Institution Press.

McFarland Symington, M. 1987. Sex ratio and maternal rank in wild spider monkeys: When daughters disperse. *Behavioral Ecology and Sociobiology* 20:421–425.

Mead, M. 1935. *Sex and Temperament in Three Primitive Societies.* New York: Morrow.

Trivers, R. L., and D. E. Willard. 1973. Natural selection of parental ability to vary the sex ratio of offspring. *Science* 179:90–92.

Vinovskis, M. A. 1972. Mortality rates and trends in Massachusetts before 1860. *Journal of Economic History* 32:184–218.

Blaming the Victim: Ideology and Sexual Discrimination in the Contemporary United States

Maxine Margolis

Women are a problem not only as individuals, but collectively as a separate group with special functions within the structure of society. As a group and generally, they are a problem to themselves, to their children and families, to each other, to society as a whole.

Lundberg and Farnham
1947, p. 1

Only an equal society can save the victim from being the victim.

Gloria Steinem
PBS Program on wife beating
May, 1977

It has long been a cardinal rule of anthropology that one of the main functions of a culture's social and economic structure is the creation of ideologies that perpetuate, or at least do not threaten, the status quo. The need for system-maintaining ideologies is particularly acute in stratified societies where the divisions between haves and have-nots always present potential challenges to the established order.

Blaming the Victim is one such system-maintaining ideology. It helps to preserve the status quo in the United States and other stratified societies by attributing myriad social ills—poverty, delinquency, illegitimacy, low educa-tional attainment—to the norms and values of the victimized group, rather than to the external conditions of inequality and discrimination under which that group lives. According to William Ryan (1971:xii), who was the first to recognize and label this phenomenon, Blaming the Victim is "an ideology, a mythology" consisting of a "set of official certified non-facts and respected untruths."

The primary function of this ideology is to obscure the victimizing effects of social forces. Rather than analyzing the socially induced inequalities that need changing, it focuses instead on the group or individual that is being victimized. This results in distracting attention from the social injustice, thus allowing it to continue. To change things, according to the ideology, we must change the victims, rather than the circumstances under which they live.

In American society this ideology is most often applied to minority groups, particularly blacks. It is used to "explain" their low socioeconomic status, their "aberrant" family structure, and their general failure to reap the benefits of all—it is said—this society so freely offers. Then too, Blaming the Victim is a convenient tool used to account for the underdevelopment of the third world. According to the ideology, underdevelopment is due to some defect in the national character of the nations affected, to their people's lack of achievement motivation or openness to innovation.

Here I will argue that in the contemporary United States Blaming the Victim is also used widely to rationalize the continued economic, political, and social inequality of women. The application of this ideology to women is somewhat problematic in that, unlike other minority groups, women, at least until recently, have not regarded themselves as the objects of collective victimization. Moreover, through the process of socialization, most women have internalized victim blaming—they blame themselves and other female victims for their economic, social, and political problems. Essentially they ask: "What am I doing to make people discriminate against me?"

In writing this paper, I soon realized

that women are blamed for a host of society's ills which, strictly speaking, only indirectly victimize women. Rather, in such cases, the victims are their children, their husbands, and their close associates who, it is said, are damaged by female behavior. The best known example of this type of thinking is the claim that women who work neglect their children and, therefore, are entirely responsible for whatever emotional and behavioral problems arise in their offspring. But this is simply a new twist of the victim-blaming mentality since its function is the same: to obscure the current social order's role in creating all manner of social and psychological problems by placing the blame where it is often not warranted.

Then too, it is sometimes difficult to distinguish the tendency to blame the female victim from outright misogyny. Is, for example, Philip Wylie's (1955: chap. 11) charge that men and boys are infantilized by their archtypical "Moms"—whom he describes as women who are "twenty-five pounds overweight," who have "beady brains behind their beady eyes," and who spend their time playing bridge "with the stupid voracity of a hammerhead shark"—simple misogyny or does it have an element of the victim-blaming mentality in it? It is clear why the line between the two is often blurred: it is far easier to victimize a group whom you dislike. By defining women as inferior, less trustworthy, more emotional, and less motivated than men, mistreatment or, at least, unequal treatment is justified and the status quo is preserved.

It is not particularly important to a great many working women whether or not they earn as much as men, or have equal opportunities for training and promotion. [Smuts 1974:108]

Blaming the female victim finds its widest application in the world of work. Here it comes in a variety of guises and is used to "explain" why women are paid less than men and have fewer opportunities for occupational advancement. Women, it is said, work only for "pin money" since they have husbands to support them and, there-

fore, do not really "need" their jobs. Similarly, it is claimed that women have higher rates of absenteeism and job turnover than men do, along with less interest in moving up the career ladder. These purported characteristics of the female labor force are then used to rationalize the fact that women are overwhelmingly confined to low-paying, tedious, dead-end positions.

According to the "pin money" argument, men must provide for their families, while women only work to supplement their husbands' income or for pocket money to buy "extras." Using this logic, employers rationalize paying women low wages on the grounds that they do not need their earnings to live on. And, lest it be thought that this justification for salary discrimination has succumbed to more enlightened thinking in this era of the Equal Pay Act and the feminist movement, the comments of a county commissioner in Utah should lay such hopes aside. When asked to explain why male employees had received a 22 percent wage increase and female employees a 5 percent increase, he replied: "We felt that with their husbands working, the ladies could stand the squeeze a little better" (quoted in *Ms. Magazine* 3 December, 1975).

This reasoning is specious since it misinterprets why women enter the labor force: the reasons are over-whelmingly economic. Of the nearly 38 million women employed in 1976, 84 percent were the sole support of themselves and their families, or were married to men whose 1975 incomes were under $15,000. Women's median contribution to family income was 40 percent, with 12 percent contributing one-half or more. Moreover, the only reason many families are able to maintain a middle-class standard of living is that they have two incomes. "Women flocking to work account for the vital margin between solvency and insolvency," says economic analyst Eliot Janeway (1977:66).

One of the most pernicious results of the pin money myth is the failure to take high levels of female unemployment seriously. The belief that women's jobless rates are less worri-

some than those of "household heads" again belies the fact that most women work not for pocket money, but because they are the sole support of their families or because their earnings make up a substantial proportion of their household income. By ignoring these factors, a delegate to the 1976 Republican National Convention could pooh-pooh high unemployment rates.

The unemployment rate tells a dangerously false story for which women are particularly to blame. It's not an economic problem. It's a sociological problem. [Quoted in Porter 1976]

Another component of the Blaming the Victim mentality in the world of work is the purported tendency of women to have higher rates of absenteeism and job turnover than men. These supposed liabilities of employing female labor also have been used to justify lower wages for women as well as employers' reluctance to promote them to more responsible, better-paying positions. Here, it is argued that women are not attached to the labor force, that they just "up and quit their jobs" to get married, or, if already married, to have babies. Why then, it is asked, should employers invest in expensive job-training programs for women or allow them to take on positions of responsibility?

Once again, the facts are ignored by the victimizers. A Department of Labor study of job turnover over one year found that 10 percent of male workers and 7 percent of female workers had changed jobs during that period (U.S. Department of Labor 1975). The number of women who leave work when they marry or have children has declined in the last two decades, and even with breaks in employment, the average woman now spends twenty-five years in the labor force.

It is also claimed that women miss work more than men do since they are subject to "female problems" and are more likely to stay home under the pretext of one minor ailment or another. Here too, the facts speak to the contrary. A recent survey by the Public Health Service found little difference in absentee rates due to illness or injury; women averaged 5.6 days annually and men averaged 5.2 days annually (U.S. Department of Labor 1975). Moreover, women over forty-five had a lower absentee rate than did men in the same age bracket.

Although ideas have changed since the early years of this century, when menstruation, pregnancy, and menopause were viewed as serious illnesses that disabled women and made them ill-suited for paid employment, many hiring and promotion policies still view women as baby makers who, if they are not pregnant, will soon become so. This assumption then becomes the employer's rationale for passing over women for promotion. Nor does the situation improve for older women since the belief that menopausal women suffer emotional disturbances is often used to justify denying them good jobs.

In a similar vein, Dr. Edgar Berman, a member of the Democratic party's Committee on National Priorities, received widespread publicity in 1970 when he questioned women's ability to hold certain responsible positions due to their "raging hormonal influences." "Take a woman surgeon," said the illustrious doctor, "if she had premenstrual tension . . . I wouldn't want her operating on me." Of course, Dr. Berman ignores the research which suggests that men have four- to six-week cycles that vary predictably and also seem to be caused by changing hormonal levels (quoted in Corea 1977:98–99).

Victim blamers also assert that women don't get ahead in their jobs because they lack the ambition to do so. They claim that women don't want promotions, job training, or job changes that add to their work load: "What they seek first in work," says sociologist Robert W. Smuts (1974:108), "is an agreeable job that makes limited demands. . . . Since they have little desire for a successful career," Smuts continues, "they are likely to drift into traditional women's occupations." George Meany offered a similar rationale in commenting on the lack of women on the thirty-three-member executive council of the AFL-CIO: "We have some very capable women in our

unions, but they only go up to a certain level. . . . They don't seem to have any desire to go further" (quoted in *Ms. Magazine*, July, 1977).

Data regarding women's purported lack of ambition are difficult to come by, given that relatively few women have been offered positions of responsibility in the business world. Nevertheless, there is no evidence that the 5.1 million women who held professional and technical jobs and the 1.6 million who worked as managers and administrators in 1974 performed any less ably than men in comparable positions.

Yet another assertion made by Blaming the Victim ideologues is that women are "naturally" good at tedious, repetitive jobs; that they have an aptitude, if not an affinity, for typing, filing, assembling small items, packaging, labeling, and so forth. This view is clearly spelled out in a pamphlet entitled *The Feminine Touch* issued by Employer's Insurance of Wausau.

The female sex tends to be better suited for the unvarying routine that many . . . jobs require. Women are not bored by repetitive tasks as easily as men.

It was also echoed by the chief detective in the notorious "Son of Sam" case who, in a *New York* article, was quoted as saying that he sent two female detectives to the hack bureau to go through tens of thousands of licenses because they were "judged better able to withstand such drudgery than men" (quoted in Daley 1977).

These stereotypes lack any data to back them up and are simply rationalizations that allow men to assign women to such tasks without guilt. They also help justify the continued ghettoization of women workers in certain "appropriate" female occupations where their purported aptitude for tedium can be put to good use.

Many women . . . exaggerate the severity of their complaints to gratify neurotic desires. The woman who is at odds with her biological self develops psychosomatic and gynecologic problems. [Greenhill 1965:154, 158]

Psychiatry and gynecology have provided lucrative settings for victim-blaming ideologues. Blaming the female victim is the unifying theme in the perception and treatment of such medically diverse spheres as depression, childbirth, contraception, abortion, menstruation, and menopause. The common thread in all is that women's psychological and medical complaints are suspect, that they exaggerate their ills to get attention, and that most female ailments are of a psychogenic rather than a biogenic origin.

Most psychotherapists, wittingly or unwittingly, ignore the objective conditions under which female neurosis and depression arise, and help maintain the sexual status quo by suggesting individual rather than collective solutions to female discontent. The patient is encouraged to think that her depression, her neurosis, is unique, that they are conditions of her own making.

Nowhere is the Blaming the Victim syndrome more evident in the profession than in the diagnosis and treatment of female sexual problems. Lundberg and Farnham, in their misogynist tome *Modern Woman: The Lost Sex,* claimed that the failure of women to achieve sexual satisfaction is a neurosis that stems from a negative view of childbearing and from attempts to "emulate the male in seeking a sense of personal value by objective exploit" (1947:265). Similarly, Freudian psychoanalyst Helene Deutsch (1944) believed that frigidity in women resulted from nonconformity to the feminine role.

Blaming the individual woman for emotional problems that in many cases are related to her fulfillment of traditional, socially accepted female roles obscures the dilemmas inherent in these roles and relieves society of responsibility for her unhappiness. The psychiatrist Robert Seidenberg suggests that the housewife-mother role often gives rise to emotional problems in women who adhere to it. He found that the "trauma of eventlessness"—that is, the absence of stimuli, challenges, choices, and decision making, which characterizes many women's lives—can threaten their mental well-being as much as physical danger (quoted in Sklar 1976).

When women are used as guinea pigs—as in the case of the birth control pill and other contraceptive devices—their complaints of side effects are often dismissed as the reaction of neurotic females. For example, depression, a fairly common side effect of the pill, is discussed in a medical text in these terms:

Recent evidence suggests that a significant number of these depressive reactions are due to an unrecognized and deeply rooted wish for another child. [Ciriacy and Hughes 1973:300]

The fact that the development of birth control pills and other contraceptive methods has been largely aimed at women is the result of a number of assumptions made by the largely male research establishment. Not only do they believe that conception control is the responsibility of women, they fear the untoward effects of interfering with the male sex drive. Having a healthy supply of sperm is more important to men than ovulation is to women, claim these authorities.

Although the medical profession encourages women to employ problematic contraceptive techniques, it is far more reticent about permitting them to undergo early, medically safe abortions. The reasons are often of the victim-blaming ilk. A staff physician at a county hospital in Milwaukee compared abortions to such cosmetic procedures as face lifts and breast enlargements. "Women know what makes them pregnant and they should have responsibility," he is quoted as saying (quoted in the *Milwaukee Sentinel,* July, 1976).

Even pregnancy and childbirth do not escape the net cast by the medical victim blamers. Morning sickness, for example, is described in one gynecological text as possibly indicating "resentment, ambivalence, and inadequacy in women ill-prepared for motherhood" (quoted in Corea 1977:77). Thus, a condition that is experienced by 75 to 80 percent of all pregnant women, and seems to be related to higher levels of estrogen during pregnancy, is dismissed as a psychosomatic

aberration. Others have claimed that many women exaggerate the pain of childbirth: "Exaggeration of the rigors of the process is self-enhancing and . . . affords a new and powerful means of control over the male," say Lundberg and Farnham (1947:294).

Menstrual cramps also are suspect. One gynecologic text writer (Greenhill 1965:154) argues that they often "reflect the unhealthy attitude toward femininity that is so predominant in our society." Other medical texts adopt a similar view. One attributes menstrual pain to a "faulty outlook . . . leading to an exaggeration of minor discomfort," while another states "the pain is always secondary to an emotional problem" (quoted in Lenanne and Lenanne 1973:288).

Victim blaming by the medical establishment reached a crescendo during Senate subcommittee hearings looking into unnecessary surgical procedures. There, the highest ranking staff physician of the American Medical Association argued that hysterectomy is justified—though the uterus was healthy—in women who feared pregnancy or cancer. The chief of obstetrics and gynecology at a Rhode Island hospital agrees: "The uterus is just a muscle" and "It's a liability after children are born because it's a cancer site." The doctor added that his reasoning "ideally" applied to breasts as well, but "this would be a hard concept to sell in this society" (quoted in *Ms. Magazine,* November, 1977). One fact little noted in these discussion is that while it is true that hysterectomy eliminates the possibility of later uterine cancer, the death rate from uterine cancer is lower than the mortality rate from hysterectomies.

Menopause is another medical area in which victim-blaming health practitioners have had a field day. The common medical depiction of menopausal women as aged hags suffering from hot flashes and severe depression has been adopted by the public at large. A judge in Toronto, for example, dismissed the testimony of a forty-eight-year-old woman, stating: "There comes a certain age in a woman's life . . . when the evidence is not too reliable"

(quoted in *Ms Magazine,* July, 1977). This stereotype overlooks the fact that only between 20 and 30 percent of the female population have such symptoms. Moreover, it is usually assumed that depression is caused by the loss of reproductive capacity, while little attention is paid to the objective life conditions of many middle-aged women—their "empty nests," their husbands' inattention, their lack of challenging employment opportunities, and society's glorification of female youth and beauty. Surely these conditions do much to account for depression in middle-aged women. But rather than question traditional sex roles, or the unequal distribution of power between men and women in our society, the medical establishment appeals to the "empty uterus" as the source of female discontent.

Whether they like it or not, a woman's a sex object, and they're the ones who turn the men on. [Judge Archie Simonson, Dane County, Wisconsin, 1977]

Nowhere is victim blaming more pernicious than when it is used to rationalize sexual and physical aggression against women. The courtroom statements of Judge Archie Simonson of Wisconsin show that Blaming the Victim is still too often the norm in the perception of rape and the treatment of its victims. This is also true of wife beating. In fact, attitudes toward abused wives and rape victims are strikingly similar; just as the rape victim is supposed to be an irresistible temptress who deserves what she got, so, it is said, the abused wife provokes her husband into beating her. Then too, it is said that women secretly enjoy being beaten, just as they are supposed to be "turned on" by rape.

There are two components to victim blaming as a rationalization for rape. For one, it is assumed that all women covertly desire rape, and, for another, that no woman can be raped against her will, so that forcible rape doesn't really exist. In combination, these assumptions lead to the conclusion that if a woman is raped, she is at fault, or, as Brownmiller (1976:374) says: "She was asking for it" is the classic rapist's remark as he "shifts the burden of blame from himself to his victim."

Victim precipitation, a concept in criminology often used in rape cases, tries to determine if the victim's behavior contributed in any way to the crime. While an unlawful act has occurred, goes the argument, if the victim had acted differently—had not walked alone at night or allowed a strange male to enter her house—the crime might not have taken place. This point is illustrated by a court case in California in which the judge overturned the conviction of a man who had picked up a female hitchhiker and raped her. The ruling read, in part:

The lone female hitchhiker . . . advises all who pass by that she is willing to enter the vehicle of anyone who stops, and . . . so advertises that she has less concern for the consequences than the average female. Under such circumstances, it would not be unreasonable for a man in the position of the defendant . . . to believe that the female would consent to sexual relations. [*New York Times,* July 10, 1977]

Another example of this mentality is the minister who wrote in a letter to "Dear Abby" that a young girl whose father had sexually abused her had "tempted" him by "wearing tight fitting, revealing clothes." In light of these opinions, which reflect the deeply ingrained notion that women provoke rape by their behavior and dress, it is little wonder that rape victims often agonize over what they did to cause themselves to be raped.

These attitudes are also evident in the way rape victims are handled by the courts and the police: the victim is more often treated like the criminal than is the rapist. Some states still permit testimony about the victim's prior sexual experience and general moral demeanor, and Brownmiller (1976:419) cites a study of the jury system which reported that in cases of rape "the jury closely scrutinizes the female complainant" and "weighs the conduct of the victims in judging the guilt of the defendant."

Similar attitudes are reflected in a California police manual which states that "forcible rape is the most falsely reported crime," and Brownmiller (1976:408) notes that many police assume that rape complaints are made by "prostitutes who didn't get paid." If a woman is raped by a stranger, the charge usually is taken more seriously than if she is raped by a man she knows. The latter, the police claim, is a "woman who changed her mind."

No matter how women behave in rape cases they are still held responsible for the outcome. While popular opinions denies the possibility of forcible rape, a judge in England recently suggested that a woman who was seriously injured fighting off a rapist had only herself to blame for being hurt. She should have given in to the rapist, said the judge. The *London Times* editorialized, "This almost suggests that refusing to be raped is a kind of contributory negligence" (quoted in *Ms. Magazine,* November, 1977). The accused rapist, a soldier in the Coldstream Guards, was freed pending appeal on the grounds that he has a "promising career"!

In dealing with sexual violence the victim blamers once again ignore the facts. As a whole, according to the National Commission of the Causes and Prevention of Violence, rape victims are responsible for less precipitant behavior than victims of other kinds of crimes (Brownmiller 1976:396). Nor are the vast majority of rape charges brought by "women who changed their mind"; a study showed that only 2 percent of rape complaints proved to be false, which is about the same rate as for other felonies (Brownmiller 1976:410). Finally, the idea that women secretly "enjoy" rape is too preposterous to take seriously. I heartily concur with Herschberger's (1970:24) remark that

the notion that a victim of sexual aggression is forced into an experience of sensory delight should be relegated to the land where candy grows on trees.

Since the evidence negates the widespread belief that rape victims are "responsible" for what happens to them, it is senseless to argue that if women took special precautions in their dress and behavior the problem would disappear. As Brownmiller (1976:449) convincingly argues: "there can be no private solutions to the problems of rape." Yet

these attitudes persist since, by viewing rape as a "woman's problem" brought on by the victims themselves, both men and society are relieved of guilt.

As I suggested earlier, the explanation for and treatment of wife abuse are remarkably similar to that of rape, and the victim blaming is just as loud and clear. Police, who are notoriously loath to intervene in domestic disputes, too often take the attitude "well, if her husband beat her, she probably deserved it." They often assume that women who accuse their husbands of beating them are vindictive, and will only prosecute if they are convinced that the wife is a "worthy victim." And in courtroom after courtroom, it is the battered woman's responsibility to persuade the judge that she is really a victim—a judge who may ask her what she did to provoke her husband's attack.

These attitudes are sometimes shared by members of the abused woman's family as well as society at large. In a newspaper article on wife abuse, a woman whose husband beat her while she was pregnant told of getting no support from her family or her doctor.

My mother said I must be doing things to make him mad, and my sister said it was all right for a man to beat his wife. I told my gynecologist that my husband was extremely violent and I was mortally afraid of him. Guess what he said? I should relax more. He prescribed tranquilizers. [*Gainesville Sun,* September 5, 1977]

Victim blamers have had a field day in looking for culprits in wife-abuse cases. A member of the New Hampshire Commission on the Status of Women, for example, suggested that the women's liberation movement was responsible for the increased incidence of wife beating and rape (reported on the "Today Show," September 16, 1977).

In fact that a mere two percent of battering husbands are ever prosecuted is clearly related to these attitudes. While assault and battery are quickly punished when they occur between strangers, punitive action is rare within a marital relationship. The extreme to which this can go is evidenced in a recent court decision in England. A man who killed his wife and pleaded guilty to "manslaughter" was sentenced to only three years probation on the grounds that his wife had "nagged him constantly for seventeen years." "I don't think I have ever come across a case where provocation has gone on for so long," said the judge (reported in the *Independent Florida Alligator*, October 20, 1977).

Many who are otherwise sympathetic to the battered wife are perplexed as to why she takes the abuse. But the reasons are not too difficult to discern. Not only are many women economically dependent on their husbands, but they also have been socialized to be victims. As Marjory Fields, a lawyer involved in wife abuse cases, has noted, "they not only take the beatings, they tend to feel responsible for them" (quoted in Gingold 1976:52).

Should something go wrong, as in the production of a Hitler, a woman is said to be at the root of the trouble—in this case Hitler's mother. [Herschberger 1970:16]

Victims blamers have devoted a good deal of their time and rhetoric to what can be termed "mother blame." In this category of victim blaming, it is not women themselves who are said to be adversely affected by their behavior, but rather their children and, ultimately, society at large. The psychiatric profession, in particular, has been responsible for popularizing the view that, in Chesler's (1972:378) words, "the lack of or superabundance of mother love causes neurotic, criminal . . . and psychopathic children." The absent or uncaring father and other forms of deprivation rarely are blamed for problem children and problem adults.

Mother blame is a natural outgrowth of the traditional, socially approved sexual division of labor that sees child rearing as exclusively "woman's work"; if something goes wrong, it must be mother who is to blame. Moreover, women are held responsible for their children's problems no matter what they do. If they work, they are accused of child neglect, while if they stay home and devote their time to child care, they are berated for smothering their offspring.

The theory that attributes juvenile delinquency and other behavior problems to maternal employment has been around for quite some time. During World War II, working mothers were widely criticized for rearing "latchkey children" who got into trouble for lack of supervision. Mother blame reached a peak shortly after the war with the publication of *Modern Woman: The Lost Sex*. In it, Lundberg and Farnham (1947:304–305) estimate that between 40 and 50 percent of all mothers are "rejecting, over-solicitous, or dominating," and that they produce "the delinquents, the behavior problem children, and some substantial proportion of criminals."

Some years later psychiatrist Abram Kardiner (1954:224) agreed with these sentiments when he wrote that "children reared on a part-time basis will show the effects of such care in the distortions of personality that inevitably result." After all, "motherhood is a full-time job."

Lest it be thought that mother blame is merely an artifact of the days of the feminine mystique, a recent newspaper editorial espoused it when attempting to explain the high crime rate.

Let's speculate that the workaday grind makes Mom more inaccessible, irritable . . . and spiteful, thereby rendering family life less pleasant . . . than the good old days when she stayed in the kitchen and baked apple pies. What could that be doing to the rising crime rate? Say fellows, could it be Mom's fault? [Editorial, *Gainesville Sun*, March 25, 1977]

These views, of course, ignore the studies that indicate that absent and low profile fathers are more responsible for delinquency in their children than are working mothers. Moreover, the most comprehensive study of maternal employment, *The Employed Mother in America* (Nye and Hoffman 1963), effectively rebuts the myths concerning the supposed ill effects of working mothers on their offspring, and concludes that "maternal employment . . . is not the overwhelming influential factor in children's lives that some have thought it to be" (Burchinal 1963:118; Siegal et al. 1963:80). But, as we have seen, victim blamers have little use for facts that contradict their strongly held beliefs.

What of the woman who stays home and devotes full time to child raising? She too is the target of the mother blamers who hold her accountable for an incredible variety of social problems. In his book *Generation of Vipers*, Phillip Wylie (1955) characterized such women as "Moms" who led empty lives and preyed upon their offspring, keeping them tied to their proverbial apron strings. This theme was also sounded by Edward Strecker (1946), a psychiatric consultant to the Army and Navy Surgeons General during World War II. In trying to account for the emotional disorders of 600,000 men unable to continue in military service, Strecker wrote, "in the vast majority of case histories, a Mom is at fault." But what causes "Moms" to be the way they are in the first place? In most cases, a Mom is a Mom because she is the immature result of a Mom, says Strecker (1946:23, 70).

If it weren't for Martha, there'd have been no Watergate. [Richard Nixon on David Frost interview, September, 1977]

Richard Nixon's statement holding Martha Mitchell responsible for Watergate is a timely reminder of the length to which victim blamers sometimes go. According to Nixon, Watergate occurred because "John Mitchell wasn't minding the store," but was preoccupied with his wife's emotional problems. This claim is particularly malicious given the often-noted fact that the large Watergate case was *all* male. A similarly absurd remark was made during the "Son of Sam" episode, when it was automatically assumed that a woman was at the root of "Sam's" problem. The killer "must have been terribly provoked by a woman," New York psychiatrist Hyman Spotnitz was quoted as saying in *Time* (July 11, 1977).

While Nixon's assertion was widely seen as self-serving, the opinions of psychiatrists and other authoritative victim blamers are taken quite seriously by the general public, including women. Women not only participate in this ideology, they often internalize it, blaming themselves and other women for a host of problems. This shows the effectiveness of the ideology in rationalizing subordination to the victims themselves. The very persistence of victim blaming, in fact, is partly due to the implicit participation of its targets. And men, of course, perpetuate the ideology since it is clearly in their own self-interest to do so. It helps maintain the status quo from which they benefit.

In recent years the ability of victim blaming to deflect attention from social institutions and obscure societal processes has been particularly valuable in "explaining" women's failure to make significant advances in employment and other realms. Despite the existence of the feminist movement and a plethora of equal opportunity laws, women still overwhelmingly remain in low-paid, low-prestige, female job ghettos. But, say the victim blamers, that is because they have no interest in getting ahead, they fear success, and don't want the added responsibility that comes with promotions. The goal of the victim blamers is clear: these purported qualities of the victimized group conveniently mask the fact of continued widespread sexual discrimination. But it must be emphasized that although the Blaming the Victim ideology does distort reality by covering up the inequalities in contemporary American life, it is not the *cause* of these deeply rooted social and economic inequalities: it is a rationalization for them.

Religion, Belief, and Ritual

The anthropological concern for religion, belief, and ritual does not have to do with the scientific validity of such phenomena, but rather the way in which people relate various concepts of the "supernatural" to their everyday lives. With this more practical perspective, some anthropologists have found that traditional spiritual healing is just as helpful in the treatment of illness as modern medicine, that voodoo is a form of social control, and that the ritual and spiritual preparation for playing the game of baseball can be just as important as spring training.

Every society is composed of feeling, thinking, and acting human beings who at one time or another are either conforming to or altering the social order into which they were born. Religion is an ideological framework that gives special legitimacy and validity to human experience within any given sociocultural system. In this way, monogamy as a marriage form or monarchy as a political form ceases to be simply one of many alternative ways in which a society can be organized, but becomes, for the believer, the only legitimate way. Religion renders certain human values and activities sacred and inviolable, and it is this "mythic" function that helps to explain the strong ideological attachments that some people have regardless of the scientific merits of their points of view.

While, under some conditions, religion may in fact be "the opiate of the masses," under other conditions such a belief system may be a rallying point for social and economic protest. A contemporary example of the former might be the "Moonies" (members of the Unification Church), while a good example of the latter is the role of the black church in the American civil rights movement, along with the prominence of such religious figures as Martin Luther King Jr. and Jesse Jackson.

Finally, a word of caution must be set forth concerning attempts to understand the belief systems of other cultures. At times, the prevailing attitude seems to be that "what I believe in is religion, and what you believe in is superstition." While anthropologists generally do not subscribe to this view, there is a tendency within the field to explain that which seems, on the surface, to be incomprehensible, impractical behavior as some form of "religious ritual." The following articles should serve as a strong warning concerning the pitfalls of that approach.

"Psychotherapy in Africa" shows how important traditional belief systems, combined with community involvement, can be to the physical and psychological well-being of the individual. This perspective is so important that the treatment of illness is hindered without it. In a related manner, "The Body's War and Peace" demonstrates how a system of belief can make a difference in how we view disease and, therefore, treat it.

"The Mbuti Pygmies: Change and Adaptation" involves ritual that is subtle, informal, and yet absolutely necessary for social harmony and stability. In contrast, in "The Initiation of a Maasai Warrior," what seems to be a highly formal circumcision ceremony is ultimately revealed to be a deeply personal experience. The emphasis in "The Secrets of Haiti's Living Dead" is upon both individual conformity and community solidarity.

Mystical beliefs and rituals are not absent from modern society. "Rituals of Death" draws striking parallels between capital punishment in the United States and human sacrifice among the Aztecs of Mexico. "Body Ritual Among the Nacirema" reveals that even our daily routines have mystic overtones. Finally, "Superstition and Ritual in American Baseball" examines the need for ritual and taboo in the "great American pastime."

In summary, the articles in this section will show religion, belief, and ritual in relationship to practical human affairs.

Looking Ahead: Challenge Questions

How can modern medicine be combined with traditional healing to take advantage of the best aspects of both?

In what respects do perceptions of disease affect treatment and recovery?

How does ritual contribute to a sense of personal security, individual responsibility, and social equality?

How has voodoo become such an important form of social control in rural Haiti?

In what ways can capital punishment be seen as a ritual with social functions?

How do rituals and taboos get established in the first place?

In what ways are magic rituals practical and rational?

How important are ritual and taboo in our modern industrial society?

Psychotherapy in Africa

Thomas Adeoye Lambo

Thomas Adeoye Lambo is deputy director-general of the World Health Organization in Geneva and an advisory editor of Human Nature. *He was born in Abeokuta, Nigeria, in 1923 and lived there until he finished secondary school. He studied medicine at the University of Birmingham in England, later specializing in psychiatry. Lambo first received international acclaim in 1954 when he published reports on the neuropsychiatric problems of Nigeria's Yoruba tribe and on the establishment of the Aro village hospital. Lambo served as medical director of Aro until 1962, when he was appointed to the first Chair of Psychiatry at Nigeria's Ibadan University; in 1968 he became vice-chancellor of the University. Lambo's psychiatric research and approach to therapy have consistently blended biology, culture, and social psychology.*

Some years ago, a Nigerian patient came to see me in a state of extreme anxiety. He had been educated at Cambridge University and was, to all intents and purposes, thoroughly "Westernized." He had recently been promoted to a top-level position in the administrative service, by-passing many of his able peers. A few weeks after his promotion, however, he had had an unusual accident from which he barely escaped with his life. He suddenly became terrified that his colleagues had formed a conspiracy and were trying to kill him.

His paranoia resisted the usual methods of Western psychiatry, and he had to be sedated to relieve his anxiety. But one day he came to see me, obviously feeling much better. A few nights before, he said, his grandfather had appeared to him in a dream and had assured him of a long and healthy life. He had been promised relief from fear and anxiety if he would sacrifice a goat. My patient bought a goat the following day, carried out all of the detailed instructions of his grandfather, and quickly recovered. The young man does not like to discuss this experience because he feels it conflicts with his educational background, but occasionally, in confidence, he says: "There is something in these native things, you know."

To the Western eye, such lingering beliefs in ritual and magic seem antiquated and possibly harmful—obstacles in the path of modern medicine. But the fact is that African cultures have developed indigenous forms of psychotherapy that are highly effective because they are woven into the social fabric. Although Western therapeutic methods are being adopted by many African therapists, few Africans are simply substituting new methods for traditional modes of treatment. Instead, they have attempted to combine the two for maximum effectiveness.

The character and effectiveness of medicine for the mind and the body always and everywhere depend on the culture in which the medicine is practiced. In the West, healing is often considered to be a private matter between patient and therapist. In

 From *Human Nature*, March 1978. © 1978 by Human Nature, Inc. Reprinted by permission of the publisher.

Africa, healing is an integral part of society and religion, a matter in which the whole community is involved. To understand African psychotherapy one must understand African thought and its social roots.

It seems impossible to speak of a single African viewpoint because the continent contains a broad range of cultures. The Ga, the Masai, and the Kikuyu, for example, are as different in their specific ceremonies and customs as are the Bantus and the Belgians. Yet in sub-Saharan black Africa the different cultures do share a consciousness of the world. They have in common a characteristic perception of life and death that makes it possible to describe their overriding philosophy. (In the United States, Southern Baptists and Episcopalians are far apart in many of their rituals and beliefs, yet one could legitimately say that both share a Christian concept of life.)

The basis of most African value systems is the concept of the unity of life and time. Phenomena that are regarded as opposites in the West exist on a single continuum in Africa. African thought draws no sharp distinction between animate and inanimate, natural and supernatural, material and mental, conscious and unconscious. All things exist in dynamic correspondence, whether they are visible or not. Past, present, and future blend in harmony; the world does not change between one's dreams and the daylight.

Essential to this view of the world is the belief that there is continuous communion between the dead and the living. Most African cultures share the idea that the strength and influence of every clan is anchored by the spirits of its deceased heroes. These heroes are omnipotent and indestructible, and their importance is comparable to that of the Catholic saints. But to Africans, spirits and deities are ever present in human affairs; they are the guardians of the established social order.

The common element in rituals throughout the continent—ancestor cults, deity cults, funeral rites, agricultural rites—is the unity of the people with the world of spirits, the mystical and emotional bond between the natural and supernatural worlds.

Because of the African belief in deities and ancestral spirits, many Westerners think that African thought is more concerned with the supernatural causes of events than with their natural causes. On one level this is true. Africans attribute nearly all forms of illness and disease, as well as personal and communal catastrophes, accidents, and deaths to the magical machinations of their enemies and to the intervention of gods and ghosts. As a result there is a deep faith in the power of symbols to produce the effects that are desired. If a man finds a hair, or a piece of material, or a bit of a fingernail belonging to his enemy, he believes he has only to use the object ritualistically in order to bring about the enemy's injury or death.

As my educated Nigerian patient revealed by sacrificing a goat, the belief in the power of the supernatural is not confined to uneducated Africans. In a survey of African students in British universities conducted some years ago, I found that the majority of them firmly believed that their emotional problems had their origin in, or could at least be influenced by, charms and diabolical activities of other African students or of people who were still in Africa. I recently interviewed the student officers at the Nigeria House in London and found no change in attitude.

The belief in the power of symbols and magic is inculcated at an early age. I surveyed 1,300 elementary-school children over a four-year period and found that 85 percent used native medicine of some sort—incantations, charms, magic—to help them pass exams, to be liked by teachers, or to ward off the evil effects of other student "medicines." More than half of these children came from Westernized homes, yet they held firmly to the power of magic ritual.

Although most Africans believe in supernatural forces and seem to deny natural causality, their belief system is internally consistent. In the Western world, reality rests on the human ability to master things, to conquer objects, to subordinate the outer world to human will. In the African world, reality is found in the soul, in a religious acquiescence to life, not in its mastery. Reality rests on the relations between one human being and another, and between all people and spirits.

The practice of medicine in Africa is consistent with African philosophy. Across the African continent, sick people go to acknowledged diviners and healers—they are often called witch doctors in the West—in order to discover the nature of their illness. In almost every instance, the explanation involves a deity or an ancestral spirit. But this is only one aspect of the diagnosis, because the explanation given by the diviner is also grounded in natural phenomena. As anthropologist Robin Horton observes: "The diviner who diagnoses the intervention of a spiritual agency is also expected to give some acceptable account of what moved the agency in question to intervene. And this account very commonly involves reference to some event in the world of visible, tangible happenings. Thus if a diviner diagnoses the action of witchcraft influence or lethal medicine spirits, it is usual for him to add something about the human hatreds, jealousies, and misdeeds that have brought such agencies into play. Or, if he diagnoses the wrath of an ancestor, it is usual for him to point to the human breach of kinship morality which has called down this wrath."

The causes of illness are not simply attributed to the unknown or dropped into the laps of the gods. Causes are always linked to the patient's immediate world of social events. As Victor Turner's study of the Ndembu people of central Africa revealed, diviners believe a patient "will not get better until all the tensions and aggressions in the group's interrelations have been brought to light and exposed to ritual treatment." In my work with the Yoruba culture, I too found that supernatural forces are regarded as the agents and consequences of human will. Sickness is the natural effect of some social mistake—breaching a taboo or breaking a kinship rule.

African concepts of health and illness, like those of life and death, are intertwined. Health is not regarded as an isolated phenomenon but reflects the integration of the community. It is not the mere absence of disease but a sign that a person is living in peace and harmony with his neighbors, that he is keeping the laws of the gods and the tribe. The practice of medicine is more than the administration of drugs and potions. It encompasses all activities—personal and communal —that are directed toward the promotion of human well-being. As S.R. Burstein wrote, to be healthy requires "averting the wrath of gods or spirits, making rain, purifying streams or habitations, improving sex potency or fecundity or the fertility of fields and crops—in short, it is bound up with the whole interpretation of life."

Native healers are called upon to treat a wide range of psychiatric disorders, from schizophrenia to neurotic syndromes. Their labels may not be the same, but they recognize the difference between an incapacitating psychosis and a temporary neurosis, and between a problem that can be cured (anxiety) and one that cannot (congenital retardation or idiocy). In many tribes a person is defined as mad when he talks nonsense, acts foolishly and irresponsibly, and is unable to look after himself.

It is often assumed that tribal societies are a psychological paradise and that mental illness is the offspring of modern civilization and its myriad stresses. The African scenes in Alex Haley's *Roots* tend to portray a Garden of Eden, full of healthy tribesmen. But all gardens have snakes. Small societies have their own peculiar and powerful sources of mental stress. Robin Horton notes that tribal societies have a limited number of roles to be filled, and that there are limited choices for individuals. As a result each tribe usually has a substantial number of social misfits. Traditional communities also have a built-in set of conflicting values: aggressive ambition versus a reluctance to rise above one's neighbor; ruthless individualism versus acceptance of one's place in the lineage system. Inconsistencies such as these, Horton believes, "are often as sharp as those so well known in modern industrial societies. . . .One may even suspect that some of the young Africans currently rushing from the country to the towns are in fact escaping from a more oppressive to a less oppressive psychological environment."

Under typical tribal conditions, traditional methods are perfectly effective in the diagnosis and treatment of mental illness. The patient goes to the tribal diviner, who follows a complex procedure. First the diviner (who may be a man or a woman) determines the "immediate" cause of the illness—that is, whether it comes from physical devitalization or from spiritual possession. Next he or she diagnoses the "remote" cause of the ailment: Had the patient offended one of his ancestor spirits or gods? Had a taboo been violated? Was some human agent in the village using magic or invoking the help of evil spirits to take revenge for an offense?

The African diviner makes a diagnosis much as a Western psychoanalyst does: through the analysis of dreams, projective techniques, trances and hypnotic states (undergone by patient and healer alike), and the potent power of words. With these methods, the diviner defines the psychodynamics of the patient and gains insight into the complete life situation of the sick person.

One projective technique of diagnosis—which has much in common with the Rorschach test—occurs in *Ifa* divination, a procedure used by Yoruba healers. There are 256 *Odus* (incantations) that are poetically structured; each is a dramatic series of words that evoke the patient's emotions. Sometimes the power of the *Odus* lies in the way the words are used, the order in which they are arranged, or the starkness with which they express a deep feeling. The incantations are used to gain insight into the patient's problem. Their main therapeutic value, as in the case with the Rorschach ink blots, is to interpret omens, bring up unconscious motives, and make unknown desires and fears explicit.

Once the immediate and remote causes are established, the diagnosis is complete and the healer decides on the course of therapy. Usually this involves an expiatory sacrifice meant to restore the unity between man and deity. Everyone takes part in the treatment; the ritual involves the healer, the patient, his family, and the community at large. The group rituals —singing and dancing, confessions, trances, storytelling, and the like— that follow are powerful therapeutic measures for the patient. They release tensions and pressures and promote positive mental health by tying all individuals to the larger group. Group rituals are effective because they are the basis of African social life, an essential part of the lives of "healthy" Africans.

Some cultures, such as the N'jayei society of the Mende in Sierra Leone and the Yassi society of the Sherbro, have always had formal group therapy for their mentally ill. When one person falls ill, the whole tribe attends to his physical and spiritual needs.

Presiding over all forms of treatment is the healer, or *nganga*. My colleagues and I have studied and worked with these men and women for many years, and we are consistently impressed by their abilities.

Many of those we observed are extraordinary individuals of great common sense, eloquence, boldness, and charisma. They are highly respected within their communities as people who through self-denial, dedication, and prolonged meditation and training have discovered the secrets of the healing art and its magic (a description of Western healers as well, one might say).

The traditional *nganga* has supreme self-confidence, which he or she transmits to the patient. By professing an ability to commune with supernatural beings—and therefore to control or influence them—the healer holds boundless power over members of the tribe. Africans regard the *nganga*'s mystical qualities and eccentricities fondly, and with awe. So strongly do people believe in the *nganga*'s ability to find out which ancestral spirit is responsible for the psychological distress of the patient, that pure suggestion alone can be very effective.

For centuries the tribal practice of communal psychotherapy served African society well. Little social stigma was attached to mental illness; even chronic psychotics were tolerated in their communities and were able to function at a minimal level. (Such tolerance is true of many rural cultures.) But as the British, Germans, French, Belgians, and Portuguese colonized many African countries, they brought a European concept of mental illness along with their religious, economic, and educational systems.

They built prisons with special sections set aside for "lunatics"—usually vagrant psychotics and criminals with demonstrable mental disorders—who were restricted with handcuffs and ankle shackles. The African healers had always drawn a distinction between mental illness and criminality, but the European colonizers did not.

In many African cultures today, the traditional beliefs in magic and religion are dying. Their remaining influence serves only to create anxiety and ambivalence among Africans who are living through a period of rapid social and economic change. With the disruption and disorganization of family units, we have begun to see clinical problems that once were rare: severe depression, obsessional neurosis, and emotional incapacity. Western medicine has come a long way from the shackle solution, but it is not the best kind of therapy for people under such stress. In spite of its high technological and material advancement, modern science does not satisfy the basic metaphysical and social needs of many people, no matter how sophisticated they are.

In 1954 my colleagues and I established a therapeutic program designed to wed the best practices of traditional and contemporary psychology. Our guiding premise was to make use of the therapeutic practices that already existed in the indigenous culture, and to recognize the power of the group in healing.

We began our experiment at Aro, a rural suburb of the ancient town of Abeokuta, in western Nigeria. Aro consists of four villages that lie in close proximity in the beautiful rolling countryside. The villages are home Yoruba tribesmen and their relatives, most of whom are peasant farmers, fishermen, and craftsmen.

Near these four villages we built a day hospital that could accommodate up to 300 patients, and then we set up a village care system for their treatment. Our plan was to preserve the fundamental structure of African culture: closely knit groups, well-defined kin networks, an interlocking system of mutual obligations and traditional roles.

Patients came to the hospital every morning for treatment and spent their afternoons in occupational therapy, but they were not confined to the hospital. Patients lived in homes in the four villages or, if necessary, with hospital staff members who lived on hospital grounds—ambulance drivers, clerks, dispensary attendants, and gardeners. (This boarding-out procedure resembles a system that has been practiced for several hundred years in Gheel, a town in Belgium, where the mentally ill live in local households surrounding a central institution.)

We required the patients, who came from all over Nigeria, to arrive at the village hospital with at least one relative—a mother, sister, brother, or aunt—who would be able to cook for them, wash their clothes, take them to the hospital in the morning, and pick them up in the afternoon.

These relatives, along with the patients, took part in all the social activities of the villages: parties, plays, dances, storytelling. Family participation was successful from the beginning. We were able to learn about the family influences and stresses on the patient, and the family members learned how to adjust to the sick relative and deal with his or her emotional needs.

The hospital staff was drawn from the four villages, which meant that the hospital employees were the "landlords" of most of the patients, in constant contact with them at home and at work. After a while, the distinction between the two therapeutic arenas blurred and the villages became extensions of the hospital wards.

Doctors, nurses, and superintendents visited the villages every day and set up "therapy" groups—often for dancing, storytelling, and other rituals—as well as occupational programs that taught patients traditional African crafts.

It is not enough to treat patients on a boarding-out or outpatient basis. If services are not offered to them outside of the hospital, an undue burden is placed on their families and neighbors. This increases the tension to which patients are exposed. An essential feature of our plan was to regard the villages as an extension of the hospital, subject to equally close supervision and control.

But we neither imposed the system

on the local people nor asked them to give their time and involvement without giving them something in return. We were determined to inflict no hardships. The hosptial staff took full responsibility for the administration of the villages and for the health of the local people. They held regular monthly meetings with the village elders and their councils to give the villagers a say in the system. The hospital also arranged loans to the villagers to expand, repair, or build new houses to take care of the patients; it paid for the installation of water pipes and latrines; it paid for a mosquito eradication squad; it offered jobs to many local people and paid the "landlords" a small stipend.

Although these economic benefits aided the community, no attempt was ever made to structure the villages in any way, or to tell the villagers what to do with the patients or how to treat them. As a result of economic benefits, hospital guidance, and a voice in their own management, village members supported the experiment.

In a study made after the program began, we learned that patients who were boarded out under this system adapted more quickly and responded more readily to treatment than patients who lived in the hospital. Although the facilities available in the hospital were extensive—drug medication, group therapy sessions, modified insulin therapy, electroconvulsive shock treatments—we found that the most important therapeutic factor was the patient's social contacts, especially with people who were healthier than the patient. The village groups, unlike the hospital group, were unrehearsed, unexpected, and voluntary. Patients could choose their friends and activities; they were not thrown together arbitrarily and asked to "work things out." We believe that the boarded-out patients improved so quickly because of their daily contact with settled, tolerant, healthy people. They learned to function in society again without overwhelming anxiety.

One of the more effective and controversial methods we used was to colaborate with native healers. Just as New Yorkers have faith in their psychoanalysts, and pilgrims have faith in their priests, the Yoruba have faith in the *nganga;* and faith, as we are learning, is half the battle toward cure.

Our unorthodox alliance proved to be highly successful. The local diviners and religious leaders helped many of the patients recover, sometimes through a simple ceremony at a village shrine, sometimes in elaborate forms of ritual sacrifice, sometimes by interpreting the spiritual or magical causes of their dreams and illnesses.

At the beginning of the program patients were carefully selected for admission, but now patients of every sort are accepted: violent persons, catatonics, schizophrenics, and others whose symptoms make them socially unacceptable or emotionally withdrawn. The system is particularly effective with emotionally disturbed and psychotic children, who always come to the hospital with a great number of concerned relatives. Children who have minor neurotic disorders are kept out of the hospital entirely and treated exclusively and successfully in village homes.

The village care system was designed primarily for the acutely ill and for those whose illness was manageable, and the average stay for patients at Aro was, and is, about six months. But patients who were chronically ill and could not recover in a relatively short time posed a problem. For one thing, their relatives could not stay with them in the villages because of family and financial obligations in their home communities. We are working out solutions for such people on a trial-and-error basis. Some of the incapacitated psychotic patients now live on special farms; others live in Aro villages near the hospital and earn their keep while receiving regular supervision. The traditional

healers keep watch over these individuals and maintain follow-up treatment.

We have found many economic, medical, and social advantages to our program. The cost has been low because we have concentrated on using human resources in the most effective and strategic manner. Medically and therapeutically, the program provides a positive environment for the treatment of character disorders, sociopathy, alcoholism, neuroses, and anxiety. Follow-up studies show that the program fosters a relatively quick recovery for these problems and that the recidivism rate and the need for aftercare are significantly reduced. The length of stay at Aro, and speed of recovery, is roughly one third of the average stay in other hospitals, especially for all forms of schizophrenia. Patients with neurotic disorders respond most rapidly. Because of its effectiveness, the Aro system has been extended to four states in Nigeria and to five countries in Africa, including Kenya, Ghana, and Zambia. At each new hospital the program is modified to fit local conditions.

Some observers of the Aro system argue that it can operate only in nonindustrial agrarian communities, like those in Africa and Asia, where families and villages are tightly knit. They say that countries marked by high alienation and individualism could not import such a program. Part of this argument is correct. The Aro approach to mental health rests on particularly African traditions, such as the *nganga,* and on the belief in the continuum of life and death, sickness and health, the natural and the supernatural.

But some lessons of the Aro plan have already found their way into Western psychotherapy. Many therapists recognize the need to place the sick person in a social context; a therapist cannot heal the patient without attending to his beliefs, family, work, and environment. Various forms of group therapy are being developed in an attempt to counteract the Western emphasis on curing the individual in isolation. Lately, family therapy has been expanded into a new procedure called network therapy in which the patient's entire network of relatives, coworkers, and friends become involved in the treatment.

Another lesson of Aro is less obvious than the benefits of group support. It is the understanding that treatment begins with a people's indigenous beliefs and their world view, which underlie psychological functioning and provide the basis for healing. Religious values that give meaning and coherence to life can be the healthiest route for many people. As Jung observed years ago, religious

factors are inherent in the path toward healing, and the native therapies of Africa support his view.

A supernatural belief system, Western or Eastern, is not a sphere of arbitrary dreams but a sphere of laws that dictate the rules of kinship, the order of the universe, the route of happiness. The Westerner sees only part of the African belief system, such as the witch doctor, and wonders how wild fictions can take root in a reasonable mind. (His own fictions seem perfectly reasonable, of course.) But to the African, the religious-magical system is a great poem, allegorical of human experience, wise in its portrayal of the world and its creatures. There is more method, more reason,

in such madness than in the sanity of most people today.

REFERENCES

Burstein, S.R. "Public Health and Prevention of Disease in Primitive Communities." *The Advancement of Science,* Vol. 9, 1952, pp. 75- 81.

Horton, Robin. "African Traditional Thought and Western Science." *Africa,* Vol. 37, 1967, pp. 50-71.

Horton, Robin. *The Traditional Background of Medical Practice in Nigeria.* Institute of Africa Studies, 1966.

Lambo, T.A. "A World View of Mental Health: Recent Developments and Future Trends." *American Journal of Orthopsychiatry,* Vol. 43, 1973, pp. 706-716.

Lambo, T.A. "Psychotherapy in Africa." *Psychotherapy and Psychosomatics,* Vol. 24, 1974, pp. 311-326.

The Body's War and Peace

Ronald Grunloh

Ronald L. Grunloh is an anthropologist who teaches at Quinnipiac College in Connecticut. He has lived in and learned from traditional cultures in the American Southwest, Mexico, Peru, India, and Nepal. He received his Ph.D. from Columbia University, where he studied shamanism with Michael Harner.

When I was a schoolchild I remember seeing a movie about the benefits of vaccination. It was an animated film produced by the Walt Disney studios. In bright colors it depicted the body as a city, the organs as factories, and the blood corpuscles as laborers happily going off to work in the morning. All went well until a germ, depicted as an evil-looking black octopus, jumped onto an item of food entering the body's mouth by conveyor belt. Once inside, the germ lurked in the dark alleyways of the city, multiplying itself at a prodigious rate. When their numbers were sufficiently great, the germs began to ambush and destroy the happy workers. When the body's managers became aware of the attacks on their workers, they attempted to change the economy to wartime production. A few factories were converted and some corpuscles were armed, but it was a situation of too little too late. The evil hordes easily overwhelmed the poorly-armed workers.

With vaccination, things were different. The introduction of a few weakened germs set off the body's alarm systems early enough so that a successful conversion to a war economy could be made. Factories began turning out guns, tanks, and fighter planes. Ranks of workers were trained and equipped. When active germs did manage to enter the body, they were immediately met by a militant and well-armed citizenry who were able to control and destroy the evil invaders before they became too numerous. The victory was celebrated by the happy workers.

This image of disease as an invasion, of medicine as war, and of health as victory was simplified in the Disney movie, but I maintain that the image is generally characteristic of the cultural assumptions underlying Western medicine. In a recent article on the immune system, the lead sentence was, "Besieged by a vast array of invisible enemies, the human body enlists a remarkably complex corps of internal bodyguards to battle the invaders."[1] The body as a fortress to be vigilantly defended; disease as hostile external organisms; medicine as weapons in the fight—the language abounds with images of war.

However, our relationship to the natural world of microorganisms is not a war. This relationship is of a different order of phenomena—in many ways mysterious. The human mind, individually and collectively, is ill at ease with mystery, so when confronted with the unknown, we deal with it by comparing it to more familiar things. War is hell, but it's a known hell. The experience of war is a familiar one in Western civilization. In America, at least until recently, our war record has been "successful." We conquered the Indians and appropriated their land. We fought the Hispanics and annexed their land. We defeated the central European powers and took over industrial and commercial dominance. Superior technology, disciplined aggressiveness, tough-minded leadership paid off. In this we were the inheritors of western Europe's successful drive for power and expansion. Western history is the story of crusades against pagans, Moslems, or atheists. Military success was followed by economic expansion and material prosperity. The destruction and bloodshed was, of course, lamentable but, unfortunately, necessary. To the victor passed the spoils and the lamp of civilization.

It was natural that this image be projected from the politics of warfare onto the politics of our relationship to nature.[2] Human progress has often been viewed as the result of our scientific and technological victory over nature. Nature itself was seen to exhibit a kind of strife and competition comparable to war. Charles Darwin's early writings describe nature as "the war of all against all." In formulating his theories on the origin of species and evolution of various life forms, he saw competition between individuals and populations as the principal mechanism leading to evolutionary progress. Darwin collected much of his data as a naturalist working on a British navy survey ship. What a naturalist of that time did was to hunt and kill specimens, and preserve and classify them according to the Linnean taxonomic system.[3] This process tended to emphasize the distinguishing characteristics of individual specimens, separateness rather than continuity. The relationship between naturalist-hunter and specimen-prey was also an aggressive one.

When Darwin is discussed in the history of science, emphasis is usually placed on the influence of his scientific predecessors, Lamarck, Cuvier, and Lyell.[4] Darwin, his predecessors, and his successors were all part of a world whose politics and economy were characterized by competition and military conflict. By force of arms the

From *The Quest*, Summer 1991, pp. 59-62. © 1991 by Ronald Grunloh. Reprinted by permission of the author.

British Empire was expanding into Africa, Asia, and the Pacific. At home, London was a world center of trade and industry with a dominant ideology of *laissez-faire* capitalism. Every individual and every company worked hard in their own interest. Through the pressure of competition and differential success came economic progress. Confronted with the mystery of nature, Darwin organized it along lines that paralleled political and economic wisdom.

In the scientific and historical literature much is made of the conflict between Darwinian evolution and the proponents of biblical creationism. I'm more interested in the difference between the Darwinian scientific naturalists and the romantic literary naturalists of about the same time. Writers like Emerson, Thoreau, and Muir saw in nature not war, but a vision of peace and harmony.[5] Their method was not to hunt and collect, but rather to travel or dwell contemplatively in the midst of nature, learning its lessons and glorying in its beauty. This practice put the emphasis on interrelationship and mutual adjustment rather than competition, on the whole rather than the parts. It is out of this tradition that we get the modern idea of ecology, of nature as a system in which all the parts fit and tend toward harmony.

Medicine followed the trend in biology toward aggressive, mechanistic models of natural processes. In Virchow's *Cellular Pathology,* which came out about the same time as Darwin's *The Origin of Species,* disease was presented as a war of cells, not so very different from the Disney movie I saw as a child. As a young man, Virchow had visited the site of Troy with the pioneering archaeologist Schlieman. Later he imagined a Trojan war going on in the arteries and tissues of the body.[6] The great medical discoveries of the late nineteenth and the early twentieth centuries were all based on the war model. Pasteur and Koch identified the enemy as germs. Their strategy of first isolating a single disease-causing microorganism, then exploiting the weaknesses of this enemy to develop an effective cure, is still followed even though the technol-ogy of the process has become more sophisticated. With the discovery of radiation, penicillin, its antibiotic offspring, and the host of drugs that make up the modern *materia medica,* the weapons have improved, but they are still envisioned as weapons, and the goal is still thought to be some kind of unconditional victory.[7]

The advances made in the treatment of infectious disease were real. The battles won against such maladies as smallpox, tuberculosis, syphilis, and polio were major contributions to the welfare of humanity. But now there are signs that we are approaching the limits of the usefulness of the war model of medicine. The old germs have been vanquished, but new disease agents, even more insidious, appear to take their place. The degenerative diseases like heart disease, diabetes, and the various forms of cancer don't fit the paradigm. In these cases the enemy is not an external army of invading cells. The enemy is a part of ourselves which no longer fits into the harmonious pattern of the whole. To wage war on alienated aspects of ourselves is like shooting our own rebellious children. It's not a strategy which promises a long-term solution. If we can change our models of disease we may find it easier to reintegrate our so-called enemies within. We may even be able to see a different, friendlier face on those ever-changing, ever-renewed enemies without.

In our search for new models of our relationship to nature and the process of disease, we can turn to the ancient civilizations of Asia. Of course, they've also had wars in Asia, but perhaps because these were, until recently, agricultural civilizations, or perhaps because of the greater time depth during which they were able to see not only war and expansion but the dissolution and contraction that always followed, the medical models that developed in Asia were not based on war.

Ayurvedic medicine, the traditional system of India, has close ties to the spiritual discipline of Tantra. Tantra, like biology, sees an evolution going on in nature. However, it's not an evolution in which higher forms dominate lower forms. The tantric cycle of creation begins with a vibration set up between consciousness and energy. As this vibration becomes cruder and cruder, various densities of physical substances are formed—light, air, liquid, solid. But even in its most bound and solid form, consciousness is still present. Under special circumstances this consciousness can begin to wake up. This is the beginning of life. The simple, early forms of life are not very conscious. Cells, by combining and becoming more specialized in their functioning, are able to increase their consciousness. Animals are more conscious than plants. Humans are the most conscious of the animals. Human beings are aware enough of their own consciousness to be able to strive toward increasing it. Through the purifying practices of yoga and meditation, human consciousness can be raised and expanded toward union with the original consciousness which pervades the universe. This is the goal and direction of all life.[8]

When this view is translated into medical terms, health is seen as movement toward consciousness, and ill health as movement away from consciousness and back toward crudification. The cause of disease is not sought in attacking microorganisms, but in blockages and pollutions. Treatments don't arm the body against invaders, but seek to purify and cleanse. The exercise positions of Hatha yoga, an aspect of Tantra now familiar to many in America, are often prescribed to unblock the flow of energy from the body's lower to higher psychic centers.

Instead of germs, Ayurvedic medicine finds the primary cause of disease to be a substance called *ama.* When food remains undigested and unabsorbed by the body, it degrades into sticky noxious ama. If it's not cleared, ama further degrades into a variety of toxins which accumulate in the weaker parts of the body and cause disease. The cleansing procedures practiced by yogis, and the dietary restrictions recommended by Ayurvedic physicians, aim to reduce and prevent the accumulation of ama. The ultimate treatment is the fast. Fasting allows the body's metabolism to burn away impurities.[9]

In seeking the cause and cure of cancer, Ayurvedic medicine looks not for illusive external agents. Cancer is attributed to a dissolute and self-indulgent life-style—lack of proper exercise, irregular hours, non-vegetarian diet, the use of alcohol, tobacco, and other intoxicants. Its treatment consists of a fairly strenuous regimen of exercise in the fresh air, sunbaths, yoga postures, cleansing procedures, and a diet of fresh fruit (especially citrus), vegetables, and milk. The symptoms of the common cold, which we ascribe to a proliferating host of viruses, are viewed by Ayurvedic as the body's natural means of cleaning itself. Instead of stopping the flow of mucus with its attendant sniffles and coughs, the flow is encouraged. Liquids should be taken and fasting should be practiced to aid the body's attempt to rid itself of toxins.[10]

Besides this model of purity vs. pollution, Ayurvedic also has an overlapping model of humoral balance, the *tri dosha*. However, for a look at a balance system par excellence, let us turn to the other great Asian civilization, China. The Chinese view of nature and the body is rooted in the Chinese philosophical notion of Yin/Yang. Yin and Yang are qualities rather than substances. Yin is cool, dark, contracting, interior, female, autumn, and winter. Yang is warm, light, expanding, exterior, male, spring, and summer. The dynamic interplay between these two qualities is behind the creation both of outside nature and the inside, personal nature of our bodies. Health is the harmonious balance of the many structures and flows, material and non-material, which sustain our bodies and relate them to their environment. Disease is imbalance.[11]

Chinese medicine is wholistic in that it seeks the cause of disease not in a single isolable factor but in a complex pattern of disharmony which involves many factors both inside and outside the patient. Diet is important; so are emotional states. The physical surroundings are taken into account as are the patient's social circumstances. The diagnostic process results in the classification of ailments like "deficient yin affecting the stomach" or "exhausted fire of the middle burner." The Chinese visualize the body's substances and processes in terms some of which correspond to our Western mechanistic view and some of which we would call psychic or spiritual.[12]

In a balance system, the goal of disease treatment is not a quick victory using the most powerful weapon at hand. Harsh measures are likely to lead to overreaction and further loss of equilibrium. Chinese medical treatment—including acupuncture, exercise, herbs, and massage—seeks to make relatively gentle adjustments to bring the body back into balance. It is comforting to know that diseases which in the Western view are incurable are, from the Chinese perspective, perfectly susceptible to treatment.

The cultural models which influence the way we view nature and our place in it do make a difference. When searching for the cause and cure for a mysterious disease, we turn in the direction and reach for the means suggested by our dominant cultural model. If we feel ourselves to be locked in a warlike struggle with hostile natural organisms, then we search for the enemy responsible and reach for a weapon capable of vanquishing this enemy. If we feel that the purpose of all life is an evolution towards higher consciousness, then our response will be quite different. There is no enemy, just different levels of realization in a common process. If the universe is seen as a system of ever-changing balances, a different kind of light is cast upon the mystery of disease. It becomes easier to see why the elimination of major infectious disease led to the rise of degenerative ailments; how the excessively harsh cure for one problem might be partly the cause of another problem.

As human beings we use the models and analogies of culture to understand and adapt to the world around and within us. No single model can ever be perfectly representative of that which it seeks to portray. All analogies are limited. At this time in our history we are lucky to have relatively easy access to the alternative analogies developed over thousands of years by cultures previously isolated from us by distance and language. If we approach these other ways with an open mind and a willingness to learn, we will be able to see our world and ourselves in a new way. We can relax, for a moment, our fighting stance and see the mysterious beauty of nature, without and within, in a healthier way.

REFERENCES

1. Peter Jaret, "Our Immune System: The Wars Within," *National Geographic Magazine,* June 1986.

2. Fritjof Capra, *The Turning Point.* New York: Simon and Schuster, 1982.

3. Alan Moorehead, *Darwin and the Beagle.* New York: Harper and Row, 1969.

4. Loren Eiseley, *Darwin's Century: Evolution and the Men Who Discovered It.* New York: Doubleday, 1958.

5. Francis Otto Matthiessen, *American Renaissance: Art and Expression in the Age of Emerson and Whitman.* London and New York: Oxford University Press, 1968.

6. Rudolf Ludwig Karl Virchow, *Cellular Pathology.* New York: Dover, 1971.

7. Logan Clendening, *The Source Book of Medical History.* New York: Dover, 1960.

8. Shrii Shrii Anandamurti, *Ananda Sutram.* Denver: Ananda Marga Publications, 1981.

9. Vasant Lad, *Ayurveda: The Science of Self Healing.* Santa Fe: Lotus Press, 1984.

10. Prabhat Rainjan Sarkar, *Yogic Treatments and Natural Remedies.* Howrah, India: Ananda Press, 1983.

11. Iona Teeguarden, *Jin Shin Do: Acupressure Way of Health.* New York: Japan Publications, 1978.

12. Ted Kaptchuk, *The Web That Has No Weaver: Understanding Chinese Medicine.* New York: Congdon & Weed, 1983.

The Mbuti Pygmies: Change and Adaptation

Colin M. Turnbull

THE EDUCATIONAL PROCESS

. . . In the first three years of life every Mbuti alive experiences almost total security. The infant is breast-fed for those three years, and is allowed almost every freedom. Regardless of gender, the infant learns to have absolute trust in both male and female parent. If anything, the father is just another kind of mother, for in the second year the father formally introduces the child to its first solid food. There used to be a beautiful ritual in which the mother presented the child to the father in the middle of the camp, where all important statements are made (anyone speaking from the middle of the camp must be listened to). The father took the child and held it to his breast, and the child would try to suckle, crying "*ema, ema*," or "mother." The father would shake his head, and say "no, father . . . *eba*," but like a mother (the Mbuti said), then give the child its first solid food.

At three the child ventures out into the world on its own and enters the *bopi*, what we mght call a playground, a tiny camp perhaps a hundred yards from the main camp, often on the edge of a stream. The *bopi* were indeed playgrounds, and often very noisy ones, full of fun and high spirits. But they were also rigorous training grounds for eventual economic responsibility. On entry to the *bopi*, for one thing, the child discovers the importance of age as a structural principle, and the relative unimportance of gender and biological kinship. The *bopi* is the private world of the children. Younger youths may occasionally venture in, but if adults or elders try, as they sometimes do when angry at having their afternoon snooze interrupted, they invariably get driven out, taunted, and ridiculed. Children, among the Mbuti, have rights, but they also learn that they have responsibilities. Before the hunt sets out each day it is the children, sometimes the younger youths, who light the hunting fire.

Ritual among the Mbuti is often so informal and apparently casual that it may pass unnoticed at first. Yet insofar as ritual involves symbolic acts that represent unspoken, perhaps even unthought, concepts or ideals, or invoke other states of being, alternative frames of mind and reference, then Mbuti life is full of ritual. The hunting fire is one of the more obvious of such rituals. Early in the morning children would take firebrands from the *bopi*, where they always lit their own fire with embers from their family hearths, and set off on the trail by which the hunt was to leave that day (the direction of each day's hunt was always settled by discussion the night before). Just a short distance from the camp they lit a fire at the base of a large tree, and covered it with special leaves that made it give off a column of dense smoke. Hunters leaving the camp, both men and women, and such youths and children as were going with them, had to pass by this fire. Some did so casually, without stopping or looking, but passing through the smoke. Others reached into the smoke with their hands as they passed, rubbing the smoke into their bodies. A few always stopped, for a moment, and let the smoke envelop them, only then almost dreamily moving off.

And indeed is *was* a form of intoxication, for the smoke invoked the spirit of the forest, and by passing through it the hunters sought to fill themselves with that spirit, not so much to make the hunt successful as to minimize the sacrilege of killing. Yet they, the hunters, could not light the fire themselves. After all, they were already contaminated by death. Even youths, who daily joined the hunt at the edges, catching any game that escaped the nets, by hand, if they could, were not pure enough to invoke the spirits of forestness. But young children were uncontaminated, as yet untainted by contact with the original sin of the Mbuti. It was their responsibility to light the fire, and if it was not lit then the hunt would not take place, or as the Mbuti put it, the hunt *could* not take place.

In this way even the children in Mbuti society, at the first of the four age levels that dominate Mbuti social structure, are given very real social responsibility and see themselves as a part of that structure, by virtue of their purity. After all, they have just been born from the source of all purity, the forest itself. By the same reasoning, the elders, who are about to return to that ultimate source of all being, through death, are at least closer to purity than the adults, who are daily contaminated by killing. Elders no longer go on the hunt. So, like the children, the elders have important sacred ritual responsibilities in the Mbuti division of labor by age.

In the *bopi* the children play, but they have no "games" in the strict sense of the word. Levi-Strauss has perceptively compared games with rituals, suggesting that whereas in a game the players start theoretically equal but end up unequal, in a ritual just the reverse takes place. All are equalized. Mbuti children could be seen every day playing in the *bopi*, but not once did I see a game, not one activity that smacked of any kind of competition, except perhaps that competition that it is necessary for us all to feel from time to time, competition with our own private and personal inadequacies. One such pastime (rather than game) was tree climbing. A dozen or so children would climb up a young sapling. Reaching the top, their weight brought the sapling bending down until it almost touched the ground. Then all the children leapt off together, shrieking as the young tree sprang upright again with a rush. Sometimes one child, male or female, might stay on a

little too long, either out of fear, or out of bravado, or from sheer carelessness or bad timing. Whatever the reason, it was a lesson most children only needed to be taught once, for the result was that you got flung upward with the tree, and were lucky to escape with no more than a few bruises and a very bad fright.

Other pastimes taught the children the rules of hunting and gathering. Frequently elders, who stayed in camp when the hunt went off, called the children into the main camp and enacted a mock hunt with them there. Stretching a discarded piece of net across the camp, they pretended to be animals, showing the children how to drive them into the nets. And, of course, the children played house, learning the patterns of cooperation that would be necessary for them later in life. They also learned the prime lesson of egality, other than for purposes of division of labor making no distinction between male and female, this nuclear family or that. All in the *bopi* were *apua'i* to each other, and so they would remain throughout their lives. At every age level—childhood, youth, adulthood, or old age—everyone of that level is *apua'i* to all the others. Only adults sometimes (but so rarely that I think it was only done as a kind of joke, or possibly insult) made the distinction that the Bira do, using *apua'i* for male and *amua'i* for female. Male or female, for the Mbuti, if you are the same age you are *apua'i*, and that means that you share everything equally, regardless of kinship or gender.

YOUTH AND POLITICS

Sometime before the age of puberty boys or girls, whenever they feel ready, move back into the main camp from the *bopi* and join the youths. This is when they must assume new responsibilities, which for the youths are primarily political. Already, in the *bopi*, the children become involved in disputes, and are sometimes instrumental in settling them by ridicule, for nothing hurts an adult more than being ridiculed by children. The art of reason, however, is something they learn from the youths,

and it is the youths who apply the art of reason to the settlement of disputes.

When puberty comes it separates them, for the first time in their experience, from each other as *apua'i*. Very plainly girls are different from boys. When a girl has her first menstrual period the whole camp celebrates with the wild *elima* festival, in which the girl, and some of her chosen girl friends, are the center of all attention, living together in a special *elima* house. Male youths sit outside the *elima* house and wait for the girls to come out, usually in the afternoon, for the *elima* singing. They sing in antiphony, the girls leading, the boys responding. Boys come from neighboring territories all around, for this is a time of courtship. But there are always eligible youths within the camp as well, and the *elima* girl may well choose girls from other territories to come and join her, so there is more than enough excuse for every youth to carry on several flirtations, legitimate or illegitimate. I have known even first cousins to flirt with each other, but learned to be prudent enough not to pull out my kinship charts and point this out—well, not in public anyway.

The *elima* is more than a premarital festival, more than a joint initiation of youth into adulthood, and more than a rite of passage through puberty, though it is all those things. It is a public recognition of the opposition of male and female, and every *elima* is used to highlight the *potential* for conflict that lies in that opposition. As at other times of crisis, at puberty, a time of change and uncertainty, the Mbuti bring all the major forms of conflict out into the open. And the one that evidently most concerns them is the male/female opposition.

The adults begin to play a special form of "tug of war" that is clearly a ritual rather than a game. All the men are on one side, the women on the other. At first it looks like a game, but quickly it becomes clear that the objective is for *neither* side to win. As soon as the women begin to win, one of them will leave the end of the line and run around to join the men, assuming a deep male voice and in other ways ridicul-

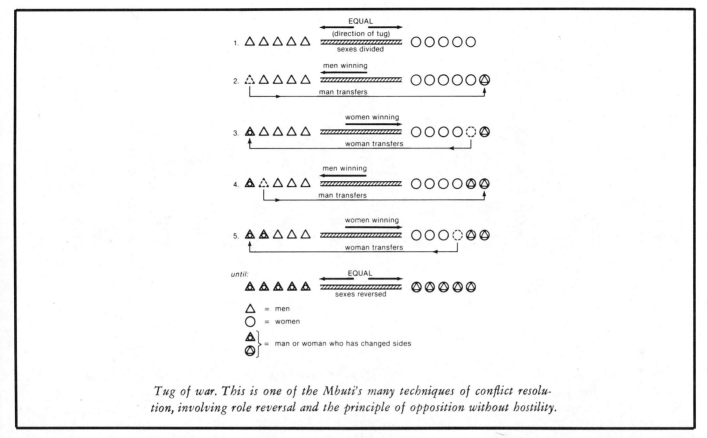

Tug of war. This is one of the Mbuti's many techniques of conflict resolution, involving role reversal and the principle of opposition without hostility.

ing manhood. Then, as the men begin to win, a male will similarly join the women, making fun of womanhood as he does so. Each adult on changing sides attempts to outdo all the others in ridiculing the opposite sex. Finally, when nearly all have switched sides, and sexes, the ritual battle between the genders simply collapses into hysterical laughter, the contestants letting go of the rope, falling onto the ground, and rolling over with mirth. Neither side wins, both are equalized very nicely, and each learns the essential lesson, that there should be *no* contest. . . .

The Initiation
of a Maasai Warrior

Tepilit Ole Saitoti

"Tepilit, circumcision means a sharp knife cutting into the skin of the most sensitive part of your body. You must not budge; don't move a muscle or even blink. You can face only one direction until the operation is completed. The slightest movement on your part will mean you are a coward, incompetent and unworthy to be a Maasai man. Ours has always been a proud family, and we would like to keep it that way. We will not tolerate unnecessary embarrassment, so you had better be ready. If you are not, tell us now so that we will not proceed. Imagine yourself alone remaining uncircumcised like the water youth [white people]. I hear they are not circumcised. Such a thing is not known in Maasailand; therefore, circumcision will have to take place even if it means holding you down until it is completed."

My father continued to speak and every one of us kept quiet. "The pain you will feel is symbolic. There is a deeper meaning in all this. Circumcision means a break between childhood and adulthood. For the first time in your life, you are regarded as a grownup, a complete man or woman. You will be expected to give and not just to receive. To protect the family always, not just to be protected yourself. And your wise judgment will for the first time be taken into consideration. No family affairs will be discussed without your being consult-

ed. If you are ready for all these responsibilities, tell us now. Coming into manhood is not simply a matter of growth and maturity. It is a heavy load on your shoulders and especially a burden on the mind. Too much of this—I am done. I have said all I wanted to say. Fellows, if you have anything to add, go ahead and tell your brother, because I am through. I have spoken."

After a prolonged silence, one of my half-brothers said awkwardly, "Face it, man . . . it's painful. I won't lie about it, but it is not the end. We all went through it, after all. Only blood will flow, not milk." There was laughter and my father left.

My brother Lellia said, "Men, there are many things we must acquire and preparations we must make before the ceremony, and we will need the cooperation and help of all of you. Ostrich feathers for the crown and wax for the arrows must be collected."

"Are you *orkirekenyi?*" one of my brothers asked. I quickly replied no, and there was laughter. *Orkirekenyi* is a person who has transgressed sexually. For you must not have sexual intercourse with any circumcised woman before you yourself are circumcised. You must wait until you are circumcised. If you have not waited, you will be fined. Your father, mother, and the circumciser will take a cow from you as punishment.

Just before we departed, one of my closest friends said, "If you kick the knife, you will be in trouble." There was laughter. "By the way, if you have decided to kick the circumciser, do it well. Silence him once and for all." "Do it the way you kick a football in school." "That will fix him," another added, and we all laughed our heads off again as we departed.

The following month was a month of preparation. I and others collected wax, ostrich feathers, honey to be made into honey beer for the elders to drink on the day of circumcision, and all the other required articles.

Three days before the ceremony my head was shaved and I discarded all my belongings, such as my necklaces, garments, spear, and sword. I even had to shave my pubic hair. Circumcision in many ways is similar to Christian baptism. You must put all the sins you have committed during childhood behind and embark as a new person with a different outlook on a new life.

The circumciser came the following day and handed the ritual knives to me. He left drinking a calabash of beer. I stared at the knives uneasily. It was hard to accept that he was going to use them on my organ. I was to sharpen them and protect them from people of ill will who might try to blunt them, thus rendering them inefficient during the ritual and thereby bringing shame on our family. The knives threw a chill down my spine; I was not sure I was sharpening them properly, so I took them to my closest brother for him to check out, and he assured me that the knives were all right. I hid them well and waited.

Tension started building between me and my relatives, most of whom worried that I wouldn't make it through the ceremony valiantly. Some even snarled at me, which was their way of encouraging me. Others threw insults and abusive words my way. My sister Loiyan in particular was more troubled by the whole affair than anyone in the whole family. She had to assume my mother's role during the circumcision. Were I to fail my initiation, she would have to face the consequences. She would be spat upon and even beaten for representing the mother of an unworthy son. The same fate would befall my father, but he seemed unconcerned. He had this weird belief that because I was not particularly handsome, I must be brave. He kept saying, "God is not so bad as to have made him ugly and a coward at the same time."

Failure to be brave during circumcision would have other unfortunate consequences: the herd of cattle belonging to the family still in the compound would be beaten until they stampeded; the slaughtered oxen and honey beer prepared during the month before the ritual would go to waste; the initiate's food would be spat upon and he would have to eat it or else get a severe beating. Everyone would call him Olkasiodoi, the knife kicker.

Kicking the knife of the circumciser would not help you anyway. If you struggle and try to get away during the ritual, you will be held down until the operation is completed. Such failure of nerve would haunt you in the future. For example, no one will choose a person who kicked the knife for a position of leadership. However, there have been instances in which a person who failed to go through circumcision successfully became very brave afterwards because he was filled with anger over the incident; no one dares to scold him or remind him of it. His agemates, particularly the warriors, will act as if nothing had happened.

During the circumcision of a woman, on the other hand, she is allowed to cry as long as she does not hinder the operation. It is common to see a woman crying and kicking during circumcision. Warriors are usually summoned to help hold her down.

For woman, circumcision means an end to the company of Maasai warriors. After they recuperate, they soon get married, and often to men twice their age.

The closer it came to the hour of truth, the more I was hated, particularly by those closest to me. I was deeply troubled by the withdrawal of all the support I needed. My annoyance turned into anger and resolve. I decided not to budge or blink, even if I were to see my intestines flowing before me. My resolve was hardened when newly circumcised warriors came to sing for me. Their songs were utterly insulting, intended to annoy me further. They tucked their wax arrows under my crotch and rubbed them on my nose. They repeatedly called me names.

By the end of the singing, I was fuming. Crying would have meant I was a coward. After midnight they left me alone and I went into the house and tried to sleep but could not. I was exhausted and numb but remained awake all night.

At dawn I was summoned once again by the newly circumcised warriors. They piled more and more insults on me. They sang their weird songs with even more vigor and excitement than before. The songs praised warriorhood and encouraged one to achieve it at all costs. The songs continued until the sun shone on the cattle horns clearly. I was summoned to the main cattle gate, in my hand a ritual cowhide from a cow that had been properly slaughtered during my naming ceremony. I went past Loiyan, who was milking a cow, and she muttered something. She was shaking all over. There was so much tension that people could hardly breathe.

I laid the hide down and a boy was ordered to pour ice-cold water, known as *engare entolu* (ax water), over my head. It dripped all over my naked body and I shook furiously. In a matter of seconds I was summoned to sit down. A large crowd of boys and men formed a semicircle in front of me; women are

not allowed to watch male circumcision and vice-versa. That was the last thing I saw clearly. As soon as I sat down, the circumciser appeared, his knives at the ready. He spread my legs and said, "One cut," a pronouncement necessary to prevent an initiate from claiming that he had been taken by surprise. He splashed a white liquid, a ceremonial paint called *enturoto*, across my face. Almost immediately I felt a spark of pain under my belly as the knife cut through my penis' foreskin. I happened to choose to look in the direction of the operation. I continued to observe the circumciser's fingers working mechanically. The pain became numbness and my lower body felt heavy, as if I were weighed down by a heavy burden. After fifteen minutes or so, a man who had been supporting from behind pointed at something, as if to assist the circumciser. I came to learn later that the circumciser's eyesight had been failing him and that my brothers had been mad at him because the operation had taken longer than was usually necessary. All the same, I remained pinned down until the operation was over. I heard a call for milk to wash the knives, which signaled the end, and soon the ceremony was over.

With words of praise, I was told to wake up, but I remained seated. I waited for the customary presents in appreciation of my bravery. My father gave me a cow and so did my brother Lillia. The man who had supported my back and my brother-in-law gave me a heifer. In all I had eight animals given to me. I was carried inside the house to my own bed to recuperate as activities intensified to celebrate my bravery.

I laid on my own bed and bled profusely. The blood must be retained within the bed, for according to Maasai tradition, it must not spill to the ground. I was drenched in my own blood. I stopped bleeding after about half an hour but soon was in intolerable pain. I was supposed to squeeze my organ and force blood to flow out of the wound, but no one had told me, so the blood coagulated and caused unbearable pain. The circumciser was brought to my aid and showed me what to do, and soon the pain subsided.

The following morning, I was escorted by a small boy to a nearby valley to walk and relax, allowing my wound to drain. This was common for everyone who had been circumcised, as well as for women who had just given birth. Having lost a lot of blood, I was extremely weak. I walked very slowly, but in spite of my caution I fainted. I tried to hang on to bushes and shrubs, but I fell, irritating my wound. I came out of unconsciousness quickly, and the boy who was escorting me never realized what had happened. I was so scared that I told him to lead me back home. I could have died without there being anyone around who could have helped me. From that day on, I was selective of my company while I was feeble.

In two weeks I was able to walk and was taken to join other newly circumcised boys far away from our settlement. By tradition Maasai initiates are required to decorate their headdresses with all kinds of colorful birds they have killed. On our way to the settlement, we hunted birds and teased girls by shooting them with our wax blunt arrows. We danced and ate and were well treated wherever we went. We were protected from the cold and rain during the healing period. We were not allowed to touch food, as we were regarded as unclean, so whenever we ate we had to use specially prepared sticks instead. We remained in this pampered state until our wounds healed and our headdresses were removed. Our heads were shaved, we discarded our black cloaks and bird headdresses and embarked as newly shaven warriors, Irkeleani.

As long as I live I will never forget the day my head was shaved and I emerged a man, a Maasai warrior. I felt a sense of control over my destiny so great that no words can accurately describe it. I now stood with confidence, pride, and happiness of being, for all around me I was desired and loved by beautiful, sensuous Maasai maidens. I could now interact with women and even have sex with them, which I not been allowed before. I was now regarded as a responsible person.

In the old days, warriors were like gods, and women and men wanted only to be the parent of a warrior. Everything else would be taken care of as a result. When a poor family had a warrior, they

ceased to be poor. The warrior would go on raids and bring cattle back. The warrior would defend the family against all odds. When a society respects the individual and displays confidence in him the way the Maasai do their warriors, the individual can grow to his fullest potential. Whenever there was a task requiring physical strength or bravery, the Maasai would call upon their warriors. They hardly ever fall short of what is demanded of them and so are characterized by pride, confidence, and an extreme sense of freedom. But there is an old saying in Maasai: "You are never a free man until your father dies." In other words, your father is paramount while he is alive and you are obligated to respect him. My father took advantage of this principle and held a tight grip on all his warriors, including myself. He always wanted to know where we all were at any given time. We fought against his restrictions, but without success. I, being the youngest of my father's five warriors, tried even harder to get loose repeatedly, but each time I was punished severely.

Roaming the plains with other warriors in pursuit of girls and adventure was a warrior's pastime. We would wander from one settlement to another, singing, wrestling, hunting, and just playing. Often I was ready to risk my father's punishment for this wonderful freedom.

One clear day my father sent me to take sick children and one of his wives to the dispensary in the Korongoro Highlands. We rode in the L.S.B. Leakey lorry. We ascended the highlands and were soon attended to in the local hospital. Near the conservation offices I met several acquaintances, and one of them told me of an unusual circumcision that was about to take place in a day or two. All the local warriors and girls were preparing to attend it.

The highlands were a lush green from the seasonal rains and the sky was a purple-blue with no clouds in sight. The land was overflowing with milk, and the warriors felt and looked their best, as they always did when there was plenty to eat and drink. Everyone was at ease. The demands the community usually made on warriors during the dry sea-

son when water was scarce and wells had to be dug were now not necessary. Herds and flocks were entrusted to youths to look after. The warriors had all the time for themselves. But my father was so strict that even at times like these he still insisted on overworking us in one way or another. He believed that by keeping us busy, he would keep us out of trouble.

When I heard about the impending ceremony, I decided to remain behind in the Korongoro Highlands and attend it now that the children had been treated. I knew very well that I would have to make up a story for my father upon my return, but I would worry about that later. I had left my spear at home when I boarded the bus, thinking that I would be coming back that very day. I felt lighter but now regretted having left it behind; I was so used to carrying it wherever I went. In gales of laughter resulting from our continuous teasing of each other, we made our way toward a distant kraal. We walked at a leisurely pace and reveled in the breeze. As usual we talked about the women we desired, among other things.

The following day we were joined by a long line of colorfully dressed girls and warriors from the kraal and the neighborhood where we had spent the night, and we left the highland and headed to Ingorienito to the rolling hills on the lower slopes to attend the circumcision ceremony. From there one could see Oldopai Gorge, where my parents lived, and the Inaapi hills in the middle of the Serengeti Plain.

Three girls and a boy were to be initiated on the same day, an unusual occasion. Four oxen were to be slaughtered, and many people would therefore attend. As we descended, we saw the kraal where the ceremony would take place. All those people dressed in red seemed from a distance like flamingos standing in a lake. We could see lines of other guests heading to the settlements. Warriors made gallant cries of happiness known as *enkiseer*. Our line of warriors and girls responded to their cries even more gallantly.

In serpentine fashion, we entered the gates of the settlement. Holding spears in our left hands, we warriors walked proudly, taking small steps, swaying like palm trees, impressing our girls, who walked parallel to us in another line, and of course the spectators, who gazed at us approvingly.

We stopped in the center of the kraal and waited to be greeted. Women and children welcomed us. We put our hands on the children's heads, which is how children are commonly saluted. After the greetings were completed, we started dancing.

Our singing echoed off the kraal fence and nearby trees. Another line of warriors came up the hill and entered the compound, also singing and moving slowly toward us. Our singing grew in intensity. Both lines of warriors moved parallel to each other, and our feet pounded the ground with style. We stamped vigorously, as if to tell the next line and the spectators that we were the best.

The singing continued until the hot sun was overhead. We recessed and ate food already prepared for us by other warriors. Roasted meat was for those who were to eat meat, and milk for the others. By our tradition, meat and milk must not be consumed at the same time, for this would be a betrayal of the animal. It was regarded as cruel to consume a product of the animal that could be obtained while it was alive, such as milk, and meat, which was only available after the animal had been killed.

After eating we resumed singing, and I spotted a tall, beautiful *esiankiki* (young maiden) of Masiaya whose family was one of the largest and richest in our area. She stood very erect and seemed taller than the rest.

One of her breasts could be seen just above her dress, which was knotted at the shoulder. While I was supposed to dance generally to please all the spectators, I took it upon myself to please her especially. I stared at and flirted with her, and she and I danced in unison at times. We complemented each other very well.

During a break, I introduced myself to the *esiankiki* and told her I would like to see her after the dance. "Won't you need a warrior to escort you home later when the evening threatens?" I said. She replied, "Perhaps, but the evening is still far away."

I waited patiently. When the dance ended, I saw her departing with a group of other women her age. She gave me a sidelong glance, and I took that to mean come later and not now. With so many others around, I would not have been able to confer with her as I would have liked anyway.

With another warrior, I wandered around the kraal killing time until the herds returned from pasture. Before the sun dropped out of sight, we departed. As the kraal of the *esiankiki* was in the lowlands, a place called Enkoloa, we descended leisurely, our spears resting on our shoulders.

We arrived at the woman's kraal and found that cows were now being milked. One could hear the women trying to appease the cows by singing to them. Singing calms cows down, making it easier to milk them. There were no warriors in the whole kraal except for the two of us. Girls went around into warriors' houses as usual and collected milk for us. I was so eager to go and meet my *esiankiki* that I could hardly wait for nightfall. The warriors' girls were trying hard to be sociable, but my mind was not with them. I found them to be childish, loud, bothersome, and boring.

As the only warriors present, we had to keep them company and sing for them, at least for a while, as required by custom. I told the other warrior to sing while I tried to figure out how to approach my *esiankiki*. Still a novice warrior, I was not experienced with women and was in fact still afraid of them. I could flirt from a distance, of course. But sitting down with a woman and trying to seduce her was another matter. I had already tried twice to approach women soon after my circumcision and had failed. I got as far as the door of one woman's house and felt my heart beating like a Congolese drum; breathing became difficult and I had to turn back. Another time I managed to get in the house and suceeded in sitting on the bed, but then I started trembling until the whole bed was shaking, and conversation became difficult. I left the house and the woman, amazed and speechless, and never went back to her again.

Tonight I promised myself I would be brave and would not make any silly, ridiculous moves. "I must be mature and not afraid," I kept reminding myself, as I remembered an incident involving one of my relatives when he was still very young and, like me, afraid of women. He went to a woman's house and sat on a stool for a whole hour; he was afraid to awaken her, as his heart was pounding and he was having difficulty breathing.

When he finally calmed down, he woke her up, and their conversation went something like this:

"Woman, wake up."

"Why should I?"

"To light the fire."

"For what?"

"So you can see me."

"I already know who you are. Why don't *you* light the fire, as you're nearer to it than me?"

"It's your house and it's only proper that you light it yourself."

"I don't feel like it."

"At least wake up so we can talk, as I have something to tell you."

"Say it."

"I need you."

"I do not need one-eyed types like yourself."

"One-eyed people are people too."

"That might be so, but they are not to my taste."

They continued talking for quite some time, and the more they spoke, the braver he became. He did not sleep with her that night, but later on he persisted until he won her over. I doubted whether I was as strong-willed as he, but the fact that he had met with success encouraged me. I told my warrior friend where to find me should he need me, and then I departed.

When I entered the house of my *esiankiki,* I called for the woman of the house, and as luck would have it, my lady responded. She was waiting for me. I felt better, and I proceeded to talk to her like a professional. After much talking back and forth, I joined her in bed.

The night was calm, tender, and loving, like most nights after initiation ceremonies as big as this one. There must have been a lot of courting and lovemaking.

Maasai women can be very hard to deal with sometimes. They can simply reject a man outright and refuse to change their minds. Some play hard to get, but in reality are testing the man to see whether he is worth their while. Once a friend of mine while still young was powerfully attracted to a woman nearly his mother's age. He put a bold move on her. At first the woman could not believe his intention, or rather was amazed by his courage. The name of the warrior was Ngengeiya, or Drizzle.

"Drizzle, what do you want?"

The warrior stared her right in the eye and said, "You."

"For what?"

"To make love to you."

"I am your mother's age."

"The choice was either her or you."

This remark took the woman by surprise. She had underestimated the saying "There is no such thing as a young warrior." When you are a warrior, you are expected to perform bravely in any situation. Your age and size are immaterial.

"You mean you could really love me like a grown-up man?"

"Try me, woman."

He moved in on her. Soon the woman started moaning with excitement, calling out his name. "Honey Drizzle, Honey Drizzle, you *are* a man." In a breathy, stammering voice, she said, "A real man."

Her attractiveness made Honey Drizzle ignore her relative old age. The Maasai believe that if an older and a younger person have intercourse, it is the older person who stands to gain. For instance, it is believed that an older woman having an affair with a young man starts to appear younger and healthier, while the young man grows older and unhealthy.

The following day when the initiation rites had ended, I decided to return home. I had offended my father by staying away from home without his consent, so I prepared myself for whatever punishment he might inflict on me. I walked home alone.

The Secrets of Haiti's Living Dead

A Harvard botanist investigates mystic potions, voodoo rites, and the making of zombies.

Gino Del Guercio

Gino Del Guercio is a national science writer for United Press International, currently on leave studying television production as a Macy fellow at Boston's WGBH.

Five years ago, a man walked into l'Estère, a village in central Haiti, approached a peasant woman named Angelina Narcisse, and identified himself as her brother Clairvius. If he had not introduced himself using a boyhood nickname and mentioned facts only intimate family members knew, she would not have believed him. Because, eighteen years earlier, Angelina had stood in a small cemetery north of her village and watched as her brother Clairvius was buried.

The man told Angelina he remembered that night well. He knew when he was lowered into his grave, because he was fully conscious, although he could not speak or move. As the earth was thrown over his coffin, he felt as if he were floating over the grave. The scar on his right cheek, he said, was caused by a nail driven through his casket.

The night he was buried, he told Angelina, a voodoo priest raised him from the grave. He was beaten with a sisal whip and carried off to a sugar plantation in northern Haiti where, with other zombies, he was forced to work as a slave. Only with the death of the zombie master were they able to escape, and Narcisse eventually returned home.

Legend has it that zombies are the living dead, raised from their graves and animated by malevolent voodoo sorcerers, usually for some evil purpose. Most Haitians believe in zombies, and Narcisse's claim is not unique. At about the time he reappeared, in 1980, two women turned up in other villages saying they were zombies. In the same year, in northern Haiti, the local peasants claimed to have found a group of zombies wandering aimlessly in the fields.

But Narcisse's case was different in one crucial respect; it was documented. His death had been recorded by doctors at the American-directed Schweitzer Hospital in Deschapelles. On April 30, 1962, hospital records show, Narcisse walked into the hospital's emergency room spitting up blood. He was feverish and full of aches. His doctors could not diagnose his illness, and his symptoms grew steadily worse. Three days after he entered the hospital, according to the records, he died. The attending physicians, an American among them, signed his death certificate. His body was placed in cold storage for twenty hours, and then he was buried. He said he remembered hearing his doctors pronounce him dead while his sister wept at his bedside.

At the Centre de Psychiatrie et Neurologie in Port-au-Prince, Dr. Lamarque Douyon, a Haitian-born, Canadian-trained psychiatrist, has been systematically investigating all reports of zombies since 1961. Though convinced zombies were real, he had been unable to find a scientific explanation for the phenomenon. He did not believe zombies were people raised from the dead, but that did not make them any less interesting. He speculated that victims were only made to *look* dead, probably by means of a drug that dramatically slowed metabolism. The victim was buried, dug up within a few hours, and somehow reawakened.

The Narcisse case provided Douyon with evidence strong enough to warrant a request for assistance from colleagues in New York. Douyon wanted to find an ethnobotanist, a traditional-medicines expert, who could track down the zombie potion he was sure existed. Aware of the medical potential of a drug that could dramatically lower metabolism, a group organized by the late Dr. Nathan Kline—a New York psychiatrist and pioneer in the field of psychopharmacology—raised the funds necessary to send someone to investigate.

The search for that someone led to the Harvard Botanical Museum, one of the world's foremost institutes of ethnobiology. Its director, Richard Evans Schultes, Jeffrey professor of biology, had spent thirteen years in the tropics studying native medicines. Some of his best-known work is the investigation of curare, the substance used by the nomadic people of the Amazon to poison their darts. Refined into a powerful muscle relaxant called D-tubocurarine, it is now an essential component of the anesthesia used during almost all surgery.

Schultes would have been a natural for the Haitian investigation, but he was too busy. He recommended another Harvard ethnobotanist for the assignment, Wade Davis, a 28-year-old Canadian pursuing a doctorate in biology.

Davis grew up in the tall pine forests of British Columbia and entered Harvard in 1971, influenced by a Life magazine story on the student strike of 1969. Before Harvard, the only Americans he had known were draft dodgers, who seemed very exotic. "I used to fight forest fires with them," Davis says. "Like everybody else, I thought America was where it was at. And I wanted to go to Harvard because of that Life article. When I got there, I realized it wasn't quite what I had in mind."

Davis took a course from Schultes, and when he decided to go to South America to study plants, he approached his professor for guidance. "He was an extraordinary figure," Davis remembers. "He was a man who had done it all. He had lived alone for years in the Amazon." Schultes sent Davis to the rain forest with two letters of introduction and two pieces of advice: wear a pith helmet and try ayahuasca, a powerful hallucinogenic vine. During that expedition and others, Davis proved himself an "outstanding field man," says his mentor. Now, in early 1982, Schultes called him into his office and asked if he had plans for spring break.

"I always took to Schultes's assignments like a plant takes to water," says Davis, tall and blond, with inquisitive blue eyes. "Whatever Shultes told me to do, I did. His letters of introduction opened up a whole world." This time the world was Haiti.

Davis knew nothing about the Caribbean island—and nothing about African traditions, which serve as Haiti's cultural basis. He certainly did not believe in zombies. "I thought it was a lark," he says now.

Davis landed in Haiti a week after his conversation with Schultes, armed with a hypothesis about how the zombie drug—if it existed—might be made. Setting out to explore, he discovered a country materially impoverished, but rich in culture and mystery. He was impressed by the cohesion of Haitian society; he found none of the crime,

social disorder, and rampant drug and alcohol abuse so common in many of the other Caribbean islands. The cultural wealth and cohesion, he believes, spring from the country's turbulent history.

During the French occupation of the late eighteenth century, 370,000 African-born slaves were imported to Haiti between 1780 and 1790. In 1791, the black population launched one of the few successful slave revolts in history, forming secret societies and overcoming first the French plantation owners and then a detachment of troops from Napoleon's army, sent to quell the revolt. For the next hundred years Haiti was the only independent black republic in the Caribbean, populated by people who did not forget their African heritage. "You can almost argue that Haiti is more African than Africa," Davis says. "When the west coast of Africa was being disrupted by colonialism and the slave trade, Haiti was essentially left alone. The amalgam of beliefs in Haiti is unique, but it's very, very African."

Davis discovered that the vast majority of Haitian peasants practice voodoo, a sophisticated religion with African roots. Says Davis, "It was immediately obvious that the stereotypes of voodoo weren't true. Going around the countryside, I found clues to a whole complex social world." Vodounists believe they communicate directly with, indeed are often possessed by, the many spirits who populate the everyday world. Vodoun society is a system of education, law, and medicine; it embodies a code of ethics that regulates social behavior. In rural areas, secret vodoun societies, much like those found on the west coast of Africa, are as much or more in control of everyday life as the Haitian government.

Although most outsiders dismissed the zombie phenomenon as folklore, some early investigators, convinced of its reality, tried to find a scientific explanation. The few who sought a zombie drug failed. Nathan Kline, who helped finance Davis's expedition, had searched unsuccessfully, as had Lamarque Douyon, the Haitian psychiatrist. Zora Neale Hurston, an American black woman, may have come closest. An anthropological pioneer, she went to Haiti in the Thirties, studied vodoun

society, and wrote a book on the subject, *Tell My Horse,* first published in 1938. She knew about the secret societies and was convinced zombies were real, but if a powder existed, she too failed to obtain it.

Davis obtained a sample in a few weeks.

He arrived in Haiti with the names of several contacts. A BBC reporter familiar with the Narcisse case had suggested he talk with Marcel Pierre. Pierre owned the Eagle Bar, a bordello in the city of Saint Marc. He was also a voodoo sorcerer and had supplied the BBC with a physiologically active powder of unknown ingredients. Davis found him willing to negotiate. He told Pierre he was a representative of "powerful but anonymous interests in New York," willing to pay generously for the priest's services, provided no questions were asked. Pierre agreed to be helpful for what Davis will only say was a "sizable sum." Davis spent a day watching Pierre gather the ingredients—including human bones—and grind them together with mortar and pestle. However, from his knowledge of poison, Davis knew immediately that nothing in the formula could produce the powerful effects of zombification.

Three weeks later, Davis went back to the Eagle Bar, where he found Pierre sitting with three associates. Davis challenged him. He called him a charlatan. Enraged, the priest gave him a second vial, claiming that this was the real poison. Davis pretended to pour the powder into his palm and rub it into his skin. "You're a dead man," Pierre told him, and he might have been, because this powder proved to be genuine. But, as the substance had not actually touched him, Davis was able to maintain his bravado, and Pierre was impressed. He agreed to make the poison and show Davis how it was done.

The powder, which Davis keeps in a small vial, looks like dry black dirt. It contains parts of toads, sea worms, lizards, tarantulas, and human bones. (To obtain the last ingredient, he and Pierre unearthed a child's grave on a nocturnal trip to the cemetery.) The poison is rubbed into the victim's skin. Within hours he begins to feel nauseated and has difficulty breathing. A pins-

and-needles sensation afflicts his arms and legs, then progresses to the whole body. The subject becomes paralyzed; his lips turn blue for lack of oxygen. Quickly—sometimes within six hours—his metabolism is lowered to a level almost indistinguishable from death.

As Davis discovered, making the poison is an inexact science. Ingredients varied in the five samples he eventually acquired, although the active agents were always the same. And the poison came with no guarantee. Davis speculates that sometimes instead of merely paralyzing the victim, the compound kills him. Sometimes the victim suffocates in the coffin before he can be resurrected. But clearly the potion works well enough often enough to make zombies more than a figment of Haitian imagination.

Analysis of the powder produced another surprise. "When I went down to Haiti originally," says Davis, "my hypothesis was that the formula would contain *concombre zombi,* the 'zombie's cucumber,' which is a *Datura* plant. I thought somehow *Datura* was used in putting people down." *Datura* is a powerful psychoactive plant, found in West Africa as well as other tropical areas and used there in ritual as well as criminal activities. Davis had found *Datura* growing in Haiti. Its popular name suggested the plant was used in creating zombies.

But, says Davis, "there were a lot of problems with the *Datura* hypothesis. Partly it was a question of how the drug was administered. *Datura* would create a stupor in huge doses, but it just wouldn't produce the kind of immobility that was key. These people had to appear dead, and there aren't many drugs that will do that."

One of the ingredients Pierre included in the second formula was a dried fish, a species of puffer or blowfish, common to most parts of the world. It gets its name from its ability to fill itself with water and swell to several times its normal size when threatened by predators. Many of these fish contain a powerful poison known as tetrodotoxin. One of the most powerful nonprotein poisons known to man, tetrodotoxin turned up in every sample of zombie powder that Davis acquired.

Numerous well-documented accounts of puffer fish poisoning exist, but the most famous accounts come from the Orient, where *fugu* fish, a species of puffer, is considered a delicacy. In Japan, special chefs are licensed to prepare *fugu.* The chef removes enough poison to make the fish nonlethal, yet enough remains to create exhilarating physiological effects—tingles up and down the spine, mild prickling of the tongue and lips, euphoria. Several dozen Japanese die each year, having bitten off more than they should have.

"When I got hold of the formula and saw it was the *fugu* fish, that suddenly

Richard Schultes

His students continue his tradition of pursuing botanical research in the likeliest of unlikely places.

Richard Evans Schultes, Jeffrey professor of biology emeritus, has two homes, and they could not be more different. The first is Cambridge, where he served as director of the Harvard Botanical Museum from 1970 until last year, when he became director emeritus. During his tenure he interested generations of students in the exotic botany of the Amazon rain forest. His impact on the field through his own research is worldwide. The scholarly ethnobotanist with steel-rimmed glasses, bald head, and white lab coat is as much a part of the Botanical Museum as the thousands of plant specimens and botanical texts on the museum shelves.

In his austere office is a picture of a crew-cut, younger man stripped to the waist, his arms decorated with tribal paint. This is Schultes's other persona. Starting in 1941, he spent thirteen years in the rain forests of South America, living with the Indians and studying the plants they use for medicinal and spiritual purposes.

Schultes is concerned that many of the people he has studied are giving up traditional ways. "The people of so-called primitive societies are becoming civilized and losing all their forefathers' knowledge of plant lore," he says. "We'll be losing the tremendous amounts of knowledge they've gained over thousands of years. We're interested in the practical aspects with the hope that new medicines and other things can be developed for our own civilization."

Schultes's exploits are legendary in the biology department. Once, while gathering South American plant specimens hundreds of miles from civilization, he contracted beriberi. For forty days he fought creeping paralysis and overwhelming fatigue as he paddled back to a doctor. "It was an extraordinary feat of endurance," says disciple Wade Davis. "He is really one of the last nineteenth-century naturalists."

Hallucinogenic plants are one of Schultes's primary interests. As a Harvard undergraduate in the Thirties, he lived with Oklahoma's Kiowa Indians to observe their use of plants. He participated in their peyote ceremonies and wrote his thesis on the hallucinogenic cactus. He has also studied other hallucinogens, such as morning glory seeds, sacred mushrooms, and ayahuasca, a South American vision vine. Schultes's work has led to the development of anesthetics made from curare and alternative sources of natural rubber.

Schultes's main concern these days is the scientific potential of plants in the rapidly disappearing Amazon jungle. "If chemists are going to get material on 80,000 species and then analyze them, they'll never finish the job before the jungle is gone," he says. "The short cut is to find out what the [native] people have learned about the plant properties during many years of living in the very rich flora."

—G.D.G.

threw open the whole Japanese literature," says Davis. Case histories of *fugu* poisoning read like accounts of zombification. Victims remain conscious but unable to speak or move. A man who had "died" after eating *fugu* recovered seven days later in the morgue. Several summers ago, another Japanese poisoned by *fugu* revived after he was nailed into his coffin. "Almost all of Narcisse's symptoms correlated. Even strange things such as the fact that he said he was conscious and could hear himself pronounced dead. Stuff that I thought had to be magic, that seemed crazy. But, in fact, that is what people who get *fugu*-fish poisoning experience."

Davis was certain he had solved the mystery. But far from being the end of his investigation, identifying the poison was, in fact, its starting point. "The drug alone didn't make zombies," he explains. "Japanese victims of pufferfish poisoning don't become zombies, they become poison victims. All the drug could do was set someone up for a whole series of psychological pressures that would be rooted in the culture. I wanted to know why zombification was going on," he says.

He sought a cultural answer, an explanation rooted in the structure and beliefs of Haitian society. Was zombification simply a random criminal activity? He thought not. He had discovered that Clairvius Narcisse and "Ti Femme," a second victim he interviewed, were village pariahs. Ti Femme was regarded as a thief. Narcisse had abandoned his children and deprived his brother of land that was rightfully his. Equally suggestive, Narcisse claimed that his aggrieved brother had sold him to a *bokor,* a voodoo priest who dealt in black magic; he made cryptic reference to having been tried and found guilty by the "masters of the land."

Gathering poisons from various parts of the country, Davis had come into direct contact with the vodoun secret societies. Returning to the anthropological literature on Haiti and pursuing his contacts with informants, Davis came to understand the social matrix within which zombies were created.

Davis's investigations uncovered the importance of the secret societies. These groups trace their origins to the bands of escaped slaves that organized the revolt against the French in the late eighteenth century. Open to both men and women, the societies control specific territories of the country. Their meetings take place at night, and in many rural parts of Haiti the drums and wild celebrations that characterize the gatherings can be heard for miles.

Davis believes the secret societies are responsible for policing their communities, and the threat of zombification is one way they maintain order. Says Davis, "Zombification has a material basis, but it also has a societal logic." To the uninitiated, the practice may appear a random criminal activity, but in rural vodoun society, it is exactly the opposite—a sanction imposed by recognized authorities, a form of capital punishment. For rural Haitians, zombification is an even more severe punishment than death, because it deprives the subject of his most valued possessions: his free will and independence.

The vodounists believe that when a person dies, his spirit splits into several different parts. If a priest is powerful enough, the spiritual aspect that controls a person's character and individuality, known as *ti bon ange,* the "good little angel," can be captured and the corporeal aspect, deprived of its will, held as a slave.

From studying the medical literature on tetrodotoxin poisoning, Davis discovered that if a victim survives the first few hours of the poisoning, he is likely to recover fully from the ordeal. The subject simply revives spontaneously. But zombies remain without will, in a trance-like state, a condition vodounists attribute to the power of the priest. Davis thinks it possible that the psychological trauma of zombification may be augmented by *Datura* or some other drug; he thinks zombies may be fed a *Datura* paste that accentuates their disorientation. Still, he puts the material basis of zombification in perspective: "Tetrodotoxin and *Datura* are only templates on which cultural forces and beliefs may be amplified a thousand times."

Davis has not been able to discover how prevalent zombification is in Haiti.

"How many zombies there are is not the question," he says. He compares it to capital punishment in the United States: "It doesn't really matter how many people are electrocuted, as long as it's a possibility." As a sanction in Haiti, the fear is not of zombies, it's of becoming one.

Davis attributes his success in solving the zombie mystery to his approach. He went to Haiti with an open mind and immersed himself in the culture. "My intuition unhindered by biases served me well," he says. "I didn't make any judgments." He combined this attitude with what he had learned earlier from his experiences in the Amazon. "Schultes's lesson is to go and live with the Indians as an Indian." Davis was able to participate in the vodoun society to a surprising degree, eventually even penetrating one of the Bizango societies and dancing in their nocturnal rituals. His appreciation of Haitian culture is apparent. "Everybody asks me how did a white person get this information? To ask the question means you don't understand Haitians—they don't judge you by the color of your skin."

As a result of the exotic nature of his discoveries, Davis has gained a certain notoriety. He plans to complete his dissertation soon, but he has already finished writing a popular account of his adventures. To be published in January by Simon and Schuster, it is called *The Serpent and the Rainbow,* after the serpent that vodounists believe created the earth and the rainbow spirit it married. Film rights have already been optioned; in October Davis went back to Haiti with a screenwriter. But Davis takes the notoriety in stride. "All this attention is funny," he says. "For years, not just me, but all Schultes's students have had extraordinary adventures in the line of work. The adventure is not the end point, it's just along the way of getting the data. At the Botanical Museum, Schultes created a world unto itself. We didn't think we were doing anything above the ordinary. I still don't think we do. And you know," he adds, "the Haiti episode does not begin to compare to what others have accomplished—particularly Schultes himself."

Rituals of Death

Capital Punishment and Human Sacrifice

Elizabeth D. Purdum and J. Anthony Paredes

We were perplexed by the resurgence of enthusiasm for the death penalty in the United States. According to a 1986 *Gallup Report,* support for the death penalty in America has reached a near-record high in 50 years of polling, with 70 percent of Americans favoring execution of convicted murderers (Gallup, 1986). In a 1983 poll conducted in Florida, 72 percent of respondents were found to support the death penalty, compared with 45 percent in 1964 (Cambridge Survey Research, 1985). Still more perplexing is the finding that nearly half of those supporting the death penalty agree that "only the poor and unfortunate are likely to be executed" (Ellsworth and Ross, 1983:153). Equally startling is the revelation that although deterrence is often given as a primary justification for the death penalty, most people would continue to support it even if convinced that it had no greater deterrent effect than that of a life sentence (P. Harris, 1986). In addition, there is little if any evidence that capital punishment reduces the crime rate; there seems, rather, to be some historical evidence for a reverse correlation. Pickpocketing, a crime then punishable by hanging, was rampant among spectators at executions in England circa 1700 (Lofland, 1977). Bowers and Pierce (1980) argue, on the basis of increased murder rates in New York State in the month following executions, that capital punishment has a

"brutalizing" effect and leads to more, not less, violence. Why, then, does capital punishment receive such widespread support in modern America?

Capital Punishment—Another "Riddle of Culture"

In theory, capital punishment should be no more a puzzle than any other seemingly bizarre, nonrational custom. Either human cultures are amenable to scientific explanation or they are not. And we anthropologists have not been timid about tackling everything from Arunta penile subincision to Hindu cow love as problems for scientific explication. As a first step in this task, we will compare capital punishment in Florida, the leader in the United States in death sentencing since Florida's 1972 capital punishment statute was affirmed by the U.S. Supreme Court in 1976, with certain forms of human sacrifice as practiced by the Aztecs of Mexico in the sixteenth century. This is not a capricious comparison. John Cooper (1976) pointedly seeks the "socio-religious origins of capital punishment" in ancient rites of, to use his term, "propitiatory death." But his study is narrowly constrained by canons of Western philosophy and history. By making a more exotic comparison, we hope to point the way to more nomothetic principles for understanding state-sanctioned homicide in complex societies. Albert Camus (1959) also perceived elements of religious ritual in French capital punishment, but argued that the practice continued

only because hidden from the view of the general public. Anticipating our comparisons here, anthropologist Colin Turnbull concludes in his article "Death by Decree" that the key to understanding capital punishment is to be found in its ritual element (1978). John Lofland (1977) has compared the dramaturgy of state executions circa 1700 in England with those of contemporary America, concluding that modern executions in their impersonal, unemotional, and private aspects appear humane, yet deny the reality of death and strip the condemned of any opportunity to die with dignity or courage.

It was the public media spectacle surrounding recent executions in Florida that triggered the thoughts leading to this paper. Detailed, minute-by-minute accounts of Florida's first post–1976 execution, widely reported press conferences with death row inmates, television images of the ambulance bearing the body of an executed criminal, news photos of mourners and revelers outside the prison on the night before an execution—all these served to transform a closely guarded, hidden expression of the ultimate power of the state into a very public ceremonial event. We were reminded of the pomp and circumstance for the masses accompanying the weird rites of Tenochtitlan that greeted sixteenth-century Spaniards. In such similarities, we thought, might lie the key to a dispassionate, anthropological understanding of capital punishment in modern America.

From *Facing the Death Penalty: Essays on Cruel and Unusual Punishment,* edited by Michael Radelet, 1989, Chapter 10, pp. 139-155. © 1989 by Temple University Press. Reprinted by permission.

Before proceeding we must note that the Aztec state itself imposed capital punishment for a variety of crimes, ranging from murder to fornication to violations of the dress code for commoners. The available sources indicate, however, that among the Aztecs capital punishment was swift, rather unceremonious, and even brutish. It is the high drama of Aztec rituals of human sacrifice that shows the closest parallels with the bureaucratically regulated procedures for electrocution of the condemned at Starke, Florida, in the 1980s.

The Victims of Execution and Sacrifice

The death penalty is imposed on only a small percentage of Americans convicted of homicide—5 percent, according to a 1980 Georgia study (Baldus et al., 1983). Today there are 2,182 people on death row in the United States; 296 of these are in Florida (NAACP Legal Defense and Educational Fund, 1988). Since 1976, 18 persons have been executed in Florida. Prior to 1972, when the Supreme Court voided state death penalty statutes, it was clear that the death penalty was disproportionately applied to black men. Fifty-four percent of the 3,859 people executed in the United States between 1930 and 1967 were nonwhite. Among those executed for rape during the same period, 405 of 455 were black (U.S. Department of Justice, 1986). Nakell and Hardy's study of homicide cases in North Carolina from 1977 and 1978 revealed the effects of race of victim and race of defendant throughout the criminal justice process (1987). The relationship between race and execution consistently holds even when one controls for such factors as differential conviction rates and the relationship between the defendant and the victim (Radelet, 1981).

Recent studies (for example, Baldus et al., 1983a; Bowers and Pierce, 1980b; Gross and Mauro, 1984; Pasternoster, 1983; and Radelet, 1981) suggest that the defendant's race, since the reinstatement of the death penalty in 1976, is less important than it once was

in predicting death sentences. These studies conclude that a more significant factor is the race of the victim: that is, people who kill whites are more likely to receive the death penalty than people who kill blacks.

Statistics aside, people familiar with death row inmates readily acknowledge that they are marginal members of society—economically, socially, and, even, in the case of Florida, geographically. Many come from backgrounds of extreme poverty and abuse. Michael Radelet and his colleagues (1983) report one common denominator among families who have members in prison: low socioeconomic status. Poverty makes it hard, if not impossible, for families to maintain ties with prisoners. Many inmates on death row have few family or social ties. Only about 15 of the 208 men on death row in Florida in 1983 had visitors each week; 60 others had visitors about once a month; and fewer than half received a visitor in any given year (Radelet et al., 1983). Many of Florida's inmates are from out of state. More than a few of Florida's death row inmates are also crazy, retarded, or both. For instance, Arthur Goode, who was convicted of murdering a nine-year-old boy, ate a half-gallon of butter pecan ice cream, his requested "last meal," then gave as his final statement his desire to marry a young boy. In the three weeks before his execution, Goode wrote letters to the governor and other prominent officials complaining of the lack of toilet paper to blow his nose (Radelet and Barnard, 1986). There is an inmate who believes that one of the people helping him with his court appeals is alternately a dead disc jockey or one of his own seven wives. Or, there is James Douglas Hill, a 26-year-old with an IQ of 66 and a serious speech impediment, who, having learned to read and write while in prison, sent to his mother this message:

Hi mom me hour are you doing to day fine i hope i am doing ok for now But i miss you so varry varry much that i can cry But i am to Big to cry. . . . i miss you i miss you love James all way. By now. (Sherrill, 1984:555)

In 1987 James Douglas Hill was released on bail when substantial doubt about his guilt surfaced.

Detailed statistics on *whom* the Aztecs put to death in their rites of human sacrifice are not available, nor is the exact number of sacrificial victims. Nonetheless, the Aztecs of Central Mexico sacrificed humans on a scale unprecedented in any other society. Putting aside the question of whether the Aztecs were nutritionally motivated toward this human slaughter (Harner, 1977), annual estimates for central Mexico in the first decades of the sixteenth century vary from 20,000 (Cortes, as quoted by Fagan, 1984:230) to 250,000 sacrificed victims (Woodrow Borah, as quoted by Harner, 1977:119).

Most of the sacrificial victims were able-bodied male war captives from neighboring kingdoms, but the Aztecs reportedly also sacrificed large numbers of children—sold to the priests by the poor. The children's tears were believed to be particularly appealing to Tlaloc, the rain god. Women were also sometimes sacrificed, some of them presented as impersonations of certain female deities. Similarly, one of the most frequently recounted, and often highly romanticized, forms of Aztec human sacrifice was that in which a flawless young war captive was pampered and indulged for a year as the embodiment of a god, then killed with great ritual and sadness while the victim dutifully played his role in the deicidal drama. Most Aztec war captives enjoyed no such protracted special treatment. How god-impersonators were selected we do not know. Neither do we know how many war captives' lives were spared, if any, nor how many were doomed to a life of slavery.

Paralleling the numerous means of execution employed in the United States—electrocution, hanging, firing squad, deadly gas, lethal injection—the Aztecs sacrificed their victims with a variety of techniques. These included beheading, burning, and flights of arrows, but the most common method was to spread the victim on a large, elaborately carved stone, cut open his chest with an obsidian knife, then tear out his heart. We present here a brief, composite account of "ordinary" war captive sacrifice using the method of coronary excision.

Announcement of Death

According to Fray Diego Duran's account of the aftermath of a battle between the Aztecs and the Tepeacas, the Tepeacan captives were taken back to the Aztec capital, Tenochtitlan, with collars around their necks and their hands bound behind them. The captives "went along singing sadly, weeping and lamenting their fate," knowing they were to be sacrificed. Once they were in the capital, priests threw incense on them, offered them maize bread, and said:

We welcome you
To this city of Mexico Tenochtitlan
. . . .
Do you think that you have come to live;
You have come to die.
. . . .
We salute you and comfort you with these words:
You have not come because of weakness,
But because of your manliness.
You will die here but your fame will live forever.
(Duran, 1964:101)

The announcement of a Florida death row inmate's impending death comes with the signing of a death warrant by the state governor, once all routine appeals and bids for clemency have failed. The criteria by which the decision is made to sign a warrant against a particular person at a particular time are not publicly known.

A death warrant is a single-page document in legal language, bordered in black. Each one bears the state seal and is officially witnessed by the secretary of state—not by some seemingly more likely authority such as the attorney general. Each death warrant is publicized by a news release issued shortly after the governor signs. Between 1972 and the end of 1988, Florida's three governors signed over two hundred death warrants. Once the warrant is signed in Tallahassee, the superintendent of Florida State Prison at Starke, 150 miles away, is immediately notified. Prison guards are sent to get

the person named in the warrant from his or her cell. They bring the prisoner, who may have no forewarning of what is about to happen, to the assistant superintendent's office. There the superintendent or his designee reads the warrant aloud to the condemned. Following a string of "whereas's" tracing the history of the case, the warrant concludes:

Now, therefore, I, [names governor], as Governor of the State of Florida and pursuant to the authority and responsibility vested by the Constitution and the laws of Florida do hereby issue this warrant directing the Superintendent of the Florida State Prison to cause the sentence of death to be executed upon [names person] on some day of the week beginning [for instance] Noon, Tuesday, the 29th day of October, 1989, and ending Noon, Tuesday, the 5th day of November, 1989, in accord with the provisions of the laws of the State of Florida.

The warrant is usually dated four weeks before the last day the warrant is in effect. Reportedly, warrants are never issued for executions to take place during the time the state supreme court is not in session or during the Christmas season. After the warrant is read, the prisoner is permitted to telephone a lawyer and a family member, if he or she has any.

Treatment After Announcement of Death

Aztec war captives were served "Divine Wine" (probably pulque) and paraded past images of the Aztec gods and past the emperor, Montezuma. They were given cloaks, loincloths, and sandals—sandals being a mark of nobility. Next, the prisoners were taken to the central marketplace, where they were given flowers and "shields of splendid featherwork" and forced to dance upon a platform. The condemned were also given tobacco to smoke, which, according to Duran, "comforted them greatly" (Duran, 1964:102).

The war captives were dispersed among the several wards of the city, and men were assigned to guard and maintain them with the charge:

Take care that they do not escape
Take care that they do not die!
Behold, they are children of the Sun!
Feed them well; let them be fat and desirable for the sacrifice
. . . (Duran, 1964:108)

Duran (1964) reports that captives were treated well and honored as if they were gods.

Many days passed during which craftsmen were instructed to carve a stone for the sacrificial altar. A few days later the altar was ready, and temple youths were given instructions about how the sacrifice was to be conducted. Guests were invited from neighboring states, and booths were decorated for spectators.

In Florida, the reading of the death warrant initiates a period officially designated as "death watch," marked by moving the person to a cell in "Q Wing," where he or she will be closer to the electric chair and isolated from other death row inmates. Most of the person's possessions are taken away, including photographs and tennis shoes, the only personally owned item of apparel that inmates are ordinarily allowed; the condemned is allowed to retain only those items listed in the "Execution Guidelines," a 39-page single-spaced document (Florida State Prison, 1983). The only books on the list are "religious tracts as distributed by Institution Chaplain, maximum possession ten (10)." Magazine and newspaper subscriptions may continue, but no new periodicals may be ordered. In a curious specific parallel with Aztec practice, there are no special restrictions on tobacco for prisoners on Q Wing. Three meals a day are fed to all "condemned inmates," and dietary restrictions for "medical reasons" continue to be observed. Indeed, meticulous, detailed instructions are given to prison personnel to ensure that the condemned person is kept in good health and not provided with any item that might be used to harm himself or attempt suicide. Moreover, under current procedures if a prisoner is determined to have become insane on death row, he or she is spared execution until restored to mental health (Radelet and Barnard, 1986).

Once death watch begins, social visits are "noncontact" and held in the "maximum security visiting park" any two days, Monday through Friday, 9 A.M. to 3 P.M. Other death row inmates are permitted "contact" social visits for six hours on Saturdays or Sundays. Legal visits for the condemned may continue to be the "contact" type during the death warrant, but only until one week before execution, when these visits, too, become noncontact. Media visits are scheduled through prison officials on Tuesday, Wednesday, and Thursday until Phase II of death watch begins, five days before the execution is scheduled to occur.

With Phase II of death watch, more property is taken from the prisoner. The condemned is allowed only a few so-called comfort items: "one TV located outside cell, 1 radio, 1 deck of cards, 1 Bible, 1 book, periodical, magazine or newspaper." Very specific day-by-day regulations and procedures now go into effect, beginning with "Execution Day–Minus Five (5)," when the "execution squad" is identified. Likewise, on Execution Day–Minus Four (4), testing of the electrical equipment to be used for execution begins. During Phase II the inmate is subjected to further limitations on visits, but during the 48 hours before the scheduled execution, the condemned may have an interview with a media representative of his or her choice. Execution Day–Minus Four (4) is a particularly busy day: the condemned reinventories his or her property and specifies in writing its disposition; specifies in writing his or her funeral arrangements; and is measured for a suit of clothing—the suit will be cheap—in which the condemned will, if he or she wants, be buried. On Day–Minus Three (3) there are "no activities," and Day–Minus Two (2) is devoted primarily to testing the equipment and "execution squad drill." On Execution Day–Minus One (1) the pace quickens, and it is on this day that the chef takes the person's order for the last meal.

Each time the prisoner is moved during Phase II of death watch, the entire prison is locked down and the condemned undergoes a complete body search upon being returned to his or her cell. A guard sits outside the condemned inmate's cell, as one always does during an active death warrant, but now the guard records every 15 minutes what the prisoner is doing.

Final Preparations for Death

On the day of an Aztec sacrifice, the visiting nobles were seated in their decorated booths and the prisoners were placed in a line before them and made to dance. The victims were smeared with plaster; white feathers were tied to their hair; their eyelids were blackened and their lips painted red. Priests who would perform the actual sacrifice stood in a long row according to their rank. Each priest was disguised as a god and carried a richly decorated sword and shield. The priests sat under a beautifully adorned arbor erected at the summit of a large, truncated pyramid. Chanters came forth and began to dance and sing.

In Florida, sometime around midnight on the night before an execution, the condemned is usually allowed a last one-hour contact visit. The person is permitted to see his own clergyman if he has one, but only the prison chaplain will be permitted to accompany the inmate to the place of execution. At 4:30 A.M. the prisoner is served his or her last meal, to be eaten on a paper plate with a spoon; if the prisoner has requested a steak, the chef has cut the meat into bite-sized pieces beforehand and arranged them to appear to be an intact steak. No later than 5:30 A.M., the official witnesses to the execution, 12 in number (one of whom may be designated by the condemned), must assemble at the main prison gate. At 5:50 A.M. the media witnesses, also 12 in number, are picked up at the "media onlooker area." Both types of witnesses will later be "escorted to the witness room of the execution chamber." At 6:00 A.M. an administrative assistant, three designated electricians, a physician, and a physician's assistant are assembled in the death chamber. The administrative assistant establishes telephone contact with the state governor's office. Meanwhile, the condemned inmate has his or her head and right calf shaved (to better conduct electricity), takes a shower under the supervision of a high-ranking prison official, and is dressed in his or her new burial clothes, omitting the suit jacket and shoes. Until recently, by informal custom the prison superintendent would then have a drink of whiskey with the condemned in his cell, but public outcry was so great that the practice was discontinued. At 6:50 "conducting gel" is applied to the person's head and leg. The superintendent reads the death warrant to the condemned a final time.

The Moment of Death

Each Aztec victim was taken singly to the sacrificial stone and tethered to it by a rope. In one form of sacrifice, in a mockery of self-defense, the victim was then given a sword edged with feathers rather than obsidian. The high priest rose and descended to the stone, walked around it twice and returned to his seat. Next, an old man disguised as an ocelot gave the captive four wooden balls and a drink of "Divine Wine" and instructed him to defend himself. Many victims tried to defend themselves against a series of ceremonially garbed priest-warriors, but others "unwilling to undergo such ceremony cast themselves upon the stone seeking a quick death" (Duran, 1964:112). Death was inevitable: as soon as the captive was wounded, four priests painted black, with long braided hair and garments resembling chasubles, spread-eagled the victim on the stone, each priest holding a limb. The high priest cut open the victim's chest with an obsidian knife, pulled out the victim's heart and offered the organ to the sun. The heart was deposited in a jar or placed on a brazier, and the next victim was brought forward.

The superintendent of Florida State Prison at Starke and two other prison officials escort the condemned inmate to the death chamber at 6:56 A.M. The person is strapped into the electric chair. At 7:00 A.M. the condemned is permitted to make a last statement. The governor directs the superintendent to proceed with the execution, traditionally concluding with the words "God save us all." The witnesses have been seated in their peculiarly carved, white high-backed chairs. The electrician places the sponge and cap on the inmate's head. The assistant superintendent engages the circuit breaker. The electrician activates the panel, the superintendent signals the executioner to throw the switch, and the "automatic cycle will begin." The actual executioner is an anonymous private citizen dressed in a black hood and robe who will be paid $150 for his services. Once the automatic cycle has run its course, the superintendent invites the doctor to conduct the examination. If all has gone well, the condemned is pronounced dead and the time recorded. A designated prison official proclaims, "The sentence of _____ has been carried out. Please exit to the rear at this time." By custom, someone in attendance waves a white cloth just outside the prison to signal the crowd assembled in a field across from it—reporters, death penalty opponents and proponents, and any others—that the deed is done. Official guidelines for the execution of more than one inmate on a single day exist, but we will dispense with those here.

After Death

Fray Bernardino de Sahagun (1951:24) reports that after each Aztec captive had been slain, the body was taken gently away and rolled down the stairs of the sacrificial pyramid. At the bottom, the victim's head was cut off for display on a rack and the remainder of the corpse was taken to one of the special houses, *calpulli*, where "they divided [the bodies] up in order to eat them." Meanwhile, those who had taken part in the sacrifice entered a temple, removed their ritual garb, and were rewarded with fine clothes and a feast. The lords from the provinces who had been brought to observe were

"shocked and bewildered."

As soon as a Florida inmate is pronounced dead in the electric chair, ambulance attendants are called into the chamber; they remove the inmate from the chair and take the body to a waiting ambulance, which transports the corpse to the medical examiner's office. There an autopsy is performed. Until recently, portions of the brain were removed for secret study by a University of Florida researcher investigating the relationship between "head trauma and violent behavior." This procedure was followed for 11 of the 13 men executed between 1979 and 1985, but was stopped in response to negative publicity. Once the autopsy is completed, the corpse is released to the funeral home for cremation or burial. If the deceased has made no arrangements for a private funeral, his or her body is interred on the prison grounds. The executioner, meanwhile, is returned to his secret pick-up point and compensated. There is a "debriefing" at the prison of all the other participants in the execution save one.

The Native Explanations

What explanations are given by Aztecs and modern Americans for these decidedly gruesome acts? While we will probably never know what the Aztec man in the street thought of the sacrificial murders committed by his priests and nobles, official theology, if we may trust the sources, held that the gods had to be fed and placated to keep the crops growing, the sun high, and the universe in healthy order. Unfortunately for war captives, one of the gods' favorite foods was human hearts.

The explanations given by Americans for capital punishment generally are clothed in more pragmatic, secular terms. Most commonly, supporters of capital punishment invoke stimulus-response psychology and declare that such punishment will prevent others from committing heinous crimes. For instance, following the execution of an admitted child-murderer, Florida's governor declared that "he hoped the execution would be a warning to others

who harbored the desire to mistreat children" (Sherrill, 1984:553). Other explanations emphasize the lower cost of execution as compared with long-term imprisonment, the need to provide families of murder victims with a sense of justice and mental repose, and what might be called the "social hygiene" approach: "[S]ome people just ought to be eliminated—we kill rattlesnakes, we don't keep them as pets," declared one Florida Supreme Court justice (*Tallahassee Democrat,* 15 Sept. 1985).

Despite the rationalistic cast of the most common public explanations for capital punishment, at least some of the explanations, or justifications, that surface into public view are unabashedly religious. The author of a letter to the *Tallahassee Democrat* (6 Feb. 1985) cited scripture to argue that earthly governments have the God-given right and authority "to make and enforce laws, including the right to take human life." He urged his readers to submit " 'to every ordinance of man for the Lord's sake,' " for in so doing evildoers will be punished, those who do well will be praised, and " 'ye will put to silence the ignorance of foolish men' (I Peter 2:13–15)." We suspect that beneath more sophisticated explanations for capital punishment there is, if not an outright appeal to supernatural authority, the same deep-seated set of nameless fears and anxieties that motivate humans everywhere to commit ceremonial acts that reassure and give substance to the Durkheimian view that "religion is society collectively worshipping itself."

Conclusion

The perceptive reader will have recognized the sometimes startling points of similarity between the conduct of some forms of Aztec human sacrifice and capital punishment in Florida. There are, of course, some profoundly important points of difference as well. We will not belabor the obvious here, but given the many commonalities in the organization, procedures, and even physical appurtenances between Aztec human sacrifice and Florida capital punishment, it is reasonable to propose that whatever psychosocial functions human sacrifice might have served in the Aztec empire, they are matched by similar functions for capital punishment in the United States. Just as Aztec ripping out of human hearts was couched in mystical terms of maintaining universal order and well-being of the state (putting aside the question of the utility of such practices as terror tactics with which to intimidate neighboring societies), we propose that capital punishment in the United States serves to assure many that society is not out of control after all, that the majesty of the Law reigns, and that God is indeed in his heaven. Precise, emic ("native") corroboration of our interpretation of capital punishment as the ultimate validator of law is provided by an automobile bumper sticker first seen in Tallahassee in 1987, shortly after the Florida legislature passed a controversial statute requiring automobile passengers to wear safety belts:

I'LL BUCKLE UP—
WHEN BUNDY DOES
IT'S THE LAW

"Bundy" is Theodore Bundy, Florida's most famous prisoner sentenced to be "buckled up" in the electric chair.

Sources as diverse as the populist *National Enquirer* (Mitteager, 1985) and the eminent legal scholar Lawrence Friedman (1973) instruct their readers that the crime rate is actually far lower today than 100 years ago. But through the mass media, the average American is subjected to a daily diet of fanatical terrorists, crazed rapists, revolting child molesters, and ghoulish murderers, to say nothing of dishonest politicians, unruly protestors, welfare and tax cheats, greedy gurus and philandering preachers, marauding street gangs, sexual perverts, and drug fiends, while all the time having to deal with the everyday personal irritations of a society in which, as Marvin Harris (1981) tells us, nothing works, mothers leave home, and gays come out of the closet. In an ironic twist on the anthropological debate (e.g., Isaac, 1983; Ortiz de Montellano, 1982; Price, 1978) over Harner's proposed materialist ex-

planation of Aztec human sacrifice, we hypothesize that the current groundswell of support for capital punishment in the United States springs from the universal, ancient human impulse to do something in times of stress, even if it is only ritual. Bronislaw Malinowski observed that "there are no peoples however primitive without religion and magic" (1954:17); neither are there peoples so civilized that they are devoid of magic. All peoples turn to magic when knowledge, technology, and experience fail (Malinowski, 1954). In the face of all the evidence that capital punishment does no more to deter crime than the bloody rituals of Tenochtitlan did to keep the sun in the sky, we must seek some broader, noninstrumental function that the death penalty serves. We propose, in short, that modern capital punishment is an institutionalized *magical* response to perceived disorder in American life and in the world at large, an attempted magical solution that has an especial appeal to the beleaguered, white, God-fearing men and women of the working class. And in certain aspiring politicians they find their sacrificial priests.

References

Baldus, David C.; Charles A. Pulaski, Jr.; and George Woodworth. 1983. "Comparative Review of Death Sentences: An Empirical Study of the Georgia Experience." *Journal of Criminal Law and Criminology* 74:661–753.

Bowers, William, J., and Glenn L. Pierce. 1980. "Deterrence or Brutalization: What Is the Effect of Executions?" *Crime and Delinquency* 26:453–84.

———. 1980. "Arbitrariness and Discrimination Under Post-*Furman* Capital Statutes." *Crime and Delinquency* 26:563–635.

Cambridge Survey Research. 1985. "An Analysis of Attitudes Toward Capital Punishment in Florida." Prepared for Amnesty International.

Camus, Albert. 1959. *Reflections on the Guillotine.* Michigan City, Ind.: Fridtjof-Karla.

Cooper, John W. 1976. "Propitiation as Social Maintenance: A Study of Capital Punishment Through the Sociology of Religion." M.A. thesis, Florida State University.

Duran, Fray Diego. 1964. *The Aztecs.* New York: Orion Press.

Ellsworth, Phoebe C., and Lee Ross. 1983. "Public Opinion and Capital Punishment: A Close Examination of the Views of Abolitionists and Retentionists." *Crime and Delinquency* 29:116–69.

Fagan, Brian M. 1984. *The Aztecs.* New York: W. H. Freeman.

Florida State Prison. 1983. "Execution Guidelines During Active Death Warrant." Starke: Florida State Prison. Reprinted in part at pp. 235–40 of Amnesty International, *United States of America: The Death Penalty.* London: Amnesty International, 1987.

Friedman, Lawrence M. 1973. *A History of American Law.* New York: Simon and Schuster.

Gallup, George. 1986. "The Death Penalty." *Gallup Report* 244–45 (Jan.–Feb.) 10–16.

Gross, Samuel R., and Robert Mauro. 1984. "Patterns of Death: An Analysis of Racial Disparities in Capital Sentencing and Homicide Victimization." *Stanford Law Review* 37:27–153.

Harner, Michael. 1977. "The Ecological Basis for Aztec Sacrifice." *American Ethnologist* 4:117–35.

Harris, Marvin. 1981. *America Now: The Anthropology of a Changing Culture.* New York: Simon and Schuster.

Harris, Philip W. 1986. "Over-Simplification and Error in Public Opinion Surveys on Capital Punishment." *Justice Quarterly* 3:429–55.

Isaac, Barry L. 1983. "The Aztec 'Flowery War': A Geopolitical Explanation." *Journal of Anthropological Research* 39:415–32.

Lofland, John. 1977. "The Dramaturgy of State Executions." Pp. 275–325 in *State Executions Viewed Historically and Sociologically,* by Horace Bleackley. Montclair, N.J.: Patterson Smith.

Malinowski, Bronislaw. 1954. *Magic, Science and Religion and Other Essays.* Garden City, N.Y.: Doubleday.

Mitteager, James. 1985. "Think Crime Is Bad Now? It Was Much Worse 100 Years Ago." *National Enquirer,* 25 Nov., p. 25.

NAACP Legal Defense and Educational Fund. 1988. "Death Row, U.S.A." Unpublished compilation, available from 99 Hudson St., New York, N.Y. 10013.

Nakell, Barry, and Kenneth A. Hardy. 1987 *The Arbitrariness of the Death Penalty.* Philadelphia: Temple University Press.

Ortiz de Montellano, Bernard R. 1982. "The Body Dangerous: Physiology and Social Stratification." *Reviews in Anthropology* 9:97–107.

Paternoster, Raymond. 1983. "Race of Victim and Location of Crime: The Decision to Seek the Death Penalty in South Carolina." *Journal of Criminal Law and Criminology* 74:754–85.

Price, Barbara J. 1978. "Demystification, Enriddlement and Aztec Cannibalism: A

Materialist Rejoinder to Harner." *American Ethnologist* 5:98–115.

Radelet, Michael L. 1981. "Racial Characteristics and the Imposition of the Death Penalty." *American Sociological Review* 46:918–27.

Radelet, Michael L., and George W. Barnard. 1986. "Ethics and the Psychiatric Determination of Competency to Be Executed." *Bulletin of the American Academy of Psychiatry and the Law* 14:37–53.

Radelet, Michael L.; Margaret Vandiver; and Felix M. Berardo. 1983. "Families, Prisons, and Men with Death Sentences: The Human Impact of Structured Uncertainty." *Journal of Family Issues* 4:593–612.

Sahagun, Fray Bernardino de. 1951. *General History of the Things of New Spain,*

Santa Fe, N.M.: School of American Research and the University of Utah.

Sherrill, Robert. 1984. "In Florida, Insanity Is No Defense." *The Nation* 239:539, 552–56.

Turnbull, Colin. 1978. "Death by Decree." *Natural History* 87 (May):51–66.

U.S. Department of Justice. 1986. *Capital Punishment, 1984.* Washington, D.C.: U.S. Government Printing Office.

Body Ritual Among the Nacirema

Horace Miner
University of Michigan

The anthropologist has become so familiar with the diversity of ways in which different peoples behave in similar situations that he is not apt to be surprised by even the most exotic customs. In fact, if all of the logically possible combinations of behavior have not been found somewhere in the world, he is apt to suspect that they must be present in some yet undescribed tribe. This point has, in fact, been expressed with respect to clan organization by Murdock (1949:71). In this light, the magical beliefs and practices of the Nacirema present such unusual aspects that it seems desirable to describe them as an example of the extremes to which human behavior can go.

Professor Linton first brought the ritual of the Nacirema to the attention of anthropologists twenty years ago (1936:326), but the culture of this people is still very poorly understood. They are a North American group living in the territory between the Canadian Cree, the Yaqui and Tarahumare of Mexico, and the Carib and Arawak of the Antilles. Little is known of their origin, though tradition states that they came from the east. According to Nacirema mythology, their nation was originated by a culture hero, Notgnishaw, who is otherwise known for two great feats of strength—the throwing of a piece of wampum across the river Pa-To-Mac and the chopping down of a cherry tree in which the Spirit of Truth resided.

Nacirema culture is characterized by a highly developed market economy which has evolved in a rich natural habitat. While much of the people's time is devoted to economic pursuits, a large part of the fruits of these labors and a considerable portion of the day are spent in ritual activity. The focus of this activity is the human body, the appearance and health of which loom as a dominant concern in the ethos of the people. While such a concern is certainly not unusual, its ceremonial aspects and associated philosophy are unique.

The fundamental belief underlying the whole system appears to be that the human body is ugly and that its natural tendency is to debility and disease. Incarcerated in such a body, man's only hope is to avert these characteristics through the use of the powerful influences of ritual and ceremony. Every household has one or more shrines devoted to this purpose. The more powerful individuals in the society have several shrines in their houses and, in fact, the opulence of a house is often referred to in terms of the number of such ritual centers it possesses. Most houses are of wattle and daub construction, but the shrine rooms of the more wealthy are walled with stone. Poorer families imitate the rich by applying pottery plaques to their shrine walls.

While each family has at least one such shrine, the rituals associated with it are not family ceremonies but are private and secret. The rites are normally only discussed with children, and then only during the period when they are being initiated into these mysteries. I was able, however, to establish sufficient rapport with the natives to examine these shrines and to have the rituals described to me.

The focal point of the shrine is a box or chest which is built into the wall. In this chest are kept the many charms and magical potions without which no native believes he could live. These preparations are secured from a variety of specialized practitioners. The most powerful of these are the medicine men, whose assistance must be rewarded with substantial gifts. However, the medicine men do not provide the curative potions for their clients, but decide what the ingredients should be and then write them down in an ancient and secret language. This writing is understood only by the medicine men and by the herbalists who, for another gift, provide the required charm.

The charm is not disposed of after it has served its purpose, but is placed in the charm-box of the household shrine. As these magical materials are specific for certain ills, and the real or imagined maladies of the people are many, the charm-box is usually full to overflowing. The magical packets are so numerous that people forget what their purposes were and fear to use them again. While the natives are very vague on this point, we can only assume that the idea in retaining all the old magical materials is that their presence in

Reproduced by permission of the American Anthropological Association from *American Anthropologist* 58:503-507, 1956.

the charm-box, before which the body rituals are conducted, will in some way protect the worshipper.

Beneath the charm-box is a small font. Each day every member of the family, in succession, enters the shrine room, bows his head before the charm-box, mingles different sorts of holy water in the font, and proceeds with a brief rite of ablution. The holy waters are secured from the Water Temple of the community, where the priests conduct elaborate ceremonies to make the liquid ritually pure.

In the hierarchy of magical practitioners, and below the medicine men in prestige, are specialists whose designation is best translated "holy-mouth-men." The Nacirema have an almost pathological horror and fascination with the mouth, the condition of which is believed to have a supernatural influence on all social relationships. Were it not for the rituals of the mouth, they believe that their teeth would fall out, their gums bleed, their jaws shrink, their friends desert them, and their lovers reject them. (They also belive that a strong relationship exists between oral and moral characteristics. For example, there is a ritual ablution of the mouth for children which is supposed to improve their moral fiber.)

The daily body ritual performed by everyone includes a mouth-rite. Despite the fact that these people are so punctilious about care of the mouth, this rite involves a practice which strikes the uninitiated stranger as revolting. It was reported to me that the ritual consists of inserting a small bundle of hog hairs into the mouth, along with certain magical powders, and then moving the bundle in a highly formalized series of gestures.

In addition to the private mouth-rite, the people seek out a holy-mouth-man once or twice a year. These practitioners have an impressive set of paraphernalia, consisting of a variety of augers, awls, probes, and prods. The use of these objects in the exorcism of the evils of the mouth involves almost unbelievable ritual torture of the client. The holy-mouth-man opens the client's mouth and, using the above mentioned tools, en-

larges any holes which decay may have created in the teeth. Magical materials are put into these holes. If there are no naturally occurring holes in the teeth, large sections of one or more teeth are gouged out so that the supernatural substance can be applied. In the client's view, the purpose of these ministrations is to arrest decay and to draw friends. The extremely sacred and traditional character of the rite is evident in the fact that the natives return to the holy-mouth-men year after year, despite the fact that their teeth continue to decay.

It is to be hoped that, when a thorough study of the Nacirema is made, there will be a careful inquiry into the personality structure of these people. One has but to watch the gleam in the eye of a holy-mouth-man, as he jabs an awl into an exposed nerve, to suspect that a certain amount of sadism is involved. If this can be established, a very interesting pattern emerges, for most of the population shows definite masochistic tendencies. It was to these that Professor Linton referred in discussing a distinctive part of the daily body ritual which is performed only by men. This part of the rite involves scraping and lacerating the surface of the face with a sharp instrument. Special women's rites are performed only four times during each lunar month, but what they lack in frequency is made up in barbarity. As part of this ceremony, women bake their heads in small ovens for about an hour. The theoretically interesting point is that what seems to be a preponderantly masochistic people have developed sadistic specialists.

The medicine men have an imposing temple, or *latipso*, in every community of any size. The more elaborate ceremonies required to treat very sick patients can only be performed at this temple. These ceremonies involve not only the thaumaturge but a permanent group of vestal maidens who move sedately about the temple chambers in distinctive costume and headdress.

The *latipso* ceremonies are so harsh that it is phenomenal that a fair

proportion of the really sick natives who enter the temple ever recover. Small children whose indoctrination is still incomplete have been known to resist attempts to take them to the temple because "that is where you go to die." Despite this fact, sick adults are not only willing but eager to undergo the protracted ritual purification, if they can afford to do so. No matter how ill the supplicant or how grave the emergency, the guardians of many temples will not admit a client if he cannot give a rich gift to the custodian. Even after one has gained admission and survived the ceremonies, the guardians will not permit the neophyte to leave until he makes still another gift.

The supplicant entering the temple is first stripped of all his or her clothes. In every-day life the Nacirema avoids exposure of his body and its natural functions. Bathing and excretory acts are performed only in the secrecy of the household shrine, where they are ritualized as part of the body-rites. Psychological shock results from the fact that body secrecy is suddenly lost upon entry into the *latipso*. A man, whose own wife has never seen him in an excretory act, suddenly finds himself naked and assisted by a vestal maiden while he performs his natural functions into a sacred vessel. This sort of ceremonial treatment is necessitated by the fact that the excreta are used by a diviner to ascertain the course and nature of the client's sickness. Female clients, on the other hand, find their naked bodies are subjected to the scrutiny, manipulation and prodding of the medicine men.

Few supplicants in the temple are well enough to do anything but lie on their hard beds. The daily ceremonies, like the rites of the holy-mouth-men, involve discomfort and torture. With ritual precision, the vestals awaken their miserable charges each dawn and roll them about on their beds of pain while performing ablutions, in the formal movements of which the maidens are highly trained. At other times they insert magic wands in the supplicant's mouth or force him to eat substances which are supposed to be healing. From time to time the medicine men come to their clients and jab magically treated needles into their flesh. The fact that these temple ceremonies may not cure, and may even kill the neophyte, in no way decreases the people's faith in the medicine men.

There remains one other kind of practioner, known as a "listener." This witch-doctor has the power to exorcise the devils that lodge in the heads of people who have been bewitched. The Nacirema believe that parents bewitch their own children. Mothers are particularly suspected of putting a curse on children while teaching them the secret body rituals. The counter-magic of the witch-doctor is unusual in its lack of ritual. The patient simply tells the "listener" all his troubles and fears, beginning with the earliest difficulties he can remember. The memory displayed by the Nacirema in these exorcism sessions is truly remarkable. It is not uncommon for the patient to bemoan the rejection he felt upon being weaned as a babe, and a few individuals even see their troubles going back to the traumatic effects of their own birth.

In conclusion, mention must be made of certain practices which have their base in native esthetics but which depend upon the pervasive aversion to the natural body and its functions. There are ritual fasts to make fat people thin and ceremonial feasts to make thin people fat. Still other rites are used to make women's breasts large if they are small, and smaller if they are large. General dissatisfaction with breast shape is symbolized in the fact that the ideal form is virtually outside the range of human variation. A few women afflicted with almost inhuman hypermammary development are so idolized that they make a handsome living by simply going from village to village and permitting the natives to stare at them for a fee.

Reference has already been made to the fact that excretory functions are ritualized, routinized, and relegated to secrecy. Natural reproductive functions are similarly distorted. Intercourse is taboo as a topic and scheduled as an act. Efforts are made to avoid pregnancy by the use of magical materials or by limiting intercourse to certain phases of the moon. Conception is actually very infre-

quent. When pregnant, women dress so as to hide their condition. Parturition takes place in secret, without friends or relatives to assist, and the majority of women do not nurse their infants.

Our review of the ritual life of the Nacirema has certainly shown them to be a magic-ridden people. It is hard to understand how they have managed to exist so long under the burdens which they have imposed upon themselves. But even such exotic customs as these take on real meaning when they are viewed with the insight provided by Malinowski when he wrote (1948:70):

> Looking from far and above, from our high places of safety in the developed civilization, it is easy to see all the crudity and irrelevance of magic. But without its power and guidance early man could not have mastered his practical difficulties as he has done, nor could man have advanced to the higher stages of civilization.

REFERENCES

Linton, Ralph. 1936. *The Study of Man*. New York, D. Appleton-Century Co.

Malinowski, Bronislaw. 1948. *Magic, Science, and Religion*. Glencoe, The Free Press.

Murdock, George P. 1949. *Social Structure*. New York, The Macmillan Co.

Superstition and Ritual in American Baseball

George Gmelch

George Gmelch teaches anthropology at Union College in Schenectady, New York. He has just completed a book on Caribbean migration, Double Passage, *from the University of Michigan Press. He is currently doing research for a book tentatively entitled* Culture Change and Professional Baseball in America: 1960–1990.

On each pitching day for the first three months of a winning season, Dennis Grossini, a pitcher on a Detroit Tiger farm team, arose from bed at exactly 10:00 A.M. At 1:00 P.M. he went to the nearest restaurant for two glasses of iced tea and a tuna fish sandwich. Although the afternoon was free he changed into the sweatshirt and supporter he wore during his last winning game, and one hour before the game he chewed a wad of Beech-Nut chewing tobacco. During the game he touched his letters (the team name on his uniform) after each pitch and straightened his cap after each ball. Before the start of each inning he replaced the pitcher's rosin bag next to the spot where it was the inning before. And after every inning in which he gave up a run, he would wash his hands.

I asked him which part of the ritual was most important. He responded, "You can't really tell what's most important so it all becomes important. I'd be afraid to change anything. As long as I'm winning, I do everything the same. Even when I can't wash my hands (this would occur when he had to bat), it scares me going back to the mound. . . . I don't feel quite right."

Trobriand Islanders, according to anthropologist Bronislaw Malinowski, felt the same way about their fishing magic. Among the Trobrianders, fishing took two forms. In the inner lagoon fish were plentiful and there was little danger; on the open sea fishing was dangerous and yields varied widely. Malinowski found that magic was not used in lagoon fishing, where men could rely solely on their knowledge and skill. But when fishing on the open sea, Trobrianders used a great deal of magical ritual to ensure safety and increase their catch.

Baseball, the American national sport, is an arena in which the players behave remarkably like Malinowski's Trobriand fishermen. To professional baseball players, baseball is more than a game. It is an occupation. Since their livelihood depends on how well they perform, they use magic to try to control or eliminate the chance and uncertainty built into baseball.

To control uncertainty Chicago White Sox shortstop Ozzie Guillen doesn't wash his underclothes after a good game. The Boston Red Sox's Wade Boggs eats chicken before every game (that's 162 meals of chicken per year). Ex-San Francisco Giant pitcher Ron Bryant added a new stick of bubble gum to the collection in his bulging back pocket after each game he won. Jim Ohms, my teammate on the Daytona Beach Islanders in 1966, used to put another penny in the pouch of his supporter after each win. Clanging against the hard plastic genital cup, the pennies made an audible sound as the pitcher ran the bases toward the end of a winning season.

Whether they are professional baseball players, Trobriand fishermen, soldiers, or farmers, people resort to magic in situations of chance, when they believe they have limited control over the success of their activities. In technologically advanced societies that pride themselves on a scientific approach to problem solving, as well as in simple societies, rituals of magic are common. Magic is a human attempt to impose order and certainty on a chaotic, uncertain situation. This attempt is irrational in that there is no causal connection between the instruments of magic and the desired consequences of the magical practice. But it is rational in that it creates in the practitioner a sense of confidence, competence, and control, which in turn is important to successfully executing a specific activity and achieving a desired result.

I have long had a close relationship with baseball, first as a participant and then as an observer. I devoted much of my youth to the game and played professionally as first baseman for five teams in the Detroit Tiger organization over three years. I also spent two years in the Quebec Provincial League. For

Originally appeared in *Elysian Fields Quarterly: The Baseball Review,* All Star Issue, 1992, Vol. 11, No. 3, pp. 25-36, P.O. Box 45618, Madison, WI 53744, 1-800-273-1444. © 1992 by George Gmelch. Reprinted by permission.

additional information about baseball magic I interviewed twenty-eight professional ballplayers and sportswriters.

There are three essential activities in baseball—pitching, hitting, and fielding. The first two, pitching and hitting, involve a great deal of chance and are comparable to the Trobriand fishermen's open sea; in them, players use magic and ritual to increase their chances for success. The third activity, fielding, involves little uncertainty and is similar to the Trobriander inner lagoon; fielders find it unnecessary to resort to magic.

The pitcher is the player least able to control the outcome of his own efforts. His best pitch may be hit for a home run, and his worst pitch may be hit directly into the hands of a fielder for an out or be swung at and missed for a third strike. He may limit the opposing team to a few hits yet lose the game, or he may give up a dozen hits and win. Frequently pitchers perform well and lose, and perform poorly and win. One has only to look at the frequency with which pitchers end a season with poor won-lost records but good earned run averages, or vice versa. For example, in 1990 Dwight Gooden gave up more runs per game than his teammate Sid Fernandez but had a won-lost record nearly twice as good. Gooden won nineteen games and lost only seven, one of the best in the National League, while Sid Fernandez won only nine games while losing fourteen. They pitched for the same team—the New York Mets—and therefore had the same fielders behind them. Regardless of how well he performs, on every outing the pitcher depends upon the proficiency of his teammates, the inefficiency of the opposition, and caprice.

An incredible example of bad luck in pitching occurred some years ago involving former Giant outfielder Willie Mays. Mays intentionally "dove for the dirt" to avoid being hit in the head by a fastball. While he was falling the ball hit his bat and went shooting down the left field line. Mays jumped up and ran, turning the play into a double. Players shook their heads in amazement—most players can't hit when they try to, but Mays couldn't avoid

hitting even when he tried not to. The pitcher looked on in disgust.

Hitting is also full of risk and uncertainty—Red Sox outfielder and Hall of Famer Ted Williams called it the most difficult single task in the world of sports. Consider the forces and time constraints operating against the batter. A fastball travels from the pitcher's mound to the batter's box, just sixty and one-half feet, in three to four tenths of a second. For only three feet of the journey, an absurdly short two-hundredths of a second, the ball is in a position where it can be hit. And to be hit well the ball must be neither too close to the batter's body nor too far from the "meat" of his bat. Any distraction, any slip of a muscle or change in stance, can throw a swing off. Once the ball is hit chance plays a large role in determining where it will go—into a waiting glove, whistling past a fielder's diving stab, or into the wide open spaces. While the pitcher who threw the fastball to Mays was suffering, Mays was collecting the benefits of luck.

Batters also suffer from the fear of being hit by a pitch—specifically, by a fastball that often travels at speeds exceeding ninety miles per hour. Throughout baseball history the great fastball pitchers like Sandy Koufax, Bob Gibson, Nolan Ryan, and Roger Clemens have thrived on this fear and on the level of distraction it causes hitters. The well-armed pitcher inevitably captures the advantage in the psychological war of nerves that characterizes the ongoing tension between pitcher and hitter, and that determines who wins and loses the game. If a hitter is crowding the plate in order to reach balls on the outside corner, or if the batter has been hitting unusually well, pitchers try to regain control of their territory. Indeed, many pitchers intentionally throw at or "dust" a batter in order to instill this sense of fear (what hitters euphemistically call "respect") in him. On one occasion Dock Ellis of the Pittsburgh Pirates, having become convinced that the Cincinnati Reds were dominating his team, intentionally hit the first three Reds batters he faced before his manager removed him from the game.

In fielding, on the other hand, the player has almost complete control over the outcome. Once a ball has been hit in his direction, no one can intervene and ruin his chances of catching it for an out. Infielders have approximately three seconds in which to judge the flight of the fall, field it cleanly, and throw it to first base. Outfielders have almost double that amount of time to track down a fly ball. The average fielding percentage (or success rate) of .975, compared with a .250 success rate for hitters (the average batting percentage), reflects the degree of certainty in fielding. Compared with the pitcher or the hitter, the fielder has little to worry about. He knows that in better than 9.7 times out of 10, he will execute his task flawlessly.

In keeping with Malinowski's hypothesis about the relationship between magic and uncertainty, my research shows that baseball players associate magic with hitting and pitching, but not with fielding. Despite the wide assortment of magic—which includes rituals, taboos, and fetishes—associated with both hitting and pitching, I have never observed any directly connected to fielding. In my experience I have known only one player, a shortstop with fielding problems, who reported any ritual even remotely connected with fielding.

The most common form of magic in professional baseball is personal ritual—a prescribed form of behavior that players scrupulously observe in an effort to ensure that things go their way. These rituals, like those of Malinowski's Trobriand fishermen, are performed in a routine, unemotional manner, much as players do nonmagical things to improve their play: rubbing pine tar on the hands to improve a grip on the bat, or rubbing a new ball to make it more comfortable and responsive to the pitcher's grip. Rituals are infinitely varied since ballplayers may formalize any activity that they consider important to performing well.

Rituals usually grow out of exceptionally good performances. When a player does well he seldom attributes his success to skill alone. Although his skill remains constant, he may go hit-less in one game and in the next get three or four hits. Many players attribute the inconsistencies in their performances to an object, item of food, or form of behavior outside their play. Through ritual, players seek to gain control over their performance. In the 1920s and 1930s sportswriters reported that a player who tripped en route to the field would often retrace his steps and carefully walk over the stumbling block for "insurance."

The word taboo comes from a Polynesian term meaning prohibition. Failure to observe a taboo or prohibition leads to undesirable consequences or bad luck. Most players observe a number of taboos. Taboos usually grow out of exceptionally poor performances, which players often attribute to a particular behavior or food. Certain uniform numbers may become taboo. If a player has a poor spring training season or an unsuccessful year, he may refuse to wear the same number again. During my first season of professional baseball I ate pancakes before a game in which I struck out four times. Several weeks later I had a repeat performance, again after eating pancakes. The result was a pancake taboo—I never ate pancakes during the season from that day on. Another personal taboo, against holding a baseball during the national anthem (the usual practice for first basemen, who must warm up the other infielders), had a similar origin.

In earlier decades some baseball players believed that it was bad luck to go back and fasten a missed buttonhole after dressing for a game. They simply left missed buttons on shirts or pants undone. This taboo is not practiced by modern ballplayers.

Fetishes or charms are material objects believed to embody supernatural powers that aid or protect the owner. Good luck fetishes are standard equipment for many ballplayers. They include a wide assortment of objects: horsehide covers from old baseballs, coins, crucifixes, and old bats. Ordinary objects acquire power by being connected to exceptionally hot batting or pitching streaks, especially ones in which players get all the breaks. The

object is often a new possession or something a player finds and holds responsible for his new good fortune. A player who is in a slump might find a coin or an odd stone just before he begins a hitting streak, attribute an improvement in his performance to the influence of the new object, and regard it as a fetish.

While playing for Spokane, a Dodger farm team, Alan Foster forgot his baseball shoes on a road trip and borrowed a pair from a teammate. That night he pitched a no-hitter, which he attributed to the borrowed shoes. After he bought them from his teammate, they became a prized possession.

During World War II American soldiers used fetishes in much the same way. Social psychologist Samuel Stouffer and his colleagues found that in the face of great danger and uncertainty, soldiers developed magical practices, particularly the use of protective amulets and good-luck charms (crosses, Bibles, rabbits' feet, medals), and jealously guarded articles of clothing they associated with past experiences of escape from danger. Stouffer also found that prebattle preparations were carried out in a fixed "ritual" order, much as ballplayers prepare for a game.

Because most pitchers play only once every four days, they perform rituals less frequently than hitters. The rituals they do perform, however, are just as important. A pitcher cannot make up for a poor performance the next day, and having to wait three days to redeem oneself can be miserable. Moreover, the team's win or loss depends more on the performance of the pitcher than on any other single player. Considering the pressures to do well, it is not surprising that pitchers' rituals are often more complex than those of hitters.

A seventeen-game winner in the Texas Rangers organization, Mike Griffin begins his ritual preparation a full day before he pitches, by washing his hair. The next day, although he does not consider himself superstitious, he eats bacon for lunch. When Griffin dresses for the game he puts on his clothes in the same order, making certain he puts the slightly longer of his

two outer, or "stirrup," socks on his right leg. "I just wouldn't feel right mentally if I did it the other way around," he explains. He always wears the same shirt under his uniform on the day he pitches. During the game he takes off his cap after each pitch, and between innings he sits in the same place on the dugout bench.

Tug McGraw, formerly a relief pitcher for the Phillies, slapped his thigh with his glove with each step he took leaving the mound at the end of an inning. This began as a means of saying hello to his wife in the stands, but it then became ritual as McGraw slapped his thigh whether his wife was there or not.

Many of the rituals pitchers engage in—tugging their caps between pitches, touching the rosin bag after each bad pitch, smoothing the dirt on the mound before each new batter or inning—take place on the field. Most baseball fans observe this behavior regularly, never realizing that it may be as important to the pitcher as actually throwing the ball.

Uniform numbers have special significance for some pitchers. Many have a lucky number which they request. Since the choice is usually limited, pitchers may try to get a number that at least contains their lucky number, such as fourteen, four, thirty-four, or forty-four for the pitcher whose lucky number is four. Oddly enough, there is no consensus about the effect of wearing number thirteen. Some pitchers will not wear it; others such as the Mets' David Cone and Oakland's John "Blue Moon" Odom prefer it. (During a pitching slump, however, Odom asked for a new number. Later he switched back to thirteen.)

The way in which number preferences emerge varies. Occasionally a pitcher requests the number of a former professional star, hoping that—in a form of imitative magic—it will bring him the same measure of success. Or he may request a favorite number that he has always associated with good luck. Vida Blue, former Athletic and Giant, changed his uniform number from thirty-five to fourteen, the number he wore as a high-school quarterback. When the new number did not produce the better pitching performance he was looking for, he switched back to his old number.

One of the sources of his good fortune, Blue believed, was the baseball hat he had worn—since 1974. Several American League umpires refused to let him wear the faded and soiled cap. When Blue persisted he was threatened with a fine and suspension from a game. Finally he conceded, but not before he ceremoniously burned the hat on the field before a game. On the days they are scheduled to appear, many pitchers avoid activities that they believe sap their strength and therefore detract from their effectiveness, or that they otherwise generally link with poor performance. (Many pitchers avoid eating certain foods on their pitching days; actually, some food taboos make good physiological sense). Some pitchers do not shave on the day of a game. In fact, Oakland's Dave Stewart and St. Louis's Todd Worrell don't shave as long as they are winning. Early in the 1989 season Stewart had six consecutive victories and a beard before he finally lost. Ex-St. Louis Cardinal Al Hrabosky took this taboo to extreme lengths; Samsonlike, he refused to cut his hair or beard during the entire season—hence part of the reason for his nickname, the "Mad Hungarian." Many hitters go through a series of preparatory rituals before stepping into the batter's box. These include tugging on their caps, touching their uniform letters or medallions, crossing themselves, tapping or bouncing the bat on the plate, swinging the weighted warm-up bat a prescribed number of times, and smoothing the dirt in the box.

There were more than a dozen individual elements in the batting ritual of Mike Hargrove, former Cleveland Indian first baseman. And after each pitch he would step out of the batter's box and repeat the entire sequence. His rituals were so time consuming that he was called "the human rain delay."

Clothing, both the choice of clothes and the order in which they are put on, is often ritualized. During a batting streak many players wear the same clothes and uniforms for each game and put them on in exactly the same order. Once I changed sweatshirts midway through the game for seven consecutive games to keep a hitting streak going. During a sixteen-game winning streak in 1954, the New York Giants wore the same clothes in each game and refused to let them be cleaned for fear that their good fortune might be washed away with the dirt. Taking this ritual to the extreme, Leo Durocher, managing the Brooklyn Dodgers to a pennant in 1941, spent three and a half weeks in the same black shoes, gray slacks, blue coat, and knitted blue tie.

The opposite may also occur. Several of the Oakland A's players bought new street clothing in an attempt to break a fourteen-game losing streak. Most players, however, single out one or two lucky articles or quirks of dress rather than ritualizing all items of clothing. After hitting two home runs in a game, infielder Jim Davenport of the San Francisco Giants discovered that he had missed a buttonhole while dressing for the game. For the remainder of his career he left the same button undone.

A popular ritual associated with hitting is tagging a base when leaving and returning to the dugout during each inning. Mickey Mantle was in the habit of tagging second base on the way to or from the outfield. During a successful month of the season, one player stepped on third base on his way to the dugout after the third, sixth, and ninth innings of each game. Asked if he ever purposely failed to step on the bag, he replied, "Never! I wouldn't dare. It would destroy my confidence to hit." A hitter who is playing poorly may try different combinations of tagging and not tagging particular bases in an attempt to find a successful combination.

When their players are not hitting some managers will rattle the bat bin, the large wooden box containing the team's bats, as if the bats were in a stupor and could be aroused by a good shaking. Similarly, some hitters rub their hands along the handles of the bats protruding from the bin, presumably in hopes of picking up some power or luck from bats that are getting hits for their owners.

There is a taboo against crossing bats, against permitting one bat to rest on top of another. Although this superstition appears to be dying out among ballplayers today, it was religiously observed by some of my teammates. And in some cases it was elaborated even further. One former Detroit minor leaguer became quite annoyed when a teammate tossed a bat from the batting cage and it landed on top of his bat. Later he explained that the top bat might steal hits from the lower one. In his view, bats contained a finite number of hits, a sort of baseball "image of limited good." For Pirate shortstop Honus Wagner, a charter member of baseball's Hall of Fame, each bat contained only a certain number of hits, and never more than 100. Regardless of the quality of the bat, he would discard it after its 100th hit.

Hall of Famer Johnny Evers, of the Cub double-play trio Tinker to Evers to Chance, believed in saving his luck. If he was hitting well in practice, he would suddenly stop and retire to the bench to "save" his batting for the game. One player told me that many of his teammates on the Asheville Tourists in the Class A Western Carolinas League would not let pitchers touch or swing their bats, not even to loosen up. The traditionally poor-hitting pitchers were believed to pollute or weaken the bats.

Food often forms part of a hitter's ritual repertoire. Eating certain foods before a game is supposed to give the ball "eyes," that is, the ability to seek the gaps between fielders after being hit. In hopes of maintaining a batting streak I once ate chicken every day at 4:00 P.M. until the streak ended. Yankee catcher Jim Leyritz eats turkey before every game. Hitters, like pitchers, also avoid certain foods that are believed to sap their strength during the game.

There are other examples of hitters' ritualized behavior. I once kept my eyes closed during the national anthem in an effort to prolong a batting streak. A friend of mine refused to read anything on the day of a game because he believed that reading weakened his eyesight when batting.

These are personal taboos. There are some taboos, however, that all players hold and that do not develop out of individual experiences or misfortunes. These taboos are learned, some as early as Little League. Mentioning a no-hitter while one is in progress is a widely known example. It is believed that if a pitcher hears the words "no-hitter," the spell will be broken and the no-hitter lost. This taboo is still observed by many sports broadcasters, who use various linguistic subterfuges to inform their listeners that the pitcher had not given up a hit, never mentioning "no-hitter."

But superstitions, like most everything else, change over time. Many of the rituals and beliefs of early baseball are no longer remembered. A century ago players spent time off the field and on looking for items that would bring them luck. For example, to find a hairpin on the street assured a batter of hitting safely in that day's game (today women don't wear hairpins—a good reason why the belief has died out). To catch sight of a white horse or a wagonload of barrels were also good omens. In 1904 the manager of the New York Giants, John McGraw, hired a driver and a team of white horses to drive past the Polo Grounds around the time his players were arriving at the ballpark. He knew that if his players saw white horses they'd have more confidence and that could only help them play better. Belief in the power of white horses survived in a few backwaters until the 1960s. A gray haired manager of a team I played for in Quebec would drive around the countryside before important games and during the playoffs looking for a white horse. When he was successful, he'd announce it to everyone in the clubhouse before the game.

Today most professional baseball coaches or managers will not step on the chalk foul lines when going onto the field to talk to their pitcher. Detroit's manager Sparky Anderson jumps over the line. Others follow a different ritual. They intentionally step on the lines when they are going to take a pitcher out of a game.

How do these rituals and taboos get established in the first place? B. F. Skinner's early research with pigeons provides a clue. Like human beings, pigeons quickly learn to associate their behavior with rewards or punishment. By rewarding the birds at the appropriate time, Skinner taught them such elaborate games as table tennis, miniature bowling, or to play simple tunes on a toy piano.

On one occasion he decided to see what would happen if pigeons were rewarded with food pellets every fifteen seconds, regardless of what they did. He found the birds tended to associate the arrival of the food with a particular action—tucking the head under a wing, hopping from side to side, or turning in a clockwise direction. About ten seconds after the arrival of the last pellet, a bird would begin doing whatever it had associated with getting the food and keep it up until the next pellet arrived.

In the same way, baseball players tend to believe there is a causal connection between two events that are linked only temporally. If a superstitious player touches his crucifix and then gets a hit, he may decide the gesture was responsible for his good fortune and follow the same ritual the next time he comes to the plate. If he should get another hit, the chances are good that he will begin touching the crucifix each time he bats and that he will do so whether or not he hits safely each time.

The average batter hits safely approximately one quarter of the time. And if the behavior of Skinner's pigeons—or of gamblers at a Las Vegas slot machine—is any guide, that is more often than necessary to keep him believing in a ritual. Skinner found that once a pigeon associated one of its actions with the arrival of food or water, sporadic rewards would keep the connection going. One pigeon, apparently believing that hopping from side to side brought pellets into its feeding cup, hopped ten thousand times without a pellet before it gave up.

Since the batter associates his hits at least in some degree with his ritual touching of a crucifix, each hit he gets reinforces the strength of the ritual. Even if he falls into a batting slump and the hits temporarily stop, he will persist in touching the crucifix in the hope that this will change his luck.

Skinner's and Malinowski's explanations are not contradictory. Skinner focuses on how the individual comes to develop and maintain a particular ritual, taboo, or fetish. Malinowski focuses on why human beings turn to magic in precarious or uncertain situations. In their attempts to gain greater control over their performance, baseball players respond to chance and uncertainty in the same way as do people in simple societies. It is wrong to assume that magical practices are a waste of time for either group. The magic in baseball obviously does not make a pitch travel faster or more accurately, or a batted ball seek the gaps between fielders. Nor does the Trobriand brand of magic make the surrounding seas calmer and more abundant with fish. But both kinds of magic give their practitioners a sense of control—and an important element in any endeavor is confidence. —EFQ

An earlier version of this essay was originally published in *Human Nature* magazine. This version is printed with permission of the author.

Sociocultural Change: The Impact of the West

The origins of academic anthropology lie in the colonial and imperial ventures of the nineteenth and twentieth centuries. During these periods, many people of the world were brought into a relationship with Europe and the United States that was usually exploitative and often socially and culturally disruptive. For almost a century, anthropologists have witnessed this process and the transformations that have taken place in those social and cultural systems brought under the umbrella of a world economic order. Early anthropological studies—even those widely regarded as pure research—directly or indirectly served colonial interests. Many anthropologists cer-

tainly believed that they were extending the benefits of Western technology and society while preserving the cultural rights of those people whom they studied. But other representatives of poor nations challenge this view and are far less generous in describing the past role of the anthropologist. Most contemporary anthropologists, however, have a deep moral commitment to defending the legal, political, and economic rights of the people with whom they work.

When anthropologists discuss social change, they usually mean change brought about in preindustrial societies, through long-standing interaction with the nation-states of the industrialized world. In early anthropology, contact between the West and the remainder of the world was characterized by the terms "acculturation" and "culture contact." These terms were used to describe the diffusion of cultural traits between the developed and less developed countries. Often this was analyzed as a one-way process in which cultures of the Third World were seen, for better or worse, as receptacles for Western cultural traits. Nowadays, many anthropologists believe that the diffusion of cultural traits across social, political, and economic boundaries was emphasized at the expense of the real issues of dominance, subordinance, and dependence that characterized the colonial experience. Just as importantly, many anthropologists recognize that the present-day forms of cultural, economic, and political interaction between the developed and the so-called underdeveloped world are best characterized as neocolonial.

Most of the articles in this section take the perspective that anthropology should be critical as well as descriptive. They raise questions that are both interesting and troublesome about cultural contact and about the political economy of underdeveloped countries.

In keeping with the notion that the negative impact of the West on traditional cultures began with colonial domination, this section opens with "Why Can't People Feed Themselves?" This article shows that "progress" for the West has meant poverty and hunger for peasant societies.

The following articles emphasize a different aspect of culture affected by the impact of the West: "Growing Up as a Fore" points to the problems of maintaining individual identity in a changing society. "Civilization and Its Discontents" assesses the impact of Western materialism on tribal traditions. "Dark Dreams About the White Man" reveals that even the dreams of natives are invaded by the white man. "A People at Risk" and "Bicultural Conflict" describe the personal devastation inflicted upon people who are caught between two worlds, the traditional and the modern.

"Lost Tribes, Lost Knowledge" helps us to understand that traditional peoples are not the only losers in the process of cultural destruction. All of humanity stands to suffer as a vast store of human knowledge, embodied in tribal subsistence practices, medicine, and folklore, is obliterated in a manner not unlike the burning of the library of Alexandria 1,600 years ago.

Finally, "Easter Island: Scary Parable" delivers the sternest warning of all: If the downward spiral of human degradation is not broken soon, it will be too late.

Looking Ahead: Challenge Questions

What is a subsistence system?

What have been the effects of colonialism on formerly subsistence-oriented socioeconomic systems?

Do cash crops inevitably lead to class distinctions and poverty?

What was it about the Fore culture that made it so vulnerable to the harmful effects of the change from a subsistence economy to a cash-crop economy?

How has culture contact affected the dreams of the Mehinaku?

In what ways are traditional peoples struggling to maintain their cultures?

What ethical obligations do industrial societies have toward respecting the human rights and cultural diversity of traditional communities?

In what ways is the destruction of tribal cultures similar to the burning of the great library of Alexandria?

What happened to Easter Island civilization?

Why Can't People Feed Themselves?

Frances Moore Lappé and Joseph Collins

Frances Moore Lappé and Dr. Joseph Collins are founders and directors of the Institute for Food and Development Policy, located in San Francisco and New York.

Question: You have said that the hunger problem is not the result of overpopulation. But you have not yet answered the most basic and simple question of all: Why can't people feed themselves? As Senator Daniel P. Moynihan put it bluntly, when addressing himself to the Third World, "Food growing is the first thing you do when you come down out of the trees. The question is, how come the United States can grow food and you can't?"

Our Response: In the very first speech I, Frances, ever gave after writing *Diet for a Small Planet,* I tried to take my audience along the path that I had taken in attempting to understand why so many are hungry in this world. Here is the gist of that talk that was, in truth, a turning point in my life:

When I started I saw a world divided into two parts: a *minority* of nations that had "taken off" through their agricultural and industrial revolutions to reach a level of unparalleled material abundance and a *majority* that remained behind in a primitive, traditional, undeveloped state. This lagging behind of the majority of the world's peoples must be due, I thought, to some internal deficiency or even to several of them. It seemed obvious that the underdeveloped countries must be deficient in natural resources—particularly good land and climate—and in cultural development, including modern attitudes conducive to work and progress.

But when looking for the historical roots of the predicament, I learned that my picture of these two separate worlds was quite false. My "two separate worlds" were really just different sides of the same coin. One side was on top largely because the other side was on the bottom. Could this be true? How were these separate worlds related?

Colonialism appeared to me to be the link. Colonialism destroyed the cultural patterns of production and exchange by which traditional societies in "underdeveloped" countries previously had met the needs of the people. Many precolonial social structures, while dominated by exploitative elites, had evolved a system of mutual obligations among the classes that helped to ensure at least a minimal diet for all. A friend of mine once said: "Precolonial village existence in subsistence agriculture was a limited life indeed, but it's certainly not Calcutta." The misery of starvation in the streets of Calcutta can only be understood as the end-point of a long historical process—one that has destroyed a traditional social system.

"Underdeveloped," instead of being an adjective that evokes the picture of a static society, became for me a verb (to "underdevelop") meaning the *process* by which the minority of the world has transformed—indeed often robbed and degraded—the majority.

That was in 1972. I clearly recall my thoughts on my return home. I had stated publicly for the first time a world view that had taken me years of study to grasp. The sense of relief was tremendous. For me the breakthrough lay in realizing that today's "hunger crisis" could not be described in static, descriptive terms. Hunger and underdevelopment must always be thought of as a *process.*

To answer the question "why hunger?" it is counterproductive to simply *describe* the conditions in an underdeveloped country today. For these conditions, whether they be the degree of malnutrition, the levels of agricultural production, or even the country's ecological endowment, are not static factors—they are not "givens." They are rather the *results* of an ongoing historical process. As we dug ever deeper into that historical process for the preparation of this book, we began to discover the existence of scarcity-creating mechanisms that we had only vaguely intuited before.

We have gotten great satisfaction from probing into the past since we recognized it is the only way to approach a solution to hunger today. We have come to see that it is the *force* creating the condition, not the condition itself, that must be the target of change. Otherwise we might change the condition today, only to find tomorrow that it has been recreated—with a vengeance.

Asking the question "Why can't people feed themselves?" carries a sense of bewilderment that there are so many people in the world not able to feed themselves adequately. What astonished us, however, is that there are not *more* people in the world who are hungry—considering the weight of the centuries of effort by the few to undermine the capacity of the majority to feed themselves. No, we are not crying "conspiracy!" If these forces were entirely conspiratorial, they would be easier to detect and many more people would by now have risen up to resist. We are talking about something more subtle and insidious; a heritage of a colonial order in which people with the advantage of considerable power sought their own self-interest, often arrogantly believing they were acting in the interest of the people whose lives they were destroying.

THE COLONIAL MIND

The colonizer viewed agriculture in the subjugated lands as primitive and backward. Yet such a view contrasts sharply with documents from the colonial period now coming to light. For example, A. J. Voelker, a British agricultural scientist assigned to India during the 1890s, wrote:

Nowhere would one find better instances of keeping land scrupulously clean from weeds, of ingenuity in device of water-raising appliances, of knowledge of soils and their capabilities, as well as of the exact time to sow and reap, as one would find in Indian agriculture. It is wonderful, too, how much is known of rotation, the system of "mixed crops" and of fallowing. . . . I, at least, have never seen a more perfect picture of cultivation."[1]

None the less, viewing the agriculture of the vanquished as primitive and backward reinforced the colonizer's rationale for destroying it. To the colonizers of Africa, Asia, and Latin America, agriculture became merely a means to extract wealth—much as gold from a mine—on behalf of the colonizing power. Agriculture was no longer seen as a source of food for the local population, nor even as their livelihood. Indeed the English economist John Stuart Mill reasoned that colonies should not be thought of as civilizations or countries at all but as "agricultural establishments" whose sole purpose was to supply the "larger community to which they belong." The colonized society's agriculture was only a subdivision of the agricultural system of the metropolitan country. As Mill acknowledged, "Our West India colonies, for example, cannot be regarded as countries. . . . The West Indies are the place where England *finds it convenient* to carry on the production of sugar, coffee and a few other tropical commodities."[2]

Prior to European intervention, Africans practiced a diversified agriculture that included the introduction of new food plants of Asian or American origin. But colonial rule simplified this diversified production to single cash crops—often to the exclusion of staple foods—and in the process sowed the seeds of famine.[3] Rice farming once had been common

in Gambia. But with colonial rule so much of the best land was taken over by peanuts (grown for the European market) that rice had to be imported to counter the mounting prospect of famine. Northern Ghana, once famous for its yams and other foodstuffs, was forced to concentrate solely on cocoa. Most of the Gold Coast thus became dependent on cocoa. Liberia was turned into a virtual plantation subsidiary of Firestone Tire and Rubber. Food production in Dahomey and southeast Nigeria was all but abandoned in favor of palm oil; Tanganyika (now Tanzania) was forced to focus on sisal and Uganda on cotton.

The same happened in Indochina. About the time of the American Civil War the French decided that the Mekong Delta in Vietnam would be ideal for producing rice for export. Through a production system based on enriching the large landowners, Vietnam became the world's third largest exporter of rice by the 1930s; yet many landless Vietnamese went hungry.[4]

Rather than helping the peasants, colonialism's public works programs only reinforced export crop production. British irrigation works built in nineteenth-century India did help increase production, but the expansion was for spring export crops at the expense of millets and legumes grown in the fall as the basic local food crops.

Because people living on the land do not easily go against their natural and adaptive drive to grow food for themselves, colonial powers had to force the production of cash crops. The first strategy was to use physical or economic force to get the local population to grow cash crops instead of food on their own plots and then turn them over to the colonizer for export. The second strategy was the direct takeover of the land by large-scale plantations growing crops for export.

FORCED PEASANT PRODUCTION

As Walter Rodney recounts in *How Europe Underdeveloped Africa,* cash crops were often grown literally under threat of guns and whips.[5] One visitor

to the Sahel commented in 1928: "Cotton is an artificial crop and one the value of which is not entirely clear to the natives. . . ." He wryly noted the "enforced enthusiasm with which the natives. . .have thrown themselves into. . .planting cotton."[6] The forced cultivation of cotton was a major grievance leading to the Maji Maji wars in Tanzania (then Tanganyika) and behind the nationalist revolt in Angola as late as 1960.[7]

Although raw force was used, taxation was the preferred colonial technique to force Africans to grow cash crops. The colonial administrations simply levied taxes on cattle, land, houses, and even the people themselves. Since the tax had to be paid in the coin of the realm, the peasants had either to grow crops to sell or to work on the plantations or in the mines of the Europeans.[8] Taxation was both an effective tool to "stimulate" cash cropping and a source of revenue that the colonial bureaucracy needed to enforce the system. To expand their production of export crops to pay the mounting taxes, peasant producers were forced to neglect the farming of food crops. In 1830, the Dutch administration in Java made the peasants an offer they could not refuse; if they would grow government-owned export crops on one fifth of their land, the Dutch would remit their land taxes.[9] If they refused and thus could not pay the taxes, they lost their land.

Marketing boards emerged in Africa in the 1930s as another technique for getting the profit from cash crop production by native producers into the hands of the colonial government and international firms. Purchases by the marketing boards were well below the world market price. Peanuts bought by the boards from peasant cultivators in West Africa were sold in Britain for more than *seven times* what the peasants received.[10]

The marketing board concept was born with the "cocoa hold-up" in the Gold Coast in 1937. Small cocoa farmers refused to sell to the large cocoa concerns like United Africa

Company (a subsidiary of the Anglo-Dutch firm, Unilever—which we know as Lever Brothers) and Cadbury until they got a higher price. When the British government stepped in and agreed to buy the cocoa directly in place of the big business concerns, the smallholders must have thought they had scored at least a minor victory. But had they really? The following year the British formally set up the West African Cocoa Control Board. Theoretically, its purpose was to pay the peasants a reasonable price for their crops. In practice, however, the board, as sole purchaser, was able to hold down the prices paid the peasants for their crops when the world prices were rising. Rodney sums up the real "victory":

None of the benefits went to Africans, but rather to the British government itself and to the private companies. . . Big companies like the United African Company and John Holt were given. . . quotas to fulfill on behalf of the boards. As agents of the government, they were no longer exposed to direct attack, and their profits were secure.[11]

These marketing boards, set up for most export crops, were actually controlled by the companies. The chairman of the Cocoa Board was none other than John Cadbury of Cadbury Brothers (ever had a Cadbury chocolate bar?) who was part of a buying pool exploiting West African cocoa farmers.

The marketing boards funneled part of the profits from the exploitation of peasant producers indirectly into the royal treasury. While the Cocoa Board sold to the British Food Ministry at low prices, the ministry upped the price for British manufacturers, thus netting a profit as high as 11 million pounds in some years.[12]

These marketing boards of Africa were only the institutionalized rendition of what is the essence of colonialism—the extraction of wealth. While profits continued to accrue to foreign interests and local elites, prices received by those actually growing the commodities remained low.

PLANTATIONS

A second approach was direct takeover of the land either by the colonizing government or by private foreign interests. Previously self-provisioning farmers were forced to cultivate the plantation fields through either enslavement or economic coercion.

After the conquest of the Kandyan Kingdom (in present day Sri Lanka), in 1815, the British designated all the vast central part of the island as crown land. When it was determined that coffee, a profitable export crop, could be grown there, the Kandyan lands were sold off to British investors and planters at a mere five shillings per acre, the government even defraying the cost of surveying and road building.[13]

Java is also a prime example of a colonial government seizing territory and then putting it into private foreign hands. In 1870, the Dutch declared all uncultivated land—called waste land—property of the state for lease to Dutch plantation enterprises. In addition, the Agrarian Land Law of 1870 authorized foreign companies to lease village-owned land. The peasants, in chronic need of ready cash for taxes and foreign consumer goods, were only too willing to lease their land to the foreign companies for very modest sums and under terms dictated by the firms. Where land was still held communally, the village headman was tempted by high cash commissions offered by plantation companies. He would lease the village land even more cheaply than would the individual peasant or, as was frequently the case, sell out the entire village to the company.[14]

The introduction of the plantation meant the divorce of agriculture from nourishment, as the notion of food value was lost to the overriding claim of "market value" in international trade. Crops such as sugar, tobacco, and coffee were selected, not on the basis of how well they feed people, but for their high price value relative to their weight and bulk so that profit margins could be maintained even after the costs of shipping to Europe.

SUPPRESSING PEASANT FARMING

The stagnation and impoverishment of the peasant food-producing sector was not the mere by-product of benign neglect, that is, the unintended consequence of an overemphasis on export production. Plantations—just like modern "agro-industrial complexes"—needed an abundant and readily available supply of low-wage agricultural workers. Colonial administrations thus devised a variety of tactics, all to undercut self-provisioning agriculture and thus make rural populations dependent on plantation wages. Government services and even the most minimal infrastructure (access to water, roads, seeds, credit, pest and disease control information, and so on) were systematically denied. Plantations usurped most of the good land, either making much of the rural population landless or pushing them onto marginal soils. (Yet the plantations have often held much of their land idle simply to prevent the peasants from using it—even to this day. Del Monte owns 57,000 acres of Guatemala but plants only 9000. The rest lies idle except for a few thousand head of grazing cattle.)[15]

In some cases a colonial administration would go even further to guarantee itself a labor supply. In at least twelve countries in the eastern and southern parts of Africa the exploitation of mineral wealth (gold, diamonds, and copper) and the establishment of cash-crop plantations demanded a continuous supply of low-cost labor. To assure this labor supply, colonial administrations simply expropriated the land of the African communities by violence and drove the people into small reserves.[16] With neither adequate land for their traditional slash-and-burn methods nor access to the means—tools, water, and fertilizer—to make continuous farming of such limited areas viable, the indigenous population could scarcely meet subsistence needs, much less produce surplus to sell in order to cover the colonial taxes. Hundreds of thousands of Africans were forced to become the cheap labor source so "needed" by the colonial plantations. Only by laboring on plantations and in the mines could they hope to pay the colonial taxes.

The tax scheme to produce reserves of cheap plantation and mining labor was particularly effective when the Great Depression hit and the bottom dropped out of cash crop economies. In 1929 the cotton market collapsed, leaving peasant cotton producers, such as those in Upper Volta, unable to pay their colonial taxes. More and more young people, in some years as many as 80,000, were thus forced to migrate to the Gold Coast to compete with each other for low-wage jobs on cocoa plantations.[17]

The forced migration of Africa's most able-bodied workers—stripping village food farming of needed hands—was a recurring feature of colonialism. As late as 1973 the Portuguese "exported" 400,000 Mozambican peasants to work in South Africa in exchange for gold deposited in the Lisbon treasury.

The many techniques of colonialism to undercut self-provisioning agriculture in order to ensure a cheap labor supply are no better illustrated than by the story of how, in the mid-nineteenth century, sugar plantation owners in British Guiana coped with the double blow of the emancipation of slaves and the crash in the world sugar market. The story is graphically recounted by Alan Adamson in *Sugar without Slaves.*[18]

Would the ex-slaves be allowed to take over the plantation land and grow the food they needed? The planters, many ruined by the sugar slump, were determined they would not. The planter-dominated government devised several schemes for thwarting food self-sufficiency. The price of crown land was kept artificially high, and the purchase of land in parcels smaller than 100 acres was outlawed—two measures guaranteeing that newly organized ex-slave cooperatives could not hope to gain access to much land. The government also prohibited cultivation on as

much as 400,000 acres—on the grounds of "uncertain property titles." Moreover, although many planters held part of their land out of sugar production due to the depressed world price, they would not allow any alternative production on them. They feared that once the ex-slaves started growing food it would be difficult to return them to sugar production when world market prices began to recover. In addition, the government taxed peasant production, then turned around and used the funds to subsidize the immigration of laborers from India and Malaysia to replace the freed slaves, thereby making sugar production again profitable for the planters. Finally, the government neglected the infrastructure for subsistence agriculture and denied credit for small farmers.

Perhaps the most insidious tactic to "lure" the peasant away from food production—and the one with profound historical consequences—was a policy of keeping the price of imported food low through the removal of tariffs and subsidies. The policy was double-edged: first, peasants were told they need not grow food because they could always buy it cheaply with their plantation wages; second, cheap food imports destroyed the market for domestic food and thereby impoverished local food producers.

Adamson relates how both the Governor of British Guiana and the Secretary for the Colonies Earl Grey favored low duties on imports in order to erode local food production and thereby release labor for the plantations. In 1851 the governor rushed through a reduction of the duty on cereals in order to "divert" labor to the sugar estates. As Adamson comments, "Without realizing it, he [the governor] had put his finger on the most mordant feature of monoculture: . . . its convulsive need to destroy any other sector of the economy which might compete for 'its' labor."[19]

Many colonial governments succeeded in establishing dependence on imported foodstuffs. In 1647 an

observer in the West Indies wrote to Governor Winthrop of Massachusetts: "Men are so intent upon planting sugar that they had rather buy foode at very deare rates than produce it by labour, so infinite is the profitt of sugar workes. . . ."[20] By 1770, the West Indies were importing most of the continental colonies' exports of dried fish, grain, beans, and vegetables. A dependence on imported food made the West Indian colonies vulnerable to any disruption in supply. This dependence on imported food stuffs spelled disaster when the thirteen continental colonies gained independence and food exports from the continent to the West Indies were interrupted. With no diversified food system to fall back on, 15,000 plantation workers died of famine between 1780 and 1787 in Jamaica alone.[21] The dependence of the West Indies on imported food persists to this day.

SUPPRESSING PEASANT COMPETITION

We have talked about the techniques by which indigenous populations were forced to cultivate cash crops. In some countries with large plantations, however, colonial governments found it necessary to *prevent* peasants from independently growing cash crops not out of concern for their welfare, but so that they would not compete with colonial interests growing the same crop. For peasant farmers, given a modicum of opportunity, proved themselves capable of outproducing the large plantations not only in terms of output per unit of land but, more important, in terms of capital cost per unit produced.

In the Dutch East Indies (Indonesia and Dutch New Guinea) colonial policy in the middle of the nineteenth century forbade the sugar refineries to buy sugar cane from indigenous growers and imposed a discriminatory tax on rubber produced by native smallholders.[22] A recent unpublished United Nations study of agricultural development in Africa concluded that large-scale agricultural operations owned and controlled by foreign commercial interests (such as the rubber plantations of Liberia, the sisal estates of Tanganyika [Tanzania], and the coffee estates of Angola) only survived the competition of peasant producers because "the authorities actively supported them by suppressing indigenous rural development."[23]

The suppression of indigenous agricultural development served the interests of the colonizing powers in two ways. Not only did it prevent direct competition from more efficient native producers of the same crops, but it also guaranteed a labor force to work on the foreign-owned estates. Planters and foreign investors were not unaware that peasants who could survive economically by their own production would be under less pressure to sell their labor cheaply to the large estates.

The answer to the question, then, "Why can't people feed themselves?" must begin with an understanding of how colonialism actively prevented people from doing just that.

Colonialism

- forced peasants to replace food crops with cash crops that were then expropriated at very low rates;
- took over the best agricultural land for export crop plantations

and then forced the most able-bodied workers to leave the village fields to work as slaves or for very low wages on plantations;

- encouraged a dependence on imported food;
- blocked native peasant cash crop production from competing with cash crops produced by settlers or foreign firms.

These are concrete examples of the development of underdevelopment that we should have perceived as such even as we read our history schoolbooks. Why didn't we? Somehow our schoolbooks always seemed to make the flow of history appear to have its own logic—as if it could not have been any other way. I, Frances, recall, in particular, a grade-school, social studies pamphlet on the idyllic life of Pedro, a nine-year-old boy on a coffee plantation in South America. The drawings of lush vegetation and "exotic" huts made his life seem romantic indeed. Wasn't it natural and proper that South America should have plantations to supply my mother and father with coffee? Isn't that the way it was *meant* to be?

NOTES

[1] Radha Sinha, *Food and Poverty* (New York: Holmes and Meier, 1976), p. 26.

[2] John Stuart Mill, *Political Economy*, Book 3, Chapter 25 (emphasis added).

[3] Peter Feldman and David Lawrence, "Social and Economic Implications of the Large-Scale Introduction of New Varieties of Foodgrains," Africa Report, preliminary draft (Geneva: UNRISD, 1975), pp. 107–108.

[4] Edgar Owens, *The Right Side of History*, unpublished manuscript, 1976.

[5] Walter Rodney, *How Europe Underdeveloped Africa* (London: Bogle-L'Ouverture Publications, 1972), pp. 171–172.

[6] Ferdinand Ossendowski, *Slaves of the Sun* (New York: Dutton, 1928), p. 276.

[7] Rodney, *How Europe Underdeveloped Africa*, pp. 171–172.

[8] Ibid., p. 181.

[9] Clifford Geertz, *Agricultural Involution* (Berkeley and Los Angeles: University of California Press, 1963), pp. 52–53.

[10] Rodney, *How Europe Underdeveloped Africa*, p. 185.

[11] Ibid., p. 184.

[12] Ibid., p. 186.

[13] George L. Beckford, *Persistent Poverty: Underdevelopment in Plantation Economies of the Third World* (New York: Oxford University Press, 1972), p. 99.

[14] Ibid., p. 99, quoting from Erich Jacoby, *Agrarian Unrest in Southeast Asia* (New York: Asia Publishing House, 1961), p. 66.

[15] Pat Flynn and Roger Burbach, North American Congress on Latin America, Berkeley, California, recent investigation.

[16] Feldman and Lawrence, "Social and Economic Implications," p. 103.

[17] Special Sahelian Office Report, Food and Agriculture Organization, March 28, 1974, pp. 88–89.

[18] Alan Adamson, *Sugar Without Slaves: The Political Economy of British Guiana, 1838–1904* (New Haven and London: Yale University Press, 1972).

[19] Ibid., p. 41.

[20] Eric Williams, *Capitalism and Slavery* (New York: Putnam, 1966), p. 110.

[21] Ibid., p. 121.

[22] Gunnar Myrdal, *Asian Drama*, vol. 1 (New York: Pantheon, 1966), pp. 448–449.

[23] Feldman and Lawrence, "Social and Economic Implications," p. 189.

Growing up as a Fore

E. Richard Sorenson

Dr. Sorenson, director of the Smithsonian's National Anthropological Film Center, wrote The Edge of the Forest *on his Fore studies.*

Untouched by the outside world, they had lived for thousands of years in isolated mountains and valleys deep in the interior of Papua New Guinea. They had no cloth, no metal, no money, no idea that their homeland was an island—or that what surrounded it was salt water. Yet the Fore (for'ay) people had developed remarkable and sophisticated approaches to human relations, and their child-rearing practices gave their young unusual freedom to explore. Successful as hunter-gatherers and as subsistence gardeners, they also had great adaptability, which brought rapid accommodation with the outside world after their lands were opened up.

It was alone that I first visited the Fore in 1963—a day's walk from a recently built airstrip. I stayed six months. Perplexed and fascinated, I

Exploring, two youngsters walk confidently past men's house in hamlet. Smaller women's house is at right.

returned six times in the next ten years, eventually spending a year and a half living with them in their hamlets.

Theirs was a way of life different from anything I had seen or heard about before. There were no chiefs, patriarchs, priests, medicine men or the like. A striking personal freedom was enjoyed even by the very young, who could move about at will and be

where or with whom they liked. Infants rarely cried, and they played confidently with knives, axes, and fire. Conflict between old and young did not arise; there was no "generation gap."

Older children enjoyed deferring to the interests and desires of the younger, and sibling rivalry was virtually undetectable. A responsive sixth sense seemed to attune the Fore

Learning to be a toddler, a Fore baby takes its first experimental steps. No one urges him on.

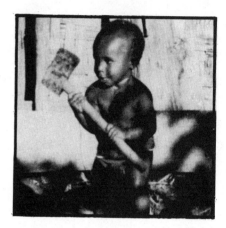

limited virgin land, and they had food plants they could introduce into it. Like hunter-gatherers they sought their sources of sustenance first in one locale and then another, across an extended range, following opportunities provided by a providential nature. But like agriculturalists they concentrated their effort and attention more narrowly on selected sites of production, on their gardens. They were both seekers and producers. A pioneer people in a pioneer land, they ranged freely into a vast territory, but they planted to live.

Cooperative groups formed hamlets and gardened together. When the fertility of a garden declined, they abandoned it. Grass sprung up to cover these abandoned sites of earlier cultivation, and, as the Fore moved on to other parts of the forest, they left uninhabited grasslands to mark their passage.

The traditional hamlets were small, with a rather fluid system of social relations. A single large men's house provided shelter for 10 to 20 men and boys and their visiting friends. The several smaller women's houses each normally sheltered two married women, their unmarried daughters and their sons up to about six years of age. Formal kinship bonds were less important than friendship was. Fraternal "gangs" of youths formed the hamlets; their "clubhouses" were the men's houses.

During the day the gardens became the center of life. Hamlets were virtually deserted as friends, relatives and children went to one or more garden plots to mingle their social, economic and erotic pursuits in a pleasant and emotionally filled Gestalt of garden life. The boys and unmarried youths preferred to explore and hunt in the outlying lands, but they also passed through and tarried in the gardens.

hamlet mates to each other's interests and needs. They did not have to directly ask, inveigle, bargain or speak out for what they needed or wanted. Subtle, even fleeting expressions of interest, desire, and discomfort were quickly read and helpfully acted on by one's associates. This spontaneous urge to share food, affection, work, trust, tools and pleasure was the social cement that held the Fore hamlets together. It was a pleasant way of life, for one could always be with those with whom one got along well.

Ranging and planting, sharing and living, the Fore diverged and expanded through high virgin lands in a pioneer region. They hunted out their gardens, tilled them while they lasted, then hunted again. Moving ever away from lands peopled and used they had a self-contained life with its own special ways.

The underlying ecological conditions were like those that must have encompassed the world before agriculture set its imprint so broadly. Abutting the Fore was virtually un-

In infancy, Fore children begin experimental play with knives and other lethal objects. Sorenson never saw a child warned away or injured by them.

Daily activities were not scheduled. No one made demands, and the land was bountiful. Not surprisingly the line between work and play was never clear. The transmission of the Fore behavioral pattern to the young began in early infancy during a period of unceasing human physical contact. The effect of being constantly "in touch" with hamlet mates and their daily life seemed to start a process which proceeded by degrees: close rapport, involvement in regular activity, ability to handle seemingly dangerous implements safely, and responsible freedom to pursue individual interests at will without danger.

While very young, infants remained in almost continuous bodily contact with their mother, her house mates or her gardening associates. At first, mothers' laps were the center of activity, and infants occupied themselves there by nursing, sleeping and playing with their own bodies or those of their caretakers. They were not put aside for the sake of other activities, as when food was being prepared or heavy loads were being carried. Remaining in close, uninterrupted physical contact with those around them, their basic needs such as rest, nourishment, stimulation and security were continuously satisfied without obstacle.

By being physically in touch from their earliest days, Fore youngsters learned to communicate needs, desires and feelings through a body language of touch and response that developed before speech. This opened the door to a much closer rapport with those around them than otherwise would have been possible, and led ultimately to the Fore brand of social cement and the sixth sense that bound groups together through spontaneous, responsive sharing.

Babies have free access to the breast and later, like this toddler being helped to kernels of corn by an older girl, can help themselves to whatever food is around—indulged by children and grown-ups.

Close, constant body contact, as between this baby and older girl, creates security in Fore children.

As the infant's awareness increased, his interests broadened to the things his mother and other caretakers did and to the objects and materials they used. Then these youngsters began crawling out to explore things that attracted their attention. By the time they were toddling, their interests continually took them on short sorties to nearby objects and persons. As soon as they could walk well, the excursions extended to the entire hamlet and its gardens, and then beyond with other children. Developing without interference or supervision, this personal exploratory learning quest freely touched on whatever was around, even axes, knives, machetes, fire, and the like. When I first went to the Fore, I was aghast.

Eventually I discovered that this capability emerged naturally from Fore infant-handling practices in their milieu of close human physical proximity and tactile interaction. Because touch and bodily contact lend themselves naturally to satisfying the basic needs of young children, an early kind of communicative experience fostered cooperative interaction between infants and their caretakers,

also kinesthetic contact with the activities at hand. This made it easy for them to learn the appropriate handling of the tools of life.

The early pattern of exploratory activity included frequent return to one of the "mothers." Serving as home base, the bastion of security, a woman might occasionally give the youngster a nod of encouragement, if he glanced in her direction with uncertainty. Yet rarely did the women attempt to control or direct, nor did they participate in the child's quests or jaunts.

As a result Fore children did not have to adjust to rule and schedule in order to find their place in life. They could pursue their interests and whims wherever they might lead and still be part of a richly responsive world of human touch which constantly provided sustenance, comfort, diversion and security.

Learning proceeded during the course of pursuing interests and exploring. Constantly "in touch" with people who were busy with daily activities, the Fore young quickly learned the skills of life from example. Muscle tone, movement and mood were components of this learning process; formal lessons and commands were not. Kinesthetic skills developed so quickly that infants were able to casually handle knives and similar objects before they could walk.

Even after several visits I continued to be surprised that the unsupervised Fore toddlers did not recklessly thrust themselves into unappreciated dangers, the way our own children tend to do. But then, why should they? From their earliest days, they enjoyed a benevolent sanctuary from which the world could be confidently viewed, tested and appreciated. This sanctuary remained ever available, but did not demand, restrain or impose. One could go and come at will.

In close harmony with their source of life, the Fore young were able confidently, not furtively, to extend their inquiry. They could widen their understanding as they chose. There was no need to play tricks or deceive in order to pursue life.

On the way to hunt birds, cuscus (a marsupial) or rats, Fore boys stride through a sweet-potato garden.

Emerging from this early childhood was a freely ranging young child rather in tune with his older and younger hamlet mates, disinclined to act out impulsively, and with a capable appreciation of the properties of potentially dangerous objects. Such children could be permitted to move out on their own, unsupervised and unrestricted. They were safe.

Such a pattern could persist indefinitely, re-creating itself in each new generation. However, hidden within the receptive character it produced was an Achilles heel; it also permitted adoption of new practices, including child-handling practices, which did *not* act to perpetuate the pattern. In only one generation after

Western contact, the cycle of Fore life was broken.

Attuned as they were to individual pursuit of economic and social good, it did not take the Fore long to recognize the value of the new materials, practices and ideas that began to flow in. Indeed, change began almost immediately with efforts to obtain steel axes, salt, medicine and cloth. The Fore were quick to shed indigenous practices in favor of Western example. They rapidly altered their ways to adapt to Western law, government, religion, materials and trade.

Sometimes change was so rapid that many people seemed to be afflicted by a kind of cultural shock. An anomie, even cultural amnesia, seemed to pervade some hamlets for a time. There were individuals who appeared temporarily to have lost memory of recent past events. Some Fore even forgot what type and style of traditional garments they had worn only a few years earlier, or that they had used stone axes and had eaten their dead close relatives.

Remarkably open-minded, the Fore so readily accepted reformulation of identity and practice that suggestion or example by the new government officers, missionaries and scientists could alter tribal affiliation, place names, conduct and hamlet style. When the first Australian patrol officer began to map the region in 1957, an error in communication led him to refer to these people as the "Fore." Actually they had had no name for themselves and the word, Fore, was their name for a quite different group, the Awa, who spoke another language and lived in another valley. They did not correct the patrol officer but adopted his usage. They all now refer to themselves as the Fore. Regional and even personal names changed just as readily.

More than anything else, it was the completion of a steep, rough, always muddy Jeep road into the Fore lands that undermined the traditional life. Almost overnight their isolated region was opened. Hamlets began to move down from their ridgetop sites in order to be nearer the road, consolidating with others.

The power of the road is hard to overestimate. It was a great artery where only restricted capillaries had existed before. And down this artery came a flood of new goods, new ideas and new people. This new road, often impassable even with four-wheel-drive vehicles, was perhaps the single most dramatic stroke wrought by the government. It was to the Fore an opening to a new world. As they began to use the road, they started to shed traditions evolved in the protective insularity of their mountain fastness, to adopt in their stead an emerging market culture.

THE COMING OF THE COFFEE ECONOMY

"Walkabout," nonexistent as an institution before contact, quickly became an accepted way of life. Fore boys began to roam hundreds of miles from their homeland in the quest for new experience, trade goods, jobs and money. Like the classic practice of the Australian aborigine, this "walkabout" took one away from his home for periods of varying length. But unlike the Australian practice, it usually took the boys to jobs and schools rather than to a solitary life in traditional lands. Obviously it sprang from the earlier pattern of individual freedom to pursue personal interests and opportunity wherever it might lead. It was a new expression of the old Fore exploratory pattern.

Some boys did not roam far, whereas others found ways to go to distant cities. The roaming boys often sought places where they might be welcomed as visitors, workers or students for a while. Mission stations and schools, plantation work camps, and the servants' quarters of the European population became way-stations in the lives of the modernizing Fore boys.

Some took jobs on coffee plantations. Impressed by the care and attention lavished on coffee by European planters and by the money they saw paid to coffee growers, these young Fore workers returned home with coffee beans to plant.

Coffee grew well on the Fore hillsides, and in the mid-1960s, when the first sizable crop matured, Fore who previously had felt lucky to earn a few dollars found themselves able to earn a few hundred dollars. A rush to coffee ensued, and when the new gardens became productive a few years later, the Fore income from coffee jumped to a quarter of a million dollars a year. The coffee revolution was established.

At first the coffee was carried on the backs of its growers (sometimes for several days) over steep, rough mountain trails to a place where it could be sold to a buyer with a jeep. However, as more and more coffee was produced, the villagers began to turn with efforts to planning and constructing roads in association with neighboring villages. The newly built roads, in turn, stimulated further economic development and the opening of new trade stores throughout the region.

Following European example, the segregated collective men's and women's houses were abandoned. Family houses were adopted. This changed the social and territorial arena for all the young children, who hitherto had been accustomed to living equally with many members of their hamlet. It gave them a narrower place to belong, and it made them more distinctly someone's children. Uncomfortable in the family houses, boys who had grown up in a freer territory began to gather in "boys' houses," away from the adult men who were now beginning to live in family houses with their wives. Mothers began to wear blouses, altering the early freer access to the breast. Episodes of infant and child frustration, not seen in traditional Fore hamlets, began to take place along with repeated incidents of anger, withdrawal, aggressiveness and stinginess.

So Western technology worked its magic on the Fore, its powerful materials and practices quickly shattering their isolated autonomy and lifestyle. It took only a few years from the time Western intruders built their first grass-thatched patrol station before the Fore way of life they found was gone.

Fortunately, enough of the Fore traditional ways were systematically documented on film to reveal how unique a flower of human creation they were. Like nothing else, film made it possible to see the behavioral patterns of this way of life. The visual record, once made, captured data which was unnoticed and unanticipated at the time of filming and which was simply impossible to study without such records. Difficult-to-spot subtle patterns and fleeting nuances of manner, mood and human relations emerged by use of repeated reexamination of related incidents, sometimes by slow motion and stopped frame. Eventually the characteristic behavioral patterns of Fore life became clear, and an important aspect of human adaptive creation was revealed.

The Fore way of life was only one of the many natural experiments in living that have come into being through thousands of years of independent development in the world. The Fore way is now gone; those which remain are threatened. Under the impact of modern technology and commerce, the entire world is now rapidly becoming one system. By the year 2000 all the independent natural experiments that have come into being during the world's history will be merging into a single world system.

One of the great tragedies of our modern time may be that most of these independent experiments in living are disappearing before we can discover the implication of their special expressions of human possibility. Ironically, the same technology responsible for the worldwide cultural convergence has also provided the means by which we may capture detailed visual records of the yet remaining independent cultures. The question is whether we will be able to seize this never-to-be repeated opportunity. Soon it will be too late. Yet, obviously, increasing our understanding of the behavioral repertoire of humankind would strengthen our ability to improve life in the world.

Civilization and Its Discontents

Amazonian Indians experience the thin wedge of materialism

Katharine Milton

Katharine Milton first traveled to Brazil in 1979 to expand her studies of howler monkeys, which she began five years earlier in Panama. [She is] a professor of anthropology at the University of California, Berkeley.

For more than a decade now, I have led a double life. I spend part of my time in the United States, living in an apartment in Berkeley and teaching anthropology classes at the University of California. The rest of my time is spent in the Amazon Basin, where I live in the company of recently contacted Indian groups, studying their traditional ecology and features of their tropical forest environment. On returning to the United States after one of these extended stays in the jungle, I always experience culture shock as I strive to regain control of my possessions, which I have totally forgotten about.

Usually my first act is to retrieve my dust-covered car, which has languished for some six to eighteen months in a garage. The battery must be charged, and then I must wash and vacuum the car, fill it with gas, and check out its many parts. Once I am mobile, I rush to a large supermarket to stock up on cleaning supplies and food. My first few days are completely taken up with chores; there never seems to be a moment when I am not contemplating some type of home repair or new purchase.

And then there is my body. What a job it is to live up to what is expected of the average American. I must visit the dentist—often more than one kind

of dentist—to be sure my teeth are performing at top level. The doctor must be seen for a checkup; my eyes must be examined, glasses and contact lenses adjusted, and so on. I begin to wonder how my friends in Berkeley manage to have any free time at all, since I have fewer possessions than they do—I own no television set, no stereo or compact disk player, no video machine, home computer, food chopper, or any number of other items my friends seem to dote on. I don't even own my apartment.

Plunged back into life in Berkeley, I see myself as a slave of material possessions, and I notice that I deeply resent the time and energy required to maintain them. Nothing could be more different from the life I have been leading with hunter-gatherers deep in the rain forests of Brazil, where people have almost no possessions, and those that they do have are made from local forest materials and are entirely biodegradable.

The groups I have visited live far from any cities, towns, or commercial enterprises. They include the Mayoruna and Maku from Amazonas State; the Arara, Parakana, and Arawete from Pará State; and the Guaja from Maranhão State—peoples so remote and little known that few outside their immediate geographic area have heard of them. Often I am one of the first nonindigenous females many members of the group have ever seen. With my pale skin and hair I am a truly terrifying apparition to younger children, who sometimes scream with fear when they first see me.

All these peoples have been recently contacted: only a few months or, at most, years have passed since the Brazilian Indian Bureau (FUNAI) managed to establish a formal relationship with them. Previously, these groups avoided or were strongly hostile to outsiders, but with contact, they have permitted a few Indian Bureau employees to live with them, to assist them, and at times, protect them in dealings with other Indian groups or members of the wider Brazilian society. Living with these people has given me the chance to see how even modest changes in their traditional lifeways—the introduction of something as innocent in appearance as a metal cooking pot or ax, a box of matches or some salt—can be the thin edge of a wedge that will gradually alter the behavior and ecological practices of an entire society.

These people typically live in small villages of fewer than a hundred inhabitants, in some cases in groups of only fifteen or twenty. Most practice slash-and-burn agriculture on a small scale, complementing crop foods with wild game and fish, forest fruits and nuts, and occasionally, wild honey. For some months life may revolve around the village, but sooner or later every group I have worked with leaves, generally in small parties, and spends weeks or even months traveling through the forest and living on forest products.

Throughout the forest there are paths that the Indians know and have used for generations. They travel mainly when wild forest fruits and nuts are most abundant and game animals are fat, but families or small groups may go on expeditions at other times of year as well. They trek a few miles, make a temporary camp, and then hunt, gather, and eat several meals in the area before moving on to a new site. At certain times of year, many groups relocate to the borders of large rivers, where they obtain turtle eggs or other seasonal river foods.

The accumulation of possessions would be an impediment to this semi-nomadic life style. Whenever individuals go on a trek, they carry everything they need. Leaving possessions behind in a thatch-and-pole hut, to be retrieved later, is not an option, since the humid climate and voracious insects would quickly destroy them. Great numbers of insects often live inside Indian dwellings, principally jungle cockroaches that hide in the roof thatch by day but come out by the thousands at night. Indians seem oblivious to them, letting them run about on their bodies and even crawl on the food so long as they are not perched on the next bite.

Granted, these are generally soft-bodied, small jungle cockroaches and not the tough, large roaches of our urban areas, but even so, I found it difficult to adjust to them. My frantic efforts to remove cockroaches from my body and clothes were regarded as strange by my Indian hosts. At one site, I resorted to storing my clothing each night in a heavy plastic bag, which I sealed shut and suspended from a piece of plastic fish line tied to a roof pole. Otherwise, at night, the roaches covered my shirt and pants so thoroughly that often the fabric could not be seen. Although the roaches would be gone the next morning, they would leave a musty smell; further, just the idea of wearing garments that I had seen coated with cockroaches gave me a squirmy, unclean feeling.

On the forest treks, the women are invariably the most burdened, something Western observers often find difficult to understand or accept. A woman will walk for hours carrying a toddler, a large palm basket containing fifty or more pounds of animal or plant foods, hammocks, a cooking utensil or two, a machete, and the family pets, such as parrots, monkeys, and young puppies. In all the groups I have observed, the women's legs and feet are deformed by the pigeon-toed walk they adopt to give them added traction and stability on the slippery, narrow forest trails. The feet of adult men turn in only slightly, because men usually carry nothing heavier than a bow and arrows (ostensibly to be free to take advantage of any hunting opportunities).

The most important possession the Indians carry with them, however, is knowledge. There is nothing coded in the genome of an Indian concerning how to make a living in a tropical forest—each individual must become a walking bank of information on the forest landscape, its plants and animals, and their habits and uses. This information must be taught anew to the members of each generation, without the benefit of books, manuals, or educational television. Indians have no stores in which to purchase the things they need for survival. Instead, each individual must learn to collect, manufacture, or produce all the things required for his or her entire lifetime.

Because people differ in their talents, the pool of community information and abilities is far greater than its component parts. Individual men and women have their own areas of expertise, as well as their share of general knowledge. Members of the group know whom to consult for special information on hunting practices, the habits of particular game animals, rituals, tool manufacture, crop varieties, and the like.

Tropical-forest Indians talk incessantly, a characteristic I believe reflects the importance of oral transmission of culture. When I lived with the Maku, I slept in a hammock inside a small communal palm shelter. If a Maku awoke in the middle of the night, he usually began to talk or sing in a very loud voice—apparently without any thought that anyone might object to this behavior. It was considered normal, what you do when you wake up in the middle of the night and aren't sleepy. Others learn, as I did, to sleep through it or, if they aren't sleepy, to listen to it. Vocal expression apparently is expected and tolerated in Maku culture, no matter what the hour, an indication to me of how much it is valued.

Unlike our economic system, in which each person typically tries to secure and control as large a share of the available resources as possible, the hunter-gatherer economic system rests on a set of highly formalized expectations regarding cooperation and sharing. This does not mean hunter-gatherers do not compete with one another for prestige, sexual partners, and the like. But individuals do not amass a surplus. For instance, no hunter fortunate enough to kill a large game animal assumes that all this food is his or belongs only to his immediate family.

Quite the reverse is true: among some forest peoples, the hunter cannot eat game he has killed or is restricted to eating only one specific portion of his kill. Game is cut up and distributed according to defined patterns particular to each group and based in large part on kinship and marriage obligations. A hunter may have amazing luck one day, moderate luck on another, and no luck at all on a third. But he can usually expect to eat meat every day because someone bound to him in this system of reciprocity may well make a kill and share the meat.

Despite the way their culture traditionally eschews possessions, forest-living peoples embrace manufactured goods with amazing enthusiasm. They seem to appreciate instantly the efficacy of a steel machete, ax, or cooking pot. It is love at first sight, and the desire to possess such objects is absolute. There are accounts of Indian groups or individuals who have turned their backs on manufactured trade goods, but such people are the exception.

When Cândido Rondon, the founder of the Indian Protection Service in Brazil, began his pacification efforts in the early 1900s, he used trade goods as bait to attract uncontacted Indians. Pots, machetes, axes, and steel knives were hung from trees or laid along trails that Indians frequented. This practice proved so successful that it is still employed (see "Overtures to the

Nambiquara," by David Price, *Natural History,* October 1984).

Whether they have been formally contacted or not, forest-living groups in the Amazon Basin are probably well aware of steel tools and metal cooking pots. After all, such goods have been in circulation along trade routes in these regions for centuries, and an Indian does not have to have seen a non-Indian in order to acquire them. However, such manufactured goods are likely to be extremely scarce among uncontacted groups. When the Arara Indians were first approached in 1975, they fled their village to escape the pacification party. Examination of their hastily abandoned dwellings showed that stone tools were still being used, but a few steel fragments were also found.

Since they already appreciate the potential utility of manufactured goods, uncontacted Indians are strongly drawn to the new and abundant items offered to lure them from isolation. Once a group has been drawn into the pacification area, all its members are presented with various trade goods—standard gifts include metal cooking pots, salt, matches, machetes, knives, axes, cloth hammocks, T-shirts, and shorts. Not all members of the group get all of these items, but most get at least two or three of them, and in a family, the cumulative mass of new goods can be considerable.

The Indians initially are overwhelmed with delight—this is the honeymoon period when suddenly, from a position in which one or two old metal implements were shared by the entire group, a new situation prevails in which almost every adult individual has some of these wonderful new items. The honeymoon is short-lived, however. Once the Indians have grown accustomed to these new items, the next step is to teach them that these gifts will not be repeated. The Indians are now told that they must work to earn money or must manufacture goods for trade so that they can purchase new items.

Unable to contemplate returning to life without steel axes, the Indians begin to produce extra arrows or blowguns or hunt additional game or weave baskets beyond what they normally need so that this new surplus can be traded. Time that might, in the past, have been used for other tasks—subsistence activities, ceremonial events, or whatever—is now devoted to production of barter goods. In addition, actual settlement patterns may be altered so that the indigenous group is in closer, more immediate contact with sources of manufactured items. Neither of these things, in itself, is necessarily good or bad, but each does alter traditional behavior.

Thus, the newly contacted forest people are rapidly drawn into the wider economic sphere (even into the international economy: for example, the preferred glass beads for personal adornment come from Czechoslovakia). The intrusion of every item—mirrors, cloth, scissors, rice, machetes, axes, pots, bowls, needles, blankets, even bicycles and radios—not only adds to the pressure on individuals to produce trade goods but also disrupts some facet of traditional production.

Anthropologist Paul Henley, who worked with the Panare, a forest-based people in Venezuela, points out that with the introduction of steel tools, particularly axes, indigenous groups suffer a breakdown in the web of cooperative interdependence. In the past, when stone axes were used, various individuals came together and worked communally to fell trees for a new garden. With the introduction of the steel ax, however, one man can clear a garden by himself. As Henley notes, collaboration is no longer mandatory nor particularly frequent.

Indians often begin to cultivate new crops, such as coffee, that they feel can be traded or sold easily. Another is rice, which the Indian Bureau encourages forest peoples to plant because, of course, all "real" Brazilians eat rice every day. Rice is an introduced crop both to Brazil and to forest Indians. Traditional crop foods, the successful cultivation of which has been worked out over generations in the forest environment and which are well suited to the soil conditions in particular regions, may become scarce, with the result that the Indian diet becomes unbalanced.

Indians who traditionally plant manioc as a staple crop may be encouraged to increase the size of their fields and plant more manioc, which can then be transformed into *farinha,* a type of cereal that can be sold in the markets. Larger fields mean more intensive agricultural work and less time to hunt—which also affects the diet. The purchase of a shotgun may temporarily improve hunting returns, but it also tends to eliminate game in the area. In addition, shotgun shells are very expensive in Brazil, costing more than $1 U.S. apiece. Dependence on the shotgun undermines a hunter's skill with traditional hunting weapons, such as blowguns and bows and arrows, as well as the ability required to manufacture them.

Clearing larger areas for fields can also lead to increased risk from diseases such as malaria and leishmanaisis, because cleared areas with standing water of low acidity permit proliferation of disease-bearing mosquitoes and flies. New diseases also appear. Anthropologist-epidemiologist Carlos Coimbra, Jr., for example, has shown that Chagas disease, which is transmitted to humans by trypanosome-carrying assassin bugs, apparently does not yet affect Indian populations in lowland areas of the Amazon Basin. Only when Indians cease their seminomadic way of life and begin to live for prolonged periods in the same dwellings can Chagas-carrying bugs adjust their feeding behavior and begin to depend on human hosts rather than small rodents for their blood meals.

The moment manufactured foods begin to intrude on the indigenous diet, health takes a downward turn. The liberal use of table salt (sodium chloride), one of the first things that Indians are given, is probably no more healthful for them than it is for Westerners. Most Indians do not have table salt; they manufacture small quantities of potassium salts by burning certain types of leaves and collecting the ash. Anthropologist Darrell Posey reports that the Kayapo Indians of Brazil make salt ash from various palm species and use each type for specific foods.

Sweets and other foods containing refined sugar (sucrose) are also given to Indians, whose wild fruits, according to research by botanists Irene and Herbert Baker, contain primarily other sugars, such as fructose. Indians find that foods containing sucrose taste exceptionally sweet, and they tend to crave them once sampled. While a strong, sugary taste in the natural environment might signal a rare, rich energy source, the indiscriminate consumption of canned foods, candies, and gums containing large amounts of refined sugar contributes to tooth decay and can lead to obesity and even health problems such as diabetes.

Results of dietary change are often difficult to anticipate. Anthropologist Dennis Werner found that the Mekranoti of central Brazil, who did not make pottery, traditionally roasted most of their food. But the introduction of metal cooking pots allowed them to switch to boiled foods. This, in turn, allowed nursing mothers to provide supplemental foods to their infants at an earlier age. Werner found that the average nursing period in the Mekranoti had dropped steadily from 19.7 months prior to 1955 to 16 months in recent years, which corresponded to the period of steady increase in the use of metal cooking pots in the village.

One of the first things the Indian Bureau doctors generally do after contact is try to protect the Indians from the Western diseases that may be communicated to them during their first prolonged interaction with outsiders. The doctors give them immunizations and may also hand out drugs to prevent or eradicate dangerous malarias. Preg-nant women, infants, and preadolescents often receive massive doses of antibiotics. Antibiotics and antimalarial drugs, although helpful in some respects, may also have detrimental effects. For example, individuals exposed to antibiotics in utero or when young generally have teeth that are abnormally dark and discolored. Some drugs are reputed to interfere with fertility among women in recently contacted groups. If this lack of fertility combines with a drop in population size due to deaths from new diseases, a population can fall to a precarious low.

Perhaps the most critical disruption suffered by these groups, however, concerns how detailed information on features of the forest environment is diluted and forgotten. This is the pool of shared knowledge that traditionally has been the bedrock, the economic currency, the patrimony of each of these nontechnological forest societies. Manuel Lizarralde, a doctoral student at the University of California, Berkeley, who has done ethnobotanical work with the Bari of Venezuela, reports that in just a single generation there was a staggering loss of information about the identity of forest trees and their uses.

Despite this tale of disruption, disease, and destruction, many of the indigenous forest cultures are proving to be far more resilient than might be expected. The indigenous peoples remaining today in the Amazon Basin are true survivors who have successfully resisted the diseases, explorers, missionaries, soldiers, slave traders, rubber tappers, loggers, gold miners, fur traders, and colonists who have persis-tently encroached on them during the past five centuries.

Anthropologist Bill Balée, for example, has found that the Ka'apor Indians of Maranhão State, in peaceful contact with outsiders since 1928, still maintain many features of their traditional economy, social organization, and ritual life. He attributes this to the continued integrity of the nuclear family and the persistence of specific ritual duties between husband and wife that prohibit certain foods at different seasons or life stages. Such ritual practices have not only spared red-legged tortoises and other wild resources from being overharvested but have also diffused hunting pressures over a large area, thereby contributing to the persistence of the traditional economy.

Unfortunately, cultural persistence will do indigenous peoples no good if their tropical forest habitat is destroyed. Deforestation is primarily the result of outside influences, such as lumbering, cattle ranching, and colonization, that are permitted by government policies. Some estimates suggest that all remaining tropical forests will be destroyed by the year 2045.

Once the technological roller coaster gets moving, it's hard to jump off or even pause to consider the situation. Some say, so what? We can't all go back to the jungle, we can't all become forest-living Indians. No, we can't. But as I stand in my apartment in Berkeley, listening to my telephone's insistent ring and contemplating my unanswered mail, dusty curtains, dripping faucets, and stacks of newspapers for recycling, I'm not sure we wouldn't be far happier if we could.

Dark Dreams About the White Man

Thomas Gregor

Thomas Gregor, associate professor of anthropology at Vanderbilt University, is the author of Mehinaku: The Drama of Daily Life in a Brazilian Indian Village, *published by the University of Chicago Press.*

Last night my dream was very bad.
I dreamed of the white man.

A Mehinaku villager

In 1500 explorer Pedro Cabral landed on the coast of Brazil and claimed its lands and native peoples for the Portuguese empire. Since that time Brazilian Indians have been killed by European diseases and bounty hunters, forced off their land by squatters and speculators, and enslaved by ranchers and mine owners. Today the Indians, numbering less than one-tenth of the precontact population, inhabit the most remote regions of the country.

I have been privileged as an anthropologist to live among the Mehinaku, a tribe of about eighty tropical-forest Indians who have thus far escaped the destruction. The Mehinaku, along with eight other single-village tribes, live in a vast government-protected reservation in the Mato Grosso, at the headwaters of the Xingu River in central Brazil. Collectively called Xinguanos by the outside world, the Mehinaku and their neighbors speak dialects of four unrelated languages. In spite of their cultural differences,

they have developed a peaceful system of relationships based on intermarriage, trade, and group rituals. This political achievement persists, thanks largely to the geographic isolation of the Xingu reservation. Even today, the Brazilian presence consists only of an outpost of the Brazilian Indian Agency and a small, dirt-strip air force base. Nearly 200 miles of forest and savanna separate the Xingu villages from Shavantina, the nearest permanent Brazilian settlement of any size.

Despite the remoteness of central Brazil and the traditional character of village life, even a casual visitor to the Mehinaku sees unexpected signs of Brazilian society: battery-operated shortwave radios (usually tuned to backwoods popular favorites), battered aluminum pots for carrying water, and discarded items of Western clothing. But these, and the other flotsam and jetsam of industrial society that drift to the center of Brazil, affect only the appearance of Indian culture. They catch the eye of the visitor, but they do not break the rhythm of traditional subsistence, ritual, and trade that are the heartbeat of Xingu life.

Although geographically and socially distant, urban Brazil peers nonetheless into the world of the Xinguanos. Popular magazines feature articles about their life in a "jungle paradise," and smiling Xingu faces adorn postcards sold at Rio newsstands. Recently, a film shot in the

Xingu reservation was woven into a *novela,* an afternoon television soap opera. So heavily exposed are the physically handsome Xingu tribes that in the popular mind they *are* the Brazilian Indian.

Brazilian officials have their own use for the Xinguanos. Faced with charges of neglect and even genocide against its native peoples, the government has used the tribes of the area for public relations. Happy, well-nourished Xinguanos decorate government publications, and when necessary, the Indians themselves can be counted on to amuse visiting dignitaries. High consular officials from the diplomatic corps in Brasília and other international elite have flown out to the Xingu reservation for adventure and entertainment. Almost invariably their visits have been a success and they have returned home with an impression of idyllic relationships between the Brazilian authorities and the Xinguanos. But if such visitors came to know their hosts more intimately, they would learn that contact with the white man has had a profound and bitter impact on the Indians' inner life.

During my work among the Mehinaku I have become increasingly aware of the villagers' anxieties about the white man. The soldiers at the nearby air force base, whom they regard as powerful and unpredictable, are especially frightening to the Mehinaku. On one occasion a rumor swept through the community that a plane from the base was going to bomb the village because one of the Mehinaku had stolen a mosquito net belonging to an air force sergeant. This wild story was believable because it drew on a reservoir of anxiety and confusion about the white man. Recently, I have been studying the villagers' dreams as a way of learning about their unconscious fears.

According to the Mehinaku, dreams are caused by the wandering of the "shadow," or soul, which is conceived of as a tiny replica of the individual living within the eye. As the villagers demonstrate to children or to the inquisitive anthropologist, the soul's image can be seen as a reflection in a pool of water or even in the iris of another person's eye. The soul is said to leave its owner at night to wander about. "Far, far away my soul wandered last night," is the opening phrase that may begin a dream narration. In the dream world of the community and the surrounding forests, the soul meets the wandering souls of animals, spirits, and other villagers. These experiences come into the dreamer's awareness in a way the villagers do not fully understand. "Dreams come up," they say, "as corn comes up from the ground."

The nightly adventures of the soul through the nocturnal village and forest are interpreted with the help of an unwritten dream book, a collection of dream symbols and their deciphered meanings. To the Mehinaku, dream symbols (patalapiri, literally "pictures," or "images") represent events to come. Frequently, the predictions resemble the dream symbol in their appearance or activity. For example, since weeds are symbols of hair, a dream of a well-cleared path is symbolic of baldness in later life. Occasionally, the dream symbol is more abstract and poetic. A dream about collecting edible flying ants suggests bereavement, since the rain of ants that descends on the village in the fall of each year is likened to the tears that fall when a kinsman dies.

As the last example suggests, many Mehinaku dream symbols are gloomy forecasts of death or misfortune. The grimmest omens of all, however, are those that deal with the white man. Any dream about a Brazilian is a bad dream. Even a dream prominently featuring an object associated with Brazilians, such as an airplane, is distressing. Dreams of the white man are, for the Mehinaku, "pictures" of disease. A person who has such a dream is likely to become sick. In support of this interpretation, the villagers point out that many illnesses—measles, colds, influenza—are brought in from the outside. These diseases have had a devastating impact on the community. In the early 1960s, nearly 20 percent of the tribe died in a measles epidemic, and the villagers continue to suffer from imported diseases for which they have neither natural nor acquired immunity. Dreams such as the following one reflect such concerns:

At the post a plane landed. Many, many passengers got off. It seemed as if there was a village in the plane. I was very frightened of them and the things they carried. I was afraid they would bring a disease to the village, the white man's "witchcraft."

The Mehinaku fear of the white man goes beyond the fear of disease, as I learned when I began to make a collection of their dreams. The villagers were willing collaborators in this effort since they regard dreams as significant and make a deliberate effort to recall them when they wake up. In the morning, as I circulated from house to house to harvest the previous night's crop of dreams, I would occasionally be summoned across the plaza ("Tommy, I have a dream for you!") by a villager with a particularly dramatic narrative. Altogether I collected 385 dreams, the majority of which (70 percent) were contributed by the men.

In thirty-one of the sample dreams, Brazilians were cast as the central characters. What is striking about these dreams is their high level of anxiety. While about half of the villagers' dreams show some level of anxiety, fully 90 percent of the dreams of the white man are tinged with fear. Furthermore, when I rated dreams on the basis of their frightening content and the dreamer's own report of distress, I found that dreams of the white man were charged with more than double the average level of anxiety. This was higher than any other comparable class of dreams, even dreams of malignant spirits and dangerous animals.

Occasionally, the mere sight or sound of an outsider creates anxiety: "I heard them speaking on the radio at the post, but I could not understand. The speech and the language were frightening to me." Within the sample of dreams, however, I found a number of terrifying themes that repeatedly appeared in the villagers' narratives. The most prominent of these are heat and fire. In the dreams, Brazilian soldiers explode incendiary devices in the village, burning houses and people. Fiery planes crash and blow up in the central plaza, covering the villagers with flames. Even when the victims throw themselves in the river, the fire continues to burn their clothes and skin.

We went to the place where the canoe was moored. A plane came overhead and broke in the sky. It crashed in the water and everything caught on fire. The gasoline floated on the water. My mother caught on fire.

Fire and heat are appropriate symbols of terror among the Mehinaku. The villagers live in large thatch houses, often as much as 100 feet long, 30 feet wide, and 20 feet high. Two narrow doors in the middle of the house and a complete lack of windows minimize the intrusion of biting insects, but make the houses firetraps. On occasion, the Mehinaku deliberately burn abandoned houses and the resultant blaze is instructive. While the villagers watch, the house owner sets fire to some of the thatch at the base of the building. Within moments, white smoke pours through the wall, and suddenly an entire side of the house bursts into flame. Seconds later, the convection of air and heat turns the building into a blazing inferno. As the Mehinaku edge back from the wall of heat and flame, they consider what would happen if an occupied house caught on fire. "If the fire begins when the people are asleep," one of the villagers told me, "then everyone burns."

Less dangerous than house fires, but almost as frightening, are fires that are deliberately set to clear the villagers' gardens. The Mehinaku are slash-and-burn agriculturists who clear a plot of land in the forest, allow the vegetation to dry, and then set it on fire. The blaze sends up towers of white smoke that can be seen for miles. Once started, the fire is totally out of control. The villagers say that it is "wildly angry," and they tell myths of how men and spirits have gone to their death, trapped in the burning fields. This danger is more than fictional, since villagers have been badly burned when the wind shifted as they were firing their gardens. Dreams that link the white man to heat and fire thus associate him with one of the most frightening and destructive forces in the Mehinaku environment.

A second recurrent theme in dreams of the white man is assault. Villagers are shot with rifles, strafed from planes, pursued by trucks, and attacked with machetes. At times, as in the following dream of a young man, the assault is sexually motivated:

We were at the air force base, and a soldier wanted to have sex with my sister. He took her arm and tried to pull her away. We shouted at the soldier and at my sister. My aunt and I tried to pull her back. But the soldier was too strong for us. He was very strong. He said "If you don't let me have sex with Mehinaku women I will shoot you." I got a gun and shot at him, many times. But he was hidden and I couldn't see him.

Another dreamer described a similar situation:

A Brazilian doctor tried to take away my sister. . . . "If you don't let me, I will kill you," he said. . . . He shot and killed my two brothers. I cried in my dream, and I cried when I woke up.

Assault, like fire and heat, has an especially potent role in the Mehinaku symbolism of fear. In comparing themselves to other Indians and to whites, the villagers invariably point out that they are a peaceful people. There is no word for war in their language

other than "many flying arrows," nor is there a historical record of the Mehinaku having participated in organized, armed violence. When attacked by the Carib-speaking Txicão tribe in the 1960s, they responded by cowering in their houses as arrows whistled through the thatch walls. After the chief sustained a serious arrow wound in his back, they moved the village closer to the Indian post in the hope that they would not be pursued.

Within the village, strong sanctions bar interpersonal violence. The man who lets his anger get the best of him is slurred as a *japujaitsi* (literally, "angry man," but also a species of nearly inedible hot pepper). There are no *japujaitsi* in the village, and in my year and a half residence in the community, I never saw a fight between men. As one villager put it, "When we are angry, we wrestle, and the anger is gone. When the white men are angry, they shoot each other."

The menace of white society is real to the Mehinaku because of the accounts they have heard at the Indian post about Brazilian atrocities against Indians. They know that in the recent past Indians have been shot, poisoned, and enslaved by bounty hunters and, during one particularly shameful period prior to the establishment of the present Indian agency in 1967, by some government employees working for the former Indian agency. They know, too, that their lands are insecure and that the boundaries of the Xingu reservation can—and do—change according to the whim of bureaucrats in Brasília. A road has already penetrated the far northern end of the reservation and has brought tribes in that area into violent conflict with white ranchers. There is thus good reason to be wary of the Brazilian. As in the case of fire, dreams of assault and aggression link the white man to very real sources of anxiety in waking life.

A final theme of fear that permeates the villagers' dreams is perhaps the most poignant. In many of the narratives, the dreamer expresses a sense of disorientation in dealing with the outsiders. The white men lack

comprehensible motivation and perform capricious acts of malice and violence. They distract mothers from their crying infants, they give presents and demand them back, and they kidnap small children. They lure a man to a distant Brazilian city, cut off his head, and send it back to his horrified kin. Disguised as Mehinaku, they tempt the dreamer to give up his life as an Indian, and urge him to accompany them to distant cities from which he will never return. A mother dreams of losing her young children to the outsider:

My children said they would go to visit the Brazilians. They said they would go to São Paulo and Rio de Janeiro, and Cuiabá. I told them not to go. But they went, far off. We waited a long time, but they did not come back. I went to find them, but I could not. My mother's sister came to help me, and we looked all over. Then I heard them crying from a far way off, but still I could not find them. Then, I awoke.

Some of the dreams border on the Kafkaesque:

A guard pointed a gun at me. He told me to go through a door. I did. The room was filled with a beautiful light. The guard gave me a watch and told me I could come out at a certain time. He locked the door. I looked at the watch, and I realized I did not know how to tell time. There was a wind and a strange smell.

The confused portrayal of the white man stems from the Mehinaku's distorted view of Brazilian life. To the villagers, everyday Brazilian conduct and ordinary material objects are both alluring and strange. Tape recorders, radios, cameras, and other gadgets sported by visitors to the Xingu reservation fascinate the Mehinaku but also perplex them. Even when these objects are dismantled and inspected, they don't give up their secrets. "Are the white men wizards?" I was once asked by one of the Mehinaku.

Those villagers who have visited São Paulo and Rio de Janeiro return home with the same sense of fascinated puzzlement. A young man, the narrator of the dream text above, spent a summer living with a vacationing upper-class family in the beach resort of Guarujá outside of São Paulo.

7. SOCIOCULTURAL CHANGE: THE IMPACT OF THE WEST

He was intrigued and attracted by what he saw, but uncomprehending. The wealth of Guarujá seemed magically produced; certainly members of the family were not making their possessions with their own hands, as do the Xinguanos. On the same trip he saw impoverished beggars on São Paulo's streets, but once he was back in the tribe, most of his stories were about the magic and glitter of the city.

The outsider visiting the Mehinaku senses the gap of understanding in another way. Let a man arrive in the community and he is immediately questioned about his kinsmen. Does he have a wife? parents? sisters? Which of his kinsmen gave him his jacket? Was it his brother-in-law? The Xingu communities are kin based, and the questions are an effort to place the white man in the orbit of under-standable social relationships. If he remains within the community, the villagers probe further, often by teasing their guest. His appearance, gait, name, and speech become the object of semihumorous (and often painful) ridicule. This period of hazing has been reported by many researchers in the Xingu, and its predictability persuades me that it is part of the effort to make the powerful outsider knowable. If he has weaknesses and can be hurt, then he is human and understandable.

The many years of friendly but superficial contact with Brazilians have not made the white man more intelligible to the Mehinaku. As of my most recent visit in 1977, none of the villagers was able to explain why the Brazilians had come to the Xingu forests. "The white man is here," the chief told me in all seriousness, "to give us presents." The economic and political forces that led the Brazilian government into the interior of the continent to construct bases such as the Indian post are mysterious to the Mehinaku. The Brazilians and their impersonal society seem nearly as bizarre and disjointed in waking life as they do in the villagers' dreams.

Mehinaku lands and culture remain largely intact, but a part of their inner tranquility has been laid to waste. Neither geographic isolation nor heroic efforts at protection could save it. Contact with Brazilian society has taken a higher toll than we might have anticipated. Certainly the Mehinaku have paid dearly for their steel tools, their cast-off clothes, and the other "gifts of civilization." By day, all appears well. But each night, we outsiders visit the sleeping villagers and haunt them in restless dreams.

A People at Risk

The Yanomami of Brazil

Peter Gorman

Peter Gorman, a free-lance writer and collector for the American Museum of Natural History, has researched and written extensively about the peoples of the Amazon.

The spiritual beliefs of the Yanomami Indians of northern Amazonia are based on a worldview in which spirits exist not only in plants, animals, and humans, but in two parallel universes located above and below the world. Those spirits who inhabit the upper world assist their creator, Omam, in keeping the world abundant so that the Yanomami may have fruitful lives; those who inhabit the lower world are vengeful and do little but bring illness and trouble to the Yanomami. To undo the trouble caused by the evil spirits, the Yanomami depend upon their shamans, tribal medicine men who not only understand the uses of medicinal plants but can call on the helpful spirits of the natural world to aid in the daily struggle to keep their universe in balance by keeping the vengeful spirits in check.

That worldview, like all aspects of Yanomami culture, grows out of their intimate relationship with the earth and all things in it. Just how complex and important that relationship is to the Yanomami is abundantly clear in their creation myth: The Yanomami not only witnessed the birth of the earth, they evolved with it. Their allies are the birds and animals; their garden the forest; the game they eat, their animal ancestors; and their demons, the spirits who have no land on which to hunt.

But in recent years that relationship has been put at great risk. During the early 1970s, Brazil's then-military government began to build a series of roads through Amazonia to open up the forest for settlement. This encroachment into Yanomami lands set into motion a series of events that today threatens the Yanomami's continued existence.

CULTURAL CLASH

One of those roads, the Perimetral Norté, built in 1983, was designed to run along Brazil's northern border, cutting through the heart of Yanomami territory. Although the Perimetral Norté was never completed, reports from Survival International, an organization that works for the rights of indigenous peoples worldwide, say that "the pre-

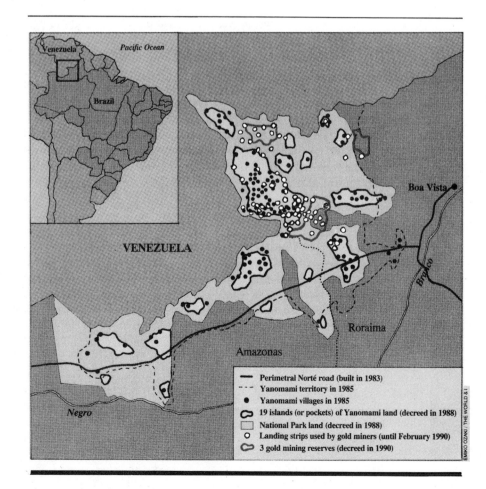

Legend:
— Perimetral Norté road (built in 1983)
--- Yanomami territory in 1985
• Yanomami villages in 1985
⌒ 19 islands (or pockets) of Yanomami land (decreed in 1988)
▢ National Park land (decreed in 1988)
○ Landing strips used by gold miners (until February 1990)
⌒ 3 gold mining reserves (decreed in 1990)

EMIKO OZAKI / THE WORLD & I

This article appeared in *The World & I*, November 1991, pp. 670-681. Reprinted with permission from *The World & I*, a publication of The Washington Times Corporation. © 1991.

Yanomami Creation Myth

A long time ago, a great shaman died. His spirit helpers were so angry about losing their chief that they began to cut a huge piece out of the sky. The ripped sky fell on top of the earth, pushing the forest and the mountains down into the underworld. The sun and the night spirits fell as well, and the people ran about in fear, screaming "aaaaaaa!"

Now in the place where the rivers are born, the fallen sky was sitting at the foot of a cacao tree, forming the mountains where the Yanomami live today. And some of the Yanomami ran to hide behind the tree to escape the falling sky, and with them was a parrot. The parrot scraped at the sky with its beak, making a hole for the Yanomami to climb through.

The Yanomami came up through the hole in the sky, and they looked around at the new world. They looked around at the new mountains and the rivers being born, and then they looked around for game to hunt, but there was none since the animals didn't exist yet. But they saw the trees of the forest and knew they were in the heart of the sky, so they spread all over the forest and began to plant gardens.

The forest was so new that it kept changing, and the people in the world kept changing like the forest. They became parrots, tapirs, and alligators. They became macaws, red deer, jaguars, toucans, sloths, and armadillos. The meat we eat today is from those people who changed into animals, from those animal ancestors.

And where the sky fell there was a new sky called *hedu ka misi*, the place where the souls of the departed go. It is the same as the earth, but only spirits live there. And the earth, *hei ka misi, is* the place we Yanomami live. The Yanomami who are on earth were created by Omam, who created us without any reason by ripping open the hollow trunk of a tall palm tree.

And underneath the earth is the underworld, *hei ta bibi,* which was created when the sky fell and pushed the old earth down. In the underworld there is only a single village where cannibal people-spirits with long teeth live. The spirits who live there have no land on which to hunt, so they capture the souls of children here on earth to eat.

How the World Began: The Yanomami Creation Myth, *told by Ikahi Yanoami; recorded by Bruce Albert; adapted by Peter Gorman.*

---

liminary works were enough to introduce a series of diseases—flu, measles, malaria—to the thirteen villages of the region. The communities were decimated by the epidemics, with a 90 percent loss of life in some places."

Even worse for the Yanomami, as part of the road building scheme, Brazil's government, under the leadership of then-President José Sarney, also began the first aerial surveys of remote Amazonia. Those surveys done in the north revealed that the Yanomami lands contained cassiterite ore (for tin), radioactive materials, and gold.

The discovery of gold quickly turned the little city of Boa Vista—the capital of Roraima, the state in which the Yanomami territory is located—into a boomtown. Miners flew in from the eastern cities and fanned out into the forest, panning for gold in the streams and rivers that crisscross the region. The rush has brought nearly fifty thousand miners to the Yanomami territory since 1985. Their presence jeopardizes not only the Yanomami culture, but the Yanomami themselves.

Since their arrival, the miners have carved more than 120 clandestine air-strips out of the tropical forest; they have dammed dozens of rivers to provide enough hydraulic pressure to strip the surface soil from the forest floor, making access to the gold easier. Water supplies have been contaminated by the mercury burned to separate the gold from impurities, destroying marine life and causing birth defects and neurological disorders among the indigenous people. Epidemics of malaria, flu, measles, and tuberculosis have spread rapidly from the mining camps to the Yanomami villages; venereal diseases, virtually unknown among the tribal peoples, have been introduced by miners to Yanomami women, who have been compelled—by economic need or physical force—to work as prostitutes. Game, which had always been plentiful, has been hunted out of whole areas, causing malnutrition and related diseases for the first time in the region. Additionally, there have been numerous substantiated reports of violent conflict between the miners and the Yanomami.

News of the plight of the Yanomami was slow to reach the outside world. That changed, however, when four Yanomami men and one miner were killed in a confrontation after the Yanomami wandered into a small mining camp in 1987. The killings sparked a public outcry demanding that Brazil's then-President Sarney take decisive action. Sarney responded by ordering the removal of all journalists, priests, anthropologists, medical personnel, and international relief organization workers from the Yanomami territory!

"Essentially, they wanted to get rid of all the inconvenient witnesses," says Bruce Albert, an anthropologist who has worked extensively with the Yanomami. But according to Albert, the reasoning behind Sarney's action was not limited to preventing the outside world from watching a tragedy of such proportions unfold: Sarney also intended to reduce the size of the Yanomami territory, something he had been unable to do under the scrutiny of the international community.

That territory, an area of 37,000 square miles in upper Brazil, was protected under rights granted to the Yanomami by the Brazilian constitution. But while the constitution guaranteed the rights of the Yanomami to their traditional lands, the land had never been demarked nor formally titled to the Yanomami, creating a legal loophole by which a large portion of those lands could be removed from their "restricted area" status and opened for public use. While Sarney had tried to implement such a land-reduction scheme for several years, it was not until 1988, after the expulsion of all nonmining outsiders, that it was successfully effected.

Sarney's 1988 plan called for the immediate reduction of Yanomami lands from 37,000 square miles to 12,000, and the creation of nineteen "islands of habitation" within the territory that would be formally titled to the Yanomami. The remainder of the land was redefined as state park and national forest land, on which gold mining was permissible by law.

Proponents of Sarney's plan saw it as a way both to appease the Yanomami and the gold miners—thousands of whom were land-poor peasants from the overcrowded cities in eastern Brazil—and to elevate world opinion with regard to Brazil's treatment of its indigenous peoples.

Opponents of the plan argued that opening up corridors of land around the Yanomami islands of habitation to the gold miners encouraged the continued spread of disease and depletion of available game. They warned that Sarney's plan threatened the entire ecology of the region by allowing the continued use of mercury and the damming of rivers.

All of the arguments, both pro and con, were rendered moot when Survival International instituted a suit on behalf of the Yanomami concerning the plan. In October 1989, the Brazilian High Court found Sarney's plan unconstitutional and ordered the removal of all gold miners from the territory.

Sarney, complying with the court's directive, ordered the expulsion of the miners and the bombing of their clandestine airstrips to begin in January 1990, in an operation called Free Forest. The operation had little federal support and was halted after just forty-eight hours, when angry miners threatened violence.

But the high court's decision was not entirely in vain: In early 1990, the ban on medical personnel in the area was lifted, and six teams of doctors were admitted to the Yanomami territory. Their initial survey of the region indicated that nearly two thousand of the nine thousand Brazilian Yanomami had already died, and thousands more would die from diseases they had already contracted.

MONEY MATTERS MORE

In March 1990, President Sarney was replaced by Fernando Collor de Mello. Early in his term President Collor admitted that it would be nearly impossible to evacuate the miners from Yanomami lands without violence, and suggested a compromise arrangement that would return all but 3,000 square miles of the territory to the Yanomami. In exchange for permission to remain on those lands, miners representatives agreed to have them deliver their firearms to the police, cut their currency use in half, and pay a gold tax to be used to build and support schools and medical clinics for the Yanomami.

Brazil's then-justice minister, Saolo Romos, hailed the compromise as "a Brazilian-style solution—with sugar and affection." Critics of the plan denounced it as a violation of the high court order and said the presence of any miners would eventually lead to the death of all the Yanomami. Some, including Survival International and the Indigenous Missionary Council, have even called the compromise genocide. And Sen. Severo Gomes, who has witnessed the Yanomami villages personally, says, "Leaving the situation as it is means the final solution to the problem of the Yanomami: extermination."

After his decision to reduce the amount of Yanomami land available to the miners, Collor took a wait-and-see attitude during his first year in office—when nearly 18,000 miners left the region voluntarily. But on April 20, 1991, in a ceremony held in the nation's capital, Brasília, he revoked the rights of all outsiders to any traditional Yanomami land. "The government now in-

tends to set an example in the treatment of indigenous lands," said Collor's justice minister, Jarbas Passarinho, at the ceremony. "By isolating the region we are protecting the Yanomami people and minimizing the problems of contact with nonindigenous peoples."

At that time, Collor failed to title the lands to the Yanomami, saying that his government needed time to survey the region's boundaries, but that the surveying would begin within six months of his decree. Neither did he explain how the removal of the miners would be affected, saying merely that "the only exception to the ban on non-Indian men entering the area will be employees of the government's National Indian Foundation."

While most Indian rights' groups cheered Collor's decision, there is some concern that the ban will include journalists, medical personnel, international relief organization workers, and others from the international community who might monitor the decree's enforcement.

The miners and their representatives have vowed to fight the evacuation. They, as well as many of Brazil's local officials, continue to claim that it is impractical to try to remove tens of thousands of miners from the Yanomami territory, and that the gold they bring out of the area is helping to develop an underdeveloped part of the country. There have been estimates, they point out, that suggest that there may be enough gold in the Yanomami region to repay Brazil's entire $134 billlon international debt.

The argument that the gold might pay to develop the area, however, or that it could in any way substantially lower the international debt, carries little weight, since almost none is taxed. According to a *London Times Sunday Magazine* report on September 9, 1990:

The Brazilian Government received only 80kg of gold from the entire 1989 mining operation, perhaps 1% of production. Hundreds of kilos are smuggled out of Brazil to gain the higher international price, or, as is strongly rumored in Boa Vista, used by the Medellin cartel in Colombia to trade cocaine.

It remains to be seen whether Collor will act decisively on his decree of April 20—whether he intends to drag out the situation through the length of his term in office, or whether he genuinely intends to survey the boundaries of the Yanomami territory, title them the land, and successfully evacuate the illegal miners. And even if he should, it remains to be seen whether the action will come in time to save the Yanomami. At best, perhaps half the remaining Yanomami could survive. At worst, they will die out before the turn of the century.

There are some who speculate that this was the government's intention from the beginning: that by allowing land-poor peasants to bring disease to the area, it believed, the Yanomami could be exterminated without any government intervention, opening up the area for industrial mining of the huge gold and uranium deposits. That is, of course, a sinister and awful scenario. But given the history of the treatment of indigenous peoples, not only in Brazil but throughout the Americas, it is not beyond possibility.

LIVING IN ISOLATION

The factors that made the Yanomami vulnerable to extermination have historically been their strength in maintaining cultural integrity. The ruggedness of the terrain and the remoteness of the region have allowed them to develop in almost complete isolation from the outside world. Until recently, little was known about them.

The earliest reports came from missionaries who made contact during the 1940s. Those reports suggested that the Yanomami were a classic example of a Stone Age tribe that had survived into the twentieth century.

During the 1950s, anthropologists followed the missionaries' lead into Yanomami territory, but it was not until 1968 that the first major study of their culture was published. Written by anthropologist Napolean Chagnon as a doctoral dissertation, the study concentrated on the violent aspects of the Yanomamo (the *o* has since been changed to an *i*), suggesting that the Yanomami proved the philosophical theory that primitive man's instincts were of a violent nature and, if unchecked by societal restrictions, would be expressed frequently and with little provocation. As samples of Yanomano violence, Chagnon pointed to ritualized blood sports, violent intravillage raiding, kidnapping, and revenge killing.

But Chagnon had been so enthralled by the violent aspects of the Yanomami that he overlooked much of the true nature of their culture, which has evolved over the course of thousands of years into a complex system of give-and-take with the forests they inhabit. And while the Yanomami are capable of violence (the jungle, after all, is a dangerous place), they are also ardent students of nature, natural conservationists. They are a people who prize generosity and imagination as the highest human characteristics.

The Yanomami live in large communities centered around a single circular dwelling called a *yano*, which may be shared by as many as four hundred people. Like many Amazonian forest dwellers, they are semiagrarian hunter-gatherers who depend upon the land for all of their needs. They cultivate a number of food and medicinal plants in communal gardens located in the forest a short distance from the village. The protein in their diet is supplied by hunting; the remainder of their needs are supplied by gathering.

Most work-related activities are well defined by gender: the clearing of the jungle for gardens, building of new yanos—constructed by covering a pole framework with braided palm fronds—hunting, and protecting the village are the province of the men. Gardening, cooking, child rearing, and weaving are done by the women. Gathering chores are shared by everyone.

Because the Yanomami men are primarily hunters and warriors, both dangerous occupations, there is a higher incidence of death among them than there is among the women, making the adult population predominantly female. To account for the excess women, the Yanomami are polygamous; the number of wives a man may take is dependent upon his abilities to protect and provide for them. It is the acquisition of wives—and the social prestige they bring—that is responsible for much of the violence in their culture; a shortage of available women in one community frequently leads to intravillage raiding and kidnapping, which in turn leads to both blood challenges and revenge killing.

Despite that aspect of their society, much of the Yanomami culture grows from a communal tradition. Hunters never eat the animals they have killed: They provide for their families, then give the remainder to someone else, who will reciprocate their generosity.

The Power of Gold

"What we call *xawara,* our ancestors kept hidden for a long time. Omam kept the xawara hidden. He kept it hidden and did not want the Yanomami to touch it. He used to say: 'No, don't touch that!' But now the *nabebe,* the white man, they have been taken over by a frenetic desire to take this xawara out of the depths of the earth. Xawara is the substance of metal, what you call ore. We are afraid of it.

"When the gold stays in the cold depths of the earth, everything is fine. It is dangerous. When the white men take the gold out of the earth, they burn it; they stir it over the fire as if it were manioc flour. Then this *xawara wakexi,* this 'smoke epidemic,' spreads through the forest where the Yanomami live. This is why they are dying. Because of the smoke.

"When the smoke reaches the breast of the heavens it will also become very sick and will also feel the effects of the xawara. The earth will also get sick. It is not just the Yanomami who will die. We will all die together."

From an interview with Davi Yanomami by anthropologist Bruce Albert in Ethnobiology in Defense of Survival: The Yanomami and Kayopo Cases *(Brasília, September, 1990)*

That tradition of dependence upon one another, as well as the communal nature of their village structure, has allowed the Yanomami to develop without having created any political or authoritative hierarchy.

The higher authority among the Yanomami has always been expressed through the earth. Now even the earth has betrayed them, allowing the evil spirits of the lower world to create gold beneath their land.

According to Albert, the Yanomami have a vision of the end of the world:

Each time a shaman dies, the spirits within him are furious; they are liberated and they are extremely angry and begin to cut the feet of the sky. Only the other shamans can contain this spirit and keep the sky on its feet. So if all the Yanomami shamans die, then soon the sky will end by falling on the heads of everyone, and not only the Yanomami but the whole of humanity will die.

ADDITIONAL READING

Action for Citizenship Committee, "Roraima, Brazil: A Death Warning," *Cultural Survival Quarterly,* vol. 13, no. 4, 1989, 59-67.

Dennison Berwick, "At Death's Door," *Longon Sunday Times Magazine,* Sept. 9, 1990.

James Brooke, "For an Amazon Indian Tribe, Civilization Brings Mostly Disease and Death," *New York Times,* Dec. 24, 1989.

Napolean Chagnon, *The Yanomamo: The Fierce People,* Holt, Rinehart & Winston, New York, 1968.

Ethnobiology in Defense of Survival: The Yanomami and Kayopo Cases, Rainforest Foundation, Brasília, September 1990.

Kenneth Good, with David Chanoff, *Into the Heart,* Simon & Schuster, New York, 1991.

Susanna Hecht and Alexander Coburn, *The Fate of the Forest—Developers, Destroyers, and Defenders of the Amazon,* Penguin, New York, 1991.

Yanomami, Survival Campaign Special Bulletin, Survival International, London, 1990.

Davi Yanomami, "Letter to All the Peoples of the Earth," *Cultural Survival Quarterly,* vol. 13, no. 4, 1989, 68, 69.

FOR MORE INFORMATION

Cultural Survival
11 Divinity Avenue
Cambridge, MA 02139

The Rainforest Foundation
1776 Broadway
New York, NY 10019

Royal Geographical Society
1 Kensington Gore
London SW7 2AR
England

Survival International
310 Edgeware Road
London W2 1DY England

Lost Tribes, Lost Knowledge

Eugene Linden

One horrible day 1,600 years ago, the wisdom of many centuries went up in flames. The great library in Alexandria burned down, a catastrophe at the time and a symbol for all ages of the vulnerability of human knowledge. The tragedy forced scholars to grope to reconstruct a grand literature and science that once lay neatly cataloged in scrolls.

Today, with little notice, more vast archives of knowledge and expertise are spilling into oblivion, leaving humanity in danger of losing its past and perhaps jeopardizing its future as well. Stored in the memories of elders, healers, midwives, farmers, fishermen and hunters in the estimated 15,000 cultures remaining on earth is an enormous trove of wisdom.

This largely undocumented knowledge base is humanity's lifeline to a time when people accepted nature's authority and learned through trial, error and observation. But the world's tribes are dying out or being absorbed into modern civilization. As they vanish, so does their irreplaceable knowledge.

Over the ages, indigenous peoples have developed innumerable technologies and arts. They have devised ways to farm deserts without irrigation and produce abundance from the rain forest without destroying the delicate balance that maintains the ecosystem; they have learned how to navigate vast distances in the Pacific using their knowledge of currents and the feel of intermittent waves that bounce off distant islands; they have explored the medicinal properties of plants; and they have acquired an understanding of the basic ecology of flora and fauna. If this knowledge had to be duplicated from scratch, it would beggar the scientific resources of the West. Much of this expertise and wisdom has already disappeared, and if neglected, most of the remainder could be gone within the next generation.

Until quite recently, few in the developed world cared much about this cultural holocaust. The prevailing attitude has been that Western science, with its powerful analytical tools, has little to learn from tribal knowledge. The developed world's disastrous mismanagement of the environment has somewhat humbled this arrogance, however, and some scientists are beginning to recognize that the world is losing an enormous amount of basic research as indigenous peoples lose their culture and traditions. Scientists may someday be struggling to reconstruct this body of wisdom to secure the developed world's future.

A VOLUNTARY CRISIS

Indigenous peoples have been threatened for centuries as development encroaches on their lands and traditions. What is different about the present situation, however, is that it goes beyond basic questions of native land rights into more ambiguous issues, such as the prerogative of individuals to decide between traditional and modern ways. Indigenous knowledge disappears when natives are stripped of their lands, but in many parts of the globe, knowledge also disappears because the young who are in contact with the outside world have embraced the view that traditional ways are illegitimate and irrelevant.

The most intractable aspect of the crisis is that it is largely voluntary. Entranced by images of the wealth and power of the First World, the young turn away from their elders, breaking an ancient but fragile chain of oral traditions. For the elders, it is difficult to persuade an ambitious young native that he is better off hunting boar with blowpipes than reaching for the fruits of "civilization," even if those fruits might translate into a menial job in a teeming city. For the well-fed, well-educated visiting scientist to make that argument can seem both hypocritical and condescending.

The pace of change is startling. According to Harrison Ngau, a member of the Malaysian Parliament concerned with the rights of tribes on the island of Borneo, as many as 10,000 members of the Penan tribe still led the seminomadic life of hunting and gathering at the beginning of the 1980s. But the logging industry has been destroying their woodlands, and the Malaysian government has encouraged them to move to villages. Now fewer than 500 Penans live in the forest. When they settle into towns, their expertise in the ways of the forest slips away. Villagers know that their elders used to watch for the appearance of a certain butterfly, which always seemed to herald the arrival of a herd of boar and the promise of good hunting. These days, most of the Penans cannot remember which butterfly to look for.

The number of different tribes around the world makes it impossible to record or otherwise preserve more than a tiny percentage of the knowledge being lost. Since 1900, 90 of Brazil's 270 Indian tribes have completely disappeared, while scores more have lost their lands or abandoned their ways. More than two-thirds of the remaining tribes have populations of fewer than 1,000. Some might disappear before anyone notices.

A recent study by M.I.T. linguist Ken Hale estimates that 3,000 of the world's 6,000 languages are doomed because no children speak them. Researchers estimate that Africa alone has 1,800 languages, Indonesia 672 and New Guinea 800. If a language disappears, traditional knowledge tends to vanish with it, since individual language groups have specialized vocabularies reflecting native people's unique solutions to the challenges of food gathering, healing and dealing with the elements in their particular ecological niche. Hale estimates that only 300 languages have a secure future.

THE PRICE OF FORGETTING

The most immediate tragedy in the loss of knowledge and traditions is for the tribes themselves. They do not always die out, but the soul of their culture withers away. Often left behind are people "who are shadows of what they once were, and shadows of what we in the developed world are," as one Peace Corps volunteer put it. The price is real as well as psychological when native peoples lose their grip on traditional knowledge. At the Catholic mission in Yalisele in equatorial Zaïre, for instance, nurses and missionaries have encountered patients brought in with burns or perforations of the lower intestine. Investigation revealed that those afflicted had been treated for a variety of ailments with traditional medicines delivered in suppository form. The problem was not the medicines but the dosages. As the old healers died off, people would try to administer traditional medicines themselves or turn to healers who had only a partial understanding of what their elders knew. This problem is likely to get worse because Western medicines and trained nurses are becoming ever more scarce in Zaïre's economically beleaguered society.

In the island nation of Papua New Guinea, in the Coral Sea, jobless people returning to highland villages from the cities often lack the most rudimentary knowledge necessary to survive, such as which rot-resistant trees to use to build huts or which poisonous woods to avoid when making fires for cooking. Many of the youths, alienated from their villages by schooling and exposure to the West, become marauding "rascals," who have made Papua New Guinea's cities among the most dangerous in the world.

The global hemorrhage of indigenous knowledge even fuels the population explosion as people ignore taboos and forget traditional methods of birth control. In many parts of Africa, tribal women who used to bear, on average, five or six children now often have more than 10.

PAPUA NEW GUINEA

A Chronicler of Elders' Wisdom

Papua New Guinea is a raucous teenager of a country, boiling with the vitality and conflict that come with its kaleidoscope of cultures. The stresses between traditional ways and the demands of modern commerce bedevil the island north of Australia with near anarchy in the cities, persistent tribal wars in the highlands and intermittent insurrection in the province of Bougainville. While many of New Guinea's people have become alienated from traditional ways during these growing pains, Saem Majnep, a simple man from the highlands, has responded by making it his cause to preserve tribal learning and restore respect for the accumulated wisdom of 800 peoples.

A diminutive man from the Kalam people of the Kaironk valley, Majnep is a living bridge between the subsistence life of a remote part of New Guinea's highlands and the world of science. In recent years, he has served as a collaborator on several scientific monographs published by Oxford University Press. Hired as an adolescent in 1959 to translate for New Zealand ornithologist Ralph Bulmer, Majnep soon found himself being interviewed for his familiarity with the feeding and breeding habits of birds that Bulmer was studying in the region.

Bulmer's respect for the knowledge of the Kalam people had a profound effect on Majnep. After assisting Bulmer, Majnep went on to work as a technician at the University of Papua New Guinea. Bulmer is now dead, and Majnep has returned to his village, where he continues to record his people's observations of animals and plants. "If you stay in your village, it is easy to pick up this learning because it is still all around you," he says. "But when people go to Madang [the nearest city], they lose it very quickly." Throughout the country, though, Majnep notes that the younger generation feels shame rather than pride in what their ancestors knew.

Alarmed at how easily this wisdom slips from its fragile perch in oral traditions, he also spends a good deal of time speaking to other tribes in New Guinea, either in person or on the radio, exhorting them to take pride in their culture. "I am an uneducated man," he tells them, "but white people value what I know."

With bountiful soils that make subsistence living an attractive alternative to workaday jobs, New Guinea's tribal life is still vibrant. Majnep says his biggest concern is the misuse of the land, as people abandon traditional crop rotation and forget about taboos that used to protect the forest. Still, people like Majnep raise hopes that the island nation may find an accord between tradition and modernity.

ALEUTIAN ISLANDS

Resurrecting a Wondrous Craft

George Dyson has set himself a task even more difficult than preserving the wisdom of a vanishing culture: reviving an art that is already lost. The son of a Princeton physicist, Dyson, 38, was fascinated by 18th century accounts of Aleutian kayakers, who were said to have sustained speeds of 10 knots on the open ocean in their 15-ft. to 30-ft. craft, defying the apparent limits imposed by the length of the boat and human endurance. For two decades, Dyson, a self-taught boatbuilder, has worked to rediscover the technological secrets of these fabled vessels, or baidarkas, as Russian colonists called them.

For more than 5,000 years, Aleut Indians plied the islands off Alaska in craft made of animal skins and bone. Over time these craft diverged in design from other kayaks. They evolved curiously split bows, sterns that were wide at the top but V-shaped at the bottom, and bone joints that made the vessels 100 times as flexible as modern boats. The Aleuts became shaped to the demands of kayaking vast distances, developing huge upper bodies from relentless paddling and bowed legs that allowed them to sit confined for hours. By the time the Russians arrived in pursuit of sea-otter pelts in 1741, the Aleuts had established a marriage of man and technology near perfect for hunting sea mammals.

The baidarka changed markedly under the influence of the Russians and then began to disappear with the end of the sea-otter hunts in the last century. After World War II, the Aleuts switched to motor-powered craft. In his efforts to reconstruct the original kayaks, Dyson, based in Bellingham, Wash., relies on early accounts of explorers and sea captains.

The most intriguing elements of baidarka design are those that show the Aleuts' rejection of typical kayak forms in favor of a distinctive approach. Dyson speculates that the forked bow prevents the boat from submarining in waves. It also gives the kayak the speed advantage of a longer, slenderer craft, and may set up a wave that counteracts the drag-inducing bow wave of ordinary designs. The oddly configured stern may help the kayak make the transition from a vessel that pushes through the water to one that planes on top of the water.

Dyson believes that the baidarka will have a robust future, influencing the shape of modern sport kayaks. Physicist Francis Clauser designed a forked-bow craft for a syndicate in the 1986-87 America's Cup race. Dyson still speaks of the genius of the Aleut kayak builders with reverence: "Modern science has recognized all the elements that went into the baidarka, but nobody put them together to achieve a synthesis the way the Aleuts did."

THE YOUNG DRIFT AWAY

It is difficult for an outsider to imagine the degree to which novel ideas and images assault the minds of tribal adolescents moving into the outside world. They get glimpses of a society their parents never encountered and cannot explain. Students who leave villages for schooling in Papua New Guinea learn that people, not the spirits of their ancestors, created the machines, dams and other so-called cargo of the modern world. Once absorbed, this realization undermines the credibility and authority of elders.

Father Frank Mihalic, a Jesuit missionary in New Guinea since 1948, views with sadness the degree to which education has alienated the young from their "one talks," as kinsmen are called. "They don't like history because history is embarrassing," he says. "They wince when I talk about the way their dad or their mom lived." Mihalic and other members of his order have intervened to prevent the government from burning spirit houses, used during tribal initiation rites. But other missionaries often tell the young people that their customs are primitive and barbaric. Relatives who have left villages for the city and return to show off their wealth and status also influence the young. Girls encounter educated women who work as clerks and are exempt from the backbreaking hauling done by their mothers' generation. How can these youngsters resist the allure of modern life? How can they make an informed judgment about which of the old ways should be respected and maintained?

John Maru, who works in Papua New Guinea's Ministry for Home Affairs and Youth recalls how during his schooling he came to see the endless gift exchanges and other traditions that marked his youth in the Sepik region as a waste of time and money and a drag on individual initiative. Now, however, he sees that such customs serve to seal bonds among families and act as a barrier to poverty and loneliness.

Sadly, tribal peoples often realize they are losing something of value too late to save it. In the village of Taï, in the Ivory Coast, three brothers from a prosperous family have tried to balance respect for the practices of their Guéré tribe with careers in the modern economy. Yet their mother, an esteemed healer, has not been able to pass on her learning. One brother said he wanted to know about the plants she used but was afraid to ask because she would think he had foreseen her death—the traditional time to pass on knowledge. Another brother would go into the forest with her but hesitated to ask what she was doing because he feared the power of her medicines; while the third, pursuing a successful engineering career, assumed that others would acquire her learning. Now with each passing year, it is more likely her knowledge will die with her.

WESTERN CONTEMPT

If the developed world is to help indigenous peoples preserve their heritage, it must first recognize that this wisdom has value. Western science is founded on the belief that knowledge inexorably progresses: the new and improved inevitably drive out the old and fallible. Western science also presumes to be objective and thus more rigorous than other systems of thought.

Guided by these conceits, scientists have often failed to notice traditional technologies even, for instance, when they are on display in the U.S. Several Andean artifacts made the rounds of American museums in the 1980s as examples of hammered gold. Then Heather Lechtman, an M.I.T. archaeologist interested in ancient technologies, examined the metal and discovered that it represented a far more sophisticated art. Lechtman's analysis revealed that the artifacts had been gilded with an incredibly thin layer of gold using a chemical technique that achieved the quality of modern electroplating. No one had previously suspected that these

Indians had the know-how to create so subtle a technology.

Nor is it only the West that has scorned traditional learning. When communist China imposed tight control over Tibet in 1959, the aggressors tried to eradicate the captive country's culture. In particular, the communists denounced Tibetan medicine as feudal superstition, and the number of doctors practicing the 2,000-year-old, herb-based discipline shrank from thousands to 500. But since the Chinese began to relent on this issue in recent years, Tibetans have returned to their traditional medicines, which they often find more effective and less harsh than Western drugs.

Even in the Third World, governments have tended to look at their indigenous cultures as an impediment to development and nationhood. In Papua New Guinea, for instance, European administrators, influenced by colonial practices in Africa, sought to discourage tribalism by consolidating power and

commerce in cities far away from the villages that are the centers of tribal life. According to John Waiko, director of Papua New Guinea's National Research Institute, this decision has fueled instability by making government seem remote and arbitrary. Among dozens of nations and regions with substantial native populations, only Greenland and Botswana stand out for their efforts to accommodate the culture and interests of these people.

GROWING APPRECIATION

Attitudes are beginning to change, however. Scientists are learning to look past the myth, superstition and ritual that often conceal the hard-won insights of indigenous peoples. Sometimes the lessons have come in handy: during the gulf war, European doctors treated some wounds with a sugar paste that traces back to Egyptian battlefield medicine of 4,000 years ago.

Michael Balick, director of the New

CENTRAL AFRICAN REPUBLIC

Proving the Worth of a Healing Art

Bernard N'donazi has the gentle manner of a country doctor, but his mildness conceals fierce commitment to a mission that began to take shape 28 years ago, following the destruction of one of his tribe's central institutions. As a boy, N'donazi endured an initiation rite of the Souma tribe in the Central African Republic, during which an incision was made in his side and his intestine was briefly exposed. This ceremony marked the transition to adulthood and followed months of instruction in the use of plants and herbs in healing. Bernard, now in his late 30s, was among the last of his cult to be initiated. Acting in deference to a Catholic abbot who regarded the traditions as pagan, N'donazi's father, a convert, ordered the destruction of the male house, where boys acquired the learning of their elders. With that, a cultural and medical tradition that extended back to antiquity went up in flames.

This might have been the end of the line had not the younger N'donazi gone on to pursue a career in Western medicine. During his training in Africa, Europe and the U.S. as a health technician, he discovered that many Western medicines are derived from plants. Angered that a European missionary might dismiss traditions that he had never witnessed, N'donazi began to direct his energies toward revalidating the healing wisdom of Central African tribes.

N'donazi's base is a clinic and research facility he founded in the remote town of Bouar. There he collects plants used by healers for laboratory analysis in order to distinguish those with biomedical value from those that have only a placebo effect. His staff dispenses both Western drugs and low-cost and proven traditional preparations.

Though modest about his work, the healer takes pleasure in recounting one triumphant moment of vindication.

Last year he was approached by nuns from a Catholic mission hospital who asked him to help an extremely sick man whose chest was being eaten away by a subcutaneous amoebic infection that had not responded to drugs. Using a method learned from his father, N'donazi applied washed and crushed soldier termites to the open wounds. The patient, Thomas Service, made a remarkable recovery. In gratitude, he now appears at the clinic every Sunday bearing a gift for N'donazi. When a visitor asks how Service feels, the diminutive man shyly shows his healed chest and says the fact that he has walked 11 miles from his village speaks for itself.

Alas, some of the secrets of the male house remain lost. During his initiation, N'donazi recalls, he was given a plant to chew that numbed the pain of the incision. He wistfully notes that he has not since been able to find that natural anesthetic.

BORNEO

The Penans Stand By Their Land

After millenniums of hunting and gathering in the forests of north Borneo, the few hundred Penans who still cling to nomadic ways find themselves besieged by the full force of the 20th century. Loggers have invaded their turf, which is part of Malaysia, scarring the land, felling fruit trees, killing game and polluting rivers. Missionaries vie for the Penans' souls, while development-minded officials disparage their existence as primitive.

These nomads, however, possess an abiding belief that their way of life is precious. During the past few years, they have mounted a stirring, nonviolent campaign to defend the forests, which are their libraries, shops and larders. "We cannot be separated from the land where our ancestors have lived," says Asik Nyelik, the headman of Sungai Ubong who has twice been arrested for joining barricades to halt the loggers. Though the lure of modern

living has reduced the nomadic Penans from 13,000 two decades ago to perhaps 500 today, those who remain see few advantages in choosing the "barren" road over the spongy, shady forest floor. Says Nyelik: "I don't see that settled Penans are doing any better than we are."

Nyelik's longhouse, as the nomads' communal bases are called, is unusual in that it has not only resisted settlement but has retained its animist beliefs. Other longhouses have converted to Christianity, a change that they find brings some practical benefits, but at a price. Gone are medicines that involved spells, as well as taboos on women's eating leopard, monkey, sun bear and python. One old hunter says Christianity has simplified life. "Before, if I went from one place to another, I had to worry about taboos," he says. "What dream did I have last night, what route should take? Now I

just go there." On the other hand, he says, since converting, he no longer has the dreams that in the past would presage a successful hunt. He also laments that fewer and fewer of the young learn the art of creating the clever, flowery songs that used to commemorate visits and noteworthy events.

Along with Christianity have come axes, cooking pots, clothing and bedding, but nomadic Penans insist that modern goods do not threaten their way of life. Most Penan hunters still prefer blowpipes to guns, and a group of headmen insists that if Western goods disappeared, their longhouses could get along just fine so long as the forest remained. This is why after years of arrests, imprisonment and fruitless legal efforts to halt the logging, the Penans continue to blockade the timber roads. "If we die," says Nyelik, "we die in the forest. There is no other place for us to go."

York Botanical Garden's Institute of Economic Botany, notes that only 1,100 of the earth's 265,000 species of plants have been thoroughly studied by Western scientists, but as many as 40,000 may have medicinal or undiscovered nutritional value for humans. Many are already used by tribal healers, who can help scientists greatly focus their search for plants with useful properties.

Balick walks tropical forests with shamans in Latin America as part of a study, sponsored by the National Cancer Institute, designed to uncover plants useful in the treatment of AIDS and cancer. The 5,000 plants collected so far, says the NCI's Gordon Cragg, have yielded some promising chemicals. If any of them turn out to be useful as medicines, the country from which the plant came would get a cut of the profits.

In the past decade, researchers in developed countries have realized that they have much to learn from traditional agriculture. Formerly, such farming was often viewed as inefficient

and downright destructive. "Slash and burn" agriculture, in particular, was viewed with contempt. Following this method, tribes burn down a section of forest, farm the land until it is exhausted and then move on to clear another patch of trees. This strategy has been blamed for the rapid loss of tropical rain forests.

Now, however, researchers have learned that if practiced carefully, the method is environmentally benign. The forests near Chiapas, Mexico, for instance, are not threatened by native Lacandon practices but by the more commercial agricultural practices of encroaching peasants, according to James Nations of Conservation International in Washington. Many indigenous farmers in Asia and South America manage to stay on one patch of land for as long as 50 years. As nutrients slowly disappear from the soil, the farmers keep switching to hardier crops and thus do not have to clear an adjacent stretch of forest.

Westerners have also come to value

traditional farmers for the rich variety of crops they produce. By cultivating numerous strains of corn, legumes, grains and other foods, they are ensuring that botanists have a vast genetic reservoir from which to breed future varieties. The genetic health of the world's potatoes, for example, depends on Quechua Indians, who cultivate more than 50 diverse strains in the high plateau country around the Andes mountains in South America. If these natives switched to modern crops, the global potato industry would lose a crucial line of defense against the threat of insects and disease.

Anthropologists studying agricultural and other traditions have been surprised to find that people sometimes retain valuable knowledge long after they have dropped the outward trappings of tribal culture. In one community in Peru studied by Christine Padoch of the Institute of Economic Botany, peasants employed all manner of traditional growing techniques, though they were generations removed from tribal life. Padoch observed almost as many combinations of crops and techniques as there were households. Similarly, a study of citified Aboriginal children in Australia revealed that they had far more knowledge about the species and habits of birds than did white children in the same neighborhood. Somehow their parents had passed along this knowledge, despite their removal from their native lands. Still, the amount of information in jeopardy dwarfs that being handed down.

LENDING A HAND

There is no way that concerned scientists can move fast enough to preserve the world's traditional knowledge. While some can be gathered in interviews and stored on tape, much information is seamlessly interwoven with a way of life. Boston anthropologist Jason Clay therefore insists that knowledge is best kept alive in the culture that produced it. Clay's solution is to promote economic incentives that also protect the ecosystems where natives live. Toward that end, Cultural Survival, an advocacy group in Cambridge, Mass., that Clay helped establish, encourages traditional uses of the Amazon rain forest by sponsoring a project to market products found there.

Clay believes that in 20 years, demand for the Amazon's nuts, oils, medicinal plants and flowers could add up to a $15 billion-a-year retail market—enough so that governments might decide it is worthwhile to leave the forests standing. The Amazon's Indians could earn perhaps $1 billion a year from the sales. That could pay legal fees to protect their lands and provide them with cash for buying goods from the outside world.

American companies are also beginning to see economic value in indigenous knowledge. In 1989 a group of scientists formed Shaman Pharmaceuticals, a California company that aims to commercialize the pharmaceutical uses of plants. Among its projects is the development of an antiviral agent for respiratory diseases and herpes infections that is used by traditional healers in Latin America.

An indigenous culture can in itself be a marketable commodity if handled with respect and sensitivity. In Papua New Guinea, Australian Peter Barter, who first came to the island in 1965, operates a tour service that takes travelers up the Sepik River to traditional villages. The company pays direct fees to villages for each visit and makes contributions to a foundation that help cover school fees and immunization costs in the region. Barter admits, however, that the 7,000 visitors a year his company brings through the region disrupt local culture to a degree. Among other things, native carvers adapt their pieces to the tastes of customers, adjusting their size to the requirements of luggage. But the entrepreneur argues that the visits are less disruptive than the activities of missionaries and development officials.

There are other perils to the commercial approach. Money is an alien and destabilizing force in many native villages. A venture like Barter's could ultimately destroy the integrity of the cultures it exhibits if, for example, rituals become performances tailored to the tourist business. Some villages in New Guinea have begun to permit tourists to visit spirit houses that were previously accessible only to initiated males. In Africa villages on bus routes will launch into ceremonial dances at the sound of an approaching motor. Forest-product concerns like those encouraged by Cultural Survival run the risk of promoting overexploitation of forests, and if the market for these products takes off, the same settlers who now push aside natives to mine gold might try to take over new enterprises as well.

Still, economic incentives already maintain traditional knowledge in some parts of the world. John and Terese Hart, who have spent 18 years in contact with Pygmies in northeastern Zaïre, note that other tribes and villagers rely on Pygmies to hunt meat and collect foods and medicines from the forests, and that this economic incentive keeps their knowledge alive.

According to John Hart, the Pygmies have an uncanny ability to find fruits and plants they may not have used for years. Says Hart: "If someone wants to buy something that comes from the forest, the Pygmies will know where to find it."

RESTORING RESPECT

Preserving tribal wisdom is as much an issue of restoring respect for traditional ways as it is of creating financial incentives. The late Egyptian architect Hassan Fathy put his prestige behind an attempt to convince his countrymen that their traditional mud-brick homes are cooler in the summer, warmer in the winter and cheaper than the prefabricated, concrete dwellings they see as modern status symbols.

Balick has made it part of his mission to enhance the status of traditional healers within their own communities. He and his colleagues hold ceremonies to honor shamans, most of whom are religious men who value respect over material reward. In one community in Belize, the local mayor was so impressed that American scientists had come to learn at the feet of an elderly healer that he asked them to give a lecture so that townspeople could learn about their own medical tradition. Balick recalls that this healer had more than 200 living descendants, but that none as yet had shown an interest in becoming an apprentice. The lecture, though, was packed. "Maybe," says Balick, "seeing the respect that scientists showed to this healer might inspire a successor to come forward."

Such deference represents a dramatic change from past scientific expeditions, which tended to treat village elders as living museum specimens. Balick and others like him recognize that communities must decide for themselves what to do with their traditions. Showing respect for the wisdom keepers can help the young of various tribes better weigh the value of their culture against blandishments of modernity. If young apprentices begin to step forward, the world might see a slowing of the slide toward oblivion.

Bicultural Conflict

Chinese cultural traits conflict with those encountered in America, posing dilemmas for immigrant children

Betty Lee Sung

Betty Lee Sung, professor of Asian studies at City College of New York, is the author of many books and articles on Chinese immigrants in the United States.

The moment a child is born, he begins to absorb the culture of his primary group; these ways are so ingrained they become a second nature to him. Imagine for a moment how wrenching it must be for an immigrant child who finds his cumulative life experiences completely invalidated, and who must learn a whole new set of speech patterns and behaviors when he settles in a new country. The severity of this culture shock is underlined by Teper's definition of culture:

Culture is called a habit system in which "truths" that have been perpetuated by a group over centuries have permeated the unconscious. This basic belief system, from which "rational" conclusions spring, may be so deeply ingrained that it becomes indistinguishable from human perception—the way one sees, feels, believes, knows. It is the continuity of cultural assumptions and patterns that gives order to one's world, reduces an infinite variety of options to a manageable stream of beliefs, gives a person a firm footing in time and space, and binds the lone individual to the communality of a group.

The language barrier was the problem most commonly mentioned by the immigrant Chinese among whom I have conducted field research. Language looms largest because it is the conduit through which people interact with other people. It is the means by which we think, learn, and express ourselves. Less obvious is the basis upon which we speak or act or think. If there are bicultural conflicts, these may engender problems and psychological difficulties, which may not be immediately apparent but may nevertheless impact on the development of immigrant children.

This article will address some of the cultural conflicts that commonly confront the Chinese child in the home and, particularly, in the schools. Oftentimes, teachers and parents are not aware of these conflicts and ascribe other meanings or other motives to the child's behavior, frequently in a disapproving fashion. Such censure confuses the child and quite often forces him to choose between what he is taught at home and what is commonly accepted by American society. In his desire to be accepted and to be liked, he may want to throw off that which is second nature to him; this may cause anguish and pain not only to himself but also to his parents and family. Teachers and parents should be aware of these differences and try to help the children resolve their conflicts, instead of exacerbating them.

AGGRESSIVENESS AND SEXUALITY

In Chinese culture, the soldier, or the man who resorts to violence, is at the bottom of the social ladder. The sage or gentleman uses his wits, not his fists. The American father will take his son out to the backyard and give him a few lessons in self-defense at the age of puberty. He teaches his son that the ability to fight is a sign of manhood. The Chinese parent teaches his son the exact opposite: Stay out of fights. Yet, when the Chinese child goes to the school playground, he becomes the victim of bullies who pick on him and call him a sissy. New York's teenagers can be pretty tough and cruel. If the child goes home with bruises and a black eye, his parents will yell at him and chastise him. What is he to do? The unresolved conflict about aggressive behavior is a major problem for Chinese-American males. They feel that their masculinity has been affected by their childhood upbringing.

What do the teachers or monitors do? In most instances, they are derisive of the Chinese boys. "Why don't the Chinese fight back?" they exclaim. "Why do they stand there and just take it?" This derision only shames the Chinese boys, who feel that their courage is questioned. This bicultural conflict may be reflected in the self-hatred of some Asian-American male activists who condemn the passivity of our forefathers in response to the discrimination and oppression they endured. Ignorant about their cultural heritage, the activists want to disassociate themselves from such "weakness," and they search for historical instances in which Asians put up a brave but costly and oftentimes futile fight to prove their manhood. The outbreak of gang violence may be another manifestation of the Chinese male's efforts to prove that he is "macho" also. He may be

This article appeared in *The World & I*, August 1989, pp. 670-679. Re-edition of Chapter 8, "Bicultural Conflict," from the book *The Experience of Adjustment: Chinese Immigrant Children in New York City.* Center for Migration Studies of New York, Inc.

overcompensating for the derision that he has suffered.

In American schools, sexuality is a very strong and pervasive force. Boys and girls start noticing each other in the junior highs; at the high school level, sexual awareness is very pronounced. School is as much a place for male/female socialization as it is an institution for learning. Not so for the Chinese. Education is highly valued, and it is a serious business. To give their children an opportunity for a better education may be the primary reason why the parents push their children to study, study, study. Interest in the opposite sex is highly distracting and, according to some old-fashioned parents, improper. Dating is an unfamiliar concept and sexual attractiveness is underplayed, not flaunted as it is according to American ways.

This difference in attitudes and customs poses another dilemma for both the Chinese boys and girls. In school, the white, black, or Hispanic girls like to talk about clothes, makeup, and the dates they had over the weekend. They talk about brassiere sizes and tampons. The popular girl is the sexy one who dates the most. She is the envy of the other girls.

For the Chinese girl, the openness with which other girls discuss boys and sex is extremely embarrassing. Chinese girls used to bind their breasts, not show them off in tight sweaters. Their attitude toward the opposite sex is quite ambivalent. They feel that they are missing something very exciting when other girls talk about phone calls from their boyfriends or about their dates over the weekends, yet they will shy away and feel very uncomfortable if a boy shows an interest in them.

Most Chinese parents have had no dating experience. Their marriages were usually arranged by their own parents or through matchmakers. Good girls simply did not go out with boys alone, so the parents are very suspicious and apprehensive about their daughters dating, and they watch them very carefully. Most Chinese girls are not permitted to date, and for the daring girl who tries to go out against her parents' wishes, there will be a price to pay.

It is no easier for Chinese boys. The pressure to succeed in school is even greater than for girls, and parental opposition to dating is even more intense. Naturally, the parents want their children to adhere to the old ways. Some children do not agree with their parents and have to carry on their high school romances on the sly. These children are bombarded by television, advertisements, stories, magazines, and real-life examples of boy-girl attraction. The teenager is undergoing puberty and experiencing the instinctive urges surging within him or her. In this society they are titillated, whereas in China they are kept under wraps until they are married.

The problem is exacerbated when teachers make fun of Chinese customs and the parents. I saw an instance of this at one of the Chinatown schools. A young Chinese girl had been forbidden by her parents to walk to school with a

Many Chinese immigrant parents walk their children to and from school, even as late as the junior high level. Some mothers come to the schools to feed their children lunch.

young Puerto Rican boy who was in the habit of accompanying her every day. To make sure that the parents were being obeyed, the grandmother would walk behind the girl to see that she did not walk with the boy. Grandma even hung around until her granddaughter went into class, and then she would peer through the window to make sure all was proper before she went home.

Naturally, this was embarrassing for the girl, and it must have been noticed by the homeroom teacher. He exploded in anger at the little old lady and made some rather uncomplimentary remarks about this being the United States and that Chinese customs should have been left behind in China. To my mind, this teacher's attitude and remarks could only push the daughter farther away from her parents. What he could have done was explain to the girl, or even to the entire class, the cultural values and traditions of her parents, so that she would understand how they thought and why they behaved in such a fashion. Putting down the parents and their customs is the worst thing he could have done.

SPORTS

The Chinese attitude toward sports is illustrated by an oft-told joke about two Englishmen who were considered somewhat mad. The two lived in Shanghai where they had gone to do business. In the afternoons, they would each take a racquet, go out in the hot sun, and bat a fuzzy ball across the net. As they ran back and forth across the court, sweat would pour from their faces, and they would be exhausted at the end of the game. To the Chinese onlookers standing on the side, this was sheer lunacy. They would shake their heads in disbelief and ask: "Why do these crazy Englishmen work so hard? They can afford to hire coolies to run around and hit the ball for them." The Chinese attitude toward sports has changed considerably, but it still does not assume the importance that it enjoys in American life.

Turn on any news program on radio or television, and you will find one-third of the air time devoted to sports. Who are the school heros? The football quarterback, the track star, the baseball pitcher. What are the big events in school? The games. What is used to rally school spirits? The games.

Yet in the traditional Chinese way of thinking, development of the mental faculties was more important than development of the physique. The image of a scholar was one with a sallow face and long fingernails, indicating that he spent long hours with his books and had not had to do physical labor. Games that required brute strength, such as football and boxing, were not even played in China. Kung fu or other disciplines of the martial arts did not call for physical strength as much as concentration, skill, and agility. In the minds of many Chinese, sports are viewed as frivolous play and a waste of time and energy. Add to this the generally smaller physique of the Chinese immigrant student in comparison to his classmates, and we do not find many of them on any of the school teams.

What does this mean to the Chinese immigrant students, especially the boys? On the one hand, they may think that the heavy emphasis upon sports is a displaced value. They may want to participate, but they are either too small in stature or unable to devote the time necessary for practice to make the school teams. If the "letter men" are the big wheels, the Chinese student will feel that his kind are just the little guys. But most important of all, an entire dimension of American school life is lost to the Chinese immigrant children.

Chinese-American students enjoy a break on the playground at Sun Yat Sen Intermediate School in New York City's Chinatown.

TATTLING

Should one report a wrongdoing? Should one tell the teacher that a schoolmate is cheating on his exam? Should one report to the school authorities that a fellow student is trying to extort money from him? The American values on this score are ambiguous and confusing. For example, in the West Point scandal a few years ago, most of the cadets involved were not cheaters themselves but they knew about the cheating and did not report it to the authorities. Their honor code required that they tell, but the unwritten code among their fellow cadets said that they should not tattle or "fink." If they had reported the cheating of their fellow cadets, they would have been socially ostracized. There is a dilemma for the American here as well.

This bicultural conflict was noted by Denise Kandel and Gerald S. Lesser in the book, *Youth in Two Worlds*, in which their reference groups were

Participation in sports—so heavily emphasized in America—frequently becomes a dilemma for Chinese immigrant students, who experience sharp contrasts in cultures when they come into contact with children from other ethnic groups in public schools.

Danish and American children. The Danish children, like the Chinese, feel duty bound to report wrongdoing. There is no dichotomy of consequences here. Authorities and peers are consistent in their attitude in this respect, and this consistency helps to maintain social control. The teacher cannot be expected to have four pairs of eyes and see everything. The parents cannot be everywhere at once to know what their child is doing during the day. If the siblings or schoolmates will help by reporting wrongdoing, the task of teaching the child is shared and made easier for the adults. But when social ostracism stands in the way of enforcing ethical values, an intense conflict ensues and contributes to the breakdown of social control.

DEMONSTRATION OF AFFECTION

A commonly voiced concern among Chinese children is, "My parents do not love me. They are so cold, distant, and remote." The children long for human warmth and affection because they see it on the movie and television screens, and they read about it in books and magazines. Because their experiences with mother and father and the other members of the family as well are so formal and distant, they come to the conclusion that love is lacking. In China, where such behavior is the norm, children do not question it. But in this country, where expressions of affection are outwardly effusive and commonly exhibited, they feel deprived.

This lack of demonstrative affection extends also to the spouse and friends. To the Chinese, physical intimacy and love are private matters never exhibited in public. Even in handshaking, the traditional Chinese way was to clasp one's own hands in greeting. Kissing and hugging a friend would be most inappropriate, and to kiss one's spouse in public would be considered shameless and ill-mannered.

Nevertheless, Chinese children in this country are attracted to the physical expressions of love and affection. While they crave it for themselves,

they are often unable to reciprocate or be demonstrative in their relations with their own spouses, children, or friends because of their detached emotional upbringing.

In the schools, this contrast in culture is made all the sharper because of the large numbers of Hispanics. In general, the Hispanics are very outgoing and are not the least bit inhibited about embracing, holding hands, or kissing even a casual acquaintance. The Chinese children may interpret these gestures of friendliness as overstepping the bounds of propriety, but more often than not they wish they could shed their reserve and reach out to others in a more informal manner.

On the other hand, the aloofness of the Chinese students is often wrongly interpreted as unfriendliness, standoffishness, as a desire to keep apart. If all the students in the schools were made aware of these cultural differences, they would not misread the intentions and behavior of one another.

EDUCATION

That education is a highly prized cultural value among the Chinese is commonly known, and the fact that Chinese children generally do well scholastically may be due to the hard push parents exert in this direction. None of this means, however, that these children do not experience a bicultural conflict regarding education when they see that the bright student is not the one who is respected and looked up to in American schools. Labels such as "bookworm," "egghead," and "teacher's pet" are applied to the intelligent students, and these terms are not laudatory, but derisive. When parents urge their children to study hard and get good grades, the children know that the payoff will not be social acceptance by their schoolmates. The rewards are not consistent with values taught at home.

Nevertheless, the Chinese immigrant high school students indicated in their survey questionnaire that they prized the opportunity to get an education. In fact, they identified the opportunity to get a free education as one of the most important reasons why they are satisfied with their schoolwork. Of 143 students who said that they were satisfied with their schoolwork, 135 mentioned this one factor. Education is not easily available to everyone in China, Hong Kong, or Taiwan. It is attained at great personal sacrifice on the part of the parents. It is costly and it is earned by diligence and industry on the part of the student. In this country, school is free through high school. Everyone has to go to school until sixteen years of age in New York, for example. It is not a matter of students trying to gain admittance by passing rigorous entrance exams, but a matter of the authorities trying to keep the dropout rates low that characterizes the educational system here.

This is ground also for conflict, however, since what is free and easy to get is often taken lightly. New York State's academic standards are lower than those in Hong Kong or Taiwan, and the schoolwork is easier to keep up with. As a result, there is less distinction attached to being able to stay in school or graduate. What the Chinese immigrant students prize highly has less value in the larger society, and again the newcomers to this country start to have doubts about the goals that they are striving for.

THRIFT

Twelve, perhaps thirteen, banks can be found within the small core area of New York's Chinatown. When the Manhattan Savings Bank opened a new branch in October 1977 it attracted to its coffers $3 million within a few months' time. Most of the large banks are aware that Chinatown is fertile ground for the accumulation of capital because the Chinese tend to save more of what they earn than other ethnic groups in America, in spite of the fact that their earnings are small.

Two major factors encourage the growth of savings among Chinese immigrants. One is the sense of insecurity common to all immigrants, who need a cushion for the uncertainties that they feel acutely. The other is the esteem with which thrift is regarded by the

Chinese. A person who is frugal is thought of more highly than is one who can sport material symbols of success.

I was once sent on an assignment to cover the story of a very wealthy Chinese man from Bangkok who was reputed to own shipping lines, rice mills, and many other industries. He was a special guest of the United States Department of State, and that evening he was to be honored at the Waldorf-Astoria. I found this gentleman in a very modestly-priced midtown hotel. When he extended his hand to shake mine, I saw that his suit sleeves were frayed.

The value placed upon thrift poses acute bicultural conflict for Chinese immigrant children who see all about them evidence of an economic system that encourages the accumulation and conspicuous consumption of material possessions. A very important segment of the consumer market is now the teenage population. The urge to have stylish clothes, a stereo, a camera, a hi-fi radio, sports equipment, and even a car creates a painful conflict in the child who is enticed by television and other advertising media, but whose parents reserve a large percentage of their meager earnings for stashing away in the banks.

In school, the girl who gets money to spend on fashionable dresses and the latest rock record feels more poised and confident about herself than do her less materially fortunate classmates. She is also admired, complimented, and envied. In the Chinese community, on the other hand, a Chinese girl who spent a lot of money on clothes and frivolities would soon be the object of grapevine gossip, stigmatized as a less-than-desirable prospective wife or daughter-in-law, whereas praises would be sung for the more modestly dressed girl who saved her money.

From my students I hear a commonly voiced complaint about their parents as "money-hungry." They give their children very little spending money. They do not buy fashionable clothing; rather, they buy only serviceable garments in which the children are ashamed to be seen. The Chinese home is generally not furnished for comfort

or aesthetics, so when Chinese children visit the homes of their non-Chinese friends and compare them with their own living quarters, they feel deprived and ashamed of their parents and their family. They certainly do not want to bring their friends home to play, and the teenagers may themselves stay away from home as much as possible, feeling more comfortable with their peers in clubhouses or on the streets.

The contrast in spending attitudes between the underdeveloped economy from which many Chinese immigrants have come and the American economy, which emphasizes mass and even wasteful consumption, is very sharp, and it creates many an unresolved conflict in the children, who do not realize that cultural differences lie behind it. They think that their parents value money more than they care for their children, and exhibit this by denying material possessions that give them pleasure and status in the eyes of their peers.

Credit is another concept foreign to immigrants from the Far East. If one does not have the money, one should not be tempted to buy. Credit is borrowing money, and borrowing should be resorted to only in extreme emergencies. The buy now, pay later idea goes against the Chinese grain. So the Chinese families postpone buying until they have saved up enough to cover the entire purchase price. This attitude is fairly common even when it comes to the purchase of a home. The family will scrimp and economize, putting aside a large portion of its income for this goal, denying itself small pleasures along the way for many, many years until the large sum is accumulated. To the Chinese way of thinking, this singleness of purpose shows character, but to the more hedonistic American mind, this habit of thrift may appear asinine and unnecessary.

DEPENDENCY

In her study, "Socialization Patterns among the Chinese in Hawaii," Nancy F. Young noted the prolonged period of dependency of the children commonly found in the child-rearing practices of the Chinese in Hawaii. She wrote:

Observations of Chinese families in Hawaii indicate that both immigrant and local parents utilize child-rearing techniques that result in parent-oriented, as opposed to peer-oriented, behavior. . . . Chinese parents maximize their control over their children by limiting their experiences with models exhibiting nonsanctioned behavior.

Analyzing and comparing the results of the Chance Independence Training Questionnaire that she administered to six ethnic groups and local (American-born) Chinese as well as immigrant Chinese, she found the mean age of independence training for American-born Chinese to be the lowest (6.78 years), while that for immigrant Chinese to be the highest (8.85 years). Among other ethnic groups in Young's study, the mean age of independence training ranged as follows: Jewish, 6.83; Protestant, 6.87 years; Negro, 7.23 years; Greek, 7.67 years; French-Canadian, 7.99 years; and Italian, 8.03 years.

Immigrant mothers exercise constant and strict supervision over their children. They take the children wherever they go, and babysitters are un-heard of. They prefer their children to say home rather than go out to play with their friends. Friends are carefully screened by the mother, and the child is not expected to do things for himself until about two years beyond the mean age that a Jewish mother would expect her child to do for himself.

On the other hand, American-born Chinese parents expect their children to cut the apron strings sooner than any of the other ethnic groups surveyed. Young did not elaborate and explain why, but it seems that Chinese parents who are American-born have assimilated the American values of independence at an early age and may even have gone overboard in rearing their own children. There are areas of dependence and independence in which Young found divergence. The immigrant Chinese child is expected to be able to take care of himself at an earlier age, but he is discouraged from socializing with people outside the family until a much later age.

The extremes exhibited between the American-born and immigrant Chinese may be indicative of the bicultural conflict that the Chinese in this country feel. As children, they may have felt that their parents were overprotective; this was frequently mentioned by the teachers to whom we talked. We saw evidence of this in the elementary schools—the previously mentioned practice of mothers coming to the school from the garment factories during their own lunch hours to feed their children lunch. Many walked their children to and from school, even as late as the junior high level, but it was not clear to us whether the parents were justifiably afraid for their children's safety from the gangs or whether they were being overprotective. The teachers thought the mothers were smothering the children and restricting their freedom of action. By adolescence, the children must have felt the same. They were chafing against parental control over what they presumed to be their own business, while the parents thought they were merely doing their parental duty.

Teachers and parents do not agree on this score, with the result that parental authority is often undermined by a teacher's scoffing attitude. A personal experience of my own reveals how damaging this can be to a parent's ability to maintain some kind of control over the growing teenager.

My seventeen-year-old son was

Many adolescents in Chinese immigrant families chafe under parental control, considering their parents overprotective. Stylish dress and dating are two issues indicative of the bicultural conflict Chinese immigrant families experience.

Chinese immigrant mothers exercise constant and strict supervision over their children and do not expect a child to do things for himself until he is nearly nine years old—the highest mean age for independence training among all ethnic groups in America.

coming home late at night, and I found it hard to fall asleep until he was home. I did not feel that he should be up so late, nor did I wish my sleep to be disturbed. My son objected strenuously to a curfew of midnight during the week and 1 A.M. on the weekends. His objection was based on the fact that no other teenagers he knew had such restrictions, that most get-togethers did not get going until 11 P.M., and that he would be the "wet blanket" if he left early. I understood his concerns and tried to get the parents of his friends to agree to a uniform time when the group should break up and go home to bed. I felt that if everybody had to go, my son would not mind leaving.

To my utter surprise, not one of the parents felt that boys or girls of seventeen years of age should have a curfew. They felt that I was being too strict and overprotective and that it was time for me to cut the apron strings. The worst part of it was that my conversation with the parents got back to my son, who immediately and gleefully confronted me with, "See, none of the other parents agree with you. You are the only old-fashioned, strict one." This lack of understanding on the part of the other parents in telling my son about our conversation undermined my authority. From that day, I was unable to set hours for him anymore.

The Chinese value of respect for one's elders and for authority is common knowledge and needs no further elaboration here. We have already mentioned that the Chinese immigrant children encountering the disrespect accorded teachers and school authorities for the first time in American classrooms find themselves extremely upset and dismayed. In our interviews with the students, this concern was voiced frequently.

Challenging established authority has been a notable feature of youth culture over the past two decades. The parents, the teachers, the police, the government, the church—all authority figures in the past—have been knocked down and even reviled. Violence against teachers is the leading problem in schools across the nation. If students

do not have respect for the teacher, neither will they have respect for the knowledge that the teacher tries to impart. The issue is a disturbing one, not only for the immigrant children but for the entire American society as well.

HEROES, HEROINES, AND INDIVIDUALISM

Who are the people who are praised, admired, looked up to, and revered? The idols of different cultures are themselves different types of people, and the values of a society may be deduced from the type of people who are respected and emulated in that culture. In the United States, the most popular figures are movie, television, and stage stars, sports figures, politicians, successful authors, inventors, and scientists; probably in that order. Who are the heroes and heroines of China? If we use literature as a guide, they are the filial sons or daughters, the sacrificing mother, the loyal minister, the patriot or war hero who saves his country, and revolutionaries who overthrow despotic rulers and set up their own dynasties. Even in modern China, the persons honored and emulated are the self-sacrificing workers who put nation above self.

Priests, ministers, and rabbis once commanded prestige in this country, but the status of these men of God has declined. In China, monks or priests have always occupied lowly positions. In contrast to the United States, in China actors were riffraff. Women did not act in the theater, so men had to play the female roles. Western influence has brought about changes in the pseudo-Chinese cultures of Hong Kong and Singapore and stage performers and movie stars are now popular and emulated, but this was not always so.

As a rule, Chinese heroes and heroines were people of high moral virtues, and they set the standards of conduct for others. In this country, the more sensational the exposé of the private lives of our national leaders or entertainment figures, the more our curiosity is aroused. How movie stars retain their popularity in spite of the

relentless campaigns to strip them naked is very difficult for someone not brought up in the United States to comprehend. An old adage says, "No man is a hero to his valet." Yet, the very fact that American heroes and heroines survive and thrive on notoriety and self-confession can only mean that the American people admire such behavior. One might say, Chinese heroes are saints; American heroes are sinners.

Noted anthropologist Francis L. K. Hsu has written extensively about individualism as a prominent characteristic of American life. According to Hsu, the basic ingredient of rugged individualism is self-reliance. The individual constantly tells himself and others that he controls his own destiny and that he does not need help from others. The individual-centered person enjoins himself to find means of fulfilling his own desires and ambitions.

Individualism is the driving force behind the competitiveness and creativity that has pushed this nation forward. Loose family ties, superficial human relationships, little community control, and weak traditions have given the individual leeway to strike out on his own without being hindered by sentimentality, convention, and tradition. Self-interest has been a powerful incentive.

In contrast, Dr. Hsu contends, the Chinese are situation-centered. Their way of life encourages the individual to find a satisfactory adjustment with the external environment of men and things. The Chinese individual sees the world in relativistic terms. He is dependent upon others and others are dependent upon him. Like bricks in a wall, one lends support to the other and they all hold up the society as a whole. If even one brick becomes loose, the wall is considerably weakened; interlocked, the wall is strong. The wall is the network of human relations. The individual subordinates his own wishes and ambitions for the common good.

Dr. Kenneth Abbott, in his book *Harmony and Individualism*, also points out that the Western ideas of creativity and individualism are not accented in Chinese and must be held within accepted norms. One of the reasons for this is the importance ascribed to maintenance of harmony. Harmony is the key concept in all relationships between god(s) and man and between man and man. It is the highest good.

To the Chinese, the sense of duty and obligation takes precedence over self-gratification. It is not uncommon to find Chinese teenagers handing over their entire paychecks to their parents for family use or for young Chinese males to pursue a course of study chosen for them by their parents rather than one of their own choosing. Responsibility toward distant kin is more keenly felt by the Chinese than by other Americans. Honor and glory accrue not only to the individual but to all those who helped him climb the ladder. This sense of being part of something

greater than oneself gives the Chinese a feeling of belonging and security in the knowledge that they do not stand alone. On the other hand, individual freedom of action is very much restricted.

Some of the better known problems that confront a Chinese immigrant to these shores, such as respect for elders, modesty and humility, and male superiority, were omitted here because they have been dealt with at length elsewhere. The foregoing examples—aggressiveness, sexuality, sports, tattling, demonstration of affection, education, thrift, independence training, respect for authority, heros and heroines, and individualism—represent other important areas of bicultural conflict that confront Chinese newcomers to these shores.

ADDITIONAL READING

Francis L. K. Hsu, "Rugged Individualism Reconsidered," *The Colorado Quarterly*, vol. 9, no. 2, Autumn 1960.

_____ *Americans and Chinese: Reflections on Two Cultures and Their People*, American Museum of Science Books, New York, 1972.

_____ "Culture Change and the Persistence of the Chinese Personality," in George DeVos, ed., *In Response to Change*, D. Van Nostrand, New York, 1976.

Denise Kandel and Gerald S. Lesser, *Youth in Two Worlds*, Jossey-Bass, Inc., San Francisco, 1972.

Richard Sollenger, "Chinese-American Child Rearing Practices and Juvenile Delinquency," *Journal of Social Psychology*, vol. 74, 1968.

Shirley Teper, "Ethnicity, Race and Human Development," N.Y. Institute on Pluralism and Group Identity of the American Jewish Committee, 1977.

Nancy F. Young, "Socialization Patterns among the Chinese in Hawaii," in *Amerasia Journal*, vol. 1, no. 4, February 1972.

Easter Island: Scary Parable

The decline of a mysterious culture contains a stunning lesson for mankind. Its people nearly destroyed their habitat and themselves. Now their island's accidental name may be prophetic.

Louise B. Young

Louise B. Young has written about Earth's environment for more than 20 years. She holds a master's degree in geophysical sciences from the University of Chicago. Her latest book is "Sowing the Wind: Reflections on the Earth's Atmosphere." Two earlier books, "Earth's Aura" and "The Blue Planet," also dealt with Earth and its halo of vital gases.

Easter Island is a little mote of land set in the middle of the widest marine solitude, the emptiest extent of ocean there is in the world. It carries the ruins of a unique Stone Age culture that flourished here four or five hundred years ago. If we could have visited the island during the classic period of this civilization we would have seen a strange, dramatic sight. Along the forbidding coast line, crowning the steep wave-lashed cliffs, great stone platforms were erected, and on these ceremonial altars the inhabitants raised giant statues, carved from brown tuff, the porous rock formed of compacted volcanic ash. Many were capped with red stone topknots. Several hundred of these effigies dominated the scant 35 miles of shoreline. They stood 35 to 60 feet tall, each one weighing at least a hundred tons. Facing inward with their backs to the sea, the austere faces with pursed lips and hypnotic eyes made of white coral and black obsidian looked out with stern and melancholy gaze at this tiny piece of the earth's surface, this triangular island pockmarked with the craters of great volcanoes.

The statues seem to be guarding the land—but from what? From demons or the ravages of storms sweeping in from the sea? Or perhaps from the awesome forces that lie hidden deep within the earth itself and erupt in sudden violence, spreading incandescent lava across the land? If so, they failed to guard it against a less expected danger: man himself.

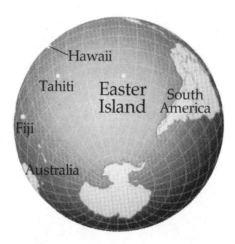

In Easter Island's tragic saga we can see many analogies to the problems faced by modern man. The whole earth is like a little island isolated in the vast seas of space. Its resources, though rich and various, are limited. And the increasing population of human beings is beginning to press hard upon these limits.

The identity of the people that settled Easter Island, and the meaning of their great stone effigies, which are called *moai* in the native language, is still a mystery. The skill used in carving them and the building of the great ceremonial platforms (called *ahus*) suggests a higher cultural heritage than has been evidenced in any other island of the South Pacific. The people responsible for this work also had some knowledge of astronomy. Several of the *ahus* are so oriented that their façades face the rising or setting sun at the equinox or the summer or winter solstices.

A form of writing was also known, but the hieroglyphics carved on pieces of wood ("talking sticks" or *rongorongo* tablets) have never been translated. No other form of ancient writing has been found in Polynesia.

These are a few of the facts that suggest an origin different from the peoples who settled the islands farther west. There are some similarities to Inca culture, as Thor Heyerdahl pointed out. The precisely fitted stonework of the *ahus* is reminiscent of examples of ancient stone walls in Cuzco, Peru. Several forms of vegetation, such as the bottle gourd and sweet potato, are typical South American plants. Totora reeds like those that grow on Lake Titicaca on the Bolivia-Peru border, and which are used there to build reed boats, are also found on Easter Island. But the language and the physical characteristics of the natives are Polynesian.

Scientists have recently unearthed facts that only deepen the mystery.

Several hundred of the many skeletons found on the island have been measured, X-rayed, and classified by anthropologists. They found distinct variations in the shape of kneecaps and pelvic girdles. These findings were interpreted as suggesting that at least two separate groups settled on Easter Island. That assumption has been challenged by other anthropologists and the question remains unresolved.

Another very interesting fact was discovered by scientists examining blood samples of the living Easter Islanders. An unusual characteristic showed up in these samples—a characteristic that is found in the blood of only one other population group in the world, the Basque people whose homeland is the northwest corner of the Iberian peninsula. It is hard to imagine how there could have been any connection between the Basques and Easter Island. But one possibility has been suggested. In the early 16th century a Spanish galleon carrying a large crew of Basque sailors was lost in these waters. Could some of these shipwrecked men have found their way to Easter Island? Science may soon have the tools to provide a definitive answer to these questions. DNA taken from samples of ancient human bones on the island could reveal the genetic origin of these peoples.

There is abundant evidence that in its original state Easter Island was heavily forested. Cores taken from the volcanic craters have revealed the presence of pollen from as many as 20 species of trees.

While many questions still remain concerning the origin of this culture, the circumstances that led to its destruction are now quite well understood. The sequence of events has been pieced together from stories handed down from generation to generation and confirmed by laboratory testing.

The story is of great human interest. It shows what can happen to a promising culture when population growth puts great stress on limited natural resources and fighting breaks out over the remaining supplies of food and fuel and water. Isolated from all other land masses, the inhabitants of Easter Island were entirely dependent on its own internal resources just as the environment of Earth itself, as it travels alone in space, is confined and limited to the natural wealth that exists here.

Easter Island is totally volcanic in origin. Like the Galapagos Islands or Surtsey off the coast of Iceland, it erupted in a cloud of smoke and fire from the bottom of the sea sometime in the last 50,000 years. And in subsequent years eruptions continued, altering the shape of the land. Geologists believe that the most recent one may have occurred within the last one or two thousand years. This volcano is known as Rano Raraku and it is from the rock at the heart of this volcanic cone that the great stone figures were carved.

The eruptions that created Easter Island were very violent in nature; the lava emerged with great explosive force, ejecting showers of "volcanic bombs" which lie in profusion across the rolling countryside. These bombs are made of porous black rocks, about the size of coconuts. They obstruct travel and are a disadvantage for agricultural development.

It is not surprising that this island bears so many marks of its volcanic origin. It sits squarely on one of the most active rift zones in the world—the East Pacific Rise. Here the earth's crust is moving at a faster rate than anywhere else on the planet. Two plates are separating from each other and new earth crust is being formed in the rift between them. At the same time the plate on which Easter Island rides is being subducted beneath the west coast of South America.

Easter Island is bathed by the cool Humboldt Current. The waters here are not warm enough to provide ideal conditions for coral growth; so there is no fringing reef like those that surround the shores of many South Pacific islands, no sheltered lagoon, no protected anchorage. The island, however, enjoys a favorable climate. Average temperatures lie in the ideal range between the high 50s and the mid 70s. And they vary only a few degrees between winter and summer. Rainfall is abundant, averaging 56 inches a year—almost twice as much as that which falls on the rich corn belt of the United States.

Given the physical characteristics of the island, one would expect to find a pleasant landscape with varied vegetation—many trees, pasture lands, perhaps fields of sugar cane, and blooming plants like those on similarly sited, volcanic Mauritius Island in the Indian Ocean. So it is surprising to find a desolate landscape covered with parched grasses. No streams, no lakes, no trees break the stark outline of the brown hills against the sky. It is a scene that bears the scars of the impact of man.

There is abundant evidence that in its original state Easter Island was heavily forested. Cores taken from the volcanic craters have revealed the presence of pollen from as many as 10 species of trees, including large deciduous trees, palms, and conifers. Many of these were useful to man: mahogany and the indigenous toromiro were both used for building purposes and for sculpture. The bark of the paper mulberry was used to make tapa cloth. Another tree, perhaps the coconut palm, yielded fiber for ropes and fishing nets. The nuts of the sandalwood tree were a staple of the early Easter Island diet, and its light-colored wood was much prized for its sweet fragrance.

But early inhabitants were so prodigal in the use of these resources that the island was gradually stripped of its forest growth at a time when the population was large and increasing. These factors are closely related not only on Easter Island but everywhere in the world. As more people must be supported, more land must be cleared to grow crops and more wood is needed as fuel to cook the food. The forests are cut down, erosion occurs, and the land becomes less able to yield abundant crops.

The soil of Easter Island, being of volcanic origin, originally contained important nutrients—lime, potash, phosphates. But this soil lies in a thin layer over very porous lava formations like a giant pumice stone. The abundant rain, falling on land without forest cover runs swiftly through the thin layer of soil, leaching out some of the essential ingredients and flowing down through the porous rock formation to the sea.

Tree roots in forested areas strike deep and are strong enough to crack the rock formations, gradually turning them into soil. The leaves of the trees break the impact of every shower. They hold the drops and little puddles, allowing it to drip softly down to the forest floor, so the soil can absorb it slowly. Trees shade the soil from the direct rays of sunlight, reducing the rate of evaporation and the land remains moist for a long period of time. As fallen leaves decay they become a soft, nutrient-rich mulch that slowly builds up into more soil. And the trees break strong winds that destroy tender young growth and further desiccate the land.

When Easter Island became stripped of forest growth it began to suffer from chronic drought, raked by the winds that sweep unimpeded over thousands of miles of open sea. Now less than an hour after every heavy shower the land is dry but the ocean all around the island is stained dark brown with the soil that has been carried with the rain out to sea. This influx of fresh water contaminated with eroded soil is a very unfavorable environment for fish and drives them away from shore.

The destruction of the forests on Easter Island, of course, did not take place all at once. It must have occurred gradually over several centuries. And this period of time seems to have coincided with the period when most of the great *moai* were carved, between the 14th and the 17th centuries. At that time the population must have been large to provide the manpower for carving and moving these enormous stone effigies. There are at least 500 of them on the island and it has been

estimated that a crew of 20 men would take almost a year to create each one. The manpower required to move one of these statues is estimated to have taken another crew of about the same size many months. The people of Easter Island did not have the wheel. They had no metal tools. For carving they used the basalt rock and obsidian, a volcanic glass that can be flaked into razor-sharp cutting edges. Although quite rare around the world, obsidian is found in abundance on Easter Island.

All of this work must have taken place in a highly disciplined and organized society. Since the island's food resources were not great even in times when it enjoyed a stand of forest growth, the work of planting, cultivating, and harvesting crops to feed a large population must also have been carefully planned and strictly carried out. It seems likely that a repressive society had evolved, with a small group of overlords and a large laboring class.

ANCIENT CLASS SYSTEM

These assumptions are supported by the stories that have been passed down from generation to generation of Easter Islanders. There were, according to these tales, two distinct classes of people: the Long-ears, the Hanau Eepe, who hung heavy ornaments in their earlobes stretching them almost to the shoulders; and the Short-ears, the Hanau Momoko, who did not engage in this practice. The Hanau Momoko were much more numerous than the Hanau Eepe, who represented a small privileged autocracy. The system, although dictatorial, worked well enough to provide sustenance for many people and countless hours of labor for carving and transporting the great stone *moai*. But as the population continued to grow, more trees were cut down to clear more land for agriculture. The moving of the *moai* required the use of long wooden poles to lever the heavy statues and to slide them over the rough terrain. Wood was also needed to build boats for fishing and for fuel to cook the food. More trees were harvested and all this time the land became less

fertile, more susceptible to periods of drought, less able to yield good crops.

At this time—about 1678, according to oral history—the ruling Long-ears ordered the Hanau Momoko to pick up all the volcanic bombs that lay strewn throughout the island and throw them into the sea. This new demand on their labor was the spark that fired the rebellion of the Hanau Momoko. All work suddenly ceased on the *moai*. Hundreds of them were left unfinished at the quarry and along the slopes of Rano Raraku. Stone tools were cast aside and still lie scattered there.

Then a terrible battle was fought on the hillside known as Poike Point. Excavations and carbon dating have verified the oral history of this brutal conflict. The Long-ears assembled on the promontory, which was surrounded on three sides by water. At the land side, at the base of the hill, they dug a series of trenches to protect themselves from invasion—a primitive Maginot Line. They filled the trenches with brush and logs, thus further stripping the forests. Their plan was to conceal themselves behind the piles of dirt thrown up by the excavations and to set the brush on fire in the event of an attack. But the plan backfired as such plans are apt to do.

A Hanau Eepe man who lived on Poike Hill had a Hanau Momoko woman working for him as a cook. She was loyal to her own people and sent them a signal when all the Eepe men were asleep. She led two bands of Momoko warriors along the shore around both ends of the line of trenches. A considerable force remained in front of the line, and at dawn they launched a frontal attack. The brush was set on fire. But Momoko warriors who had penetrated behind the lines attacked from the rear and drove the Eepe warriors into their own flaming trenches. Only one Eepe man survived. Allowed to live, he married a Momoko woman and had many descendants.

Recent excavations have found charred remains in the ditch. Carbon dating has verified a date of 1678, plus or minus a hundred years.

When the repressive regime was

wiped out the whole fabric of the society was destroyed and anarchy prevailed. The victorious Momokos broke up into tribal groups that turned on each other, fomenting almost continuous warfare. Families hid in the many caves that honeycombed the island or barricaded themselves in stone houses with doors so small that to enter them one must crawl on all fours.

Labor in the fields and gardens was dangerous and was considered degrading because all organized labor was associated with the time of autocratic rule. The food supply dwindled until it was insufficient to feed the considerable population that had survived. Cannibalism became widespread. Gnawed human bones found heaped in the caves of Easter Island bear witness to the scale of this practice.

For almost two centuries the conflict continued, becoming ever more violent as the food supply dwindled. During this time all the objects that had been held sacred were desecrated. One by one the great statues were toppled onto their faces and the ceremonial *ahus* were destroyed.

SOURCE OF SLAVES

The final tragedy occurred about 1860. During a three-year period Peruvian ships came repeatedly to Easter Island to capture and carry off slaves. They seized all the leaders of the community—the strongest men as well as those who could read and write the hieroglyphics on the *rongo-rongo* tablets. These were the guardians of whatever written knowledge remained concerning the origin and evolution of this culture.

Years later a pitiful little remnant—only 15 men—were returned to Easter Island. They carried with them small pox and tuberculosis. Epidemics swept through the remaining population, reducing it to only a few hundred. This was all that remained of a population of approximately 8,000 believed to have lived on the island during the height of the culture.

It was during these centuries of internal conflict that the first contacts with Europeans were made. In 1722 a Dutch fleet captained by Jacob Roggeveen visited the island on Easter Day and named it in honor of that occasion. An account written by Carl Friedrich Behrens, who was a member of the expedition, reported that the outward appearance of the island was not inviting: "parched-up grass and charred brushwood." A party of crewmen that went ashore were disappointed to find no sign of running streams or ponds to replenish the ship's supply. When asked for food, the natives produced sandalwood nuts, sugar cane, chickens, yams, and bananas.

CAPTAIN COOK'S ASSESSMENT

Half a century later Captain James Cook on his second voyage around the world found an even less inviting scene. Only three or four canoes could be seen on the whole island. "These were very narrow, built of many pieces sewed together with fine line . . . as small and mean as these canoes were, it was a matter of wonder to us where they got the wood to build them with; for in one of them was a board six or eight feet long, fourteen inches broad at one end and eight at the other; where I did not see a stick on the island which would have made a board half this size. . . ." The account of Captain Cook's visit gives the impression that the island had just suffered a serious major conflict. Straw houses had recently been burned and many fires lighted the skies at night.

A few years later a French mariner, Jean François de la Pérouse spent just eight to ten hours on the island, but in this short time he identified the reason for its poverty of natural resources. The inhabitants, he said, had been so imprudent as to cut down all the trees that had grown there in former times, leaving it fully exposed to the rays of the sun and the sweep of the winds. Trees do not grow again in such a situation, he observed, unless they are sheltered from the sea winds, either by other trees or an enclosure of walls. La Pérouse attempted to help the islanders amplify their small food supply. He gave them lambs, hogs, and goats as well as many seeds and tubers to start gardening. But the people were so improvident that they ate the animals before there was a chance for them to bear progeny. They were not willing to work at building protective walls for the young trees or cultivating vegetables.

In 1872 the young Frenchman, Pierre Loti, came as a crew member on a frigate that stopped at Easter Island. He was deeply moved by the tragic character of this tiny spit of land with its dying remnant of humanity. Loti, who became a prominent writer, felt instinctively that there was something sinister about the island. "The country seems an immense ossuary," he said. "Skulls and jawbones we find everywhere. It seems impossible to scratch the ground without stirring those human remains."

By the time of Loti's visit all the completed statues had been toppled. They lay on their faces where once they had stood proudly dominating the landscape. Only the unfinished *moai* where the carvers had thrown down their tools two centuries earlier still looked up at the sky with sightless eyes.

MORAL OF THE MOAI

Today forests all over the world are being cut down to make space for growing more food and to provide fuel to cook the food. In today's complex civilization trees are cut down for many special purposes in addition to the essential ones of food and fuel. To take just one example, a single Sunday edition of a newspaper with a circulation of 1 million requires the destruction of 15,000 trees. Around the world tropical forests are being destroyed at the rate of approximately 100 acres per minute. As resources become scarce wars are fought over the division of those remaining, and in the conflict more of the scarce resources are squandered.

An interesting analogy exists between the fire ditch at Poike Point and a defense plan used by Saddam Hussein. Trenches were dug along the border of Kuwait and oil was piped into them. The plan was to set the oil on fire at the time of an attack, thus providing an impenetrable barrier against the invading ground force. But as on Easter Island the plan failed. The Allied Forces set the trenches afire with napalm bombs well before the invasion. Alternative measures used by the Iraqis were more devastating but equally futile. They set on fire more than 500 oil wells in Kuwait in order to cloud the atmosphere with heavy smoke and ash, making aerial bombardment more difficult. More oil was pumped into the sea to foul the desalination plants of the Gulf states and cut off this source of fresh water. The almost incredible wanton waste of oil—this most valuable resource of the modern world—is comparable to the burning of trees (perhaps the last forest stand) in Poike Ditch. And the long-term effect on the environment, the climate, and the health of the earth casts its shadow far into the future.

But the most alarming part of the message that comes down to us from Easter Island is the way violence breeds more violence. Acts of cruelty become progressively easier to commit when they are reinforced by example and supported by tradition. On the other hand, acts of kindness and compassion can be reinforced in a civilized society. Human nature is complex, volatile, and impressionable. Capable of both good and evil, it can be influenced by life experiences. An education in violence uncovers the beast in the nature of humans.

There is, however, light at this end of the Easter Island story. The name Easter Island may have been prophetic.

A rebirth of life and a resurrection of the environment is beginning to occur here. Motivated by the lure of a tourist industry, the islanders and the Chilean government, aided by the United States, have gone to work. An airstrip has been built and several times a week commercial airlines bring in tourists. A number of small hotels have sprung up along the southwest shore. Plantings of trees and flowers around the hotels relieve the older stark landscape. Magnolia and hibiscus are thriving. Nasturtiums and tropical lilies in many bright colors grace the garden beds. Wild guava has been introduced and has taken over some of the open countryside. The fruit is eaten by birds who pass the seeds through their digestive systems and distribute them over a wide area.

Government agencies have undertaken the planting of trees along the mountain slopes. These are mostly eucalyptus, a fast-growing tree which is tolerant of dry conditions. But, unfortunately, it is not a favorable species for soil-building. Eucalyptus leaves do not rot; they lie in a smothering layer on the ground and discourage new growth.

There are also, however, several small groves of mahogany and coconut palms. The fact that they are doing well suggests that eventually the whole island may be restored.

In fact, Easter Island may serve as an example of how land that has been decimated can be returned to health and fertility. Conventional wisdom has held that once the forest has been stripped from the land a vicious circle of erosion and loss of fertility occurs and cannot be broken.

EASTER ISLAND'S HOPE

Recently, however, there is some indication that restoration can be achieved by hard work and intelligent land management. The first steps are the hardest because most seedling trees exposed to wind and direct sunlight all day cannot survive. They need some protection, such as a small stone wall, to provide some shade and to break the wind. These saplings need regular watering, cultivation, and weeding to prevent competition with other species. But as soon as the first trees attain a reasonable size, other species can take hold in their shadows. As the grove increases in size it begins to make its own environment. Litter builds up on the ground, acting as a giant sponge to hold the water and retard evaporation. The earth remains cooler beneath this litter, and the decaying leaves provide additional nutrients and soil conditioning for the young plants. Trees that bear fruit and blossoms attract birds that help to disseminate the seeds. Thus a positive cycle of cause and effect promotes the rebuilding of the environment.

Our understanding of these processes gives hope that the terrible last phases of the tragedy of Easter Island need not be repeated on Planet Earth. But the achievement of a proper balance between the natural resources and the population of mankind is a challenge that must be met soon in order to break the downward spiral leading to the depths of human degradation, and to speed the resurrection of the variety and beauty of the whole web of life on Earth.

Index

Credits/ Acknowledgments

Cover design by Charles Vitelli

1. Anthropological Perspectives

Facing overview—United Nations photo.

2. Culture and Communication

Facing overview—United Nations photo.

3. The Organization of Society and Culture

Facing overview—Courtesy of Department Library Services, American Museum of Natural History photo by Thomas Luut. 72—Jason Laure.

4. Other Families, Other Ways

Facing overview—United Nations photo. 105—Enid Schildkrout. 119—United Nations photo by Ian Steele.

5. Sex Roles and Statuses

Facing overview—United Nations photo by John Isaac.

6. Religion, Belief, and Ritual

Facing overview—United Nations photo by S. Stokes.

7. Sociocultural Change: The Impact of the West

Facing overview—United Nations photo. 203-206—photos by Dr. E. Richard Sorenson. 229-231, 233—Paolo Galli/The World & I.

ANNUAL EDITIONS ARTICLE REVIEW FORM

■ NAME: _____ DATE: _____

■ TITLE AND NUMBER OF ARTICLE: _____

■ BRIEFLY STATE THE MAIN IDEA OF THIS ARTICLE: _____

_____

_____

_____

_____

■ LIST THREE IMPORTANT FACTS THAT THE AUTHOR USES TO SUPPORT THE MAIN IDEA:

_____

_____

_____

_____

_____

_____

■ WHAT INFORMATION OR IDEAS DISCUSSED IN THIS ARTICLE ARE ALSO DISCUSSED IN YOUR
TEXTBOOK OR OTHER READING YOU HAVE DONE? LIST THE TEXTBOOK CHAPTERS AND PAGE
NUMBERS:

_____

_____

_____

_____

_____

_____

■ LIST ANY EXAMPLES OF BIAS OR FAULTY REASONING THAT YOU FOUND IN THE ARTICLE:

_____

_____

_____

_____

_____

■ LIST ANY NEW TERMS/CONCEPTS THAT WERE DISCUSSED IN THE ARTICLE AND WRITE A
SHORT DEFINITION:

_____

_____

_____

_____

_____

We Want Your Advice

ANNUAL EDITIONS:
ANTHROPOLOGY 94/95
Article Rating Form

Annual Editions revisions depend on two major opinion sources: one is our Advisory Board, listed in the front of this volume, which works with us in scanning the thousands of articles published in the public press each year; the other is you—the person actually using the book. Please help us and the users of the next edition by completing the prepaid article rating form on this page and returning it to us. Thank you.

Here is an opportunity for you to have direct input into the next revision of this volume. We would like you to rate each of the 44 articles listed below, using the following scale:

1. **Excellent: should definitely be retained**
2. **Above average: should probably be retained**
3. **Below average: should probably be deleted**
4. **Poor: should definitely be deleted**

Your ratings will play a vital part in the next revision. So please mail this prepaid form to us just as soon as you complete it.
Thanks for your help!

Rating	Article	Rating	Article
	1. Doing Fieldwork Among the Yąnomamö		23. Society and Sex Roles
	2. Doctor, Lawyer, Indian Chief		24. Why Don't We Act Like the Opposite Sex?
	3. "The White Man Will Eat You!"		
	4. Eating Christmas in the Kalahari		25. The Global War Against Women
	5. The Naked Truth		26. The Little Emperors
	6. The World's Language		27. Parental Favoritism Toward Daughters
	7. Language, Appearance, and Reality: Doublespeak in 1984		28. Blaming the Victim: Ideology and Sexual Discrimination in the Contemporary United States
	8. Shakespeare in the Bush		
	9. A Cross-Cultural Experience: A Chinese Anthropologist in the United States		29. Psychotherapy in Africa
			30. The Body's War and Peace
	10. The F Word		31. The Mbuti Pygmies: Change and Adaptation
	11. Understanding Eskimo Science		
	12. The Blood in Their Veins		32. The Initiation of a Maasai Warrior
	13. Mystique of the Masai		33. The Secrets of Haiti's Living Dead
	14. Too Many Bananas, Not Enough Pineapples, and No Watermelon at All: Three Object Lessons in Living With Reciprocity		34. Rituals of Death
			35. Body Ritual Among the Nacirema
			36. Superstition and Ritual in American Baseball
	15. Life Without Chiefs		37. Why Can't People Feed Themselves?
	16. An Unsettled People		38. Growing Up as a Fore
	17. Memories of a !Kung Girlhood		39. Civilization and Its Discontents
	18. When Brothers Share a Wife		40. Dark Dreams About the White Man
	19. Young Traders of Northern Nigeria		41. A People at Risk
	20. Family Planning, Amazon Style		42. Lost Tribes, Lost Knowledge
	21. Death Without Weeping		43. Bicultural Conflict
	22. Arranging a Marriage in India		44. Easter Island: Scary Parable

(Continued on next page)

ABOUT YOU

Name_____ Date_____

Are you a teacher? ☐ Or student? ☐

Your School Name _____

Department _____

Address _____

City _____ State _____ Zip _____

School Telephone # _____

YOUR COMMENTS ARE IMPORTANT TO US!

Please fill in the following information:

For which course did you use this book? _____

Did you use a text with this Annual Edition? ☐ yes ☐ no

The title of the text? _____

What are your general reactions to the Annual Editions concept?

Have you read any particular articles recently that you think should be included in the next edition?

Are there any articles you feel should be replaced in the next edition? Why?

Are there other areas that you feel would utilize an Annual Edition?

May we contact you for editorial input?

May we quote you from above?

ANNUAL EDITIONS: ANTHROPOLOGY 94/95

No Postage
Necessary
if Mailed
in the
United States

BUSINESS REPLY MAIL

First Class   Permit No. 84   Guilford, CT

Postage will be paid by addressee

The Dushkin Publishing Group, Inc.
Sluice Dock
DPG **Guilford, Connecticut 06437**